"*Murder in Cairo* illuminates a sinister, colourful, clandestine world."
TINA BROWN, BESTSELLING AUTHOR AND FORMER EDITOR-IN-CHIEF OF THE *NEW YORKER*, *VANITY FAIR* AND *TATLER*

"A dazzling feat of investigative journalism that reads like a le Carré. Two reporters piece together, after fifty years, the murder of the Middle East correspondent on their own newspaper – and mine – David Holden. Their hunt for the truth, which evaded a massive search at the time, broke through those brick walls to reveal the dangerous and widespread connections between the intelligence agencies, the spies among us and the journalists they targeted. Little did we know how close they were."
JAMES FOX, AUTHOR OF *WHITE MISCHIEF*

"I learned so much that I didn't know from this riveting page-turner of a book. It's a fascinating take on a genuine mystery."
DANIEL FINKELSTEIN, AUTHOR OF *HITLER, STALIN, MUM AND DAD* AND FORMER EXECUTIVE EDITOR OF *THE TIMES*

"Gripping. Gillman and Midolo's hunt for the truth behind the complicated facade of David Holden's murder reads better than any Cold War spy thriller."
CLAIRE HUBBARD-HALL, AUTHOR OF *HER SECRET SERVICE: THE FORGOTTEN WOMEN OF BRITISH INTELLIGENCE*

"A wonderful story, superbly told. A true page-turner. Emblematic of an opaque world that is all but impossible for outsiders to penetrate. Enthralling, it deserves to be read."
BOB BAER, FORMER CIA OFFICER AND AUTHOR OF *SEE NO EVIL*

"If any mystery writer were to put this in a novel, it would hardly be believed. But page by page, a dramatic story of spies, murder and betrayal unfolds in this excellently researched and gripping book."
RICHARD J. ALDRICH, AUTHOR OF *GCHQ*

MURDER IN CAIRO

Solving a Cold War Spy Mystery

Peter Gillman and **Emanuele Midolo**

with Leni Gillman

Biteback Publishing

First published in Great Britain in 2025 by
Biteback Publishing Ltd, London
Copyright © Peter Gillman and Emanuele Midolo 2025

Peter Gillman and Emanuele Midolo have asserted their rights under the Copyright, Designs and Patents Act 1988 to be identified as the authors of this work.

All rights reserved. No part of this publication may be reproduced, stored in a retrieval system or transmitted, in any form or by any means, without the publisher's prior permission in writing.

This book is sold subject to the condition that it shall not, by way of trade or otherwise, be lent, resold, hired out or otherwise circulated without the publisher's prior consent in any form of binding or cover other than that in which it is published and without a similar condition, including this condition, being imposed on the subsequent purchaser.

Every reasonable effort has been made to trace copyright holders of material reproduced in this book, but if any have been inadvertently overlooked the publisher would be glad to hear from them.

ISBN 978-1-78590-702-9

10 9 8 7 6 5 4 3 2 1

A CIP catalogue record for this book is available from the British Library.

Set in Minion Pro

Printed and bound in Great Britain by
CPI Group (UK) Ltd, Croydon CR0 4YY

To Juliette Gillman and Lorenzo Trimarchi

CONTENTS

Map of David Holden's last journey	ix
Foreword *by Tina Brown*	xi
Authors' note	xv
Prologue	xvii

PART ONE			1
Chapter 1	The vanishing of David Holden		3
Chapter 2	The warning		13
Chapter 3	Into deep waters		17
Chapter 4	On deadline		37
Chapter 5	Citadels		47
Chapter 6	An inside job?		61
Chapter 7	A man of many lives		71
Chapter 8	The Thunderer		87
Chapter 9	Roving correspondent		107
Chapter 10	Sunday papers		117
Chapter 11	The report		137
Chapter 12	'Jerusalem 1500'		159
Chapter 13	The wilderness of mirrors		169

PART TWO	185
Chapter 14 The strange case of Mr Halton	187
Chapter 15 The last of his kind	191
Chapter 16 Back on the case	199
Chapter 17 The name's Fees, James Fees	221
Chapter 18 Red and lavender	241
Chapter 19 The mockingbirds	259
Chapter 20 On Her Majesty's secret service	273
Chapter 21 Running sands	295
Chapter 22 The wrong man	317
Chapter 23 The scribe	333
Chapter 24 Under the Pyramids	345
Chapter 25 Agent of influence	365
Epilogue	409
Notes and references	413
Bibliography	421
Acknowledgements	429
Index	433

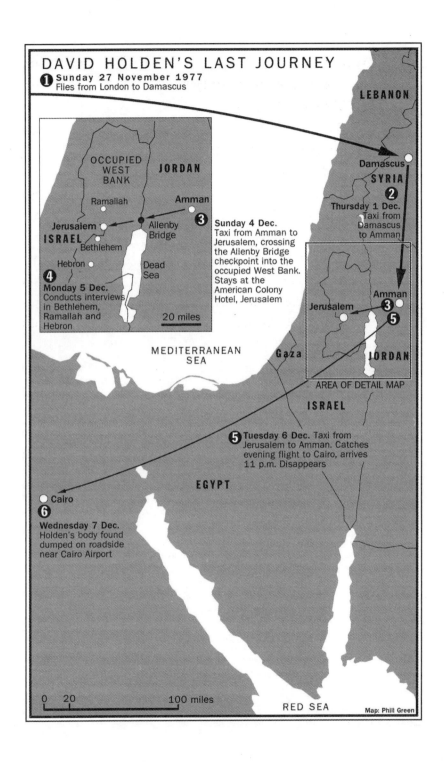

FOREWORD

'Things are not what they seem on the surface. Dig deeper, dig deeper, dig deeper.' That was the ethos – expressed in 2010 to former *Guardian* editor Alan Rusbridger – that inspired Sir Harold Evans's years as a newspaper editor at the *Northern Echo*, the *Sunday Times* and *The Times* and informed his second act in the US as the president and publisher of Random House, a bestselling author and a historian. His rigour was relentless, his curiosity insatiable and his contempt for slapdash sourcing or confirmation bias withering. In 2002, Harry's peers voted him the greatest British newspaper editor of all time. It was an accolade of which my husband was extremely proud.

As editor of the *Sunday Times* in 1967, Harry reinfused its Insight investigative unit with new ambition, a cadre of brilliant truth seekers and a tenacious mission to take on the big, daunting stories that exposed cover-ups of human injustice, corporate greed, government malfeasance and a political establishment that rested too easily on assumptions of its own inscrutability. Freedom of information was an unwelcome concept and one that Harry was determined to embrace. One of his most celebrated scoops was Insight's exposure of the Foreign Office's knowledge that Harold 'Kim' Philby, its top Soviet spymaster, was in fact an unscrupulous double agent, whose decades-long betrayal of his country was even more damaging than previously known. After the global sensation it caused, Harry was told that Ian Fleming – former intelligence officer, creator of James Bond and longtime *Sunday Times* executive – said that the real Bonds 'were pissed off at being revealed as a ship of fools'.

Harry's unshakable commitment to the truth translated into his willingness to campaign – for years, if necessary – to expose the cover-ups and, just as important, to ensure that the reporting would lead to results, including the reform of laws. In his 2009 memoir *My Paper Chase*, he asserted: 'No campaign should be ended until it had succeeded – or was proved wrong.'

As the 33-year-old editor of the *Northern Echo* in Darlington, Harry became consumed by the heartbreaking miscarriage of justice in the case of a young, barely literate Welshman, Timothy Evans, who was hanged in 1950 for the murder of his wife and baby daughter instead of the real perpetrator, serial killer John Reginald Christie, who lived in the flat downstairs. The *Northern Echo*'s posthumous campaign was so effective it contributed to Home Secretary Roy Jenkins's epic decision to abolish the death penalty in the UK.

Harry's longest and most acclaimed campaign was in the pages of the *Sunday Times* on behalf of the children born with horrific birth defects caused by the morning sickness drug thalidomide, manufactured by the German firm Chemie Grünenthal and distributed in the UK by the powerful Distillers (one of the paper's biggest advertisers). More than 20,000 babies worldwide were born with serious birth defects long after the company had been warned of the dangers, but their families were offered a pittance in compensation. Harry launched a decade-long Insight crusade that found new ways every week to tell the human story as well as expose the true scale of the human pain of the scandal and the cynical support of commercial interests by politicians. In the face of corporate suppression and legal gag orders, Harry ultimately appealed to the European Court of Human Rights, saying he was prepared to go to prison if that was

FOREWORD

the price of publishing the truth. 'It was a famous victory,' former Insight journalist Clive Irving summed it up:

> The government was obliged to pass a statutory reform that allowed reporting and comment in a civil case until a date was set for trial – a vital new freedom that other papers and media, who had in this case been notably less zealous than the *Sunday Times*, also came to enjoy.

But there was one story, very close to home, that Harry and his crack *Sunday Times* reporters were never able to solve. And it obsessed him to the end of his life. In his last years, he was still trying to seek out new leads that might shed light on the mystery of what happened to one of his own most valued reporters, David Holden, the *Sunday Times*'s chief foreign correspondent, who was murdered in Cairo on assignment when covering the peace talks between Israel and Egypt, ten years after the Six-Day War. Harry recalled in *My Paper Chase* how he first heard the news of Holden's violent end.

Late on Saturday 10 December, 'the dreaded call came. The British embassy ... had heard that on Wednesday, 7 December, the body of "an unknown European male" had been deposited in Cairo's Kasr el Ainy mortuary.' Bob Jobbins, the BBC Cairo correspondent who went to the mortuary three days later and identified Holden, 'was struck by the lack of any obvious injury, save a small exit wound in his chest. "An apparent execution," he presciently observed.'

Holden's body had been found at 8 a.m. on Wednesday, nine hours after his arrival in Cairo. He lay on a sandy patch, littered with old newspapers, by the highway that ran beside the walls of Al-Azhar University. He was on his back, his feet neatly together. His expression was calm, his hair as sleek as ever. All marks that might suggest his identity or nationality had been removed, down to the maker's label in his jacket.

Within hours, Harry dispatched six reporters to the Middle East and began peppering them with questions to answer: Who knew Holden was arriving on flight RJ 503 from Amman? Who else was on the plane with him? Could he have spotted a terrorist on board? Was he seen leaving the airport with anyone and by anyone he knew? Was the motive for his killing something to do with his private life? Or was the trigger his work? Was there something to suggest that he had been chosen as a high-profile target by Palestinian rejectionists or terrorists? Who had he seen in his swing through the Middle East? Had he alarmed somebody? Or had he perhaps been asked to carry to Cairo a message or document too sensitive for telex or telephone?

Potential clues did emerge. Holden – like so many at that time – turned out to have been hiding his true sexuality. He had sent a mysterious postcard to Jan – formerly James – Morris with the cryptic message: 'In the Middle East, citadels still have their uses.' But his murder was clearly a professional hit. And back at the *Sunday Times* office, there were mysteries too. Eight telexes about Holden's changing travel plans had gone missing. Had the *Sunday Times* office been burgled or – more concerning – was there a mole inside the *Sunday Times*? The regretful conclusion Harry eventually reached was that Holden himself had been working in intelligence – but for whom, and why was he liquidated?

This compelling investigation by Peter Gillman and Emanuele Midolo uncovers much that is new. Perhaps most significantly, it unpeels many more layers of the dark labyrinth in which the lives of journalists and spies were then so deeply interwoven and where Holden's role seems fatally to be trapped in conflicts of identity, allegiance and personal beliefs.

Deeper, deeper… I only wish Harry, who died in 2020, was alive to read it.

Tina Brown
January 2025

AUTHORS' NOTE

This book is a work of non-fiction; all characters and events depicted in these pages are real. All dialogue in quote marks is based on contemporaneous notes and/or recordings. Although this book describes our activities during the original and new investigations, we have written it in the third person, for purposes of clarity. The observant reader may deduce that Peter Gillman was the lead author in the first part, Emanuele Midolo in the second. That is correct, but we discussed and agreed what each of us would write and then commented on the resulting text. The outcome is a collaborative manuscript to which we are pleased to put both our names.

Peter Gillman and Emanuele Midolo
January 2025, London

PROLOGUE

PROLOGUE

David Holden was in a foul mood. His flight from Amman to Cairo on the evening of 6 December 1977 had been held at the departure gate for ninety minutes as the pilot waited for an overdue group of American tourists. When they finally filed on board, one of them, Mrs Willivene Bonnette, stopped beside Holden, who was ensconced in a seat on the aisle. She told Holden she wanted to take the centre-row seat, but he refused to stand up to let her pass. Bonnette, a sturdy middle-aged woman from Clyde, Ohio, was forced to squeeze past him instead.

Holden, aged fifty-three, was the chief foreign correspondent of the London *Sunday Times*. With slicked-back brown hair and china-blue eyes, he was wearing a navy corduroy jacket with a black roll-neck sweater, beige trousers and black Italian leather moccasin shoes. He was nearing the end of a hectic ten-day swing through the Middle East, covering prospective peace talks between Egypt and Israel, but he was not about to reveal that to Bonnette.

Flight RJ 503 finally took off at 9.45 p.m. Once it was in the air, Bonnette tried to strike up a conversation with Holden.

'Why are you going to Cairo?' she asked him.

'On business,' was all he would say.

Bonnette persevered. 'We're on a trip to the Holy Land.'

Holden showed a flicker of interest. 'What sites are you going to visit in Egypt?'

'I don't know,' Bonnette admitted.

'That's absurd,' Holden snapped. At that point, Bonnette gave up trying to engage with him. She later said that she found him 'sarcastic, surly and impatient'.

Just why Holden appeared so tetchy that evening, beyond the matter of the flight delay, was later to prove a central issue for a team of *Sunday Times* investigative journalists. Holden's sour demeanour cannot have been improved by the drab supper of cold chicken salad and tinned peaches which the Royal Jordanian airline served its economy passengers. At the end of the meal – the last Holden would ever eat – he was handed a coffee, which he topped up from a hip flask he retrieved from inside his jacket. After drinking that, Holden refilled his cup from the flask and swallowed the contents neat.

The flight landed in Cairo at 11 p.m. The passengers, including the forty-one American Holy Land tourists, were ferried by bus to the airport terminal. Once inside, Holden walked briskly through the echoing stone corridors to the arrivals hall. Holden had last visited Egypt five years before, but he knew the routine. First, as required by Egypt's visitor regulations, he purchased some Egyptian currency, cashing traveller's cheques to the value of $200 at the Royal Bank of Egypt desk and receiving 200 Egyptian pounds in notes plus a handful of coins in exchange. He completed a form for a temporary visitor's visa, curiously entering 'writer' rather than 'journalist' in the space asking his profession – a detail that was later to attract attention. He passed through immigration control and joined the cluster of passengers waiting for their baggage. When his venerable red Samsonite case slid into sight on the luggage belt, he retrieved it and headed for the customs area, passing unhindered through the 'nothing to declare' channel.

PROLOGUE

The route to the exit lay along yet another corridor and through a pair of swing doors. Beyond, a double line of crash barriers funnelled arriving passengers into the throng of people waiting to meet their friends or relatives, with a pair of policemen, revolvers on their belts, on hand to help clear a way through. Another few steps led to the pavement outside.

It was a warm night, around twenty degrees, with an arid tang of dust lingering from the sandstorm which had swept through Cairo the previous day. The pavement was lit by the glare of the illuminated blue lettering above the door, showing the single word 'Arrival' with its Arabic version alongside. A short distance to the left was a line of taxis, waiting to take passengers on the half-hour journey into central Cairo for a metered fare of around £3, plus tip. Before a taxi set off, a policeman would log the details – registration plate, departure time, destination – in a notebook, a measure intended to prevent passengers from being robbed or hijacked.

In a darkened area to the right, barely visible among intermittent pools of light, was a cluster of battered pirate taxis offering a bone-shaking, cut-price ride into Cairo but without the security of being logged by the police; their drivers had secured this privileged position near the arrivals exit by bribing the selfsame airport police. As passengers emerged from the terminal, the pirate drivers would walk alongside them and offer to take them into the city centre for around £2, substantially undercutting the official rate.

It is known for certain that Holden did not take an official taxi. It is far more likely that he was escorted to the shadowy area to the right of the terminal, where he boarded a battered Fiat that resembled one of the pirate taxis.

Then David Holden disappeared into the Cairo night.

PARLOURS

PART ONE

*'Things are not what they seem on the surface.
Dig deeper, dig deeper, dig deeper.'*
HAROLD EVANS

CHAPTER 1

THE VANISHING OF DAVID HOLDEN

The last time anyone at the *Sunday Times* had heard from David Holden was three days before. On Saturday 3 December 1977, he sent a report from Amman, Jordan's capital, about prospects for peace in the Middle East. He had been dispatched to the region ahead of a nine-day conference in Cairo, organised by the Egyptian President, Anwar Sadat. Journalism is said to provide the first draft of history, and it was already clear that this was an epochal moment, signalling the first rapprochement between Israel and its embattled Arab neighbours since Israel's fire-and-brimstone birth twenty-nine years before. In mid-November, Sadat had made a historic three-day visit to the country, the first ever by an Arab leader, implicitly recognising its right to exist. The geopolitical forces swirling around these events were immense, so it was appropriate for the *Sunday Times* to send its chief foreign correspondent to the Middle East.

Holden had spent a busy week researching his story, visiting Damascus and Amman where he met political leaders and diplomats and attended press conferences given by President Assad of Syria and King Hussein of Jordan. He started writing his report at the Reuters news agency office in Amman on the evening of

2 December, returning the next morning to complete it and transmit it to the newspaper. Some 2,000 words long, it was an accomplished and cautiously optimistic review of how the region was responding to the talks between Sadat and Israel's Prime Minister, Menachem Begin. Holden's piece was allocated to the top of page ten of the 4 December issue under the headline: 'Peace may break out after all'.

In an accompanying message to the newspaper's foreign desk on Saturday 3 December, Holden had outlined his travel plans: on Sunday he would travel to the occupied Palestinian West Bank and then Israel, crossing from Jordan via the Allenby Bridge. Holden would spend two nights in Jerusalem and then, on 6 December, would return across the Allenby Bridge into Jordan in time to catch the evening flight from Amman to Cairo.

At first, his editors were not unduly concerned at having no word from Holden. Journalists on overseas trips were expected to stay in contact with the foreign desk, both to enable the newspaper to plan the week's edition and to monitor their movements and check on their safety. The correspondents often found this a time-consuming distraction, given the difficulties they faced in communicating with their London office. They had two main methods of doing so. One was by telex, which meant typing a message on their portable manual typewriter and asking a hotel to transmit it, usually handing it to the telex operator with a financial sweetener to ensure it went to the top of the pile of messages waiting to be keyed. The other was to book a telephone call at the hotel, which could take hours to be placed. So Holden's silence was not considered troubling, at least for the time being.

His plans were, however, an important item at the scheduled news conference on Wednesday morning. The meetings were led by the editor, Harold Evans. By then, Evans had been in post for ten years, building the newspaper's reputation for independent journalism with a succession of dramatic investigations and revelations, which included exposing the MI6/KGB double agent Harold 'Kim' Philby and the fight to establish the truth about the pregnancy drug thalidomide, which caused severe birth defects, and to obtain compensation for its victims.

It was through his commitment to stories such as these that Evans won his journalists' loyalty and respect. They became accustomed to the way he would tilt his head and fix them with his compelling blue eyes as he quizzed them about their evidence and their sources. Approaching fifty, with a shock of neatly parted brown hair, he spoke in quietly persuasive tones, revealing only a trace of his Manchester accent. His most prized quality, once he was satisfied a story was sound, was the trust he placed in his journalists, particularly when the newspaper published controversial subjects and the inevitable rows broke.

The reporters also valued his readiness to agree to their proposals to undertake potentially dangerous assignments, although here Evans was the subject of conflicting instincts. One was to protect his journalists' safety. The other was to allow them to do what they wanted. It was profoundly wearing, he once said, 'trying and failing' to restrain his journalists when they wanted to report from the world's conflict zones and front lines. He was distraught when the writer Nick Tomalin was killed by a Syrian missile during the 1973 Arab–Israeli War, questioning both others and himself as to whether more could have been done to protect Tomalin. Two years later, the reporter Jon Swain was captured by the Khmer Rouge in Cambodia and only narrowly survived – a story later told in the film *The Killing Fields*. On that occasion, Evans later observed, Swain had ignored the newspaper's instructions to leave Phnom Penh when the Khmer Rouge approached, illustrating the difficulties of reining in his journalists and the anxieties they subjected him to. Those anxieties were about to return.

At 11 a.m. that Wednesday, the newspaper's section editors

gathered in Evans's office on the sixth floor of the *Sunday Times*' building in Gray's Inn Road, half a mile north of the traditional newspaper milieu of Fleet Street. The home news editor, Derrik Mercer, was usually the first to pitch his stories, followed by the foreign editor, Peter Wilsher, or his deputy, Cal McCrystal. By the standards of Fleet Street, where bullying and profane language were rampant, these morning meetings were civilised affairs. It was nonetheless an uncomfortable moment for the foreign desk pair when Evans asked what Holden intended to write that week. They told Evans that Holden had planned to visit the occupied Palestinian West Bank to test reactions to the prospective peace deal between Israel and Egypt. But they had no information beyond that and were still waiting to hear from him.

At first, the foreign desk assumed that Holden had been preoccupied with his travel arrangements and may even have arrived in Cairo a day later than planned. But when they returned to the *Sunday Times* office on Thursday morning to discover there was no overnight message from him, their concern mounted and they embarked on a search. So far as they knew, Holden had been planning to stay at one of two hotels: the Cairo Hilton or the Cairo Méridien. They found that he had not checked in at either hotel; nor had he contacted the Cairo office of the Reuters international press agency – a vital calling point for journalists anxious to secure their lines of communication.

Throughout Thursday, the search continued with increasing urgency. The foreign staff called the British Embassies in Amman and Cairo, but they had no news of him. The foreign desk located several British journalists whose paths had crossed with Holden's during his trip, but none had any useful information. They enlisted other journalists at the *Sunday Times* office, among them Peter Gillman, a member of the Insight investigative team, who had made several trips to the Middle East that year. Gillman called a contact in Jerusalem who offered to visit the taxi rank where drivers plied the run to and from Amman via the Allenby Bridge. Holden had presumably taken a taxi for his return to Amman on 6 December, but none of the drivers remembered carrying him that day.

By Friday, it was clear that something was seriously amiss. The *Sunday Times* had managed to establish the bare essentials: yes, Holden had been recorded crossing the Allenby Bridge and yes, he had taken flight RJ 503 to Egypt, although it had been unable to confirm any of his arrival details in Cairo. Otherwise it had nothing. The foreign desk speculated that Holden was following up a story so sensitive that he deemed it unwise to contact the office. On Saturday, as response after response to its inquiries came back negative, it abandoned the theory. Then came a new hope, when the British Embassy in Amman suggested that Holden could have been detained at Cairo Airport because his cholera certificate was out of date – a member of the embassy staff had been held incommunicado at the airport for three days for exactly that reason. The deputy foreign editor, McCrystal, believed that within a few hours, a 'tired and exasperated' Holden would telephone from Cairo with just such an explanation.

Meanwhile, preparations for that week's edition continued. As a hands-on editor, Evans could usually be found in the newspaper's composing room. Amid the sweet smell of printing ink and the clatter of metal type, stories were being cut to fit the available space and headlines rewritten, with the printers lifting and trimming slabs of metal type to the journalists' instructions. The first edition went to press at 5 p.m. – a deadline timed to accommodate the afternoon's football results – with a front-page lead about how the UK's Labour government was teaming up with trade union leaders to launch a propaganda assault on the neo-Nazi National Front, which was gaining ground among working-class voters. There was a largely unchanged second edition at around 9 p.m. Shortly afterwards,

Evans left the office for the five-minute journey to a nearby apartment which was rented for overnight stays. He was still settling in when, as he later remarked, 'the dreaded call came'.

Earlier that day, the BBC's Middle East correspondent, Bob Jobbins, had been called to the mortuary in Cairo where the bodies of accident victims were deposited. Jobbins drove there from his office accompanied by an Egyptian journalist, Fuad al Gawhary, the Cairo correspondent, or 'stringer', of the *Sunday Times*. Al Gawhary was among the journalists enlisted by the newspaper in the search for Holden, and he had placed calls to his contacts in the Cairo police and security services. That morning one of them had called back with the news that the body of a European man had been taken to the mortuary three days earlier.

Al Gawhary had never met Holden; so he in turn called Jobbins. Jobbins had met Holden just once, some seven years before, when they spent a frustrating week together in Tripoli, trying – and failing – to obtain an interview with Libya's Colonel Gaddafi. Jobbins considered that was enough to enable him to identify Holden, if indeed his body was now in the mortuary.

More than forty-five years on, details of Jobbins's visit were imprinted in his memory. The mortuary adjoined Cairo's Kasr el Ainy Hospital, a run-down building close to the west bank of the Nile. Jobbins and al Gawhary were shown into a tiled room, poorly lit and reeking of disinfectant, where a series of giant refrigerated drawers lined the walls. The mortuary superintendent, a middle-aged Egyptian wearing a clinician's apron, pulled open one of the drawers, which was green on the outside, steel-lined on the inside. Jobbins saw a man's body covered in a white sheet, which the superintendent lifted back to reveal his face.

At first, Jobbins felt sure it was Holden. Then, in a moment of self-doubt, he hesitated. Aware of the responsibility he was assuming, he asked himself: 'Could it be someone else?' He silently answered his own question: 'No, it's David.' Jobbins repeated his answer, this time aloud, to al Gawhary, who translated it for the superintendent.

Jobbins looked at the body again. The mortuary embalmer had done his work well. Holden had rosy cheeks, his hair had been parted and his face was set in a parodic semblance of repose. Jobbins thought how peaceful he looked but could not help comparing his inert figure with the sociable companion he had spent a week with holed up in Libya.

Questions were already racing through Jobbins's mind. Before he could voice them, the superintendent pulled the sheet further down. Holden was wearing a singlet which the superintendent lifted to reveal a small, neat wound below his left nipple – together with a bullet which was now caught up in the folds of the singlet.

The superintendent spoke to al Gawhary, who translated again for Jobbins's benefit. 'He says this is the exit wound,' al Gawhary reported. 'And this is the bullet which killed him. The entry wound is in his back. He would have died at once.'

Jobbins was struck by two aspects of what he had seen and heard. First, the bullet that killed Holden was a small calibre, possibly a 9mm. Second, this looked like a professional hit, suggesting that Holden was the victim of an execution. After returning to his office, Jobbins telephoned the press attaché at the British Embassy in Cairo. It was the Foreign Office which in turn telephoned the *Sunday Times* in London shortly before 10 p.m. The call was answered by McCrystal, who heard the stark message: Holden's body had been found. McCrystal then made the fateful call to Evans.

The shock, Evans later wrote, was 'profound'. For the moment, professionalism kicked in. The front page of the next morning's newspaper was redesigned and the news of Holden's death was posted at the top under the headline: 'Sunday Times man found shot in Egypt'. It was illustrated with a photo of Holden looking up at the camera from beneath a furrowed brow, with a quizzical half-smile on his lips: 'eminent and admired', read the caption. Meanwhile, a distressed Evans asked the senior editors still at the office to call the journalists who had been assisting in the search during the week.

One was Gillman, who was at home when the telephone rang. It was the features editor, John Barry, who told him that Holden's body had been found in Cairo, adding some details which Jobbins had acquired. Holden had apparently been shot soon after he arrived at Cairo Airport on 6 December. His body had been stripped of all means of identification and dumped in the dirt beside a road near the airport, where it had been found on the morning of Wednesday 7 December. Barry told Gillman that the newspaper was still formulating its plans for covering Holden's death, but he should expect a call from Evans in the morning.

After a fitful night at the apartment, Evans swung into action. Baffled and concerned though he was, his journalistic instincts took over. He began calling some of his most experienced reporters, requesting them to travel to the Middle East to reconstruct Holden's last week and look for answers as to why he was killed. Barry and McCrystal would go to Cairo, Gillman and his Insight colleague Paul Eddy to Amman. The veteran reporter Antony Terry would go to Israel, while Helena Cobban, a correspondent based in Beirut, would cover Lebanon.

When Evans called Gillman, he told him that he and Eddy should establish, in as much detail as possible, how Holden had spent his three days in Jordan before flying to Cairo on 6 December. Gillman reminded Evans that he had visited Jordan several times already that year and had contacts he was sure would help. Evans said that was good to hear.

'Watch out for Mossad,' Evans added. 'They're the best intelligence agency in the world.'

Gillman was only too aware of the implications of Evans's warning. Six months before, the *Sunday Times* had published a lengthy and meticulously researched article which concluded that Israel's security service habitually tortured Palestinian prisoners. The report was unprecedented in the British media for its criticism of Israel, whose President termed it 'the single most damaging article' published about Israel since its creation in 1948. Israel was nothing if not vengeful in taking reprisals against those it deemed its enemies. If that was the case now, Holden was the victim of a mistake. The Israeli press had mistakenly named Holden as one of the authors of the article. The two principal reporters who conducted the investigation were in fact Gillman and his colleague Eddy. This raised one immediate question: if they tried to follow Holden's footsteps on his final Middle East trip, would they walk into the same trap?

CHAPTER 2

THE WARNING

Emanuele Midolo did not notice him at first. The man was sitting, alone, at a table a few metres away. The first thing Midolo saw were his sunglasses. It was early afternoon and the sky was covered by a thin haze. There was no need for shades, he thought, even by the swimming pool where they were sitting. The man wore a white polo shirt and blue jeans. He had two mobile phones on the table, one on top of the other. His brown hair was parted in the middle and neatly combed. Clean shaven, he looked like a young Arab version of Sylvester Stallone. Despite the sunglasses, he could see that the man had his eyes set on him. He was not eating or drinking, and he sat very still, his head not moving. The only thing he seemed to be doing was staring. For the first time since arriving in Cairo, Midolo felt uneasy. It was September 2023 and Midolo, thirty-five, a reporter at *The Times* and the *Sunday Times* in London, was in Egypt to investigate a murder that had happened there more than four decades earlier.

He decided to take a photograph of the man and send it to his writing partner, Peter Gillman, who was forty-five years his senior and had been Midolo's age when he was first assigned to the case. Holding his phone low and close to the table, as if he were reading a message, Midolo managed to take a clear shot of the man – he could even see his eyes looking at him beneath the glasses. But as soon as he had done that, the man signalled to a waiter. Midolo panicked. Did he see him taking the photo? The man spoke to the waiter who, to Midolo's relief, soon returned with a shisha, from which the man started pulling white puffs of smoke. Was he going crazy? Imagining it all?

He was not naturally prone to paranoia, but there had been many signs – and warnings too. People he had contacted did not want to meet him, nor even speak to him over the phone. Local fixers had refused to help. *The Times*'s Middle Eastern correspondent, who had been banned from Egypt years earlier after he had conducted investigations of the current regime, told him he was likely to be followed at all times. 'They assume that every British journalist, and especially from *The Times*, is MI6,' he told him. 'So you are going to be watched.'

One Western journalist based in Egypt, who had previously investigated the same story, had sounded particularly paranoid. She had first agreed to meet but urged: 'Do remember that you need to be super careful, yes?' As Midolo's visit approached, she backtracked, saying she was not sure she would be able to meet him after all. 'People here are not going to help you with this, sorry to say.'

The day before flying to Cairo, he messaged her again, using an encrypted app.

'I'm going to take a pass on this,' she replied. 'Good luck, but it's just not the right time for these kinds of inquiries.'

Midolo chose not to press her, but the wording left him wondering what she meant. The day before leaving London, he had received another warning, this time from a colleague at the paper who was known in the office to be close to MI6. 'I've been talking to "a friend in the Foreign Office" (as they call themselves) and need to pass on a rather important message about your proposed inquiries in Egypt,' the colleague texted him.

When Midolo called, the colleague relayed his conversation with the 'friend': 'Do not pursue any kind of obvious snooping around. Every second person is an informer. You have no idea, the control... it's all around. It's still a police state, don't ever forget that.'

The colleague went on to explain that the 'friend' had run a number of operations in Egypt but that he only ever did that 'from outside'. If ever he went to Egypt, he was extremely careful. 'He just looked at things and didn't ask too many questions,' the colleague said. 'They're watching foreigners. They're pretty jumpy there, particularly after the story with the poor Italian.' He was referring to Giulio Regeni, a young journalist and Cambridge PhD student who had been abducted, tortured and murdered in Egypt in 2016. But Regeni's murder was different. It had happened under the current regime, after General Abdul Fattah al-Sisi had seized power in a military coup d'état in 2013, overthrowing the first-ever democratically elected government in the country. The Egyptian intelligence services were suspected of having a hand in the killing of the Italian journalist, therefore putting General Sisi under international pressure.

Holden had been murdered almost half a century before. At first, it felt like a different time and place, where the past was another country. Holden had died in an era when, in the midst of the Cold War, the two great powers of the US and the USSR were jostling for dominance in a turbulent region. For a luminous moment, after the fall of the Iron Curtain in 1989, that world seemed to have ended. The CIA was not busy plotting coups and toppling regimes in faraway places, while the KGB was no longer assassinating dissidents at home and abroad. There was relative peace in the Middle East and the Prime Minister of Israel and the leader of Palestine were shaking hands on the lawn of the White House.

But now, the old days had returned. The CIA and the new Russian secret service were as active as ever and at each other's throats again. The Middle East was on fire and Israel and Palestine were locked in an all-out war. It was Holden's world. The same world that had killed him and dumped him on the side of a desert road. Midolo was in Cairo to find out, once and for all, who had done it and why.

The Times had taken things seriously enough to arrange safety measures for him. For starters, the phone Midolo had used to take the man's picture was not his phone. It was a 'burner' phone given to him by the newspaper. Before his trip, he sat down with Chris Kemp, the paper's head of safety and security, and told him about the story he was working on. Kemp explained that with the latest monitoring technology, courtesy of China, the authorities in Egypt could hack into his phone remotely. They could listen in on his calls, read his texts, steal his passwords and even turn on his microphone to eavesdrop on him. The burner phone would be equipped with a software, called Lookout, to shield it from any of these cybersecurity threats and alert him if anyone was trying to hack their way in.

Sitting on the terrace of the Four Seasons Hotel in the Garden City quarter in West Cairo, Midolo was glad he did not have his personal phone with him, full of details of the Holden case. That was the only thing he was glad about. To be warned about state surveillance was one thing; to have that crawling feeling on his skin was another altogether. The staring contest with the man was still on. Midolo had finished his lunch but decided to stay at the table until his watcher left. After a while, the man stood up, paid and walked away, this time not even glancing at him.

Feeling the tension ease, Midolo sipped from his glass and realised his hand was shaking. He waited a few more minutes then headed towards the exit. The man was there too and was about to get into a lift. Midolo slowed down, hoping the doors would close, but the man placed a hand over the sensor and kept them open. Midolo had no choice but to get in. As the doors closed on him, all he could think was: 'What am I doing here?'

CHAPTER 3

INTO DEEP WATERS

Peter Gillman was packing. He did not know how long he would be in Amman – at a guess, a week to ten days, taking him close to Christmas. Strewn out beside his travel-worn suitcase was a range of clothing that he hoped would cover all eventualities. One item stood ready: his portable typewriter, in its case labelled 'Peter Gillman *Sunday Times* London England'.

Gillman enjoyed the challenge, the thrill, of overseas reporting: step off the plane, negotiate the passport checks, find your bearings at the airport exit, rely on a mix of procedure and wit to see you through. But this was no ordinary assignment. He had hardly known Holden, other than as a face he occasionally glimpsed in the *Sunday Times* office. Even so, the fact remained that a journalist had been killed. For the sake of other journalists, for the sake of journalism itself, the murderers had to be found, the reason revealed.

Why should someone want Holden dead so badly that he was lured into a car and executed some hours later, his body unceremoniously dumped in the dirt beside a road? What did the manner of his execution say about his killer's motives? Hovering over all of this was Evans's warning about Mossad, with the implication that Holden could have been the wrong target, leaving open the question of whether Israel would strike again.

Gillman, thirty-five, with owlish glasses and dark curly hair that was beginning to recede, had been writing for the *Sunday Times* for twelve years. He started as a freelancer on its weekend colour magazine, specialising in long-form features and developing a niche in true-crime reporting. Then he joined the magazine staff and, in 1973, graduated to the news desk of the newspaper where his beat included covering the Troubles, the lethal inter-communal strife between Catholics and Protestants in Northern Ireland that raged for much of the decade. A year or so later, his career took a step up when he met Evans in the office lift. Evans clapped him on the shoulders and asked him to join the newspaper's Insight team, its renowned investigative unit, which was then being revitalised. Gillman hardly had time to ask any questions by the time the lift reached its destination but thought it politic to agree.

A second recruit for the Insight team was Paul Eddy, who had joined the *Sunday Times* in 1971. It was a tight-knit pairing, referred to sometimes as 'Giddy' or 'the twins', and they had complementary backgrounds. Gillman, from suburban south London, went to Dulwich College and Oxford University; Eddy, from Leamington in the Midlands, left school at fifteen and performed stints in local papers and news agencies before setting up his own agency in the West Midlands. After working for the *Sunday Mirror* and the Associated Press bureau in Athens, he started part-time shifts at the *Sunday Times*, where his talent was spotted and he was taken on the staff. A lean figure, always well-dressed, he was known for his inordinate consumption of both cigarettes and coffee, which helped sustain him during the long Friday-night writing stints that Insight required, often lasting through to the Saturday afternoon deadline as well. 'I don't mind if I kill myself early, so long as I can live the life I want,' Eddy would say to people who warned him about his lifestyle.

Gillman and Eddy began their investigation of Israel's treatment of Palestinian prisoners in April 1977. They spent three weeks working undercover in Israel and the occupied West Bank and Gaza, interviewing forty-four Palestinians who had been arrested and interrogated. They described interrogations that included beatings, sexual abuse, electric shocks, being held in tiny cells with serrated floors where they were unable to stand up and other methods amounting to torture. Their four-page report was published on 1 June. It was headlined 'Israel and Torture' and unequivocally concluded that Israel's security service, Shin Bet, routinely and systematically deployed brutality and torture against Palestinian prisoners.

The report was greeted with a furore. On one side were those who felt that Israel had held the British media in its thrall for far too long, exempting its practices as an occupying power from scrutiny. Others contended that the article was antisemitic and that the *Sunday Times* had been corrupted by Middle East money. Prime Minister Begin delivered his statement that it was the most damaging article ever published about Israel to a meeting of senior British Jewry. The Israeli Embassy delivered a purported rebuttal to the article which the *Sunday Times* published on 3 July and which the Insight team demolished, point by point, the following week. In the US, President Carter raised the report in a meeting with Begin, telling him that all such interrogation methods should stop.

It was in this period that Holden was named in the Israeli press as one of the authors of the piece. The *Sunday Times* did publish a correction, naming Gillman and Eddy instead. But maybe the belief that Holden was involved had stuck? Or perhaps the chief foreign correspondent of the *Sunday Times* was still judged a suitable target? Either way, Gillman knew he should take heed of Evans's warning, which he coupled with another he had received in Amman just three months before. Gillman had been conducting further inquiries in the aftermath of the Insight report, with the discreet assistance of the chief Jordan delegate of the International Committee of the Red Cross (ICRC), Jean Courvoisier. 'Mr Gillman,' Courvoisier had urged, 'I caution you with all seriousness against ever going to Israel again. You would be in the greatest danger if you did.'

Gillman had absolutely no plans to visit Israel on this trip. But the warnings served as an intimation that shadowy and ruthless forces were involved in Holden's killing, Israeli or otherwise. So how was he to conduct himself on such an assignment? The closest comparison for Gillman lay in his reporting from Northern Ireland, where he had covered both sides in the conflict, as well as the British Army. In internecine conflicts such as that, where suspicion of betrayal and double-dealing could be fatal, the overriding principle for journalists was to be open and above board in all they did. It followed that they should decline any invitations to become an informant for the British intelligence and security services, as Gillman did when propositioned by Peter Imbert, then a senior Special Branch officer who specialised in Northern Ireland. If those were the rules for operating in Northern Ireland, what were they for inquiring into a journalist's murder in the Middle East? What were the pitfalls and dangers? Other than Evans's warning, Gillman had been given no guidance by the *Sunday Times*, which presumably assumed that he was sensible and experienced enough to work these things out for himself.

'How are you getting on?' Gillman's wife Leni had come into the room.

'It's going well,' Gillman told her. 'All under control.'

'Let me fold these up for you.' Leni picked up a pair of shirts, straightened and folded them, then placed them neatly in her husband's suitcase.

'How long will you be away?'

'Not sure,' Gillman replied. 'A week or so, at a guess.'

They had been married for fifteen years, Gillman a journalist for thirteen. Their parting the next morning was practised, a hug and a kiss, as they juggled their respective departures: hers to the nearby secondary school, attended by their two sons, where she worked as a teacher; his to Heathrow, where he was booked into Alia's 10 a.m. flight to Amman.

By then, two of the *Sunday Times*'s most experienced journalists were already in Cairo, having flown there on 11 December: Cal McCrystal, from the newspaper's foreign department, and John Barry, a former Insight editor. Another was dispatched to Israel: Tony Terry, who had been a reporter with the *Sunday Times* since the 1940s. The *Sunday Times* had also enlisted its experienced Beirut correspondent Helena Cobban, and Gillman's Insight colleague Paul Eddy was due to follow him to Amman a day or so later. The work would be coordinated by the foreign department manager Steve Boyd, a dependable, good-humoured character who would also conduct further inquiries from London.

It was a commitment of resources that spoke of Evans's determination to find out all he could about Holden's murder. The journalists would follow what had become a tried-and-tested formula: gather every available scrap of information, assemble it into a coherent narrative and trust that the answers to the central question would become clear.

It fell to McCrystal and Barry to deal with the immediate aftermath of Holden's murder in Cairo. McCrystal, forty-two, came from a Catholic family in Belfast. After working on the *Belfast Telegraph*, he joined the *Sunday Times* in 1964 and was appointed its crime reporter. He later moved to New York as the *Sunday Times* US editor. When he returned to London, he became the deputy foreign editor, playing a key role in running the foreign department and managing its correspondents. Balding, with an engaging smile, his softly spoken persona, with a hint of Irish speech rhythms, belied his determination as a journalist; he was also a superb writer.

Barry, aged thirty-five, joined the newspaper in the same year as McCrystal and, following a lengthy stint heading Insight, was now an editor in the features department. He had a disconcertingly young face, with piercing eyes; an Oxford drop-out, Evans later called him 'a contrarian with a quicksilver mind'.

The pair's primary aim, once they arrived in Cairo, was to piece together all they could of Holden's plans and the circumstances of his death. Their mission swiftly expanded. They found themselves embroiled in the formalities and procedures entailed by the high-profile murder of a British citizen on Egyptian soil, liaising between the British Embassy and the Cairo police, as well as between the Cairo police and the authorities in Amman and London. They performed those duties against the ticking background of a deadline to write and transmit all their information to the *Sunday Times* in London in time for the major report the newspaper intended to publish the following Sunday.

Their work began as soon as they arrived at Cairo Airport on 11 December, following in Holden's footsteps from five days before. Once outside the departure building, they found themselves, McCrystal later wrote, 'in a swirling mass of people' who included drivers of the official regulated taxis and those plying for trade with their gypsy cabs, parked diagonally to the right of the main airport exit. They took an official taxi to the Cairo Sheraton, where they were told that the hotel was overbooked and so they were required to share a room.

The next day, they paid their first visits to the British Embassy, finding its officials in a state of consternation at the murder of a British subject, and to the Cairo police, who asked them 'urgently' for a list of Holden's possessions, so that they could identify any if they were found. At that early stage, Barry reported to London, the police had an open mind about the motives for the murder. 'General point is that violent crime of that nature is so unusual here and missing hours are so mysterious that all possibilities should be borne in mind.'

Both Barry and the Cairo police considered it vital to reconstruct Holden's movements, from his arrival in Jordan via the Allenby Bridge from Israel on the morning of 6 December to him boarding the plane to Cairo that evening. Barry sent an urgent 'brief' for Gillman to work on as soon as he arrived in Amman, written in the abbreviated cablese that reduced the word length and, consequently, the cost:

Start at bridge, get David's entry records and fullest passport details of all those who came over with him. Trace him to Amman. We must get passenger list with again fullest details addresses etc. of all who travelled on flight. Any late bookings? Trace any phone calls from Intercontinental. Then him onto plane. Crucial details are first whether he was accompanied wittingly or otherwise and second whether anyone could have expected his arrival at that time in Cairo.

In London, Boyd forwarded Barry's telex to the Amman Intercontinental Hotel, where Gillman was booked to stay. In reply to Barry's query over who knew Holden was travelling to Cairo and when he expected to arrive, Boyd pointed out that his plans were known in the *Sunday Times* foreign department: Holden had been meticulous about informing it about his movements and the foreign department had been in touch with two Cairo hotels, the Hilton and the Méridien, which would also be aware that he was coming.

Boyd had already traced a journalist who had met Holden in Amman on 2 December. Gavin Scott of *Time* magazine had lunched with Holden, together with Edward Mortimer of *The Times* and an American journalist, Joe Kraft. Boyd had one troubling item of conversation from Kraft to pass on. Holden had joked about returning to Cairo for the first time in years 'and how he expected to be public enemy number one'.

Boyd also forwarded a list of Holden's belongings which the Cairo police had requested via the British Embassy, meticulously documented by his wife Ruth. A dark blue corduroy suit made by Austin Reed. A pale blue/grey check suit from Burton's. A dark green and brown check sports jacket made by Adeney and Boutroy, Sackville Street. For shoes, two pairs of moccasin-style shoes, one reddish brown made in Venice, the other a black Gucci type. Three knitted silk ties – one brown, one fawn, one blue – all made in Madrid. A black and white sponge bag containing a Gillette Techmatic razor and *Acqua di Selva* aftershave in a dark green flask.

The following morning, 13 December, McCrystal and Barry, accompanied by a British Embassy official, went to the Kasr el Ainy mortuary. Like Jobbins three days before, they found it musty with the smell of formaldehyde and so short of space that a corpse was lying on the floor because all the tables were occupied. The embassy official explained that the police had given them permission to view Holden's body. When the mortuary attendant said he needed to see the authorisation in writing, McCrystal took the hint, handing over a few Egyptian pounds, which appeared to suffice.

Holden's body was in a steel-lined drawer within a giant filing cabinet. At first, the attendant pulled it back far enough to reveal Holden's face. 'Recognition was not immediate,' McCrystal subsequently noted. 'He had lost a lot of blood and his face was very thin.' His hair seemed to have thinned too and was very straggly. 'The face was in repose, but we were first struck with the fact that it was only vaguely like the David we knew.' The exit wound was clearly visible, close to his left nipple. The attendant turned the body on to its side, revealing the entry wound, with a slight ooze of blood. McCrystal and Barry felt more confident that this was Holden, and the matter was settled when the attendant pointed out a small, wart-like lump on the right side of his nose – a feature McCrystal remembered. The attendants appeared anxious to return Holden's body into the filing cabinet, so McCrystal and Barry thanked them and left.

What they saw accorded with the police autopsy, which concluded that Holden had been shot once from behind by a 9mm automatic and at such close range that it left a scorch mark just below the left shoulder blade. As Jobbins had concluded three days before, it had to be a professional hit. McCrystal and Barry had little time to think through the implications, as they needed to obtain the documents required to secure clearance for Holden's body to be released and returned to London.

McCrystal and Barry next visited the site where Holden's body had been found on the morning of 7 December. It was on a roadside in Nasr City, a housing estate composed of monolithic blocks of flats which also contained Cairo's Al-Azhar University. 'Nasr City is notorious as a dumping ground for murder victims,' McCrystal later wrote. 'But the murder of foreigners is quite unusual in Cairo.' The body, which was lying among sand and litter below a wall of the university, had been found by a medical student who informed the Nasr police station. The detective who arrived observed that the body had been carefully placed on the ground with arms at its side and feet out straight, an apparent indication that the killers wanted the body to be found that morning.

Barry and McCrystal were questioning some students at a nearby bus stop when two police cars drew up and several senior police officers climbed out. The two journalists were expecting to be reprimanded for doing their own detective work, but the police proved very welcoming. They included the head of criminal investigations in the Cairo police, General Ahmed Hassan, and the head of Cairo security, Brigadier Mustafa Kamal. Before long, still standing at the roadside, the group began discussing the murder and possible motives.

The police theories, as summarised in a telex by Barry, included 'theft (no one believes it); political; and most private is hormonal' – a coded reference to a possible sexual encounter, which Barry added 'is just at rumour stage'. Under the political rubric, Holden could have been murdered by fanatical opponents of Sadat's peace moves; or he knew something explosive and had been followed to Cairo. Finally, there was Israel, seeking revenge for the Insight torture articles. Here, Barry confided that this could have been 'a joint job' carried out by Israel and Egypt – which he diplomatically referred to as 'our hosts'.

Hassan had some queries for Barry, starting with who knew Holden was coming to Cairo during his final trip. 'Please assemble anything which will piece those days together,' Barry told London. 'We must rpt must trace exactly what he did who he saw etc. on West Bank, as well as tracing Amman.'

Hassan also asked about Holden's spectacles. 'Could London confirm that they were square with heavy black rims – and under what circumstances did he wear them? Did he wear them for reading, driving, writing, looking at maps? Did he wear them all the time, when he was tired or only for certain specified functions?' Hassan wanted to know, Barry explained, because Holden was still wearing his glasses when his body was found.

There was a seemingly minor detail that the police had observed, namely that when Holden completed his visa form at Cairo Airport, he had given his occupation as 'writer', not 'journalist' – thus enabling him to bypass the Ministry of Information team waiting to escort journalists into the city. In addition, Hassan said, the police had checked the records at the airport and were almost certain that Holden had not taken an official taxi. Instead, Hassan believed, Holden had travelled from Amman with someone he knew or had met on the flight. This person was met at Cairo Airport by someone with a car, and Holden accepted a lift from them. In summary,

Holden had been targeted by someone who knew he was coming, reinforcing the need to track his movements and who knew about them. 'This raises fearful questions,' Barry wrote to London. 'They think that at least two people involved. We are moving into very deep waters indeed and everyone now in the field should watch themselves.'

• • •

'Everyone now in the field' included Gillman, who arrived in Amman, following the five-hour flight from London, on the evening of 13 December. He felt he at least had the reassurance of familiarity, as he had visited Amman twice in the previous six months. He had found it a compact, manageable city in comparison with the sprawling metropolis of Cairo, with its near-permanent traffic gridlock and its erratic telephones. He took a taxi to the Intercontinental Hotel – known as 'the Intercon' – to find two telexes from London waiting for him at the front desk: one relaying Barry's instructions, the other warning him about the 'deep waters' and needing to watch himself.

It was hardly a reassuring welcome. Gillman was still considering its implications when a woman approached him at the reception desk. She said she was a French journalist, her name was Kenizé Mourad and she had spent time with Holden during his trip. 'He was a wonderful man,' she told Gillman.

Mourad, a slight, handsome figure with fair curly hair framing her face, somewhere in her thirties, said she had met Holden while covering the Middle East for *Le Nouvel Observateur*, a leftist French weekly. After checking in, Gillman sat down with Mourad in the hotel coffee shop. Mourad gave Gillman a detailed account of all she knew about Holden's movements from Damascus on 30 November to Amman on 4 December – two days before his flight to Cairo.

Mourad said that she first met Holden at a briefing delivered by Robert Pelletreau, the political officer at the US Embassy in Damascus, on 30 November. She and Holden were staying at the Hotel Méridien and she chanced upon him there again that evening. Mourad suggested they have a drink, but Holden declined, saying he was due to have dinner with the British ambassador. Holden travelled from Syria to Jordan the next morning, taking a taxi with two other journalists for the bone-shaking four-hour ride to Amman.

Mourad made the same journey the following day, 2 December, once again bumping into Holden at around 5 p.m. in the lobby of the Intercontinental Hotel. An hour or so later, they took a taxi to the Reuters office, where they inspected incoming telex messages for any significant news. Then Holden began drafting the article that he was due to dispatch to the *Sunday Times* the following day. They returned to the Intercontinental together, where Holden disappeared to his room to do more writing. At 8.30 p.m., they had dinner in the hotel coffee shop. At 10.30 p.m., Holden said goodnight, explaining he had to be up early the next morning to work on his article.

The following morning, 3 December, Holden returned to the Reuters office to finish writing his article, handing the opening pages to the Reuters operator who began telexing them to London. At 1.30 p.m., Holden called Mourad at the hotel, telling her – with manifest relief – that he had finished the article and asking if she would care to have dinner with him that evening.

Holden and Mourad met in the hotel bar at 8.30 p.m. They walked the short distance to the New Oriental restaurant, which served a fusion of Chinese and Middle Eastern food. When they returned to the hotel at 11 p.m., Holden asked if Mourad would like to come to his room for a drink. She accepted the invitation and spent two hours with him before returning to her own room.

Mourad saw Holden for the last time later the next morning, 4 December. Holden had arranged to take a taxi with some other journalists to the occupied West Bank, where he was keen to discover how Palestinians felt about the impending peace talks between Egypt and Israel. Mourad angled for an invitation to join Holden on the trip, but he did not take the hint. She did not see Holden again and returned to Damascus the following day, 5 December.

This was an encouraging start, providing detailed information about Holden's itinerary during five days as he moved between Syria, Jordan and the West Bank. But Gillman could see nothing untoward about Holden's activities: he had been assiduous in covering the bases in respect of the impending peace talks. He had evidently made a strong impression on Mourad as they discussed the Middle East and the article she was writing for *Le Nouvel Observateur*. She added a vital detail which hinted at a possible motive for his murder: Holden had talked about a book he was writing about Saudi Arabia. He said he had found evidence of corruption 'in high places' but was uncertain how much he could include in the book.

To Gillman, Mourad's eagerness to help spoke of a sense of loss or grief. Although she appeared to give full expression to her feelings, Gillman was left unsure if there were other things left unsaid. He wondered what had happened during her two hours in Holden's room on the night of 3 December. Although he did not ask the question directly, he deduced from what Mourad said that this had been a celibate encounter.

Gillman's first move the next morning, 14 December, was to call a Jordanian journalist, Rami Khouri, the editor of the English-language newspaper the *Jordan Times*. Khouri, a Palestinian with both US and Jordanian citizenship, had helped Gillman when he was conducting interviews in Amman for the Insight investigation of Israeli torture. Gillman now told Khouri that he had come to Jordan to reconstruct Holden's visit, and they agreed to meet later that day.

Gillman also called the British Embassy and learned that it had arranged for him to meet Brigadier Alalawi, the officer heading the

Jordanian inquiries into Holden's death. When Gillman met Alalawi at Amman's central police station, Gillman soon discerned that he was an Anglophile, like many Jordanians at the time. As an intelligence officer, he had learned intelligence techniques at a centre in Uckfield, Sussex, followed by a stint in a safe house in London where he was instructed in elements of subversion and countersubversion. Following a spell as head of Jordan's intelligence in Aqaba, he was now head of Amman's judicial police.

Alalawi seemed anxious to show that he was on the case, telling Gillman he would help as much as he could. Alalawi was keen to discuss the reasons for the killing and advanced two possible motives. One was to disrupt the peace initiative between Israel and Egypt; the second was as revenge for the Insight torture articles published six months before. Alalawi said he was eager to cooperate with the Egyptian police and told Gillman that a senior Egyptian officer was due in Amman imminently. But Alalawi also asked Gillman to pass on any information about the investigations by the police in Cairo. Uneasily aware that he was being co-opted as a liaison officer between the two police forces, Gillman said he would do his best.

Gillman next visited the office of the *Jordan Times*, where Khouri had discovered that Holden had met a Palestinian writer, Raymonda Tawil, in Ramallah on 5 December. Tawil, who had been placed under house arrest by the Israelis for her open support of the Palestinian cause, had been one of Holden's sources for his assessment of sentiment on the West Bank towards the peace moves. Khouri also had news of what appeared to be a significant sighting of Holden on 6 December, the day he flew to Cairo. As Gillman related in a telex to London, Holden had been seen in the company of 'Mr and Mrs Festier who work for Jordan tourist board in Beirut. Am attempting to confirm but there are no repeat no telephones Amman to Beirut so canst try from London and advise.'

Gillman also asked if Tony Terry in Israel could check the lead to

Raymonda Tawil. Then he received a telex saying that Eddy would arrive in Amman that evening. Gillman, who had hired a car, met him at Amman Airport and gave him a run-down of what he had done so far, focusing on his meeting with Mourad. Eddy seemed suitably impressed but agreed there was much work to do – and barely two days to do it in, as they were due to send their findings to the *Sunday Times* in London by the evening of Friday, 16 December, in time for that weekend's edition.

• • •

In Cairo that day, McCrystal and Barry were doing their best to stay abreast of fast-moving events. They had a meeting that morning with Egypt's deputy Minister of the Interior, Brigadier Ismail, a burly figure who had suppressed the bread riots which had gripped Cairo the previous January. Ismail told them the police were doing all they could to solve the murder. The investigation had been split into teams: one to examine Holden's clothing, others to analyse the ballistic evidence, trace Holden's contacts, search for the car or cars used by the killers and explore possible motives. All the identifying labels had been cut from Holden's clothing; the only mark that could be found was inside the waistband of his corduroy trousers.

Ismail showed McCrystal and Barry a set of photographs taken of Holden's body after it had been found by the roadside. In some, Holden was fully clothed; in others, he was naked. There was also a difference in his eyes. In one photo, they were wide open and his glasses were still on his face. In another, his eyes were half-closed, presumably because the body had been moved so that it could be photographed from different angles. Even so, Holden looked placid in all the shots. Ismail said that this was how he had appeared to police when they first saw his body, leading them to believe that

Holden was asleep or had been drugged. The lack of signs of alarm or fear on Holden's face suggested he had no warning he was about to die. McCrystal and Barry found Ismail sympathetic and interpreted the meeting with such a high-ranking figure as a sign of how seriously the Egyptians were treating the murder.

Having sent requests to other members of the *Sunday Times* to discover all they could about Holden's movements, McCrystal and Barry now found answers close at hand. Also in Cairo was Edward Mortimer, a roving Middle East correspondent for *The Times*, who had followed a similar itinerary to Holden and had been with him in Syria, Jordan, Jerusalem and the occupied West Bank. Mortimer, a tall figure with a mop of dark hair and glasses, had been at Oxford University at the same time as Gillman and had joined *The Times* in 1967.

In two lengthy interviews with McCrystal, Mortimer provided details which matched and complemented the itinerary Gillman had constructed from his meeting with Mourad. Mortimer first encountered Holden in Damascus on 29 November, two days after Holden arrived, and the day before he met Mourad. On 1 December, Holden and Mortimer travelled by taxi to Amman – confirming what Mourad had said – where they attended a press conference given by Jordan's King Hussein. That evening, over dinner in a Chinese restaurant, Holden told Mortimer he intended to return to Damascus the next day, 2 December. So Mortimer was surprised to find Holden still at the hotel the following evening. Mortimer had dinner with Holden and Mourad at the hotel coffee shop (Mourad had described the dinner but did not mention Mortimer).

Mortimer did not see Holden the next day, 3 December, when Holden was writing his *Sunday Times* report before dining with Mourad that evening. He met him again on 4 December, joining him on his taxi ride to the West Bank, together with two fellow journalists – but excluding Mourad, despite her hints to Holden.

Once they had crossed the Allenby Bridge, the two pairs split up. Mortimer and Holden continued to Jerusalem where they were staying at the American Colony Hotel – known to be Holden's favourite. After making phone calls, they met Ma'amoun al-Sayyid, editor of the Palestinian newspaper *Al Fajr*, at his office in East Jerusalem. Al-Sayyid showed them a set of proofs covered in red ink, marks from the Israeli censor ordering that an extensive series of passages should be deleted. Mortimer and Holden then visited Jericho together, returning for dinner at the American Colony.

The following morning, 5 December, Holden and Mortimer conducted a series of interviews together in Bethlehem, Hebron and Ramallah. Holden bought several presents in Bethlehem, including a necklace for his wife, Ruth. That afternoon, after returning to Jerusalem, Holden and Mortimer separated. Holden told Mortimer that he wanted to visit Jerusalem's Old City, as he had not been there in twenty years.

At around 6 p.m., they met the American journalist Michael Elkins, who worked for *Newsweek* and the BBC. Elkins was a controversial figure, an avowed Zionist who delivered radio reports for the BBC in a portentous manner that was styled on the wartime broadcasts from London of the US correspondent Ed Murrow. Mortimer said that Elkins repeatedly pressed Holden to tell him where he would be staying in Cairo. Holden had been prevaricating over when to go there, finally confirming his plans with the *Sunday Times* the previous day. He was hoping to stay at the Cairo Hilton but deflected Elkins's questions, first saying he was not sure he was going to Cairo at all, then finally saying that he would most likely stay 'with friends'. Mortimer was puzzled by these exchanges.

That evening, Holden and Mortimer had drinks and dinner with a Palestinian who ran the Jerusalem Young Women's Christian Association. The next morning, 6 December, Holden paid his bill at the American Colony and booked a seat on a service taxi going to the Allenby Bridge (and so not using the taxi rank where the drivers had not remembered him). Holden and Mortimer then took a stroll around the Old City – apparently a second visit for Holden, given that he had told Mortimer he was going there the previous afternoon. After losing their bearings in the Jewish Quarter, they headed along David Street towards the Jaffa Gate. Holden remarked how dismayed he was that the area had become a 'big souvenir shop'. Holden and Mortimer parted company at 10 a.m. As Holden turned to walk back towards the Damascus Gate, he said to Mortimer, 'See you in Cairo.'

In Amman the next day, 15 December, Gillman was now working with Eddy. With assistance from Brigadier Alalawi, Gillman had fulfilled Barry's request to obtain a list of all foreigners who crossed from Jordan to the West Bank on the same day as Holden, 4 December, and those who made the return crossing, like Holden, from the West Bank to Jordan on 6 December. Gillman now turned to Alalawi again, this time producing a list of passengers on Holden's flight to Cairo. He and Eddy started combing through them to see if any names other than Holden's appeared on all three lists.

Later that day, they met another senior Jordanian official, Major General Ghazi Arabiyat, head of public security. Gillman had told London that the Amman police had 'offered the *Sunday Times* all possible cooperation'. But the cooperation between Jordan and Egypt was far from smooth. Arabiyat was fuming over reports from Cairo that two or more Jordanian nationals had been arrested as suspects. 'The Egyptians have no basis for this,' he stormed. The Egyptians had not asked for any help over the suspects; what was more, the Egyptian policeman who was due in Amman the previous day never arrived. Gillman asked the Egyptian Embassy if the officer was still expected to arrive from Cairo and was told 'he may come Friday or Saturday'.

Gillman was disconcerted, fearing that the investigation could be hampered by these bureaucratic complications and rivalries. He relayed the news to the *Sunday Times* in a telex which he concluded by asking if someone could call his wife Leni to report that he was OK. Leni thanked the person who passed on this minimal news, the first she had received since Gillman had left for Amman. But it also served to revive the anxiety she felt about an assignment intended to find a fellow journalist's killer, where there were so many questions to answer. In the morning, as she helped their two sons get ready for school, one asked if she knew when their father was coming home.

'Not yet,' she said. 'But I expect we will have some more news soon.'

CHAPTER 4

ON DEADLINE

The photograph showed the body of a middle-aged man with injuries that clearly indicated he had been stabbed to death. Large enough to occupy a substantial space on the wall, it had been framed and hung in the corridor outside the office of General Hassan, the senior detective John Barry and Cal McCrystal had met two days before at the roadside location where Holden's body had been found. Hassan had shared his initial thoughts with the *Sunday Times* pair, then posed them a series of questions. He told them he would come to see them at the Sheraton Hotel but did not turn up. McCrystal was preoccupied with completing the arrangements for returning Holden's body to London, so Barry was now visiting Hassan alone.

Hassan saw that Barry was struck by the gory image. He had already told Barry and McCrystal that murders in Cairo were 'very rare', the main exception being 'honour killings' in the city's municipal housing areas. The murder of foreigners was even more unusual, which suggested why he had gone out of his way to display the photograph. He now explained further: it showed the last foreigner to be killed in Cairo, some two years before. The victim was an American teacher who was gay and had been stabbed by his partner.

Barry took that information in his stride as the meeting proceeded. He presented Hassan with the latest information he had received, including the details from Ruth in London about Holden's spectacles. As relayed by Steve Boyd in a telex, 'he did not need them for reading, writing or map-reading etc. but did wear them for driving or when out walking. He would not wear them usually if he was being driven for instance in a taxi. He did not wear them merely when tired.' McCrystal and Barry guessed that Holden had put on his glasses to help see where he was being driven, a detail that indicated the fear or bewilderment he must have felt, and Hassan agreed. Hassan restated his belief that Holden must have been targeted and asked Barry what the *Sunday Times* had learned about who knew he was going to Cairo. Barry passed on the information he already had but warned Hassan that it looked like a long list which the other reporters were still compiling.

As he left the meeting, Barry wondered what Hassan had been trying to convey with his remarks about the photograph. It was, after all, a factual description of what it depicted. Was there more? Was he indicating that he knew more about Holden than he was letting on? Was he trying to suggest that Holden was gay? But Hassan had already discussed, and dismissed, 'hormonal' or sexual theories for the killing. For the time being, Barry let the suggestion pass.

Meanwhile, McCrystal had collected the final document he needed to secure the release of Holden's body. He departed for Amman that afternoon, hoping that nothing would prevent him and the body from returning to London on the same flight. For once, the formalities were concluded without further difficulty, and by the evening, both he and the body were in the air.

Barry too felt relieved that no last-minute hitches had arisen. 'Things have been rather hectic,' he remarked in his latest progress report to London. But at around 11 p.m., just as he felt it was safe to relax, he was called by the Cairo police, asking him to come to the police station in the Dokki quarter of central Cairo. There, Barry met Brigadier Ismail, flanked by a dozen senior detectives and security officials.

'We promised results,' a beaming Ismail told Barry, 'and we have got them.' Illuminated by spotlights was a battered white Fiat 128 car, stripped of its licence plates, missing a headlight and much of its body trim, which had been dumped nearby. Inside the boot, the police had found Holden's red Samsonite suitcase, which had been ransacked. His cameras and lenses were missing, as were his passport, traveller's cheques and notebooks. Other items, so far as Barry could tell, remained intact, including his clothing, unexposed film, pages from his contacts book and two packages that Barry guessed were presents for Ruth. His typewriter was in the car too.

From the chassis number, the police had swiftly traced the car owner, who had reported it stolen three days before. A 22-year-old Jordanian engineering student, he had already been picked up, together with two of his friends who were in his Cairo apartment when the police arrived. These proved to be the Jordanians Gillman had been told about in Amman that afternoon by the fuming head of security, Major General Arabiyat. But it was soon clear that they were not connected with the murder, and the state of Holden's belongings appeared to rule out a simple case of theft. 'It looks as though the killers knew what they were looking for,' Ismail remarked. Barry sent an urgent telex to the *Sunday Times* office in London, asking it to call Evans, Peter Wilsher and McCrystal with the news, which should also be forwarded to Gillman and Paul Eddy in Amman.

The next day, 16 December, was deadline day, when the reporters were due to start filing their accounts. News was still arriving from all quarters. From Amman, Gillman sent London a holding telex, saying he and Eddy were 'filling in the gaps'. From Beirut, Helena Cobban reported she had tracked down the couple Gillman had identified as 'the Festiers'. Cobban advised that they were in fact an American couple named John and Isobel Fistere, who told her they had seen Holden for about five minutes on the evening he left Amman for Cairo. He was in the government press centre in the lobby of the Intercontinental Hotel, anxiously trying to telex the Cairo Hilton to confirm his room reservation. Holden looked dirty and worn-out from his travels and in a desperate hurry to catch the Cairo flight. But he had said nothing about where he had been and did not appear to be travelling with anyone else.

From Israel, Tony Terry sent photocopies of the Israeli entry and exit forms which showed Holden arriving over the Allenby Bridge on 4 December and leaving via the bridge on 6 December. Terry had also found the taxi driver who took Holden to Amman via the Allenby Bridge on 6 December, sharing it with a couple from Jordan and their children who had made a family trip to Israel. The driver had stopped at a post office to purchase the thirty-five Israeli pound stamp Holden required for his visa form at the crossing point; Holden had no Israeli money left, so the driver changed some British sterling for him.

In Cairo, now working alone, Barry was having a frustrating time, having been asked to find photographs for the report that would appear on Sunday. 'Don't think you quite realise what Cairo like to operate in on Friday especially when major phone breakdown,' he told London. He finally obtained 'two boring pix of car and possessions', which he dispatched via a British Airways flight to Heathrow. He included a sketch map of the location where the body was found but had been unable to obtain photographs of the airport, since it was a forbidden military area.

Barry asked London to tell the 'Jordan pair' to send their account as soon as possible. Boyd relayed his request to Gillman and Eddy. 'Please start moving your copy, not just for us but have just had

Barry on the line saying the Egyptian police are going spare for info and hassling him beyond endurance.'

By then, Gillman and Eddy had assembled a chronology which covered most of Holden's time in Amman. He attended a press conference held by Jordan's ruler King Hussein and dined with the British ambassador. He had devoted most of one day to writing his article for the *Sunday Times*, and he also spent time with Kenizé Mourad. Holden appeared assiduous in filling his working day with interviews and appointments, convivial when relaxing with fellow journalists over drinks or a meal. But Gillman and Eddy had been unable to account for Holden's last afternoon in Amman on 6 December, from the time he arrived after crossing the Allenby Bridge to his departure for the airport in the evening, as described by the Fisteres. All of this they set out in their account, which they took to the Reuters office for transmitting to London. Reuters sent part of their dispatch that night and resumed transmission in the morning.

On Saturday morning, fresh information was still arriving in London. From Jerusalem, Terry sent a report of Holden's movements on the West Bank on the afternoon of 5 December, when he had met Ahmed Rahman, an academic from Birzeit University, who told him about the persistent Israeli harassment of Palestinians and took him to a village where this had occurred. Rahman told Holden that most Palestinians were in favour of President Sadat's peace initiative – 'but DH appeared to doubt this', Terry reported. From Jordan, Gillman added the latest news in the saga over the Cairo police officer supposedly going to Amman. An Egyptian Embassy official had spent three hours waiting for him at Amman Airport, but he had still not arrived. From Cairo, Barry sent his own detailed chronology of Holden's final trip.

In London, the task of stitching together the flood of dispatches into one composite narrative for the following day's *Sunday Times* fell to Peter Wilsher, a practised hand in compiling such collaborative accounts. Wilsher began the article with a chilling quote from a book review written by Holden the previous month, where he remarked that he had 'never suffered either bullets or steel tearing into my flesh ... but I know how sickening the fear of such moments can be'. Wilsher summarised Holden's career – 'at fifty-three, he was right at the top of his profession' – and included all known details of how Holden had been shot and his body found and identified. During his final trip, Holden had apparently voiced no 'fear, preoccupation or concern', apart from over what he would write in the piece he filed for the newspaper's 4 December edition. Afterwards, he appeared 'relaxed and happy', looking forward to seeing Jerusalem and staying at the American Colony, 'his favourite hotel'.

There was nothing in Holden's demeanour to suggest any reason for his killing, Wilsher observed. Nor was it yet to be found in the details of his ten-day trip, so laboriously compiled by the teams on the ground in the Middle East and the London office. Wilsher accordingly compressed their account, covering his two days on the West Bank in a single paragraph – but pointing out that nothing was known about how Holden had spent his final afternoon in Amman. The reporters had also done their best to answer the second key question: who knew the details of Holden's plans? But the list was now immensely long and included the foreign staff of the *Sunday Times*; the staff of the *New York Times Magazine*; the London travel agency Kendal's, which made most of the arrangements for *Sunday Times* journalists travelling abroad; the Egyptian Embassies in London and Washington, which had helped arrange Holden's visas; the Hilton and Méridien hotels in Cairo; and a number of journalists who had met Holden or travelled with him during his final trip. Rather than try to focus on any one of these, Wilsher simply ignored the issue.

As for the motives for Holden's killing, Wilsher wrote that robbery had been 'virtually eliminated' by the Cairo police. They considered the murder to be political, but pinning it down to any particular organisation or group remained unresolved. 'In the tense, jumpy, unpredictable Middle East, anything is possible.'

So, Wilsher asked, was Holden's death 'to do with him as a person, the tragic result of some catastrophe in his private life?' Was it the result of his work as a journalist – 'something he had learned, somebody he had seen, some document he had discovered?' Or was it a blow aimed 'at wider things ... such as embarrassing President Sadat on the eve of the Cairo peace conference?' Wilsher remarked that Holden's private life was 'irreproachable' – so a killing as a result of some romantic or sexual encounter was 'the least likely' possibility.

Wilsher did not consider a possible motive that the Middle East team had discussed with police and other officials, namely that Holden was killed in revenge for Insight's torture report – although Wilsher did note that Holden had been 'wrongly but bitterly' blamed for masterminding the piece. As for the theories Wilsher did summarise, he did not steer readers to any one in particular, leaving the impression that most were equally plausible.

Wilsher had nearly completed the piece when the news broke that the Cairo police had found a second car involved in the murder. Wilsher tacked on a concluding paragraph reporting that the car had been found at Tanta, in the delta farmlands north of Cairo. 'There were rumours of bloodstains and cartridges in the car – but, again, the police would not confirm this.'

The article ended with those words. Impressively fluent, it was some 3,000 words long, occupying two pages at the centre of the edition, beneath the headline: 'Who killed David Holden?' Questions like these are posed to lure readers in to seeking the answer. In this case, the answer was notably lacking. The same went for the further question that journalists consider fundamental: 'Why?' Here too the piece was inconclusive. The inescapable truth was that for all its endeavours that week, the *Sunday Times* team had proved unable to explain either who or why.

In Amman, Gillman did not yet know how the material he and Eddy had provided had been incorporated in the final narrative. Nor did he know what conclusions Wilsher had reached. In the belief that the investigation would continue the following week, he and Eddy were preparing to fly to Damascus the next day, where they intended to flesh out the second-hand reports the *Sunday Times* had received on Holden's time there. That plan was put in doubt by a telex from Barry in Cairo. He was still chasing details of the second car the police had found and urged that either Gillman or Eddy should stay in Amman to follow the new lead.

That evening, everything changed again. A telex from the *Sunday Times* directed Gillman and Eddy to return to London the next day. It gave no reason, but Gillman deduced that since the newspaper would not be published the following Sunday, as it was Christmas Day, Evans had decided it was time to take stock. For the time being, Barry was to remain in Cairo. Evans asked him to stay there over Christmas, with the inducement that the *Sunday Times* would pay for his wife Pat to join him. Barry respectfully declined, saying he needed to return to London by Wednesday at the latest.

Back at home in South Norwood, Leni had been phoned by the *Sunday Times* to say that Gillman would be home that evening. Gillman had been away for just six days, but compared with other absences, this had been one of the more stressful, given that his inquiries could have led him into an encounter with Holden's killers. Over dinner that evening, with their sons Danny and Seth, Gillman said little about his trip. Afterwards, once their children had gone to bed, he told Leni more. They had found out a lot, but there was much that remained unknown. Leni had deduced that the story was incomplete, given the inconclusive report in that morning's *Sunday Times*. When Gillman read it too, he was compelled to agree. There were too many gaps and inconsistencies, and the central issues of who killed Holden and why had gone unresolved. Their efforts were not entirely in vain, but he could see only too well that the article raised far more questions than answers.

'Will you have to go back?' Leni asked.

'It's looking that way,' he replied.

'Any idea when?'

'Most likely in the New Year.'

'How long do you think you will be away?'

'It's hard to tell.'

Beneath these coded exchanges lay a truth that neither was yet ready to acknowledge: the quest for Holden's killers had only just begun.

CHAPTER 5

CITADELS

Gillman's homecoming on 18 December brought only a brief respite. With John Barry still in Cairo, and the various resident correspondents responding to follow-up queries, the quest continued. On Monday 19 December, Gillman went into the *Sunday Times* office, mostly deserted, as was usual for a Monday, but with an odour of cigarette fumes lingering from the Saturday press night. Gillman was carrying a crucial prize which he had obtained in Amman: the passenger manifest for Holden's flight to Cairo. The standout item was a list of forty-one Americans from Cleveland, Ohio. Their tickets had been purchased on 1 December from Alpha Omega Travel in New York, at a cost of $701.90. The list began with 'The Rev. Stewart' and ended with 'Miss E. Robinson'. Gillman telexed to the New York office of the *Sunday Times*, with the note that it showed 'Yanks who were on board David's flight to be upchased by the New York office in the hope that they remember him and any companions.'

The 'upchasing' was undertaken by the New York staff reporter, Peter Pringle, an engaging man in his thirties who formed part of the talented coterie of staff enlisted by Harold Evans. Pringle worked fast and by that evening had conducted a key telephone interview with passenger number eleven on the list, 'Mrs J. Bonnette'. Her full name was Barbara Willivene Bonnette, she worked as a welder in

Ohio and she and her husband, James, were part of a travel group to the Holy Land led by the Rev. James Stewart, a clergyman author who specialised in Bible studies. She explained to Pringle that because their flight from New York had arrived late in Amman, no seats had been allocated for the group, leaving Bonnette to search for one when she went on board. Unable to find one next to her husband, she saw that a centre seat was free, with an Arab-looking passenger in the window seat and a European at the aisle.

Bonnette had been forced to push her way past the European in order to reach the centre seat. She told Pringle that he appeared to be about fifty, 'rather shabbily dressed', with a dark jacket that did not match his trousers, and hair that was 'receding and fair, a bit tousled'. She noted that he took swigs from a hip flask during their meal and then emptied the flask into his coffee cup before finishing it off. Since Bonnette never drank alcohol, this was a telling detail for her – as was the fact that he did not smoke, since she was allergic to tobacco fumes. She did not notice if he had any hand luggage, because her first thought after the flight touched down in Cairo was to rejoin her husband. She did not see the man again.

A few days later, Bonnette saw a newspaper report that a man named David Holden had been found dead near Cairo Airport. From the accompanying photograph, she realised that he was the surly Englishman she had sat next to on the flight. It was a mark of Pringle's tenacity that he also found the person who showed Bonnette the news report. Another member of the Holy Land tour group, her name was Mrs Anita Lawrence, from Gibsonburg, Ohio, and the newspaper was the *Jerusalem Post*, dated 12 December. Bonnette, she said, seemed shocked.

To Gillman, the details of Bonnette's account were intriguing. Here was Holden in an unpleasant mood, gratuitously rude to his fellow passenger. He had also consumed a stiff measure of alcohol. It was consistent with the account given by the Fistere couple in Amman, who had seen him anxiously trying to confirm his hotel booking in Cairo. But it was in marked contrast with the Holden who came across as professional, urbane and composed in the office – and with the glimpses fellow journalists had provided from his travels the previous week, when he was jovial and sociable, wise-cracking over lunch. There could have been ample justification for his bad temper: the flight had been delayed by a group of US tourists, one of whom was now trying to make conversation with him; and he may still not have known where he would be staying that night.

For the moment, the enigma rested there, and there was already more to ponder. That day, news reached the *Sunday Times* of the preliminary findings of a post-mortem examination conducted on Holden's body by Professor James Cameron the previous Friday, 16 December – the day after the body had arrived in London. Cameron had been impressed by how well it was preserved: Egyptian pathologists had removed and retained Holden's stomach but left the other organs intact. Cameron noted that there were marks on the body which were consistent with Holden having been held and also bruises on his left knuckles. Beyond that, any further findings would have to wait until Cameron completed his report. Cameron gave his consent for Holden's body to be cremated, which took place the next day.

There were two police detectives at the post-mortem: Detective Chief Inspector Ray Small and Detective Inspector Tony Comben, who had been assigned to the case by Scotland Yard. The lines of protocol for investigating the murder of a British subject abroad are blurred and can raise issues of territorial rivalry. But in Holden's case, the Egyptian police had already asked Scotland Yard for assistance, which legitimised the role of Small and Comben. For their part, the Egyptians had appointed an army colonel as their liaison officer, who had been due in London the previous evening. However – in a familiar repeat of events in Amman – he had not arrived, nor sent any word as to why he had been delayed. Small and Comben were keen to pursue their inquiries and asked the *Sunday Times* to pass their request to the Egyptians.

The next day, 20 December, there was further news from Beirut. Helena Cobban had met John and Isobel Fistere again, following a request from London to clarify their account of seeing an anxious Holden in the lobby of the Intercontinental Hotel in Amman. The Fisteres timed the meeting at 6.30 p.m. and remembered Holden saying he had to leave for the airport within twenty minutes. After a five-minute conversation, they claimed, Holden had set off with an official of the government press centre in order to send a telex to the Cairo Hilton to confirm his reservation for that night. They didn't know if Holden had succeeded in sending his telex. Here, there was a detail that was in dispute between the Fisteres: John thought that Holden was trying to send his telex from the hotel, rather than the press centre. But Cobban preferred Isobel's account, as her husband was 'stone drunk on both occasions that I saw him'.

There was, however, a clash between the evidence of the Fisteres and that of the manager of the Bisharat travel agency in the lobby of the Intercontinental Hotel. Mr Bisharat, who knew Holden, said he had seen him around lunchtime, shortly after he had arrived in Amman. Holden was with the Fisteres, and they had gone into the hotel coffee bar together. He did not see him again. For the time being, it was impossible to resolve the contradiction.

In Cairo, meanwhile, Barry was continuing his own inquiries. That same day, 20 December, he had a further meeting in the office of the Cairo security chief, Brigadier Kamal. Barry had shown the police Gillman's list of the American tourists on the 6 December Amman to Cairo flight, together with the information obtained from Bonnette. On 21 December, Barry telexed London to report that this had 'transformed the situation'. Apparently galvanised by the cooperation the *Sunday Times* had received in Amman, Kamal promised that he would provide the full passenger details from the flight's arrival in Cairo. Kamal was 'pretty desperate' to help and asked if the Scotland Yard team could pass on any theories about Holden's killing – 'likewise Special Boys', Barry added, a reference to MI5 and MI6.

The Cairo police had now concluded that the killing was 'a very skilful and premeditated operation' and they passed on a warning that Edward Mortimer, correspondent for *The Times*, could also be in danger, on the grounds that 'he almost certainly knows without realising why'. One final detail intrigued the Egyptians: the description that Holden had been drinking from a hip flask during the Cairo flight. As Barry reported, 'Muslims' immediate conclusion is that he was a lush.'

All of this Barry reported in a telex on 22 December, before flying home that evening to London. 'Let's regroup London and assess situation and divide mammoth task,' he proposed in a telex. In the foreign department, Boyd had called Ruth to ask for any information she could provide about Holden's hip flask. She told Boyd that it was 'leather covered, bought from Aspreys. Although David was a moderate drinker, he liked to have some Scotch with him when travelling.' In his note of the conversation, Boyd added: 'Must stress that David normally drank sparingly. He was not, repeat not, a lush.'

The inquiry team met up again early in the New Year. By then, Professor Cameron had completed the findings of his post-mortem. In summary, Holden had been shot from behind by a gun angled downwards. The wound track extended at an angle of forty-five degrees from the middle of the upper back, passing through the aorta, to the exit point by the left nipple. The injuries were consistent with a 9mm calibre weapon. Cameron confirmed that there were bruises on the knuckle and fingers of his left hand, on his left arm above the elbow and on the knuckle of his right thumb – which perhaps indicated a fight or were caused when his body was lifted from the car.

Cameron's summary was brief and to the point: 'Well-nourished middle-aged man, 5ft 7in., no evidence of natural causes, died from gunshot wound to the chest.'

Cameron's report was a sombre prelude to the journalists' meeting, which had to confront the fact that a collection of the *Sunday Times*' most experienced reporters had spent the best part of ten days scouring the ground Holden had covered and talking to official investigators in several countries. They had amassed a wealth of information but so far had not made much progress in answering the two key questions: who had killed Holden and why? They were impressed by the verdict of the Cairo police that this was a thoroughly skilful and professional operation. They were also only too aware, as Barry had presciently observed at an early stage, that they were venturing into some very deep waters, and they shared the unease that they could stumble on the answers without realising it – the same concern that had led *The Times* to summon Mortimer back to London.

There was nothing for it but to press on. The *Sunday Times* was renowned for its commitment and determination to go wherever a story led and for however long it took. At such an early stage, this was not a time to feel daunted. Instead, the team would use its tried-and-tested investigative methods and a mix of diligence, determination and instinct to arrive at the truth.

The next move was to return to the Middle East for a less frenetic visit than before Christmas. Gillman and Barry were to make the trip, going to the four capital cities, Cairo, Amman, Damascus and Beirut. There was a range of questions to be addressed, some persisting from the inquiries of the first week, some arising from them.

In respect of Cairo, there were two key issues. The list of those who knew Holden was going there was immensely long. But who knew exactly when he planned to arrive was a far shorter list. Holden had typically juggled his options during the trip, only confirming that he would fly to Cairo on the evening of 6 December at a late stage. If Gillman and Barry focused on that narrower question, some meaningful answers might emerge. There was a related question of whether Holden had been met at Cairo Airport. The Cairo police were now confident he had been driven in a car that resembled one of the unofficial taxis that plied their bribe-oiled trade at the airport. But who had met him and persuaded him to get into the car – most likely the one in which some of his belongings had later been found? That could prove massively revealing.

Questions were arising in Amman. Gillman knew all too well that the tireless inquiries he had conducted with Eddy had failed to resolve one major puzzle: how did Holden spend the afternoon of December 6? His last confirmed location was when he reached the Allenby Bridge, the crossing point into Jordan from Palestine's occupied West Bank, at around 1 p.m. The next known sighting was in the lobby of the Intercontinental Hotel in Amman, either around lunchtime with the Fisteres, as related by the Bisharat travel agency manager, or at 6.30 p.m., as claimed by the Fisteres themselves. Could he and Barry fill that gap?

There were similar questions about Holden's time in Jerusalem and the West Bank. One concerned what he had done on the afternoon of 5 December, when he had apparently been in two places at once. That was when he had reportedly met the Palestinian academic Ahmed Rahman, who told him about Israeli harassment of Palestinian villagers and took him to a village where this had occurred. Yet Holden told Mortimer that he had spent the afternoon in the Old City of Jerusalem, commenting on how much it had changed since his last visit. The mystery was compounded by a further item of information from Jan (formerly James) Morris, who had known Holden since the 1950s. Morris had received a postcard which Holden had sent from Jerusalem on 5 December. It depicted a fortress that formed part of the stone wall around the Old City that was captioned 'Jerusalem, The Citadel'. (The fortress was known by alternative names: The Tower of David or The Citadel.) Holden had written a terse message: 'In the Middle East, citadels still have their uses.' Morris said that she was not accustomed to receiving cryptic messages from Holden and had no idea what this could mean.

Gillman felt it unlikely that he and Barry could resolve these questions, as they were not due to visit Jerusalem or the West Bank. As for Damascus, that was something of an open book. No reporter from the *Sunday Times* had been assigned there during the initial week's inquiries. Several journalists who had been there with Holden had provided information, including Mortimer and Mourad. Gillman and Barry would try to retrace those steps and talk to the people Holden had met.

There was one outstanding interview to be conducted. While in Damascus, Holden had paid a brief visit to the office of the Palestine Liberation Organization (PLO), formally the main representative body of the Palestinian people, divided between those living in the territory occupied by Israel in the West Bank and Gaza and those living in Israel itself. The PLO was committed to securing the original territory of Palestine for its people, including by armed struggle.

Until 1971, the PLO's headquarters had been in Amman. Then it was expelled from Jordan and so had to set up a new base in Beirut, the capital of Lebanon. Since 1975, Lebanon had been gripped by a civil war between a mix of political and religious factions, and Beirut was no longer the fun-loving garden city that Holden had known in the 1960s. As the PLO was clearly a major player in the region, it seemed essential for Gillman and Barry to find out what it knew about Holden's murder.

On 11 January, Gillman met Barry at the check-in desk at Heathrow for the 11.05 a.m. Lufthansa flight to Cairo. Gillman had worked on stories with Barry before. He was impressed by Barry's knowledge on a wide range of subjects and admired his journalistic skills.

It was an important basis for a partnership where the two men would spend three weeks together that were likely to be testing, possibly dangerous too.

Gillman and Barry fared poorly on their first test. Their flight touched down at around 6 p.m. Cairo time. Gillman was keenly aware that he was following the path taken at the airport by Holden four weeks before, as described by McCrystal during his own Cairo visit. After collecting their baggage and completing the immigration procedures, he and Barry picked their way through the throng of people waiting at the arrivals exit. As they paused to get their bearings, a man came up to them and asked if they needed a ride into Cairo. It would cost £2, he told them. Gillman and Barry glanced at each other and agreed. They were led to an assortment of cars that lay to the right of the official taxi rank. The man opened the door to a somewhat dilapidated car and they clambered inside.

'Where to, mister?' the driver asked.

'Hilton Hotel,' Barry replied.

After they had been travelling for a few minutes, Gillman looked at Barry and said, 'Do you realise what we just did?'

'Yes,' Barry replied.

The ride to the Hilton, which passed without further incident, took some forty minutes. When they checked in at the hotel desk, asking for their two rooms, the receptionist shook his head in a sorrowful manner.

'We are very full tonight, sir,' he said. 'Would you mind sharing a room?' Gillman and Barry agreed.

The pair spent three days in Cairo. Their most significant encounter was with General Hassan, the head of criminal investigations in Cairo whom Barry had previously met in December. This time, Barry and Gillman were summoned to meet him in a cavernous office building at 2 a.m., where Hassan told them that the police had now found a third car related to Holden's abduction and murder. Its owner had reported it missing on 6 December, it had probably been stolen the previous night and it contained documents relating to one of the two previously stolen cars.

Barry had already passed on the judgment from the Cairo police that the murder was both skilful and premeditated, and the news of the third car theft served to underline that view. Barry had been told about the first car, the white Fiat which had been stripped of its licence plates, in Cairo on 15 December. He had learned about the second car on the afternoon of 17 December, just in time to send the bare facts to the *Sunday Times* for its report on 18 December. He had since acquired more details of that car; taken with the new discovery, this added up to a composite picture that was ever more chilling.

Car One, found on 15 December, contained some items of Holden's luggage, including his red Samsonite suitcase, which had been ransacked. His documents and cameras were missing but most of the clothing was still in the car, together with his typewriter. It had most likely been stolen on the night of 5 December, twenty-four hours before Holden arrived in Cairo.

Car Two, found on 17 December, contained bloodstains between the two front seats, together with a cartridge case matching the 9mm bullet that killed Holden. The car had been resprayed from white to green and was found in the city of Tanta, between Cairo and Alexandria. It had been reported stolen on 18 November – nine days before Holden left London.

Car Three, found in Cairo on 7 January, contained documents relating to Car Two. It had been resprayed, from green to red, and had been most likely stolen the night of 5 December – the same timing as for Car One.

These bare facts carried the following implications. Holden's killers had begun their preparations no later than 18 November, more than a week before Holden's departure, when they stole the first car used in the murder. Two further cars had been stolen just twenty-four hours before he arrived in Cairo, strongly indicating that the killers knew precisely when he was coming. They were organised enough to steal and store three cars and to respray two of them. There was a consistent methodology in the manner of the thefts: all three had been stolen by someone who had broken open a quarter light and hot-wired the ignition. The killer group had also retained Car Three, which they had probably used to flee the scene, for more than four weeks, as it had apparently not been dumped until 5 or 6 January.

Gillman and Barry returned to the Hilton shortly before dawn, still coming to terms with what they now knew about the scale of the operation that had killed Holden. That perspective tended to overwhelm two of the questions they had hoped to answer. On the first, how the killers knew precisely when he was due to arrive at Cairo, they were no further forward. As for how the killers had persuaded Holden to go with them in one of the cars, they and the Cairo police were inclined to the view that Holden had done so willingly. So how had they persuaded him to do so? Or did he know them already? Those questions remained tantalisingly open.

Later that day, they met the Egyptian Interior Minister, Brigadier Ismail, whom Barry had seen several times during his initial visit. It was an important meeting for one reason: the two Scotland Yard detectives, Small and Comben, had said they were keen to go to Cairo as part of their investigation. This raised a sensitive territorial matter, as police are habitually reluctant to admit intruders from other forces. Barry duly relayed the Scotland Yard request as tactfully as he could, but Ismail declined to take the hint.

That weekend, the pair moved on to Amman. Here it was Gillman who felt he was on familiar ground. He and Barry touched some of the bases Gillman had previously visited, meeting a senior British Embassy official, Geoffrey Tantum, and Brigadier Alalawi, head of the Jordanian inquiries. Alalawi passed them on to the head of Jordan's interior security, Izadeen Zaza, who listened to their questions intently and then gently advised them not to try to do detective work in Amman – or in Cairo, for that matter.

'That's our job,' he told them. 'You should find out all you can about Holden's background, who he was, which we can't do.' To show there were no hard feelings, Zaza invited them to his squad's weekly lunch, where the main dish was a whole roast lamb stuffed with roasted chickens and rice. Zaza gave them a plate each but indicated that they should extricate the food and eat it by hand. Gillman, for one, felt it would be churlish not to take part and did as he was instructed.

Gillman took Barry to meet several of his previous interviewees, including Rami Khouri, editor of the *Jordan Times*. They had nothing new to offer, but another encounter served to deepen one of the core mysteries: what did Holden do on the afternoon of 6 December? At the Reuters office, a staff member told them that he had asked Holden for a favour. The Reuters man was ill and needed to send a blood sample to a hospital in Jerusalem for analysis. Holden took the package before he left Amman on 6 December, promising he would deliver it that afternoon and would call to confirm that he had done so. But Holden never called the Reuters man as he had promised and it turned out that he had not delivered the sample either.

Gillman also took Barry to meet a key source in the Insight torture investigation, which had been published the previous June and which now figured in the speculation around Holden's murder, notably the theory that this had been the work of a vengeful Israel. Barry had edited the article as it was prepared for print, so Gillman introduced him to Jean Courvoisier, the chief delegate in Amman of the International Committee of the Red Cross (ICRC). Courvoisier had given Gillman discreet but crucial assistance during the row that followed publication, allowing him to inspect the ICRC's confidential reports to the Israel government about the treatment of Palestinian prisoners. Barry was delighted to meet Courvoisier, who was both welcoming and charming. He reprised the ICRC's concerns while apologising that he knew nothing that would help their inquiry into Holden's murder. Afterwards, Barry told Gillman how impressed he was that Courvoisier was so frank and open with them. 'Normally these guys won't even tell you the time of day.'

After Gillman and Barry had spent a week in Amman, their next stop was Damascus, where they stayed at the same hotel, the Méridien, as Holden. Their aim was to establish or confirm Holden's movements between arriving from London on Sunday 27 November and departing on the four-hour taxi ride to Amman on Thursday 1 December. As Gillman and Barry covered Holden's tracks, two of their encounters stood out. One was with John Bunney, a British press attaché, whom Holden met both at the British Embassy on the morning of 29 November and over dinner that evening with Bunney and his wife Pamela at their home. They recalled that Holden had told them he was going to visit the Damascus souk, the street market that is the oldest and most celebrated of its kind in the Middle East. That evening, Holden described his visit, remarking on how much he had been struck by the beauty of the ancient Umayyad Mosque on the north side of the souk. Much later, as Gillman looked for patterns in Holden's final trip, these remarks came to assume a new significance.

Their second notable meeting was with the US political officer, Bob Pelletreau. Four journalists, including Holden, had attended his briefing on 30 November. Gillman and Barry had presumed that it was a standard occasion, when Pelletreau provided the US perspective on the prospective peace movements in the region. But Pelletreau declined to provide any details about the briefing and would only respond when Gillman or Barry asked questions that led with their own information. Pelletreau did appear interested when they volunteered material about Holden. It was a classic instance,

Gillman and Barry concluded afterwards, of an official who wanted to find out what they knew while being prepared to offer nothing himself.

On 24 January, Gillman and Barry prepared to leave Damascus and move on to their final calling point, Beirut. They felt that they had made reasonable progress in adding to Holden's itinerary and were also intrigued by Pelletreau's performance. Their main objective in Beirut was to visit the office of the PLO. That evening, however, news came from London which led them to reconsider much of what they knew, or thought they knew, taking them still further into the deep waters Barry had foreseen in Cairo.

CHAPTER 6

AN INSIDE JOB?

The foreign department at the *Sunday Times* occupied a long office on the fifth floor. It was on the opposite side of the building from the newsroom, a gloomy space illuminated by strip lights and a window overlooking a central well. The foreign department, by contrast, had an array of windows looking onto Gray's Inn Road so was always a bright and seemingly cheerful place. There was a line of desks and a sprinkling of cupboards and filing cabinets. (Frank Giles, foreign editor, had his own office on the floor above.) It had an air of friendly informality and although you may have had to push open a door to enter it, the door was never locked.

On the morning of Tuesday 24 January, the department staff made a startling discovery. There had been a theft. Missing from a cupboard were a folder containing information about the *Sunday Times* foreign reporters, giving their addresses, telex numbers, bank details and other information, and, more troubling, copies of telexes which had arrived in the department since Sunday. These included two messages sent by Gillman and John Barry from Damascus, in which they gave a progress report and their travel plans.

The theft was alarming enough in itself. But it also led the staff to reconsider an earlier incident. The previous Tuesday, 17 January, they had found other items had gone missing. These were the foreign department's contacts book, containing the names and addresses of freelancers, and a folder containing stories written by foreign correspondents since the beginning of the year. Although puzzling, the foreign staff did not connect it with the Holden inquiry and did not raise the alarm.

It got worse. The staff now checked back through their collection of telexes, particularly those relating to Holden. From a set of carbons, they realised that eight of those were also missing – and every single one concerned Holden's arrival plans for Cairo. The first, on 26 November, consisted of a message from Holden which he had sent from the *Sunday Times* to the Cairo Hilton giving his date of arrival in Cairo as 4 December. The last, on 5 December, was a note from the Méridien Hotel in Cairo, confirming that Holden had altered his arrival date, and his booking, to 6 December.

The implications of this new discovery were multiple and devastating. At their simplest, someone had gained secret access to the *Sunday Times* offices in order to steal material relating to Holden and the subsequent investigation of his death. That person had acquired information about Holden's travel plans which vitiated the inquiry team's prolonged endeavours to discover who had known when Holden was due to arrive in Cairo.

All these considerations were discussed in a meeting that same day, 24 January, between Paul Eddy and Evans in his sixth-floor office. As Evans later recorded, Eddy, 'in his cool, cryptic style, proceeded to astonish me'. Eddy told him that the killers knew exactly when Holden would arrive in Cairo, 'because they got the information from the horse's mouth – us'.

Evans wondered if the loss of the crucial telexes could have been the result of a mix up or carelessness. Eddy admitted that the same thought had occurred to him – but since there had been at least three thefts in all, this could not apply. On reflection, it was only too easy for someone to reach the editorial floors of the *Sunday Times*.

AN INSIDE JOB?

There were at least six entrances to the Gray's Inn Road offices from the surrounding streets. Especially on Saturdays, when the newspaper was being produced, print workers – many of them casual or part-time employees, paid in cash that night for their shift – would flood in and out of the building. Even so, the person or persons who committed the theft would have had to know their way around the editorial offices – and, in particular, the foreign department, where the telexes had been removed from an unmarked cupboard. It was Eddy who voiced the hovering, troubling thought: could there be a spy on the *Sunday Times* staff?

Evans and Eddy agreed that they needed to act fast. That afternoon, Eddy moved all Holden material from the foreign department to Insight's own office, locking it into a filing cabinet to which he had the only key. He arranged for the foreign department door to be fitted with new locks and insisted that it should be locked at night. He sent a telex to Gillman and Barry informing them of thefts and advising: 'Pse be discreet and do not rpt not file telexes overnight.'

At the Méridien Hotel that evening, Gillman and Barry were shocked by Eddy's message. As Gillman saw it, whoever had killed Holden had the organisational ability to monitor Holden's travel plans and movements. He and Barry discussed whether they should stick to their plan of moving on to Beirut the next morning. As there was no way of telling whether they were safer in Damascus or Beirut, they decided to do so. They arrived in Beirut around midday on 25 January and checked into the Commodore Hotel, renowned as a haven for journalists since the start of the Lebanese Civil War some three years before.

Their first call was to Helena Cobban, the *Sunday Times* correspondent in Beirut, who had assisted with the initial week's inquiries into Holden's death. Cobban had developed excellent contacts with the Palestine Liberation Organization, as had the Western embassies in Beirut, which had discreetly arranged with the PLO security apparatus to help protect their diplomats in west Beirut, given the total breakdown of the official security forces. In Cobban's case, those arrangements were particularly intimate. Following Holden's murder, on the insistence of the British Embassy, the PLO provided her and her husband with a squad of guards armed with Kalashnikov rifles who moved into their apartment in the Verdun area of Beirut. Cobban was pregnant, with the birth expected in a matter of weeks, and a female PLO guard accompanied her to hospital appointments.

Cobban had agreed to assist Gillman and Barry in their goal of questioning the PLO leadership about the Holden killing. She asked the security officers at the British Embassy to help with the arrangements, and so it proved. Gillman and Barry were collected at the Commodore Hotel by car from which, after driving a due distance, they were transferred to another car. They eventually pulled up outside an apartment block that bore signs of damage from the civil war. They were met by two men who led them up several echoing flights of stairs and gestured to them to enter a room.

Once inside, Gillman's eyes adjusted to semi-darkness, the result of heavy curtains draped over the windows – presumably to protect those inside from flying glass in the event of an attack. The central figure, who greeted them as he sat at a heavy desk, was Abu Jihad, the trusted deputy of Yasser Arafat, leader of the PLO. Standing against a wall beside Abu Jihad was a tall man with a neat crop of black hair who, Gillman realised with a jolt, was Ali Hassan Salameh, accused by Israel of helping to organise the kidnapping of Israeli athletes at the Munich Olympic Games of 1972. Gillman had co-authored a book which included an account of the Israelis' subsequent attempts to kill Salameh, during which they mistakenly gunned down a Moroccan waiter in the Norwegian town of Lillehammer. Gillman was in little doubt that the Israelis would have redoubled their efforts to find Salameh and take their revenge.

The principal question which Gillman and Barry intended to ask was whether the PLO had killed Holden. But without being asked, Abu Jihad said he could assure them, following inquiries requested by Arafat himself, that no 'arm of the resistance' had participated in the murder. An emboldened Barry asked how he could be so sure. Abu Jihad provided two reasons. First, the PLO had a policy of not killing journalists. Second, that particularly applied to the *Sunday Times*, given its revelations about Israeli torture the previous year. Since Gillman, with Eddy, had been the principal author of the report, and Barry its editor, they felt relieved to hear this. The Palestinian resistance, Abu Jihad continued, considered the *Sunday Times* 'a friend'.

After the meeting, blinking as they emerged into the sunlight, Gillman and Barry were ferried back to the Commodore Hotel. Over dinner on the seafront that evening, they discussed whether they could accept the PLO's assurances at face value. They were uncertain how flattered they should feel about receiving the PLO's seal of approval, but they considered that the PLO's denial that it had killed Holden was plausible, if not yet conclusive.

Gillman and Barry were in a relaxed mood as their taxi headed back to their hotel. Abruptly, the taxi jolted to a halt. The offside rear door was thrown open and a man wearing a keffiyeh peered inside. Gesturing at Gillman and Barry with a Kalashnikov rifle, he barked a question at the driver. As they tensed in their seats, Gillman and Barry discerned the word 'Sahafi' in the driver's reply. The gunman briefly stared at Gillman and Barry, then slammed the door shut. The driver eased into gear and moved on. 'He asked who you were,' he told Gillman and Barry in passable English. 'I told him you were journalists.' Once back at the hotel, Gillman and

Barry treated themselves to a nightcap in the bar before heading to their rooms.

In London the following morning, there was yet another troubling development: despite all the precautions, there had been a further theft. Especially disturbing was the intimate knowledge the thief displayed of the office layout and the procedures for handling telexes – and they were clearly more au fait with them than Eddy, who had overlooked the fact that copies of all telexes were retained in the wire room where they first arrived. The wire room was tucked away in a windowless office several floors down from the foreign department, and only an insider, or someone briefed by one, would have known this. The theft must have occurred between 9.30 p.m. on 26 January, when the last telex operator went home, and 9 a.m. on 27 January, when the first operator of the day shift arrived. Eddy discovered that all outgoing and incoming messages from 22 January onwards were missing from the spikes where they were placed. Among them was copious material relating to Holden, including summaries from Gillman and Barry on what they had discovered and updates on their travel plans.

Eddy learned from the wire room operators that the door, which had a Yale lock, should have been secured overnight; but procedures were lax and sometimes the door was not fully closed. There were no signs of a forced entry. When Eddy discussed the latest theft with Evans, he conceded that it was not certain that the Holden material had been targeted, as all the *Sunday Times* telexes for that period had been removed. But early that afternoon came confirmation that the thefts were focused on the Holden inquiry. At some time between 8 a.m. and midday, yet another telex was stolen. It was from Gillman in Beirut, telling Eddy that he intended to return to London on 30 January and giving details of his flight plans. There were normally six copies of each telex: five were distributed to the respective editorial departments and one retained in the wire room.

AN INSIDE JOB?

After receiving all five copies of Gillman's telex, Eddy decided to check that the sixth was still in the wire room. It was not. After discussions with the wire room operators, Eddy concluded that it had been removed that very morning, even though the room had been staffed at the time.

The truth was starker than ever. Going back perhaps six weeks, someone had been stealing key telexes from the *Sunday Times*. The first batch contained Holden's travel plans and could have been used to plan and time his assassination. The subsequent thefts would have revealed details of the newspaper's investigation of Holden's murder – and, most disturbing of all, the investigators' own travel plans. By one theory, the thief or thieves had taken advantage of the absence of any security at the *Sunday Times* entrances and had gained access to the foreign department and the wire room without being challenged or disturbed. Along the way, they had acquired vital information about the geography of the newspaper's offices and its procedures for handling incoming and outgoing telexes. The other theory was simpler but profoundly disturbing: as proposed by Eddy, the thefts were an inside job. Contemplation of the respective theories led inevitably to paranoia.

Eddy sent news of the latest thefts to Gillman and Barry, who saw at once that the killers' reach was even greater than they had previously imagined. After discussing what precautions they might take, Gillman altered his travel plans. He had been due to fly to London on 30 January but switched to a flight a day earlier, on Sunday 29 January. Barry, meanwhile, would go back to Cairo for a few days before returning to London.

Over their dinner at home on Sunday evening, Gillman told Leni about the highlights of his three-week trip. Despite some misgivings, he revealed the disappearing telexes, culminating in the final theft which had brought him home a day early. Leni had a heightened sense of anxiety: this was getting personal; this was coming near to home. The following evening, they went to see a production of Shakespeare's *Macbeth* at the Donmar Warehouse in Covent Garden, where the stellar actors Ian McKellen and Judi Dench took the two lead roles. It was an intimate performance, with the actors at times entwined as they wove their murderous plot, and pervasive symbols of darkness conveying the evil they were embracing. For the Gillmans, it felt a little too close for comfort.

The next day, Gillman had lunch with Eddy at the Brasserie du Coin, five minutes' walk from the *Sunday Times* office. Eddy spelled out the details of the thefts, as well as the implication that someone was taking a close interest in their own discoveries and movements. Later that week, Evans convened a meeting with Gillman, Eddy and Barry. It was a disconcerting juncture and one that threatened to divert them from their principal task. Now the focus was moving from Holden to themselves, as they had become the object of someone's malevolent attention. It was nonetheless vital to see if they could discover who that was – which could also lead them to Holden's killers. They formulated a plan to do precisely that. In short, they would set up a fake investigative trip abroad, then dispatch telexes in the normal manner. They would arrange surveillance so that if the thefts continued, they could see and hopefully identify who was carrying them out.

It would be an elaborate and complex scheme, made trickier because only a very limited number of people should know about it. They included the detectives Tony Comben and Ray Small, whose help was required in the planning. Evans also informed the Foreign Office and was promised cooperation from a group known as 'the watchers', who conducted surveillance and who would install security cameras in the newsroom.

The surveillance plan was ready towards the end of February. At the Tuesday morning news conference, it was announced that Gillman and Eddy had made an important breakthrough in their continuing investigations and that Eddy would be visiting Amman and Cairo to follow this up. It was a charade. On 8 March, Eddy left his home in west London by car, took a convoluted route through the neighbouring streets to ensure he was not being followed, then headed for the seaside resort of Rhyl on the north Wales coast. The only person on the newspaper who knew the location was Gillman. Not even Evans had been told, and he later revealed the coincidence that Rhyl was where he spent his earliest family holidays.

A day or so later, Eddy began sending a series of telexes datelined Amman, Beirut and then Cairo. They were written in the vernacular of the telexes from the previous visits: 'Have checked arrival and departure lists for Damascus and Amman hotels plus entry and exit lists for Syria–Jordan and Jordan–Egypt. As we thought there are some interesting names...' Another related: 'Some disturbing news in last hours. Will explain in detail later but meanwhile suggest you obtain full (repeat full) Scot Yard autopsy report.' Some of the fake telexes required quick thinking, as when Israel invaded Lebanon in mid-March. Since Eddy was supposedly in Beirut, he contrived to find an excuse not to cover it.

It was all in vain. At the *Sunday Times* office, Gillman kept a checklist of Eddy's incoming telexes and listed where they were distributed. Not one went missing. Whoever was stealing the telexes had outwitted them once more. Maybe they had spotted the ruse. Maybe they concluded that the telexes were not worth stealing. The Scotland Yard duo, Small and Comben, reviewed the footage from the clandestine cameras that had been installed and reported nothing untoward.

Eddy returned from Rhyl and yet another conference was convened. Once again Evans, Barry, Gillman and Eddy went over what was now familiar ground. A highly organised group, with immense resources, had conducted a meticulous operation in Cairo to kill Holden. Now it appeared that the same group had penetrated the subsequent inquiry by the *Sunday Times*, obtaining information about its findings and its members' movements, and had then escaped detection in a meticulous sting. It carried one major implication, namely that all the team's laborious research into who knew Holden was going to Cairo and when was now rendered irrelevant. So who could be behind the thefts? The most likely explanation was a security or intelligence agency. In which case, what did that tell them about Holden? Did it mean that he was part of that world too?

Gillman, for one, felt chastened as the four discussed this thought. Was he naive, he asked himself, in not considering it at an earlier stage? Was it commonplace for journalists to act as spies? If so, then that should inform the next stage of the newspaper's inquiries, which were now to be broadened to encompass the whole of Holden's life. Until then, the investigation had been conducted by the Insight team and other members of the newspaper's reporting staff. Now it would be undertaken by Gillman and Eddy of the Insight team, together with its newest recruit, Isabel Hilton. A talented and versatile journalist from Scotland, who had studied in China and spoke fluent Mandarin, she had been recruited by the *Sunday Times* after working as a presenter for Scottish Television and then, briefly, at the *Daily Express*.

As Evans discussed with Gillman and Eddy how the team should proceed, it felt like a watershed moment.

'Are you sure you want to carry on?' Evans asked.

'Of course,' Gillman replied.

'Then do nothing else,' Evans told them. 'No expense spared.'

CHAPTER 7

A MAN OF MANY LIVES

The quest to construct an account of David Holden's life began in Sunderland, north-east England, where he was born on 20 November 1924. His father Thomas was a journalist who fought in the First World War and rose to the post of editor of the *Sunderland Echo* during the Second World War. His mother Ethel was a teacher and the family lived in a terraced house at 26 Park Place East, a mile or so inland from the Sunderland Docks, later moving to a larger house in a leafier area in Barnes View, near Barnes Park. Holden made clear his admiration for his father when he wrote in a university application that 'he left school when he was twelve, but with real enthusiasm and much hard work he became a man well read in literature and history, with a keen interest in music and an extensive knowledge of current affairs'.

Much of what Gillman and his colleagues learned about Holden's childhood in 1978 came from his older brother Geoffrey, then a retired solicitor, who told them that David had been frequently ill from an early age. He contracted polio, which left him with a limp when he became tired. A bout of diphtheria left him deaf in one ear and he had a 'leaky heart' resulting from scarlet fever. Holden attended a local primary school, with frequent absences caused by his illnesses. In 1936, aged eleven, he passed an exam to attend Bede College Boys' School, where he spent the next three years.

In September 1939, shortly after the start of the First World War, he moved to the Friends' School, a boarding school run by Quakers in Great Ayton, close to Middlesbrough. It was a spartan institution, but Holden's health improved, which he attributed to the school's 'open air regime'.

Among the signs of war, the pupils regularly practised air-raid drills and the school took in refugees from Germany, Austria and Spain. The Friends' School headmistress, Evelyn Nicholson, who had taught Holden English, told Isabel Hilton that she remembered him as 'clever, modest and humorous'. His first published writing dates from that time: three articles for the school magazine, including an account of an eight-mile train journey to the village of Danby, where the pupils picnicked from food hampers which awaited them in a cottage, despite the limitations of food rationing. 'After three hearty cheers for the old lady of the cottage, we trudged back to the station, hot, dusty, tired but happy,' Holden wrote.

Holden also played clarinet in the school orchestra and enjoyed walks across the moors. A history teacher, Robin Pedley, later a renowned advocate of comprehensive schooling, remembered Holden with clear affection. He spoke to Gillman warmly about their excursions to give music recitals in nearby villages and of his dismay for teachers who did not hold Holden in the same high esteem. Holden and Pedley maintained their friendship after Holden left the school and sustained it through the 1940s. In 1946, when Pedley was an education lecturer at Leicester University, they made a boat trip together to Shetland. In 1947, they visited south-west France and in 1949, together with another former Great Ayton pupil, they went on a motoring holiday to France, Germany, Switzerland and Italy.

In spring 1941, Holden moved on to another Quaker boarding school, Bootham School in York, with the aim – encouraged by

Pedley – of going to Cambridge University. In early 1943, after attending a round of interviews, he was given a place to read geography at Emmanuel College. He spent much of the intervening six months in Bristol, where he enrolled in a youth leadership training course. He divided his time between studying and working as a farm labourer and said he was especially proud when a farm official said he was 'an expert milker'. At the age of nineteen, he was still liable to be conscripted into the armed forces but was rejected on medical grounds, his examiner describing him as 'a perambulating museum of past ailments'.

Emmanuel College, when Holden arrived in September 1943, had readied itself for war. There was a fire watchtower on the roof of the Front Court, the basements were prepared as air-raid shelters and the nightly blackout was strictly enforced. Beside his course – Holden had selected the specialities of historical, political and economic geography – he pursued his interest in music, playing clarinet and singing with a choir which specialised in Gilbert and Sullivan. He took up acting, joining the university drama group The Mummers and becoming president in his last year. During one summer vacation, he spent five weeks as a paid actor with the Newcastle Repertory. He completed his geography course in June 1946, gaining a respectable upper-second honours degree.

At this point, the Insight team came upon an episode that raised what appeared to be some highly relevant questions. In September 1946, Holden returned to Emmanuel College to take a one-year teaching diploma course. However, this was evidently not his first choice of action. In 1978, his brother Geoffrey told Gillman that he had met David at 'a north-eastern port' in the summer of 1946 to help him make arrangements for a trip to Czechoslovakia. Later that year, the report of the Ayton Old Scholars' Association (AOSA) recorded that Holden had returned to Cambridge for the diploma course, 'plans to spend a year of study at a Czech University having fallen through'.

What was noteworthy about the episode, Gillman discovered, was that it precisely matched a method employed by British intelligence to recruit potential agents. Usually with the aid of college tutors, the secret service would 'spot' a likely recruit at Oxford or Cambridge and place them for a year in a university in Eastern Europe to gain familiarity with the country and make contacts for possible future use. Then it would help them find a teaching job in England where they would wait to be called. The spy-turned-author John le Carré described just such a process in his novel *Tinker Tailor Soldier Spy*, where a prospective agent was recruited at Cambridge shortly after the Second World War, placed at a university in Hungary for a year, then 'put out to grass' as a teacher at a rural prep school. It was all uncannily close to the episode involving Holden.

At some point, the plan for Holden was evidently aborted. Whatever the reason, he took up his teaching diploma course at Cambridge. He qualified as a teacher in June 1947 and, now emulating his mother's career path, found a job at Duns High School in Berwickshire, where he taught geography and social studies. He also embarked on a range of cultural activities. He joined the local drama society and continued to play the clarinet. A fellow teacher, Harold Cranswick, told Gillman that Holden was 'an excellent teacher and of course he could write'. Holden reported on the Edinburgh Festival one summer for the *Sunderland Echo*, where his father was still the editor.

Holden himself later complained that, despite all his efforts, he felt cut off from cultural life at Duns. 'No theatres, no concerts, hardly any societies,' he wrote. 'I was lost.' After little more than a year at Duns, Holden moved to Edinburgh, where he took up a new teaching post at Leith Academy in Duke Street, Leith. Cranswick felt that Holden did so to gain access to a wider cultural life, but it seemed clear by then that Holden had little enthusiasm for teaching, either at Duns or at Leith. In that summer's AOSA report, which

Holden edited, he wrote that he often met his old Ayton friend John Watson 'for a comforting grouse about life in general'. In July, he, Watson and Pedley embarked on their motoring tour of Europe, driving 3,000 miles in three weeks. Six months later, in December 1949, Holden quit both Leith and teaching.

The year 1950 was a watershed in Holden's life. Having given up teaching, he decided to return to university – not in the UK but in the US, where he applied to take a graduate course at Northwestern University, Illinois. Holden was clearly determined to make a break with the stultifying life at Leith Academy in particular and with teaching in general. His motor tour of Europe had given him a taste for foreign travel. To spend a year or more at a university on the edge of Chicago could be seen as a new adventure. His principal testimonial came from Pedley, who wrote that he was 'a man of quite exceptional insight ... It is with particular pleasure and confidence that I support his nomination.' Gillman's interview with Pedley in 1978 had left him wondering just how close his friendship with Holden had been. There was a particular irony in Pedley providing such a lavish endorsement, as Holden was in the process of moving on to another deep personal relationship. From its subsequent inquiries, the Insight team concluded that it was the most important of his whole life, one that potentially held the key to many of the questions that the team pursued.

• • •

Leo Silberman was a striking figure, immaculately dressed and groomed when posing for family photographs. In the 1950s, when he was close to Holden, he was described as 'a slight man weighing about 110 pounds, bald on top of his head, about 5ft 6in. tall. He has sharp features, penetrating black eyes and rather nervous mannerisms.' An examination of his life shows a man of undoubted academic brilliance, of multiple interests and notable achievements. It also reveals someone who exaggerated his credentials and constantly juggled his options. Others described him as loud, flamboyant and determined to be the centre of attention. An academic colleague, while praising his charm and wit, found him utterly unreliable, evasive and dishonest.

Silberman came from a Jewish family and had radical political views that derived in part from his family's turbulent experiences in Germany during the First World War and the rise of the Nazis. Friends said he belonged to the 'Bohemian left', a term that encompassed Silberman's sexuality, as he was both gay and promiscuous.

A key aspect of Silberman's relationship with Holden was revealed near the start of the first of two long interviews Gillman conducted in 1978 with Silberman's brother Freddy and his wife Moyra. The relationship, Freddy told Gillman, was both 'strong and physical'. In short, Holden and Silberman were lovers.

Freddy's assertion, made without prevarication or embarrassment, provided the first direct confirmation of something Gillman and his colleagues had begun to suspect, namely that Holden was gay or bisexual. It cast light on his friendship with his former teacher, Robin Pedley, although they did not know if that had been physical too. During his interview with Freddy, Gillman did his best to take the revelation in his stride, even while the possible implications were taking shape in his mind. Freddy told Gillman that the relationship was established 'by 1950'. He was confident about the timing, which he confirmed by relating it to two key family events: the date when his parents moved into a new home in north London, a mansion in Avenue Road, St John's Wood; and the date when he and his first wife, Elisabeth Lewsen, were married. He also described two incidents from the early stage of the relationship.

Shortly after Holden and Silberman met, Freddy told Gillman, Silberman's parents needed a new butler at their home in Avenue

Road. At Silberman's prompting, Holden applied for the position. But Silberman's parents felt that it would be embarrassing for a friend of Leo to work as a house servant and turned Holden down. Then Holden asked Silberman if he could work in the family company, L. S. Mayer, high-end dealers and traders in furs, leathers, jewellery and other luxury goods. Freddy, who was its managing director, created a job for Holden – and was both surprised and irritated when Holden said that he had changed his mind. Holden was in fact about to go to the US – and it is another aspect of their relationship that he and Silberman tracked each other across the globe, seeking excuses to be together while both pursued peripatetic careers.

Silberman was born in Frankfurt, Germany, in May 1915. At that time, his father Fred was a prisoner in an internment camp at Ruhleben, near Berlin. Fred was originally from South Africa and was interned at the start of the First World War in 1914 because the German authorities deemed him to be British. His wife Hilda – Leo's mother – was German, and her family owned the L. S. Mayer company. Fred became managing director after he and Hilda were married in 1913, just a year before he was interned.

When Fred was released at the end of the war, the family moved to Britain. Fred set up a British division of the company, with offices in the City of London and a factory in Tottenham. In 1922, the family returned to Germany, settling into a new home near Frankfurt. By then, Leo had a brother, Gordon, born in 1920; Freddy, his second brother, whom Gillman met in 1978, was born in 1927. With Hitler and the Nazis on the rise, Fred began to prepare to move again. The day after Hitler became Chancellor in January 1933, Fred sent his family to Switzerland. After settling as much business in Germany as he could, Fred joined them there, then again moved his family to Britain, where they went to live in Hampstead. Fred built up the British end of the company and assisted German employees who were desperate to escape the Nazis. In one audacious episode, he smuggled the wife of one of his directors out of Germany into Basel in Switzerland. He then bribed airport officials to allow her to fly to London, where he secured Home Office permission for her to settle in Britain.

At the time when his family moved to Britain, Leo was at school in Switzerland, his father having sent him to the Schmidt Institute in St Gallen to escape the Nazis' 'singing and marching and flag-waving'. Leo rejoined his family in the summer of 1933 and soon became politically active, taking part in an anti-fascist march on May Day 1934 that ended with a rally at Hyde Park. Shortly afterwards, with the backing of the British Trades Union Congress (TUC), he asked the Paris left-wing periodical *Le Peuple* to help him research socialist politics and trade unionism. He also wrote a pamphlet for the Fabian Society about the aims of Nazi Germany and attended an international trades union summer school in the Netherlands, where a fellow student was Vic Feather, later general secretary of the TUC. Leo worked for a Birmingham metalware company for a time but, so his brother Freddy told Gillman, his political activities cost him several possible jobs.

The Second World War disrupted the family once again. Freddy went to live with a relative in the US while Leo at first remained in London. After his father's company offices were destroyed during the Blitz in December 1940, he went to Johannesburg in South Africa, where he obtained several degrees and became a college lecturer specialising in town planning. He travelled widely in Africa and wrote papers that challenged the racist policies of the South African government. At the end of the war, his father returned to Germany to take back control of the family company. He also opened a manufacturing plant in Dundee and bought a mansion in Avenue Road, St John's Wood. Leo returned to Britain in 1946 and applied for a research post at Liverpool University.

A former colleague, Betty Spice, provided Gillman with revealing memories of working with Silberman at Liverpool. Between 1947 and 1949, they were researchers on a race relations project funded by the Nuffield Foundation. Spice remembered Silberman as 'smallish and wiry, neat, quite good-looking – his eyes were an attractive feature'. He wore a Harris tweed sports jacket 'which looked wrong on him' and in winter 'an odd-looking overcoat that was too long'. Silberman had told Spice that this was his first time in Britain. He explained that his family were German Jews who had fled to South Africa in the 1930s and came to Britain after the Second World War. Spice thought it strange that Silberman seemed to know Britain so well and did not appear shocked on seeing the extensive bomb damage in Liverpool.

Spice gave Gillman a graphic account of the two sides of Silberman. As a friend, he was 'funny and witty, lively and buoyant at a depressing time'. He was also kind, generous, gentle and quiet. As a colleague, he was utterly unreliable, testing Spice's patience to the limit. 'He never showed up at the time he said he would, never had a piece of work done in time, let everyone down all the time.' In one spectacular incident, he and Spice travelled to London to discuss their research project with officials at the Colonial Office. After lunch at their hotel, Spice left Silberman in the foyer while she went to the toilet. 'When I returned a few minutes later, he was gone. The manager of the hotel was quite upset and called a taxi as I had no idea where I was.' Spice attended the meetings by herself and when she returned to Liverpool, Silberman wasn't there. 'No explanation was ever offered, much less an apology. This kind of behaviour was typical of him and annoyed me and my colleagues very much.'

On another occasion, Spice was with Silberman during a visit to the Seamen's Mission in Liverpool. An elderly man who clearly recognised Silberman approached him and greeted him as 'Brother Silberman'. 'Leo pretended not to know him and the man reminded him that they had worked together on a TUC committee,' Spice told Gillman. Silberman denied this, saying there must be some mistake. 'He seized my arm and hastily took his leave.' When Spice asked Silberman to explain, he insisted that the old man had been mistaken. 'But I had seen how flabbergasted he had been at Leo's denial and knew it couldn't be true,' Spice recalled. 'The incident remained in my mind as it was one of the few times I ever saw Leo rattled.'

The incident puzzled Gillman as much as it had Spice. Why was Silberman attempting to deny his left-wing activities and beliefs? The image of a man juggling or concealing the multiple facets of his life was confirmed when Gillman learned more about his time at Liverpool. In 1947, Silberman wrote a pamphlet for the Fabian Society about Africa. In August, he wrote from Liverpool to say that he was going to Spain 'to study the sixteenth century'. He also began to claim that he was alternately studying and teaching at Balliol College, Oxford; he said he had formally registered with Oxford University and had been made a 'Beit fellow', a form of scholarship, to study at the college. Extensive checking by Gillman and his colleagues in 1978 could find no trace of this. Silberman supposedly intended to write a thesis on the care of tuberculosis patients in Britain but never submitted it. Later, he was deemed to have 'lapsed' from the university.

Even so, Silberman continued to use Balliol College as an address. In May 1951, a letter addressed to him there thanked him for giving a talk at a college in Berkhamsted the previous week. Silberman did in fact apply for a junior research fellowship at Balliol in June 1951 but was turned down. He was still cashing in on the supposed Balliol College connection years later: letters were mailed to him there addressed to 'Professor Leo Silberman'. For Gillman, it added up to a man constructing different versions of himself, using charm and brilliance as well as dissimulation and deceit – characteristics he would come to discern in Holden himself.

By 1950, Silberman and Holden had embarked on their relationship, with Holden's failed attempt to become the Silbermans' butler and his decision not to take up the job Freddy found for him at L. S. Mayer. Freddy also remembered heated arguments about the state of Israel, created in 1948. At first, Leo supported Israel but abruptly switched sides, becoming 'anti-Zionist and pro-Arab'. Freddy believed that he did so perversely, in order to rile his father who supported the Zionist cause. Freddy also remembered that Holden too was pro-Zionist, at least during the intense family discussions on the topic.

Hovering over Holden's relationship with Silberman was his application to go to Northwestern, which he had made as soon as he quit teaching in December 1949. Holden was clearly considering other options, as when he asked to become the Silbermans' butler and to join the family firm. His mind was made up in June when he learned that an application he had made to the English-Speaking Union for a grant had succeeded. It looked as though his relationship with Silberman was at risk; but the ever-resourceful Silberman soon found an answer.

Holden arrived at Northwestern in September. Founded a century before, it had a mix of mock-Oxbridge and stylish interwar buildings, located on a privileged site beside Lake Michigan. Holden had enrolled to study education, history and philosophy, which required him to write a thesis. He joined the students' theatre group and appeared in several plays, including Cocteau's *The Infernal Machine* and Ibsen's *An Enemy of the People*, in which he played Dr Stockmann, the lead role.

In 1978, during a visit to the US, Gillman and his wife Leni interviewed a number of Holden's fellow students from Northwestern. While some remembered his interest in acting, their most striking recollections, among women at least, concerned Holden's sexuality. One woman, whom the Gillmans met in Maine, said she had been a 'regular girlfriend' of Holden for about a year. At one stage, she felt strongly enough about him to want to marry him. Yet not once did Holden make any kind of physical proposal or advance – and this, she made a point of saying, cannot have been for the lack of opportunity or volition on her part. A second woman told the Gillmans that she had been strongly attracted to Holden and had believed that he felt the same. She described a long walk beside Lake Michigan where she made it quite clear to him that she was 'available', but Holden did not take up her offer.

These testimonies accorded with what the Gillmans were learning about Holden's sexuality. They did not hear of any men who may have had a close relationship with him, leaving them to surmise that he was remaining faithful to Silberman. If so, Silberman did not reciprocate. In March 1951, he met an Irish student named John Jordan. Aged twenty-one, Jordan had sharp aquiline features and dark swept-back hair. He was a talented writer and poet who later won widespread acclaim in Ireland. After he and Silberman met in London, they began a short-lived but passionate affair. In a letter dated 10 April 1951, written after Jordan had returned to Dublin, Silberman wrote of 'my laughter at your acting, my eyes popping at your knowledge, my heart melting in your sweetness'. Two months later, Jordan told Silberman he planned to visit Oxford. 'My dearest, sweetest,' Silberman replied, 'I am eaten up by longing for you ... and that lovely body of yours.' Jordan secured a place to study at Oxford for 1951–52 but by then his relationship with Silberman was at an end, as Silberman focused his energies on joining Holden at Northwestern.

In June 1951, at the end of the academic year, Holden was awarded a master's degree in education. In a letter to his brother Geoffrey, he complained that he was depressed, life was monotonous and his colleagues 'lacked breadth and intellectual zest'. Despite his disillusionment, he applied to remain at Northwestern for a second year.

The reason for Holden's decision to remain at the university was not hard to find. Silberman had secured a job as a lecturer there, beginning in September. Silberman later described knowing Holden at Northwestern: 'He is intelligent, reliable, has good sense and a great deal of sensibility and a lively and engaging style.' Silberman's praise for Holden, which he wrote when Holden applied for a job at *The Times*, concealed as much as it revealed. Silberman claimed he first knew Holden 'when he was teaching at Northwestern University'. That was manifestly untrue, given that his brother Freddy was certain that he and Holden were lovers by 1950.

While Silberman embarked on his course as a lecturer, Holden was nominally attending lectures and seminars in connection with his second-year graduate course. He was also supposed to be writing another thesis but was spending far more time on non-academic pursuits, including joining a touring Irish theatre company. Gillman was therefore struck by the aplomb with which, in February 1952, Holden applied for a further year's grant so that he could complete his thesis, which would also allow him to continue his relationship with Silberman. Holden was granted his extension but continued to do the bare minimum of academic work. In November, he took up a job for the *Encyclopaedia Britannica* in Chicago, acting and narrating for its film division. In prospect was a trip to Mexico with Silberman, which was the subject of further subterfuge and obfuscation. In the testimonial Silberman wrote for *The Times*, he observed: 'It was at my suggestion that [Holden] went to Mexico to work with the Friends Unit.' This fitted with what Holden himself told *The Times*, namely that he had spent three months in Mexico in early 1953, 'working with the American Friends' Service Committee in their voluntary labour project'.

Holden was lying about the dates. The project he was referring to was run by Quakers in the state of Nayarit on Mexico's Pacific coast. It was true that Holden worked there – but not for three months. The project's records showed that he had worked there from 10 May to 4 June 1953. Holden did write to his brother Geoffrey from the project on 21 May, telling him that he was working as a labourer for stonemasons who were building a village school. What both Holden and Silberman were at pains to conceal was a trip they conducted to Mexico City in April. Letters by Silberman reveal that he was there on 18 and 22 April and there can be little doubt that Holden was with him.

Exactly what they sought to conceal was another matter of interest for Gillman and his Insight colleagues in light of their discovery that in the 1950s, Mexico City was notorious as a spying base for the Soviet Union. Despite conducting minimal trade with Mexico, the USSR maintained an enormous staff at its embassy, including around 100 members of its clandestine intelligence operation, the KGB, whose aim was to undertake covert activities in North America. It was in Mexico City that a Soviet agent assassinated Leon Trotsky with an ice axe in 1940; and it was there that Fidel Castro and Ernesto 'Che' Guevara took refuge in July 1953 after their first unsuccessful attempt to overthrow the Cuban dictator Fulgencio Batista, going on to cultivate a relationship with a KGB officer, Nikolai Leonov. The Mexico City KGB outpost notoriously came to public attention a decade later when it was discovered that Lee Harvey Oswald, the assassin of J. F. Kennedy, visited it a month before the assassination, in October 1963.

This fragmentary information led Gillman to speculate further on Holden's relationship with Silberman. It was now clear that they were in a committed relationship, albeit one punctured with absences and, in Silberman's case, with other sexual affairs. Silberman had shown his leftist political credentials at several stages too. Was Silberman linked to the KGB? If so, had he used their relationship to enlist Holden to the cause? And did they travel to Mexico City to meet KGB agents? Lacking any proof, these remained no more than enticing possibilities.

Whatever the truth, it was clear that by the time of his visit to Mexico City with Silberman, Holden had abandoned his doctorate at Northwestern. From Mexico, Holden travelled to New Orleans, writing to Geoffrey on 12 July to say that he was heading for Chicago. From there, he returned to London, enabling him to meet Silberman during the Northwestern summer vacation. Silberman himself clearly alluded to this period when he told *The Times* in 1954: 'I have seen him often in London ... He has an excellent character; a good friend and also a good judge of persons; modest and sincere, he will make a loyal colleague.'

After spending time in London, Holden returned to Sunderland. His father had died, at the age of sixty, in June 1952. Holden had been unable to attend his funeral as it had been held just three days later. His brother Geoffrey was there, together with numerous journalists and local dignitaries. In the summer of 1953, Holden joined his mother in the family home in Barnes View where, so she told his brother Geoffrey, he spent 'a long time upstairs trying to write'. Holden had resolved to become a journalist, like his father. And in 1954, the Ayton Old Scholars' Association recorded that Holden would now be able to say: 'Sucks to you', to all the doubting Thomases who had beset him in the previous nine months. He had obtained a job at *The Times*.

CHAPTER 8

THE THUNDERER

It was in June 1954 that Holden approached *The Times*, the austere and grandiose flagship of British upmarket journalism, still relishing its fading epithet 'The Thunderer' and its place at the heart of the political establishment. The narrative that emerged in 1978 was that, after Holden decided to abandon acting and follow his father into journalism, he had made the most of the old boy network, the relationships established in public schools and at Oxbridge that were supposed to rule the country. Holden, it was said, made an unashamed appeal to the Quaker version of the network after learning that Donald Tyerman, the deputy editor, had – like Holden – been a pupil at the Friends' School in Great Ayton. Upon reading Holden's letter, Tyerman promptly offered him a job.

In 1978, Tyerman told Gillman and his colleagues that he had relied on his 'instinct' to conclude that Holden deserved a job. But when they asked to see Holden's application letter, Tyerman said he felt embarrassed at how he had hired Holden and declined to produce it. After a lengthy delay, the *Sunday Times* team was finally permitted to look at Holden's personnel file at *The Times*. The crucial letter was missing.

Tyerman had form when it came to problematic appointments. In 1956, as editor of *The Economist*, he was the man who hired Kim

Philby, the most damaging of all British double agents working for the USSR. Philby had been previously cleared by the British government of being the 'third man' who had tipped off the fellow Soviet spies Guy Burgess and Donald Maclean, betrayers of Britain's nuclear secrets to the USSR, enabling them to escape to Moscow. MI6 assisted in the supposed rehabilitation of Philby, helping him to find employment as a journalist with both *The Economist* and *The Observer*. Tyerman later protested that he knew nothing untoward about Philby when he hired him, but not everyone believed his denials.

In the case of Holden, the theory considered by the Insight team was that he had been placed at *The Times* by British intelligence. It fitted with the abortive attempt to send him to Czechoslovakia in 1946 and matched other intelligence placements in the British press of that time. Once again short of further proof, it remained a possibility to be added to the growing list the team was now considering.

The job Tyerman offered Holden was with the Special Issues and Supplements Department at *The Times*. The department produced reports on subjects such as the colonies, agriculture, science, aviation and motoring and was considered a suitable apprenticeship for aspirant journalists. Tyerman did tell Holden that he needed to make a formal application but made clear that it was most likely to succeed. Holden listed four people who could provide references. The first was 'Dr Leo Silberman, Balliol College, Oxford'. Second was 'Mr E. Welbourne, Master of Emmanuel College, Cambridge'. Then came his professor at Northwestern, Baker Brownell, followed by a 'Mr W. R. Hutton'. In the event, *The Times* only followed up Silberman and Welbourne. As we have seen, Silberman was fulsome in his praise, recommending Holden 'in the warmest possible terms'. Ironically, Silberman need not have written in such extravagant terms, as Holden was offered the job before the references arrived.

Holden began working at *The Times* for a trial period of six months on a salary of £600 a year. His subsequent seven-year career at *The Times* provided some telling insights. He was ostensibly a diligent and conscientious foreign correspondent, reporting from countries that were variously chaotic and corrupt, where even making a telephone call could consume hours of his time, and his dispatches had to be sent by cable or air mail. While Holden's articles rarely hinted at these difficulties, his internal communications with *The Times* seethed with anger at the problems he faced. These were not just the difficulties presented by the country he was operating from but extended to those caused by *The Times* itself, ranging from its persistent meanness towards its correspondents to the damage perpetrated on their copy by its subeditors. To Gillman, Holden appeared to have two personalities: the confident outward-looking version and the profoundly dissatisfied inner character, struggling to contain his sense of alienation and anomie. He was dissembling in other ways: hiding his relationship with Silberman from scrutiny while trying to manipulate his career at *The Times* in order to follow it. The saving grace, for Holden, was his family, with whom he corresponded regularly in letters expressing affection and empathy, recalling their shared times and conversing on matters of mutual interest and concern.

Just as Holden's appointment to *The Times* had been made with remarkable speed, his rise within the newspaper was equally rapid. His time with the Special Issues and Supplements Department lasted for barely half of his supposed probationary period of six months. Just days before Christmas 1954, he was plucked out of the department and assigned to the Washington bureau of *The Times*. On 23 December, the newspaper's foreign editor, Iverach McDonald, asked Harold Nockolds, the head of the supplements department, if he would release Holden at once, and Nockolds agreed.

In a brisk memo, McDonald proposed to *The Times* manager Francis Mathew that Holden spend three weeks working as a subeditor and a further two weeks in the foreign newsroom, headed by Gerald Norman, before heading to Washington at the end of January. The next day, Holden was sent a letter confirming his appointment as assistant correspondent in Washington, on a salary of £900 a year, plus $3,400 running expenses. Holden accepted with alacrity, although in a curious coda, he wrote to Mathew to make it clear that he was not married: 'I wish to reassure you that I am not now married and that I have no intention of marrying in the foreseeable future.'

As Gillman and his Insight colleagues attempted to probe Holden's promotion, they met another brick wall. In 1978, they questioned McDonald about Holden's move to the Washington office. Contrary to what Holden's personnel file showed, McDonald denied that he had selected Holden. He described Holden as 'a likely young man' and mentioned that his death had been discussed at St Antony's College in Oxford, renowned as a gathering place of the intelligence world. During his interview with the team, McDonald referred to his work for both the Foreign Office and St Antony's, as if this were public knowledge. But when the team asked McDonald what theories had been considered at St Antony's, McDonald declined to provide any details. Much later, a former senior MI6 officer told Gillman that McDonald was 'an MI6 man on *The Times* or at least did what Six wanted'.

Holden sailed for New York on the American liner the SS *United States*. He arrived on 15 February 1955, staying there for two nights before taking the train to Washington. *The Times* office was in the Washington press building, where Holden was to be deputy to the chief US correspondent, Robert Wright Cooper. He was soon reporting on nuclear tests which the US staged in Nevada and on the patchy progress achieved in desegregating US public schools, with six southern states refusing to enact a landmark Supreme Court decision.

As the Cold War got underway, the US was heavily concerned with the potential threat from the USSR and its allies. Holden wrote several articles about the US response to a British government White Paper on Burgess and Maclean, the British diplomats who had spied for the USSR. Holden quoted a US news report declaring that the affair demonstrated that US concerns about Soviet spying were not hysteria but 'a necessary response to great, hidden danger'. He also reported on fears that the USSR was 'catching up' in the arms race, and on political moves in the Middle East, where the USSR had offered to finance a new dam for Egypt on the Nile.

Holden's reports were mostly crisp and to the point, with little attempt at any personal styling. He revealed some of his feelings in a letter to his brother Geoffrey in March 1955. He said that he was 'more Americano-phobe than ever, though don't let it be known in the Foreign Office' and raged about 'that sanctimonious old fleabag' Secretary of State John Foster Dulles. Otherwise, life was boring: 'No glamour, no excitement, this is largely a rewrite job, glued to our wire service and our morning newspapers, can rarely get out to meet anyone.' Holden also made a striking comment on a sexual theme, saying that he had heard that Washington was full of 'ravishing girls' but all the ones he had met were 'very plain and exceedingly dull'. It was one of a succession of remarks which left Gillman wondering whether, in view of Holden's true sexual preferences, he was protesting too much.

Holden revealed further frustrations in a letter to Geoffrey at New Year in 1956. He had survived the Christmas round of parties: 'Always too many of them, especially the soul-destroying cocktail affairs at which you stand forever, clutching your glass, and swap inanities with people you don't care about and who don't care about you.' Washington, he added, was an 'odd place, such an amorphous and transient society ... There is very little friendship to be found. A lonely and stultifying place.'

Holden soldiered on through 1956, until relief came in early June. Norman cabled him to ask him to take over as *The Times* Middle East correspondent as its incumbent, James Morris, wanted to leave to write books. A subsequent letter from Mathew told Holden he had been chosen for his 'political judgment and lively pen – you will need both in your new post'. As well as reporting events in Cairo, he would be expected to travel widely in the region, covering the 'intricate politics' of the Arab League and how the Middle East countries viewed the West. It looked a 'hard task', Mathew admitted, but he had little doubt that Holden would succeed. Morris was leaving Cairo in mid-July and Holden was needed there as soon as possible. Holden accepted the offer and arranged for his belongings to be shipped from Washington to Cairo.

Before leaving Washington, Holden sent Norman a five-page letter setting out a list of complaints and grievances about his spell in the US. Because the US was five hours behind the UK, Holden declared, time was always short. When writing from the US, correspondents had no idea which or how much of their previous stories had been used. Often London's story requests were trivial or merely followed up dubious reports in other newspapers. *The Times* used too many stories from the Reuters news agency instead of from its own correspondents. Any 'human' stories, steering away from the political or diplomatic circuit, were the first to be cut. It was an extraordinary list, once again revealing Holden's disenchantment as he balanced his public and private personas. Yet Holden appeared to have given little thought to conditions in Egypt. He was soon to discover that, in comparison to Cairo, working in Washington would look like a breeze.

Holden arrived in Cairo at a crucial juncture in British history. Since the Second World War, Britain had been attempting to sustain its position in the Middle East. It appeared like a victor doing its utmost to guard its spoils and at the same time trying to maintain its possessions and influence in the new realities of the post-war world. In Egypt, those overblown aspirations were about to meet their nemesis.

The Suez Canal, which forged the short-sea route between Europe and the Middle East, had been managed by Britain through the mechanism of the Suez Canal Company for eighty years. Britain had been desperate to prevent Germany from reaching it during the Second World War, seeing it as the symbolic gateway to its colonial possessions, above all India. By the mid-1950s, the canal had a new strategic importance, as the transit point for tankers carrying two-thirds of Europe's oil supplies.

Now, in British eyes, the canal was threatened again, this time by an upstart nationalist in the figure of Egypt's President, Gamal Abdel Nasser. What was more, Nasser was engaged in a courtship dance with the USSR, looking to it for funds and weaponry, while the USSR saw the opportunity to extend its influence into North Africa and the Middle East.

Holden arrived in this imbroglio in early August. *The Times* had increased his salary to £1,200, plus £3 a day running expenses – listed as 'cost-of-living, secretary, office and entertainment expenses, including trips to Alexandria'. He was to live in a houseboat beside the Nile which had previously been occupied by Morris and had use of a 1950 Rover car which Morris had warned was unreliable and costly to maintain.

Before long, Holden was encountering problems against which those in Washington paled into insignificance. If he wanted to telephone anywhere in Egypt outside Cairo, he had to book the call hours ahead and it proved quicker to do so from the Metropolitan Hotel. Telephoning London was all but impossible and he had to send his reports by cable or airmail. The Rover proved as problematic as Morris had warned. The Egyptian Information Office, the fount of official announcements, would call a press conference to be held at midnight or 1 a.m. – frequently at a moment's notice, which as often as not did not reach Holden anyway.

Meanwhile, the crisis over the Suez Canal was deepening. On 26 July, Nasser had announced that he was seizing the assets of the Suez Canal Company – effectively nationalising the canal itself. Britain and France were outraged and France began planning military action. Diplomatic talks began in an attempt to find a solution, headed by Australia's Prime Minister Robert Menzies. Holden's first piece for *The Times* from Cairo reported that Nasser was not prepared to attend a conference planned for London. Nasser did, however, agree that the conference be switched to Cairo, and Holden noted the 'amicable spirit' in which it opened on 3 September. But within a week, he was reporting that the talks had failed because Nasser refused to give up control of the canal.

Holden was also covering another downturn in British/Egyptian relationships. His report on 29 August, headlined 'More arrests in Cairo on spy ring allegations', told of the arrests of three British subjects, including James Swinburn, the business manager of the Arab News Agency (ANA). Holden later described him as 'somewhat tired, but otherwise in good health', as he was led into the national criminal court in handcuffs. Holden covered further court proceedings in a non-committal manner and it was only much later that the full truth about the ANA was revealed.

The organisation was in fact a front for a range of dirty tricks and covert action undertaken by the British in their battle with Nasser. Ostensibly, the agency served to collect and dispense news agency reports about both Egypt and the region. It had thirty-five staff members in Egypt, branch offices in the major Middle East nations and representatives in some fifteen other countries. It later emerged that the agency was an offshoot of the Information Research Department (IRD), a secret Foreign Office department created after the Second World War to support British government objectives such as opposing the USSR and anti-colonial movements. In this role, it created black propaganda, disinformation and falsehoods that today would be called fake news. The IRD operated for twenty-nine years and its secrets were still being uncovered in previously closed files some forty years on. At the same time, the British were attempting to set up an operation to assassinate Nasser and tried to bribe his main medical doctor to poison him, lining up a cabal of anti-Nasser army officers to take over if the plot succeeded. Following the Cairo arrests in August, two British Embassy officials who were said to be the ANA's contacts were abruptly expelled. Swinburn eventually pleaded guilty to spying and was sentenced to five years' hard labour. A British businessman, James Zarb, was sentenced to ten years and two other British residents in Cairo were acquitted. A 51-year-old Egyptian, Sayed Amin Mahmoud, said to be the main agent working for the British, was executed, and other Egyptians received long sentences.

Seen in retrospect, the affair served as a marker of Anthony Eden's determination to be rid of Nasser. The British Prime Minister said as much to his Foreign Secretary, Anthony Nutting: 'I want him destroyed, can't you understand? I want him murdered.' It also indicated Britain's readiness to use covert action to achieve such aims. The crossover between journalism and spying appeared to cause no embarrassment to the intelligence or newsgathering outfits involved.

On 29 October, Israel conducted a full-scale attack across the Sinai Peninsula and headed for the heavily defended canal. On 31 October, Holden reported that Nasser had rejected a proposal by the British and French to position troops in Egypt who would separate the Israeli and Egyptian forces and protect the canal. On 1 November, British and French forces invaded Egypt, sinking an Egyptian warship, bombing its airfields and occupying the canal zone. For a long time, the British and French insisted that they had acted independently of Israel; eventually, it was proved that they had colluded with Israel throughout, agreeing that it should invade Egypt and so give them cause and justification for the British and French to invade Egypt themselves and seize control of the canal.

Holden reported from Cairo on 1 November that Nasser had declared martial law and the British Embassy had been burning its files on the embassy lawn. Two days later – and in apparent retaliation for the detention of Egyptian journalists in London – the British journalists in Cairo were interned. Holden was one among seven who were driven to the Semiramis Hotel on 3 November and ordered to remain there until further notice. Holden shared a room with the *Sunday Times* correspondent John Slade-Baker, a man in his fifties who had arrived late in the profession after serving as a professional soldier in both world wars. He was delighted to find that Holden was an accomplished clarinettist who played passages from Mozart and also attempted to teach the *Manchester Guardian* correspondent, Michael Adams, how to play the guitar. Egyptian plain-clothes and armed officers guarded the hotel corridors and exits, but the internees considered they were being well treated, particularly as they were allowed to visit the hotel's two bars.

In a duplicated letter to his family, Holden wrote: 'Everyone has been most courteous and considerate ... We have been safe, well-housed and well-fed, and if we had had our freedom we couldn't have done any effective work.' Then came a stinging rider:

> My only complaint at the moment is directed against the British Government, whose actions impress us all here as being gigantically foolish at the very least; and to me seem criminally dishonest as well. It is impossible to say just how much we have lost in the Middle East – at present it is beyond computation.

Holden added a note in pencil for his brother Geoffrey: 'Words fail me in describing just how lunatic it is! You <u>must</u> write to your MP urging Eden's <u>instant dismissal or resignation</u>.'

In a further aside, he castigated 'my employers' who 'have shown a singular inability to comprehend the facts of my situation here, although other newspapers have not been so stupid'. It was a revealing comment. *The Times* had all but ignored Holden's internment, seemingly because it was preoccupied with its own discussions with members of the government, including Eden himself, and with the nuances of its editorials which were cautiously critical of the government. Such, at any rate, was the burden of *The Times*'s self-important history of the period 1939–66, published in 1984. It was written by Iverach McDonald, who revealed that he had been secretly briefed about the joint invasion plans some two weeks ahead. The internment of Holden and *The Times* stringer Alan McGregor merited one brief paragraph in McDonald's account.

On 23 November, the interned journalists were escorted out of the hotel and placed on flights home. Holden reached London via Rome and soon afterwards wrote his first dispatch in almost three weeks, with the anonymous byline: 'From our Cairo correspondent who has just been released from internment.' He reported that all British residents were being required to leave; they had to leave their possessions behind and their passports were stamped 'No return'. Holden made light of being interned, saying only that although the journalists had been notionally in prison, they were 'in such luxury that we scarcely had the courage to use the word'. And he found the airport security officers 'patient and consistently courteous'.

For Holden, it had served as an abrupt introduction to the volatile politics of the Middle East, as well as a dramatic end to his first visit to the country where he was to die twenty-one years later. He was back in the region by Christmas, celebrating Christmas Day in Jerusalem before going on to Amman and Beirut, where he stayed at the Palm Beach Hotel. Beirut was to be his base for more than two years, although he never succeeded in securing settled accommodation there. It was, in many ways, an ideal place to be, a cockpit of gossip and intrigue, where some major players in the worlds of espionage and conspiracy were to be found.

One such was none other than Kim Philby, working as a journalist while still plying his trade as a spy for Moscow and continuing to feed information to MI6. (He had another seven years to run before he was finally unmasked and fled to the Soviet Union.) Within days of arriving in Beirut, Holden himself suggested that *The Times* hire Philby, as it needed to replace its stringer there. 'Philby, the *Observer* man, would be good, probably,' Holden wrote, though adding that this might not suit Philby, 'as he lives out of town'. Philby was in fact staying in a village, Ajaltoun, a few miles outside Beirut that was the home of his father, the renowned Arabist St John Philby. Philby senior had strong connections with Saudi Arabia, and in May, Holden suggested asking him for help in obtaining a Saudi visa, but nothing came of it.

In 1978, the Insight team learned most of these details of Holden's relationship with Philby. What astonished them, however, was that Holden had never revealed them himself. In 1968, three *Sunday Times* journalists – Phillip Knightley, David Leitch and Bruce Page – wrote a book about Philby, sub-titled *The Spy Who Betrayed a Generation*. In 1978, Knightley told the Insight team that it was widely known at the paper that they were researching Philby's life, and they had appealed for anyone with information about him to come forward and assist them. Yet Holden had not done so.

As for Middle East politics after the Suez confrontation, it was a time when many of the nations were still finding their way in the post-colonial years. A mix of kingdoms, autocracies and elective democracies, they alternately sought pan-Arab alliances and jostled with each other for power. They were also becoming an arena for Cold War rivalries, as the US and the USSR competed for influence, with Britain trailing some way behind. Holden covered an impressive amount of territory as he visited Arab capitals, interviewing their leaders, while also travelling to outlying areas to ensure he was not solely occupied with city politics.

In early 1957, Holden visited Aden and then Yemen, from where he had to dispatch his reports via a nine-hour jeep journey back to Aden. He moved on to Bahrain and Baghdad before returning to Beirut, this time staying at the St George Hotel. Throughout this period, he had been trying to obtain a visa to go back to Cairo, which at last came through. On 10 March, *The Times* published his account of his return to Cairo, 'City of Ghosts'. It was an evocative piece in which he regretted the rupture between Egypt and Britain and hoped that good relations could be restored. There were nicely observed touches: returning to *The Times* houseboat was like 'donning a shroud', with the dust on his books and the calendar still showing 29 October.

Holden next reported on successive political crises in Jordan and Syria, which had been under martial law for nine months. On 24 July, he wrote of continuing disquiet about the plight of Palestinian refugees. In October, he lamented the fact that he was living out of a suitcase for much of the time and said he needed a permanent base, so that he could be 'released from the limbo of uncertainty I have been forced to inhabit for the last eleven months'.

There was an underlying reason for Holden's persistent dissatisfaction. It concerned his relationship with Leo Silberman. In January, while trying to persuade Norman that he needed a base, he argued that he should be free to travel widely around the region – including to Sudan. He had proposed visiting Sudan at least once before but found Norman sceptical. 'I am a little surprised at your reluctance over the Sudan,' Holden wrote on 7 January, arguing that it was important for its links to Egypt, for belonging to the Arab League and for its friendship with the West. Somewhat enigmatically, he framed his argument in the context of his freedom from personal ties: 'I am still single (and likely to remain so, I fear, so long as I stay in the Middle East, where a normal bachelor must either surrender his judgment or seek sublimation) and therefore not obliged to offer minimum comfort to a wife.'

Holden wanted to go to Sudan for one overriding purpose: Silberman was there. After Holden finished at Northwestern, Silberman resigned from his teaching there and secured a new research post at the nearby University of Chicago. He won approval for a project, 'The Rise and Fall of Democracy in Sudan', which took him to the country in 1957 and 1958. He witnessed parliamentary elections in February 1958 and then the turmoil which led to a military coup in November. He went on to write a thesis in which he lamented the fall of the last Arab democracy and observed how the US and the USSR were vying for influence with the new government.

When Holden made his second plea to go to Sudan, Norman did not relent. Holden tried again in October, with the same result. Norman told him: 'We do not want to over-extend your territory and feel that just now you should keep well in the Middle East area, which the Sudan is rather outside of.' On 23 December, Holden raised Sudan once more, proposing that he cover the elections there in February – the very topic that Silberman was studying. Still Norman said no, still Holden persisted, writing from Cairo on 31 January 1958 to say: 'I believe these [elections] will be important, and in any case nothing in the Sudan has had much of an airing for the past two years.'

Ironically, Silberman himself wrote an article from Sudan for *The Times* in early March, covering the results of the election in the rural provinces. It had descriptive flourishes characteristic of Holden, strongly suggesting that Silberman had sent Holden a draft for his comments or even that Holden had ghostwritten it. It appeared on 4 March, with the byline: 'From a Special Correspondent.' Soon afterwards Holden made another pitch to Norman, suggesting that he go to Sudan during a visit to Saudi Arabia. Norman remained unmoved.

Holden could not, of course, disclose his true reason for pressing to go to Sudan. He could not tell his brother either, but, shortly before Christmas 1957, he revealed his frustrations in a letter to Geoffrey that had a strong sexual theme.

> I do not really like the Arabs. Certainly not en masse ... The social atmosphere of the Arab world as a whole is repugnant to me. Partly, I think because it is still a mono-sexual (and for that matter very often homo-sexual) world. The absence of women from all forms of public life is infinitely damaging to the men. (I speak here with heartfelt sincerity, as I am sure you will understand.) The men are fundamentally effeminate, petty, impulsive and untrustworthy.

Holden planned to spend Christmas in Jerusalem and told Geoffrey and his wife Freda he would drink a toast to them in the bar of the National Hotel.

In April 1958, Holden was back in Beirut, lamenting that he still did not have a flat and so was paying expensive hotel bills instead. He did, however, renew his friendship with Michael Adams, the correspondent for the *Manchester Guardian* with whom he had been interned in Cairo. Adams's wife Celia remembered him from this period: 'He used to come to our house to chew the political fat with Michael. They were very much of the same mind over the politics of the time in the Middle East, especially over Palestine.' She continued: 'They both knew the fundamentals of that story, going way back, and had no illusions about Israel and its ambitions.'

Later in April, Holden travelled to Saudi Arabia, writing three reports from Jeddah. In early May, he was in Aden, penning his rage at the difficulties he had encountered in Jeddah. 'It was a terribly frustrating experience,' he wrote. 'I was literally close to tears with suppressed and helpless rage.' In terms of 'oriental bureaucracy nothing comes within a thousand miles of Saudi Arabia'.

A reply came not from Norman but from John Buist, who told him that Norman had left *The Times* (he moved to the BBC) and he was the new foreign news editor. For the time being, Holden's wanderings from Beirut ceased, as Lebanon itself became the story: there were riots against the ruling Christian regime, the main oil pipeline from Iraq was cut and the US sent arms for the Lebanese police. Syrian troops conducted a raid into Lebanon, bringing widespread fighting and seventy deaths.

All of this was reported by Holden, but his work was interrupted when, on 3 June, he was told he had been expelled from Lebanon. Holden and *The Times* were baffled, as they could see nothing sufficiently untoward in his writing to cause him to be expelled. In London, Iverach McDonald went to the Lebanese Embassy where he met the chargé d'affaires who appeared 'embarrassed and puzzled' by the expulsion. The order was withdrawn the next day. Despite Holden's rapid release, his expulsion posed questions about what other activities he might be pursuing, particularly in light of similar events later in his career.

After further travels, Holden spent Christmas in Cairo, and in the New Year once again raised the issue of where he should be based. Having argued persistently for Beirut, he now switched tack and favoured Cairo. He concluded with a familiar plea: 'As I have been living out of a suitcase for 2 ½ years I need a permanent home of some kind badly, even if I have to leave it frequently.' Still *The Times* prevaricated. Barely able to contain his exasperation, Holden replied that he was going to return to *The Times* houseboat, which remained at its mooring beside the Nile.

As for Sudan, Holden succeeded at last. He had told Buist in

October: 'I will keep my eyes on the Sudan, where I would like to go a little later.' In early 1959, he suggested that he set up trips to several destinations, including Sudan. Buist replied on 25 February, invoking the editor, William Haley, to quash the proposal. 'On this matter the editor's wish is that you stay in Cairo meanwhile, since it is not very long ago that Oliver Noods was in Sudan and Aden.' Even now, Holden persevered, and finally Buist weakened, allowing an opening for Holden to make a firm proposal, namely that he should visit Sudan to cover the trials of some dissident army officers and to inspect an irrigation scheme in the Gezira province.

Holden finally had his wish fulfilled. But, by a monumental irony, Silberman had moved on from Sudan. After completing his thesis about democracy in Sudan, he had secured approval for a new proposal, namely to study 'change and conflict in the Horn of Africa'. The bulk of Silberman's research was in Ethiopia, Somalia and Kenya.

Although Silberman was no longer in Sudan, Holden clearly felt he should complete his assignment. He also told Buist that if he could get as far as the city of Juba in southern Sudan, he would 'cross into Uganda and/or Kenya', paying his own expenses and using two weeks of his leave to do so. He told Buist: 'I have one or two friends in Nairobi I would like to look up.' On 14 July, Holden sent Buist a 'mailer' from the Grand Hotel in Khartoum, the capital of Sudan. It concerned a new river weed that had been found in the Nile, and he sent two more handwritten mailers on 26 July. Holden did indeed reach Juba, then moved on to Uganda and Kenya, to be reunited with Silberman once again.

Throughout this period, and unknown to Holden, *The Times* was discussing a possible change in his career. McDonald, the foreign editor, felt that it should appoint a 'roving correspondent', who would be ready to cover sudden crises, particularly in Africa. On 28 July, McDonald wrote to Holden inviting him to take up the post:

'We need a man who is fit and active, who has powers of quick and sound judgment, and writes well.' Holden replied, accepting the proposal: 'I am delighted at the prospect you outline and gratified to know that you think I am the man to whom you can trust the new assignment.' His salary would be increased from £1,750 to £2,000.

For Holden, the new post covering Africa carried another plus. If Silberman continued his research in Africa, it would provide them with further opportunities to meet. That hope was abruptly thwarted in November, when Silberman fell ill and was diagnosed with pancreatic cancer. Following a four-hour operation, he made enough of a recovery to start travelling again but not to Africa. In January 1960, he visited St Moritz with his father, then made further trips to France and Germany.

Meanwhile, Holden was busy in his new role, visiting Algeria, Northern and Southern Rhodesia, Angola and the Congo in April, all places where pushes for majority rule and independence were under way. In September, Holden was in Leopoldville, capital of the newly independent Congo Republic, where factional struggles were convulsing the country. He was preparing to move on to Lagos to cover the occasion of Nigeria's independence in a ceremony on 1 October.

Then came news from London: Leo Silberman had died. He had made a further trip to Italy in April and in July exhibited his gift for making exotic contacts when he secured a contract from David Attenborough, then a BBC TV producer, to act as an adviser on a series of films about Madagascar. A few weeks later, the pancreatic cancer returned; Silberman suffered a relapse and died on 8 September.

Holden was notified about the funeral but was unable to attend. A secular occasion, it was held at Golders Green Crematorium on 12 September. Freddy Silberman gave the principal address, referring to his brother's 'short but turbulent life', adding that 'best of all, Leo loved to talk; next to talking he loved to listen; and next to listening he loved to be talked about'.

On 18 September, Holden sent Buist an obituary notice on Silberman,

> whom you may have known slightly. I know his copy was often (probably always) impossible to sub; but he was an old and dear friend of mine with many fine qualities. He never quite achieved what he should have achieved; but I would like to record the fact that he had friends who thought a lot of him.

He asked Buist to pass his notice to the obituary department, but it was not used, and *The Times* published only a brief three-paragraph death notice.

Silberman's death brought a new watershed in Holden's life, a moment when many of his dissatisfactions crystallised, and he searched for a solution elsewhere. Once again, his career was discussed in his absence, and he was invited to spend the following year in the role of '*Times* correspondent in Africa'. On 25 October, he met the editor to discuss the proposal. Although Holden expressed some reservations, *The Times* believed that he had accepted the post. Its editors were therefore astonished when Holden wrote to Haley a week later tendering his resignation. In a notably terse letter, he told Haley he was going to work for *The Guardian*, which had offered him a job. (The newspaper had dropped 'Manchester' from its title two years before.) He understood that he had to give three months' notice, after which he would start at *The Guardian*.

On 2 January 1961, while in Kampala, Holden wrote a long letter of explanation to McDonald. 'To begin with,' he said starkly, 'I don't much like black Africa any more and I don't look forward to living out of a suitcase for months on end.' He talked of living a rootless existence: 'The endless vista of hotel rooms; the perpetual shoptalk in the bar at night; the creeping loneliness; the gradual sense of demoralisation; and the feeling of frustration and pointlessness that eventually arises.'

In addition, he listed the lack of promotion prospects and the absence of human contact within *The Times*, which was 'too inflexible, formal, stuffy for enthusiasm, creativity, gaiety and even at times ordinary humanity to flourish'. *The Times* preferred 'abstract thought and the rational façade to the concrete illustrations of the sight, smell and sound of life'. The reporters' anonymity was a further frustration. At *The Guardian*, by contrast, reporters could write 'with directness and enthusiasm' about the world they lived in; and they were free to write and broadcast elsewhere.

It was an astonishing disavowal of his work for *The Times*, a sweeping damnation that left no aspect unscathed. It also showed a determination, following Silberman's death, to embark on the next chapter in his life. Had Silberman lived and continued finding research projects in Africa, Holden might have welcomed the idea of becoming Africa correspondent for *The Times*. That no longer applied. What was more, moving to *The Guardian* resolved some of his grievances against *The Times*. It enabled him to take greater control of his working conditions and would permit him to be better known, instead of the stultifying anonymity *The Times* imposed on its writers. Perhaps aware of how churlish he might appear to McDonald, he added a postscript: 'Please believe me that I am terribly grateful for the opportunities *The Times* has given me, and that I really love the damned old thing – in a way, perhaps, that I shall never love another!'

CHAPTER 9

ROVING CORRESPONDENT

Holden had lied. He told *The Times* that he had been offered a job by *The Guardian* and by several other newspapers as well. By contrast, *The Guardian*'s editor, Alastair Hetherington, told Gillman and his colleagues in 1978 that it was Holden who had asked him for a job. Holden gave Hetherington two principal reasons, both of which he cited to William Haley in his resignation letter: he wanted a byline, and he wanted more freedom – by which he meant more free time, as well as the freedom to write for other publications. By Holden's standards, his lie to *The Times* was a minor dissimulation, hardly ranking with the deception that had governed his ten-year relationship with Leo Silberman. As it proved, 'freedom' also entailed Holden coming up with his own ideas; as *The Guardian* had no correspondent in the Middle East or most of Africa, it could give him an almost clear run to go where he liked.

Holden's first overseas assignment, in early July, took him to the Gulf oil state of Kuwait, where British troops were digging in to help protect the newly independent regime in the face of threats from Iraq. He next returned to his old stamping ground, Beirut, from where he reported the latest news from Kuwait. Then came a week in Baghdad on the third anniversary of Iraq's revolution, where Holden observed that the revolution and its leader, General Abdul

Kassem, were losing their way as their initial popularity gave way to apathy and disillusion. Holden was writing with notably more freedom, colour and descriptive detail.

In August, Holden was in Lisbon, writing about the push for independence of Portugal's African colonies and its effect on the dictatorship of António Salazar. He went on to Cairo, where he reported on President Nasser's latest bid to install Arab socialism, with moves towards land reform but also to greater state power. In October, he reported from Accra, capital of Ghana, ahead of a visit by Queen Elizabeth II, which rebels tried to disrupt with a series of bomb explosions. When she arrived on 9 November, Holden noted that there was 'no doubt of the delight she has given to the people of Accra by coming in the teeth of all the anxieties and alarms of recent weeks'. In keeping with the requirements of covering a royal event, Holden dutifully noted that – 'according to my fashion advisers' – she was wearing a slim-fitting dress in a princess line of creamy ecru lace with a matching tulle hat. Holden proceeded to Nigeria, looking to exert African leadership a year after it became independent. Then, following five months on the road, Holden returned to Britain for a spell of rest and recuperation.

By then, he had started to write for the magazine section of the *New York Times*. His first piece, published in June 1961, criticised the US as a tourist destination on the grounds that it was expensive, unfriendly, had poor food and paled by comparison with European countries such as France and Germany. It appeared like a restatement of the jaundiced view of the US he had acquired during his spell there for *The Times*. The article, headlined 'America is a bad tourist trap', so upset the US tourist business that the *New York Times* published a rejoinder shortly afterwards. Holden wrote further articles for the magazine over the next twelve months: a report from the Congo on a disastrous clash by a United Nations force in the breakaway province of Katanga; a profile of the oil-rich rulers of the Persian Gulf; and an account of the disturbing rise of neo-Nazi groups in the UK.

When the Insight team tried in 1978 to find out more about the circumstances in which Holden had been enlisted to write for the *New York Times Magazine*, they encountered a strange case of collective amnesia. The editor, Lewis Bergman, could recall nothing about Holden's commissions, despite the furore which greeted his first article about US tourism. Nor could two other editors the team spoke to. Anthony Austin, the magazine's articles editor in 1978, declined to show them any internal files relating to Holden on a series of grounds. He said that it was an invariable rule that outsiders could not look at the files; these files were rather dull and inconsequential; and, anyway, they had recently been weeded, so contained nothing earlier than 1974. It was all reminiscent of the obstruction the team had faced when inquiring into Holden's hiring by *The Times*, but the team found it hard to know what to make of it.

During a spell in London in early 1962, Holden wrote two articles about its nightlife, the first on the mildly titillating nude revues at the Windmill Theatre, the second on the Crazy Gang, a group of comics appearing at the Victoria Palace. After that respite, he spent a month in Canada, followed by a month in the Caribbean and Central America, including stays in Haiti, Panama and Cuba. Then came a further period in London, culminating in a dramatic new departure in Holden's life: he got married. The ceremony was held at the Register Office of the Royal Borough of Kensington on 24 August 1962. Holden's wife was Ruth Elaine Lynam, at thirty-seven just five months younger than Holden, and like him a journalist.

As Holden later told it, he first met Ruth in a bar in Lagos in September 1960 – just three weeks after the death of Leo Silberman. They were both covering Nigeria's independence day on 1 October, when the former British colony became the Federation of Nigeria. Holden was there for *The Times*, Ruth for the American magazine

Life, and Holden recalled that she was making herself a suitable hat to wear in order to meet Princess Alexandra, cousin of Queen Elizabeth II, who was there to formally award Nigeria its independence.

They met again in Ghana in November 1961, this time when Queen Elizabeth herself was making a tour of Africa, and once again Ruth's hat proved to be her distinguishing feature. As the Queen stepped off her plane at Accra, the first thing she noticed among the waiting spectators was Ruth's hat, so one member of her entourage reported. And it was clearly Ruth who, as Holden told *Guardian* readers, had advised him about how the Queen had dressed for the occasion. Holden said he admired 'her inborn sense of true elegance' and her 'vital sense of all that's new'.

Ruth was born on 23 April 1925 in the town of Farnborough, Hampshire, home to an aircraft research and military base, where her father worked as a designer. During the Second World War, she was a boarder at Christ's Hospital girls' school in Hertford, a partner of the equivalent boys' school in Horsham. After the war, Ruth became a general assistant at the Royal Opera House in central London, which reopened – following six war years as a dance hall – in February 1946. She worked for both the top administrator, David Webster, and Ninette de Valois, the choreographer of the ballet company which also performed there. Later, Ruth moved to public relations work and by 1950, she had switched to the Glyndebourne Opera.

A year later, she joined the staff of the American photo magazine *Life*, renowned for its global photojournalism. She was listed in *Life*'s masthead, under its foreign news services. She officially worked as a reporter, but in the *Life* hierarchy, this was often in a subordinate role to the magazine's photographers, acting as their assistants and general dogsbodies. By the time Ruth met Holden, she had a more elevated status. During a further royal tour to India and Nepal, she took part in a tiger hunt which required her to share a tent with no fewer than four photographers.

As Holden told it, he was wooed by Ruth's love of adventure and travel, her elegance and sense of style and her willingness to educate him – 'an ordinary philistine' – in elements of high culture such as ballet and opera. The witnesses at their wedding were Holden's brother Geoffrey and a fashion designer friend of Ruth's, H. G. Viall. They were living close to each other in Chelsea at the time they were married, moving to a neat Georgian terrace house in St Paul's Road, a street in Islington, north London, that was becoming fashionable. (After renting the house for a period, they purchased it in 1970.)

To outsiders, the marriage looked unlikely in several ways. Holden was still travelling and could be away for a month or more at a time. Ruth was frequently away too, and their respective returns to St Paul's Road often did not coincide. Once Ruth gave up travelling, she was able to build a social life when Holden was back. Many of the friends they acquired had not previously known Holden and none would have been aware of his clandestine relationship with Silberman. Anyone who did know might wonder if Holden had married Ruth on the bounce. Those who knew that Holden was gay believed that Ruth was gay too and that this was therefore a marriage of convenience. To Gillman, it resembled a lavender marriage, one undertaken to conceal the sexuality of one or both partners. That said, Holden and Ruth were clearly fond of each other and as their interests converged and their social circle developed, they came to be seen as a fixture whose existence did not need to be questioned.

For the equivalent of their honeymoon, they spent a rainy weekend in Dublin, where they had a chance encounter with the Irish poet and Republican Brendan Behan. Holden was evidently prompted to return, for his first reporting for *The Guardian* following the marriage was from Ireland. It was not until March 1963 that Holden hit the international road once more – and ironically, it led to an immediate pause in his reporting activities. He was intending to make a further visit to Central America and the Caribbean, starting in Cuba on 10 March. But when he arrived in Havana, he was seized by immigration officials and driven to a detention centre in the old part of the Cuban capital, which he described as a gloomy building with high ceilings and a few prison cells with white tiles and barred windows. He was given two meals a day, consisting mostly of beans and rice. When he asked why he had been detained, the guards would only say that he had tried to enter Cuba without a visa or 'special permission'.

He repeatedly asked to see the British consul, who finally visited him on the third day of his detention but professed that he was none the wiser. Eventually, on day five, Holden was woken at 6 a.m., driven back to Havana Airport and placed on a flight to Mexico City. From there, he flew to New Orleans, where he wrote a good-humoured dispatch about his experiences which led *The Guardian*'s front page in its issue of 18 March. All further attempts to find out why Holden had been detained failed. One plausible explanation may have lain in a hostile article Holden wrote in May 1962, when he contended that the idealism of Castro's revolution was being overtaken by totalitarianism, accompanied by indoctrination, poverty and food shortages – downplaying the consequences of the stranglehold exerted by the US economic boycott. 'The romantic betrayal', Holden concluded, 'is virtually complete.' Another explanation which the Insight team considered was that, just as with his expulsion from Lebanon in 1958, the Cubans knew or suspected something of Holden's clandestine activities for one or another intelligence agency.

Undeterred by his arrest, Holden continued his global peregrinations, which took him from Canada to Eastern Europe, Iraq to Jordan, and then to a lengthy stay in Greece. In December 1963, he was back in Cairo, writing a series of articles about the latest disputes between Egypt and Israel; President Nasser's attempt to establish an Arab Socialist Union, so enlarging his own political base; and the fate of the Abu Simbel monuments, threatened by the

Aswan Dam. He moved on to the Far East, visiting Indonesia, Laos and Vietnam – both Saigon and Hanoi.

Then came a long hiatus. With the agreement of *The Guardian*, Holden had taken time off to write his first book, *Farewell to Arabia*, based on his travels in the region termed Arabia, encompassing the nations bordering the Red Sea, the Gulf of Aden and the Persian Sea, including Aden, Yemen, Bahrain and Saudi Arabia. He framed it as a valediction for the decline of British influence and the resurgence of local power, interwoven with the impact of nationalism, technology, population shifts and oil. In Aden in early 1957, he had overheard British residents chatting in the Crescent Hotel in the wake of the Suez debacle, 'where gloomy prognostications of British retreat were decried in brave, imperial voices' and with racist references to 'the wogs'.

To Holden, these were 'voices from beyond the grave, pleading causes that were already dead'. Upon visiting Yemen soon afterwards, he described sitting on the floor of a palace attempting to eat a hunk of goat's meat with one hand, followed by an account of the tribal rivalries that were besetting Britain's bid to retain control of its protectorate. Holden viewed past and future with the same pessimism, concluding: 'All that remains is to say farewell to innocence and gird ourselves to understand the shape of things to come.' The death of innocence was to become a familiar theme in Holden's writing, together with the inevitable downfall of idealism and the thwarting of hopes.

In Britain, his book was published by Faber and Faber. In the US, the book was taken by a lesser-known company, Walker and Co., which, so the Insight team found, had a shadowy provenance. Its head, Charles Walker, was a former CIA agent who had been recruited while studying at Yale University. He had edited a magazine, *Eastern Europe*, which was directly published by the CIA in a bid to promote the US and its values during the Cold War. The CIA had set up a department called the Domestic Operations Division which funded publishers and subsidised books with the same aim. It had an overseas division which provided authors with the excuse and funds to visit and study a country at length. One example was a seemingly innocuous travelogue of Sweden for which the author had spent two entire years travelling at leisure around Scandinavia.

A key figure in these operations was Howard Hunt, who came to public fame through his part in the Watergate scandal of the early 1970s, eventually exposed by the *Washington Post* duo Bob Woodward and Carl Bernstein. For a period during the early 1960s, Hunt had been head of covert actions in the Domestic Operations Division, in which role he had handled Charles Walker. Hunt also had knowledge of another publishing operation, namely the funding of the British political and cultural magazine *Encounter*, which likewise promoted US values among the British intelligentsia. If Walker and Co. intended to publish Holden's *Farewell to Arabia* for the same purpose, its message was more subtle. The decline of British influence in its former imperial territories, which Holden described, was something which fitted US policy objectives – particularly if it created a power vacuum which the US could fill. It could be argued that Holden's message suited CIA objectives. As Gillman soon found, there would be some far less ambiguous examples to come in Holden's life and career.

By now, Ruth had decided that while Holden was continuing his global travels, a peripatetic career was no longer right for her. In the summer of 1964, she became the women's editor of the *Weekend Telegraph*, the Saturday colour magazine of the *Daily Telegraph*. It was not a comfortable place to be, as its editor, John Anstey, was notorious even by Fleet Street standards for his bullying and capricious behaviour, victimising staff members and blaming them for his own mistakes, all the while maintaining a façade of reason and calm. Ruth survived a year there before help came in the form of a job offer to edit the British edition of the US-led fashion magazine *Harper's Bazaar*. She was heralded in its issue of June 1965 with the assertion that she would bring 'a vital sense of all that is new and a conviction that *Harper's Bazaar* will lead the fashion field'.

Ruth later admitted that her appointment had been a dramatic mistake, as she lacked any worthwhile editing experience. But it enabled Holden to review the first three years of their marriage in an article for *The Guardian* headlined 'Darling editor'. During those three years, he wrote, he had learned that Ruth disliked skiing, slingback shoes and wrist watches for women. She refused to drive a car or travel on the London Underground as she was claustrophobic – she travelled to work by bus instead. She liked to eat gulls' eggs and smoke Egyptian cigarettes. It was a witty and enjoyable account, offering a semblance of orthodoxy that concealed as much as it revealed. It also marked his last piece for *The Guardian*, as he had been offered a job by the *Sunday Times*.

CHAPTER 10

SUNDAY PAPERS

It was Frank Giles who recruited Holden to the *Sunday Times*. Giles was the newspaper's foreign editor, having been hired by Ian Fleming in 1960, around the time Fleming left to concentrate on monetising his literary creation, James Bond. Giles had wanted to become a diplomat after the Second World War but flunked the Foreign Office exam. A sympathetic adviser suggested that a suitable alternative for a failed diplomat was a career as a journalist and Giles was duly hired as a subeditor at *The Times*. He later held foreign correspondent posts in Rome and Paris, before he was taken on by Fleming.

A Wodehousian character, Giles came across as an effete, languorous figure. He had a titled wife, Lady Katherine Sackville, daughter of the 9th Earl De La Warr, known to her friends as Lady Kitty. Once installed as foreign editor, Giles regarded any actual reporting as beneath his station. Instead, he would depart on lengthy overseas tours, visiting foreign capitals and meeting officials and diplomats, following an itinerary that was usually arranged by the long-suffering local correspondent. 'I did not see my function as a reporter of news,' he observed; it was enough that he should brief himself about the countries so that if one came into the news, 'I knew at least something of its problems and personalities.'

From the start, Giles had nurtured the ambition to become the *Sunday Times* editor, saying as much to Fleming when he was appointed foreign editor. His own writing was at best banal, and Holden appeared like the correspondent he could have been. Holden was adept at visiting the same countries as Giles and writing accomplished surveys of what he had found. His reports were also skilful in establishing a balance of views, usually with a wry cynicism, and rarely taking a pronounced position with the occasional marked exception. Giles recommended Holden to the *Sunday Times* editor, Denis Hamilton, who agreed that he should be hired.

Hamilton was initiating other changes heralding a journalistic revolution at the *Sunday Times*, facilitated by the arrival of a new proprietor. In 1959, Lord Kemsley, always an unlikely news magnate, sold the newspaper to a Canadian media owner, Roy Thomson, who had a substantial news empire in Canada and had embarked on expanding it in Britain. He had already taken over *The Scotsman* and the Scottish Television company, which he famously lauded as 'a licence to print money'. Buying the Kemsley group, including the *Sunday Times*, marked a further expansion. Unlike most media magnates, Thomson was not interested in political power or influence; only in how many advertisements his newspapers sold and how far they were in profit. He oversaw Hamilton's changes without demur. Under Hamilton, the *Sunday Times* started publishing a colour magazine in 1962, another media sea change that gave a platform to the best photographers and writers while scooping in millions in advertising revenue.

In 1963, Hamilton launched a new form of journalism: a team of reporters dedicated to explaining the news in depth and revealing misdeeds and scandals. Titled the Insight team, it elevated journalism to new levels in the ensuing decades. Giles regarded some of these developments with distaste, later commenting that the newspaper was 'happy and harmonious' until the arrival of a

'Young Turk' element who were 'much given to office intrigue and acrimony'.

One particular new arrival posed a direct threat to Giles's ambitions. That was Harold Evans, who was thirty-eight when he joined the *Sunday Times* in 1966, after five years as editor of the *Northern Echo*, based in Darlington in north-east England. Hamilton made Evans his own chief assistant, then promoted him to managing editor. At this time, Giles considered himself the first-choice candidate to replace Hamilton, failing to spot that Evans was now Hamilton's heir apparent. Hamilton, who judged that Giles 'lacked brio and sparkle', appointed Evans editor in January 1967. Giles felt 'shock and disappointment', even though he had been awarded the consolation prize of deputy editor.

For Holden, who arrived at the *Sunday Times* one year before Evans, the advantages of joining the newspaper in this expansive period were clear. He was offered more money and more space in a newspaper getting into its stride under its new apolitical owner. He had a direct internal sponsor in the shape of Giles. For his first article, on the Commonwealth leaders' conference in London in June 1965, Holden was accorded a modest welcome, a passport-sized photo with the caption: 'David Holden, who joins the *Sunday Times* as a special correspondent'.

The main focus of the conference, so Holden wrote, concerned the prospects for independence of Rhodesia, where a 5 per cent white settler elite continued to rule over the remaining 95 per cent African population. In August, he travelled to Aden and Cairo, where President Nasser was embroiled in a conflict in Yemen while Egypt's economy and his prestige in the Arab world were in decline. Next came a trip to India and Pakistan, followed by a return to Aden, and then to Salisbury, capital of Rhodesia, where he reported on the privileged life led by the whites, which they were determined to entrench, in contrast to that of the Africans. He speedily returned to Salisbury after the white regime, led by the unsavoury figure of Ian Smith, unilaterally declared independence from Britain in its bid to maintain white supremacy.

In February 1966, having completed his book *Farewell to Arabia*, Holden was given his first assignment for the *Sunday Times Magazine*, travelling to India with Lord Snowdon, husband of Princess Margaret. Snowdon was a photographer who, before he was ennobled by marrying the sister of Queen Elizabeth II, was known as Antony Armstrong-Jones and built a reputation taking photographs for *Tatler*, the house magazine of the global upper classes. His entrée into royal circles came when he was asked to photograph Queen Elizabeth and her family at their London home, Buckingham Palace, in 1957.

Holden and Snowdon spent three weeks in India, travelling from the Punjab to Kerala. After the *Sunday Times Magazine* was started in 1962, it lured high-value consumer advertising which at times sat uneasily with socially conscious articles about hunger and deprivation. Snowdon's solution to the problem was to produce images largely determined by aesthetics, rather than their social and personal content. 'The photos were very pretty,' one disaffected magazine staffer told Gillman. Holden's accompanying article was more open in discussing the difficulties faced by Gandhi and India: soaring prices, industrial failures, food riots, tribal rebellions. Holden ended with a balancing caveat: 'It is easy to be too impatient with India, and too full of doom and gloom.'

Holden's article in the magazine brought a neat coincidence, for Gillman had started writing for the magazine just a few months before. Aged twenty-three, Gillman later came to feel he was part of the fortunate generation who grew up in post-war Britain. He was a war baby, born in 1942, and still bore a diagonal scar across his nose to show it. It was caused by a V-2 which crashed to earth near the home of an aunt he was visiting in Beckenham. The blast blew in his aunt's windows and although her lace curtains protected him from most of the flying glass, one piece sliced into his nose. He was among the first cohort to benefit from the new welfare state, with free health care and education, and then from a growing consumer economy. Gillman won a scholarship to Dulwich College and later from there to Oxford University. His father, a civil servant who had fought in the First World War, died of cancer when he was eleven. His mother, a schoolteacher then in her fifties, took him on astonishing car journeys through France and Spain, taking him to the Louvre and the Prado galleries, passing on her love of art, music and literature. Gillman also reckoned she imbued him with a self-confidence and independence that were to equip him well for a career in journalism.

At Oxford, Gillman studied psychology and philosophy. His course was interrupted when his mother fell ill with cancer and he returned to be with her in her final days. By then, he had fallen in love with Leni, having met her in the Campaign for Nuclear Disarmament (CND), the peace movement calling on Britain to unilaterally renounce its nuclear weapons. CND undertook annual protest marches from the weapons research establishment in Aldermaston in Berkshire to London and it was on one such march, Gillman liked to say, that he and Leni first held hands. He was taken by her generous spirit, her intelligence and wit, not to mention her long, elegant limbs and her mysterious grey-green eyes.

At Oxford, Gillman spent at least as much time on journalism as on his degree course and was editor of the radical Oxford magazine *Isis* in the first term of 1964. After taking his degree examination, securing what was termed 'a good second', he cast around for work in journalism and was offered a job as an 'editorial assistant' at *Town Magazine*, a glossy monthly which, like the *Sunday Times Magazine*, was enlisting an array of young and talented writers and photographers. Gillman joined the staff on a salary of £850 and had articles published on topics ranging from demolition workers to surf-riding in Hawaii. After a year with *Town*, Gillman had the temerity to ask for a pay rise but was instead sacked. The editor, Clive Labovitch, co-proprietor with the future Conservative MP Michael Heseltine, told him that he was not a good investment for the magazine, but Gillman later discovered that it was in financial trouble and needed to cut back. The magazine closed two years later.

Gillman next joined the staff of the *Weekend Telegraph* magazine, shortly after Holden's wife Ruth had left it, where he too encountered the bullying and victimisation of the editor, John Anstey. Gillman's biggest success was for the *Daily Telegraph* newspaper, not its magazine. He covered an audacious winter ascent of the north face of the Eiger mountain in Switzerland by two competing teams, one German, one British-American. When the leader of the British-American team died in a fall, the two teams allied to reach the summit in a violent storm. Gillman's dispatches led the newspaper's front page three times in a week, which somehow irritated Anstey beyond measure. He alternately ostracised Gillman and blamed him for whatever mistakes were going, finally giving him the sack.

Gillman had already lined up an escape route, in the shape of the *Sunday Times Magazine*, whose features editor, Peter Crookston, had already commissioned several articles from him. In the summer of 1966, three months after Holden's article about India appeared, the magazine offered Gillman a freelance contract, guaranteeing him a minimum number of assignments per year. By then, he and Leni were married. Since they had two children and a mortgage, and Gillman had been sacked from his first two jobs in journalism, he accepted the offer. Over the next three years, he wrote some twenty articles for the magazine, covering a range of subjects with a speciality in true crime reporting, including a story about the brutal random killing of a young gay man on an outer London housing estate and another about a lethal feud between two south London scrap-dealers which culminated in a murder trial at London's Central Criminal Court, the Old Bailey.

Meanwhile, following his appearance in the magazine, Holden resumed his travels for the newspaper. In August 1966, he covered the jailing in Cairo of Mustafa Amin, the editor of the newspaper *Al-Akhbar*, who had been arrested a year before while having lunch at his village in Alexandria with an alleged CIA agent. Amin was given a life sentence on charges of espionage and currency smuggling. Holden was back in Egypt the following year, recounting an unsettling taxi ride from Cairo to Suez, where he hoped to inspect the damage caused by an Israeli raid on an Egyptian oil refinery, and the taxi got lost.

In 1968, Holden assisted the *Sunday Times*' coverage of the polarised and intransigent politics of Northern Ireland, attending a meeting and rally addressed by the hardline Protestant leader Ian Paisley in November. When Paisley discovered that Holden was reporting for the *Sunday Times*, he was physically ejected from the meeting, taking a hefty punch on his nose into the bargain. The *Sunday Times*, together with *The Guardian*, was alone among the English press in reporting the grievances of Northern Ireland's minority Catholic population. The newspaper surmised that Paisley had felt especially aggrieved over an investigation by its Insight team, headlined 'John Bull's Political Slum', which had given voice to the Catholics and criticised Paisley for his divisive and provocative activities.

In May 1969, Holden was back in Egypt once more, his visit occasioned by the latest border skirmishes with Israel. Holden judged that Nasser's hold on power appeared stable – thanks in part to his security police being firmly in control, despite earlier hints that their oppressive machinery would be dismantled. Holden's report from Cairo was his first for the *Sunday Times* in four months, as he had been preoccupied with making a film for the BBC in its *One*

Pair of Eyes series, which gave public figures the opportunity to make a personal statement about matters close to their heart.

Holden's episode, 'The Unreal Image', was broadcast on 27 September. As the title hinted, it examined the nature of political reporting of the kind Holden himself conducted. What was astonishing was the degree of cynicism in Holden's commentary, effectively condemning much of his own efforts and output. Holden's writing habitually contained an undertone of scepticism, but here it was writ large, an astonishing renunciation of his work and even his reputation. The commentary was also notable for one aside Holden made towards the end of the film: 'You can't be too careful when you have to communicate something.' To Gillman, this cryptic remark spoke volumes, suggesting as it did the importance of a key element of a spy's tradecraft. As such, it was at one with the enigmatic postcard Holden sent Jan Morris the day before he was killed.

Holden undertook further work for BBC, this time for its radio division, as a presenter and commentator for its World Service output and as an occasional presenter for its prestigious news review, *The World Tonight*. One of the producers, Alastair Lack, remembered Holden as 'extremely pleasant but quite reserved'. Holden, Lack recalled, was an accomplished professional, writing clear, simple scripts and asking clear, simple questions. But he maintained a careful distance, never indulging in chit-chat. 'To me, in a nutshell,' Lack said, 'he was a charming enigma.'

Holden also resumed his relationship with the *New York Times*, reporting from Cairo in May 1970. He observed that there was still disquiet about Nasser over Egypt's defeat in the 1967 war with Israel and resentment of the 5,000 Russian 'advisers', as they were called, in Egypt's armed forces. There was talk of corruption, but somehow the Egyptians appeared to want to make the best of things. Holden was more critical of Nasser in a subsequent article for the *Sunday Times*, following the ignominious collapse of an Arab summit conference in Rabat. Nasser appeared increasingly isolated, leading him to propose an alliance or even a merger with Gaddafi's Libya. Whatever the outcome of that proposal, Holden concluded, it made it likely that the 'old futilities' of the Arab world would continue.

That could not, however, prepare the world for the seismic shock of Nasser's sudden death, at the age of fifty-two, on 28 September. Holden hastened back to Cairo, writing a report for the *Sunday Times* which set out the daunting problems Nasser's successor would face. As for who that could be, Holden listed four contenders, who included Egypt's current Vice-President, a former army officer named Anwar Sadat.

Throughout this period, whenever Holden was taking a break from his travels, he was enjoying an increasingly elevated social life. It had received an initial boost from his work for the *Sunday Times Magazine* with Lord Snowdon, who would on occasion stop by with his wife Princess Margaret at the Holdens' home in Islington. Following Ruth's disastrous spell as editor of *Harper's Bazaar*, she had abandoned journalism and moved into public relations, first as director of advertising and publicity at the Jaeger fashion company, renowned for helping to launch the career of designer Jean Muir, then as promotion and publicity director for the hair stylist Vidal Sassoon, who was busy building a global chain of hairdressing salons. Sassoon commented that he enjoyed Ruth's 'aristocratic bearing' and her readiness to criticise 'anything that didn't suit her sense of propriety or aesthetics'. He also considered her 'frightfully posh and well-connected', as demonstrated by the Sunday evening dinner parties which the Holdens took to hosting at their home.

A *Financial Times* journalist and editor, J. D. F. Jones, made a similar comment to Gillman, describing the 'high-grade local set' who were guests at the dinners; they included the architect Denys Lasdun; the diplomat Sir Humphrey Trevelyan, who had been Britain's ambassador in Cairo at the time of the Suez invasion, later ambassador to the USSR; a second former Cairo ambassador, Sir Harold Beeley, who was in Cairo during the 1960s; and Michael Rice, a publicist with close links to the Arab world, furthered through his work as a museum designer in the region. The dinner table, Jones told Gillman, was always 'very well laid and laden'. But Jones was puzzled that an overseas journalist like Holden should want to consort with diplomats he had encountered abroad over dinner in London, rather than keep his two lives separate. The talk was very high-grade, covering matters of diplomacy and national policy. Jones was impressed that Lord Snowdon and Princess Margaret were among the guests – 'to have the Queen's sister at these dinners was obviously a coup'. And Holden, despite any internal misgivings, 'was always at his most suave and debonair'. Jones had an enticing thought to offer Gillman: if Holden were indeed working for one or other intelligence agency, he would win many kudos for having such a high-grade roster of acquaintances and contacts at his domestic dinner table.

In the autumn of 1971, Holden was back on the road, covering Africa, the Far East and the familiar territory of the Middle East. In July 1972, he was in Egypt once more, following the move by President Sadat – confirmed as Nasser's successor in 1970 – to expel the Soviet military advisers and 'experts' Holden had previously written about. Holden considered it a risky gamble and compared Sadat to 'an embarrassed squid', as he engaged in 'endless double speak' in a bid to conceal a lack of any substantial policies. Holden did not spell it out, but Sadat's move marked a key stage in Egypt's epochal shift from the Soviet to the American camp. Holden did conclude that it was the US and Israel which now held Egypt's fate in their hands, and observers should be looking to Washington or Tel Aviv to read its future, rather than 'among the rumours and confusion of Cairo'. That pay-off marked the end of Holden's last visit to Egypt for five years.

The previous year, Holden had paid his first reporting trip to Chile, one of three in the space of two years. Whereas Holden usually made a show of balancing his arguments, in the case of Chile, he was unremittingly hostile. His first report, published in July 1971 and headlined 'Marxist on a Tightrope', purported to examine the prospects of Chile's President, Salvador Allende, as Holden castigated him for illegal land seizures, industrial decline, a deteriorating economy and the prospect of violence among Chile's warring factions. He returned to Chile a year later, and this time was even more antagonistic, serving a damning summary of Allende's two years in power, which had brought a divided society, an acute economic crisis and a nation of 'fear and anger'. Holden's third piece was published on 9 September 1973, when Chile was suffering from rampant inflation and a devalued currency – 'a mighty peculiar road to socialism', Holden wrote.

Holden left Chile shortly before the article was published. It was impressive timing, as two days later, a Chilean army officer, General Augusto Pinochet, staged a coup against the elected regime and Allende allegedly shot himself rather than fall capture to the insurgents. Holden's timing proved doubly auspicious. He had once again arrived at the perfect moment to report an imminent coup. Then he had departed a day or so before the coup took place, avoiding any personal risk. So was Holden just lucky? Or brilliantly astute? Or was someone tipping him off?

Further questions arose from two subsequent articles Holden wrote about Chile. The following Sunday, 16 September, Holden asserted that Allende had been the victim of his own illusions, leaving Chile in a traumatic state of disorder which only an authoritarian government could restore. Holden took a benevolent view of the generals who staged the coup and downplayed suggestions that the US had in any way helped topple Allende from power. Holden wrote an article for *Encounter* magazine in January 1974 which was even less restrained. Allende, he concluded, had 'died a lucky man'. His life was a failure, his policies disastrous, yet in death he achieved success beyond his wildest dreams. He was the Western world's 'newest left-wing martyr, overnight the most potent political cult figure since his old friend, Che Guevara'.

Holden's writings on Chile, culminating in the onslaught in *Encounter*, appeared astonishing in light of the semblance of balance he had previously presented. Fred Halliday, a left-wing academic who specialised in the Middle East, greatly admired Holden's book *Farewell to Arabia* for its analysis of the shifting politics of the region as British colonial influence was replaced by Arab nationalism. He had come to know Holden and had dinner with him not long after Allende's downfall. Holden, he told Gillman, had been 'astonishingly crass and partisan about the fall of Allende', saying 'how much better it was in Chile' and even mentioning that it was now possible to buy cheap vicuña coats there. Halliday considered it a grotesque performance. 'It was like a strange piece of role-playing, utterly at odds with the journalist who had previously imparted secrets of the SAS.' Halliday said he could never reconcile the two Holdens he had seen.

The same thought occurred to Gillman, as did a possible answer. It was that Holden, whose book about Arabia had already been published in the US by a CIA front organisation, could be among the writers and authors who had been enlisted by the CIA in its culture war with the USSR. That case was strengthened when the Chile articles were considered alongside an extraordinary report Holden had written for *The Times* shortly before he moved to *The Guardian* in 1961. Dated 24 January, it comprised an unrestrained attack on Patrice Lumumba, the first democratically elected Prime Minister of the Congo, who had been deposed in a military coup. Lumumba was a socialist who had confronted Western interests in the Congo and threatened to take over their mines. At his time of writing, Holden did not know that Lumumba had been shot by a firing squad a week before, following lengthy torture sessions. When Holden did report Lumumba's death, he suggested that Lumumba's sordid end meant he had been 'cheated of the last moment of drama in a dramatic career'. It later emerged that both the British and US governments had sought to depose Lumumba; US President Eisenhower wished that he would 'fall into a river full of crocodiles'.

If that piece helped make the case that Holden was writing articles to suit the CIA's political agenda, there was an alternative, namely that Holden was at pains to demonstrate right-wing credentials precisely in order to conceal his true allegiance. This, Gillman felt, was a further foray for the team into the espionage game, where nothing was what it seemed and ambiguity abounded.

There was a further issue that Gillman and his colleagues considered. Holden's arrival in Chile in September 1973, together with his departure just two days before the coup that deposed Allende, appeared perfectly judged. As they looked back through his career, his timing appeared equally exquisite. He was in Egypt for the Suez Crisis in 1956; Jordan, for an attempted coup in 1957; a coup and civil war in Yemen in 1962; the colonels' coup in Greece in 1967; a coup in Oman in 1970; and an attempted coup by Milton Obote in Uganda in 1972. The most straightforward explanation, as Gillman had already pondered, was that Holden – and his editors – had a superb gift for being in the right place at the right time. The alternative version was that Holden was being assisted by tip-offs from governments or agencies which knew what was coming and wanted their man at the scene.

In 1974, Holden displayed a remarkable burst of energy, writing a series of articles for both the *Sunday Times* and the *New York Times*, with datelines in Europe that included Spain, Greece and Portugal. He proved adroit at the journalistic craft of recycling, producing two articles from the same destination for different publications, while managing to avoid any obvious repetitions. There was, however, a noticeable overlap in reviews he produced of a book by the former *Times* Cairo correspondent, whom he had known then as James Morris. Following a gender transition, which culminated in a full sex-change surgical operation performed in Casablanca in 1972, James Morris had become Jan Morris, all of which she related in her book *Conundrum*.

Once again, Holden discarded all restraint, this time to convey in powerful and affecting terms his admiration for what Morris had done. The book, Holden told his *Sunday Times* readers, 'is a story of love and of what it can do to make even the most bizarre and potentially tragic human situation both socially acceptable and individually fulfilling'. For the *New York Times*, he added that Morris was 'the latest and by any odds one of the most remarkable recruits to that tiny band of transsexuals who have negotiated successfully the ultimate exploration of the human condition, in the passage from one sex to the other'.

There seemed to be particular empathy in Holden's observation that Morris had begun to feel that 'the endless travelling of a reporter's job was becoming a kind of drug to mask his doubts about his own identity' and had therefore turned his back 'on the exposed heights of journalism, withdrawing into the greater privacy of the true writer's trade'. In a further telling comment, Holden noted that, before transitioning, Morris had been leading 'a nerve-wracking and exciting double life' – a phrase that could well apply to the dissimulation Holden had practised in respect of his sexuality and possibly other clandestine activities.

Holden continued his circuit of global capitals through 1975 and 1976. By then, his *Sunday Times* salary had reached £5,214, which was to cover six months' work each year, an arrangement Holden had negotiated to allow time for his other activities, including books, broadcasts and writing for the *New York Times*. In June 1976, he and Ruth went on holiday to Crete, followed by a trip to southern Spain in September. Holden sent his brother Geoffrey a postcard advising him: 'If you haven't been here you must come,' adding the PS: 'The sherry festival was full of sherry. So are we.'

By then, Gillman was a full-time reporter on the newspaper. In 1969, on something of a whim, he had accepted an invitation to become features editor of the *Radio Times*, the BBC's programme journal which was then being revamped. He worked there for two years, doing his best to steer clear of the vicious internal feuding that raged among the BBC's executives. He continued to write for the *Sunday Times Magazine*, with more true-crime articles and an exposé of the perils of asbestos. In 1971, he asked Crookston if he could join the staff of the *Sunday Times Magazine* and was thrilled when Crookston said yes.

Gillman spent two years with the magazine and then transferred to the newspaper. He reported on a range of domestic topics and was part of a team who regularly visited Northern Ireland. On one occasion, he was caught in an ambush staged by the IRA, who fired at a group of soldiers and instead hit a schoolgirl just a few feet from where Gillman was crouching, seriously injuring her in the thigh. Then, after two years in the newsroom, came his encounter with Evans in the office lift, when Evans asked if he would join the Insight team. This was not an offer to be refused, and Gillman moved up a floor at the *Sunday Times* building at Gray's Inn Road, graduating from the newsroom on the fifth floor to an office overlooking the well of the building on the sixth floor. The Insight office was closer to the newspaper's seats of power, with Evans some twenty strides away and other senior editors on the same corridor. Insight's editor was Peter Kellner, known as a political commentator, and another recruit was Paul Eddy, who – like Gillman – joined the team from the newsroom.

Gillman visited Israel for the first time in January 1977, reporting on the suicide of Israel's Housing Minister, who killed himself after he was revealed as corrupt. The night he arrived, Gillman visited Jerusalem's Jaffa Gate, familiar from an etching that had hung on a wall in his parents' home. It was a memento of his father's service in Palestine during the First World War: after seizing Jerusalem from the Turks, the British had staged a march through the gate to celebrate their victory.

Gillman worked on the suicide story with the newspaper's resident Jerusalem correspondent, Eric Marsden, an old-school reporter previously based in South Africa. After they had filed their report, Marsden took Gillman to meet some Palestinians who had disturbing stories about how they had been treated by Israel's security service. When Gillman returned to London, he and Eddy asked Evans if they could mount a full-scale investigation. Evans agreed but added that he hoped they would return and tell him the allegations were untrue, as it was not a story he wanted to publish. Gillman and Eddy flew to Israel in April. After conducting their forty-four interviews, they made elaborate arrangements to protect their recordings, as they could not risk taking them out via Tel Aviv Airport where they were likely to be searched. They copied the entire set and lodged one in a safe place arranged by Marsden. To transport the other set out of Israel, they enlisted the help of a Quaker aid worker, Diana Macrae, who agreed to take them to Amman. Once there, she dispatched the precious package to London.

By late May, their article was ready. Evans was in no doubt that it should be published but called all his editors to a meeting where he asked if they had any reservations about going ahead with publication. There were some questions about the methodology of the investigation, but none demurred. To no one's great surprise, the article, published on 19 June, proved massively controversial to Israel and its supporters. As the row rumbled on, Israel invoked the ICRC in its defence, whereupon Gillman returned to Amman and obtained copies of the ICRC's secret reports about Arab prisoners. The *Sunday Times* published these damning findings on 18 September under the headline: 'Israel and Torture – what the Red Cross secret reports show'. Holden was impressed by the Insight report, telling Evans in a memo on 22 June: 'It's a very thorough and courageous job that very much needed doing. I expect you'll be bombarded with hate mail – but for whatever it's worth, I'm behind you!'

By then, Holden was writing his second book, *Greece Without Columns*, which he had been mulling over ever since his extended stay in Greece in 1963. Published in 1972, it was dedicated to Ruth, 'who started it and suffered it'. It promised to debunk the myth of Ancient Greece as the cradle of Western civilisation and fount of Byronic romanticism, in the same vein Holden had followed with the Middle East in *Farewell to Arabia*. However, the result was less accomplished than his first book. Overall, it was a strange and provocative description of modern Greece from the perspective of an Englishman who professed from the start not to be 'a philhellene'.

'I happen to like Greeks on the whole,' Holden wrote in his introduction. 'I enjoy Greek sunshine, I can usually stomach Greek food and I readily acknowledge that the Parthenon is a noble site.' But he added that he suspected that much of the Parthenon's appeal lay in its state of ruin. 'I am perfectly certain that ... I should have disliked the place intensively in its original form. For it must surely have been a thing of some vulgarity in its heyday.' Gillman found the book bizarre at best but was intrigued to find in the acknowledgements the name of a known MI6 agent, C. M. Woodhouse, who was involved in the MI6/CIA 1953 coup d'état in Iran to remove the Prime Minister, Mohammad Mosaddegh. The most effective writing in the book consisted of Holden's account of the Greek junta or Regime of the Colonels, who ruled the country after a coup between 1967 and 1974. However, Holden was often apologetic towards the colonels and far less critical of their brutal fascist regime than he was about Ancient Greek temples, 'covered in gaudy paint'. His sympathy for the colonels accorded with US policy, which saw the military government as a bulwark against communism, all the more so because of Greece's proximity to the pro-Soviet Eastern Europe regimes.

Holden's third book, for which he had taken more time away from the *Sunday Times* in the mid-1970s, was to be about Saudi Arabia, the oil-rich nation which held 25 per cent of the world's oil and was courted by the industrial nations anxious to secure their own energy supplies. In the book, to be called *The House of Saud*, Holden hoped to discard the cultural preconceptions about Saudi Arabia and to penetrate the cloaks with which its ruling dynasty kept their activities from public gaze. He was aware of the allegations of systematic corruption within the ruling elite, the graft and pay-offs that were intrinsic to its dealings. He suspected that he might not get too far in revealing those and that it would be unwise to push too hard.

Holden had visited Saudi Arabia a dozen or more times in the preceding ten years and was now making his way through the middle-rank echelons of the ruling structure, filling a series of small pocket notebooks with neat, tiny handwriting. By late summer, he had written ten chapters, taking the story to the end of the Second World War and what he termed the start of 'the era of American hegemony'. In September, he found time to return to Crete with Ruth, this time telling his brother on a postcard that he was writing each morning while she went swimming and enjoyed the sun.

While Holden was immersed in Saudi Arabia, the most significant geopolitical action was elsewhere. In early November, the news broke that Egypt's President Sadat was to travel to Israel, where he would address Israel's parliament, the Knesset, in a bid to advance the cause of peace between the two countries. It was a momentous move. In prospect, encouraged and facilitated by the US, was a formal peace treaty between Egypt and Israel. Sadat was widely condemned by many of his fellow regional leaders, who promptly called a rejectionist conference which would be held in Libya in early December.

As the *Sunday Times* swung into action to cover these epochal events, its first instinct was to ask Holden to travel to the Middle East. Although Holden was officially on leave from the newspaper, he had proved flexible in the past. Two foreign department editors telephoned Holden on successive days in mid-November, receiving differing responses. When Peter Wilsher asked Holden if he would go 'to the Middle East' (Wilsher had Israel in mind), Holden turned him down flat. When Cal McCrystal called, asking Holden if he would go to Cairo, Holden prevaricated, promising an answer within twenty-four hours. At all events, the idea that Holden might go to the Middle East was current at the newspaper's editorial conference, presided over by Evans, on Thursday. Holden made it clear that he could not travel that week. The newspaper canvassed several other reporters, Gillman and Eddy among them, before McCrystal himself flew to Cairo the next day, 18 November.

That weekend, Holden changed his mind. He did so after he was called by Anthony Austin, articles editor at the *New York Times Magazine*, who had previously commissioned many of Holden's pieces. Austin asked Holden if he would go to Cairo, and this time, Holden replied that he was 'very interested' in the proposal. A day or so later, Holden told Austin he was keen to accept the assignment, which was 'precisely the kind of piece on the Middle East he had long wanted to do'.

Gillman was puzzled that Holden had been so ready to please the *New York Times*. Or was he also seeking to please other paymasters? Events now moved very quickly. On 23 November, the Egyptian Embassy in Washington telexed Cairo on behalf of the *New York*

Times to request facilities for Holden, including an interview with Sadat. Holden also approached the Cairo newspaper editor Mustafa Amin, whom he had known since the 1950s. Holden reopened discussions with the *Sunday Times*, saying he was ready to go to the Middle East after all.

The plan that emerged was for Holden to go to Damascus and Amman for the *Sunday Times* and to Cairo for both newspapers. The foreign department booked him a flight to Damascus on Sunday 27 November. From there, he would travel to Amman and then Jerusalem, returning to Amman in order to fly to Cairo. His plans were still fluid, as discussions with London and New York continued. It could also prove difficult to find hotels in Cairo, notoriously short of accommodation, all the more so in view of the intense media interest in the rapprochement between Israel and Egypt.

The foreign department told Holden it would attempt to book him rooms at both the Cairo Hilton and the Méridien in the hope that one succeeded. It also booked a flight for Holden from Amman to Cairo on the evening of Tuesday 6 December, allowing Holden a full day's work before moving on to the country that was at the heart of the potential realignment of the Middle East. It was with the Jordan airline Alia, coded RJ 503, scheduled to leave at 7.45 p.m. and to arrive in Cairo at 9.15 p.m.

CHAPTER 11

THE REPORT

Harry Evans felt torn. By June 1978, Insight's inquiry into Holden's life had lasted for the best part of six months. Evans prided himself on allowing his journalists all the time they felt they needed to bring a story home. He never put them under financial pressure either, allowing them to go wherever they thought was necessary. When an Insight member once thanked him for not setting them a budget, he replied by saying there was a budget, but he never told them what it was. His instinct was, therefore, to trust the Insight team to make its own decisions over how to proceed and how much time they needed.

Against that, other pressures were in play. Evans remained anxious to know if Holden had been an intelligence agent – and, if so, it had to be the *Sunday Times* who revealed it. The last thing he wanted was for a rival newspaper to break the news first. He was also repeatedly asked, at both formal and social occasions, what his journalists had found out about Holden and when they intended to publish. On 14 June, he dictated a memo to Gillman, Paul Eddy and John Barry which read:

> We ought to concentrate effort on the Holden story and wind it up. It's getting to be a bit silly that after all our efforts and inquiries

we have published nothing ... Let us set ourselves a target by the end of June, presumably with a final call on the Egyptian police.

Gillman and his colleagues understood where Evans was coming from. After so long, they shared his desire for a result. But the salutary fact remained that their research so far had not yielded any conclusions solid enough to be published. They had a mosaic of information that did not form a coherent picture. They had anomalies, gaps and suspicions. They did not have headlines or breakthroughs.

They also told Evans that two major elements of the inquiry were still required in the US. They consisted of approaches to both the FBI and the CIA. If Holden had in fact been involved in spying, surely one or both of these law enforcement and intelligence agencies must hold information on him? Evans agreed that the team should make the opening moves in an approach but warned that he was not prepared to wait an indefinite period for a response.

In London, the Insight team decided to split its resources. Eddy would take charge of Insight's weekly reporting while Gillman continued with the Holden inquiry. On 1 August, Gillman met Barry in Washington to plan their approaches to the FBI and the CIA. After calling the FBI, they were given an appointment with a member of the FBI's Freedom of Information section. His name was Ed Grimsley and they met him in the morning of 7 August at the J. Edgar Hoover Building, a brutalist concrete building named after the FBI's first director, on Pennsylvania Avenue.

As Gillman and Barry laid out their case, Grimsley responded with a sympathetic smile. He advised them that they should submit a written application, known as a Freedom of Information (FOI) request, for any files or information the FBI held on Holden, as well as on Leo Silberman. After completing the requisite forms, Grimsley said he hoped to have a preliminary answer that week, and they should call him on Friday 11 August.

Barry and Gillman duly made the call from the Washington office of the *Sunday Times*. Grimsley, still friendly and cooperative, told them that he had 'Holden's file' in front of him but added: 'It looks to me as if some of the stuff in here is classified.'

Proceedings now took a less friendly turn. Five days later, on 16 August, the FBI sent a formal written acknowledgement of the Freedom of Information request. Then came silence. Gillman and Barry returned to London, handing the task of chasing the FBI to the newspaper's office in New York. On 5 September, Grimsley told the office that 'some Holden files, but not all' would be released. This appeared to imply that Grimsley had personally examined Holden's file, confirming the impression he gave to Gillman and Barry. Grimsley added that the FBI had not yet located any material on Silberman.

Two weeks later, in place of the smiling Grimsley, the FBI showed its sternest bureaucratic face. In a letter dated 19 September, it declared:

> The indices to our central records disclose references to a name similar to David Shipley Holden and Dr Leo Silberman. Since we have reviewed only the index to our records and not the records themselves, we do not know at this point whether the records in question are the records you seek.

The FBI's declaration was in total contradiction to what Grimsley had told Gillman and Barry six weeks before. There was not even any locus for further dialogue; instead, the newspaper would have to seek recourse through the law. The New York office asked the Washington law firm of Williams & Connolly, renowned for challenging official institutions, to take initial action under the Freedom of Information Act – namely that the FBI had failed to respond to the newspaper's application within the specified time limit. This move was significant in terms of commitment and of time. It showed the newspaper's determination to see the Holden case through. But it also meant that there would be no speedy answer to its lawsuit, frustrating Evans's wishes once more.

Meanwhile, Barry and Gillman had contacted a serving FBI officer who was prepared to help 'on background' – the US version of the journalistic convention 'off the record'. The officer came back with one startling item of information: there was an FBI report of an 'observed meeting' between Holden and a 'known Soviet-bloc agent'. For the time being, the officer was unable to provide further details about the meeting or to say whether the FBI held other reports on Holden.

There was more. From the same officer, Gillman and Barry learned that the FBI did hold a report on Silberman. It contained a visa application to visit the US, together with a recommendation from an FBI field officer, most likely at the US Embassy in London, that Silberman should be 'investigated'. There was no record of whether Silberman had indeed been investigated, but the file did contain a note of his death. The agent could not tell if the file, as he saw it, was complete. But he was very puzzled over why the agency should 'know or care' that Silberman had died.

For Gillman, the snippets he and Barry had gleaned offered further tantalising glimpses of the world Holden occupied. But Gillman did not see any immediate way of building on those and felt daunted at how long it could be before the formal lawsuit showed any result. At the same time, the *Sunday Times* embarked on a similar path with the CIA, where the outcome proved equally enigmatic.

The formal method of approaching the CIA was, as with the FBI, to ask through a FOI request to see any documents mentioning Holden or Silberman. This could be a time-consuming and ultimately frustrating experience. Aware of this, the team first made an unofficial approach. A month or so before, while still in London, they had contacted Miles Copeland, a legendary figure in the intelligence world.

Copeland was one of the Office of Strategic Services (OSS) agents who graduated to the newly formed CIA after the Second World War. He played a key subversive role in the Middle East, helping to depose Iran's Prime Minister Mosaddegh in 1953. After retiring from the CIA in 1957, he ran a consultancy agency while still performing assignments for the agency. In 1970, he moved to London with his family and became a prominent commentator on intelligence matters.

Copeland now agreed to undertake two inquiries. The first was to approach James Jesus Angleton, a former head of counter-intelligence at the CIA. Angleton would become a notorious figure in the intelligence world, known as a former friend of the British spy Kim Philby, who became paranoid when Philby was unmasked as a Soviet mole and went on to conduct a witch-hunt for traitors within the CIA. In 1978, his reputation was less sullied and Copeland told the team that he and Angleton were working on a commercial project together. Copeland said that he asked Angleton two questions: did he know anything about the Holden case? And was he willing to meet reporters from the Insight team? The answer to both questions, as relayed by Copeland, was no.

Copeland's second approach was to a current Middle East officer at the CIA headquarters in Langley. The officer told Copeland there was nothing he could do to help, as this was 'an ongoing matter'. As for Angleton, when Evans heard of his refusal to meet an Insight reporter, he made a second attempt, this time through the writer and journalist Ed Epstein. At the time Evans approached Epstein, he was working with Angleton on a volume of memoirs. Angleton's answer, even to Epstein, was still a flat no.

On 15 August, following these rebuffs, the *Sunday Times* in New York made its formal request under the Freedom of Information

Act (FOIA) for any information the CIA held on Holden. The Act required the CIA to respond within ten days, but it did not do so. On 5 September, an official who gave his name as 'Jeff' told the New York office that the CIA had sent an acknowledgement of the request, but he added: 'It will take about six months for you to receive any information.'

The New York office pointed out that the six-month estimate was vastly longer than the FOIA permitted and threatened to take legal action unless the CIA complied with the Act. The CIA replied that it had a backlog of 2,800 unprocessed requests and added that the newspaper 'accordingly had the right to appeal on the basis of our failure to respond'. The quadrille continued. Evans protested to the CIA in a further letter to which the agency replied with an admission that it was indeed in default. It went on to say that if the newspaper insisted on appealing, its request would be sent to the back of the 2,800-long queue.

Just as they did with the FBI, the journalists tried to bypass the formal procedures for obtaining information. On a later visit to New York, Barry called the CIA in an attempt to persuade it to respond more constructively to the newspaper's inquiry. Barry was invited to meet two CIA officials in Washington's Mayflower Hotel. Barry felt this looked promising – but at the meeting, the two officials flatly said that the CIA had nothing in its files about Holden and no knowledge about his murder. Barry protested that he simply did not believe these statements: at the very least, the CIA must have taken an interest in the murder of a British newsman in Cairo. The officials conceded the point but said that all the CIA had collected were rumours which were no better than anyone else's. They then invited Barry to withdraw the FOI action. Barry declined to do so.

The team again tried to make a less formal approach. And from an unofficial CIA source, the journalists learned that the CIA *did* have a file on Holden. It showed Holden as an 'informal contact' of the CIA, which meant that he would have met 'second trade secretaries at US Embassies' on a fairly regular basis, most likely to exchange information. The source speculated that Holden 'probably knew who he was talking to' – meaning that a 'second trade secretary' was common cover for the CIA station officer. The source insisted that Holden was not in the pay of, nor under the control of, the CIA. However, they suggested that 'adverse parties' could misunderstand this relationship or come to a more sinister conclusion, since most of the 'second trade secretaries' in US Embassies had had their cover blown. What was more, any meetings outside the embassies would very likely have been observed and photographed by hostile intelligence agencies.

The team concluded that there was nothing more to be done, other than to let the FOI suit take its course. What the source said indicated that the two officials had lied to Barry in claiming that the CIA had no information on Holden. But the information it did hold, according to the source, hardly added up to a smoking gun.

Evans was pressing even more strongly for the team to deliver the results of its inquiry. He did, however, accept that it should undertake one more task, namely to make the 'final call' on the Egyptians he had referred to in his insistent memo of 14 June. Gillman arranged to go to Cairo in October, accompanied by Isabel Hilton. They arrived in Cairo on 4 October. Their first call was to the British Embassy, where they met David Blatherwick, head of Chancery. Blatherwick – later Britain's ambassador in Cairo during the 1990s – made clear the sense of surprise and shock that lingered in the embassy at the killing. The Cairo police, Blatherwick reported, were now convinced Holden had been murdered by terrorists and were directing their attention at two possible groups. The first consisted of communists; the second was a mixed group, allegedly headed by a Swiss national named Sergio Mantovani, which comprised both Arabs and Europeans. The Egyptians had arrested members of both groups, although some had since been released. Blatherwick had arranged for Gillman and Hilton to meet senior security officials at Egypt's Ministry of Interior, which had asked them to submit their questions in writing. They compiled a list of six questions, which Blatherwick agreed to pass on.

'We're not going to restrict ourselves to those, are we?' Hilton asked.

'Certainly not,' Gillman replied.

The meeting, on 8 October, was at the cavernous building Gillman remembered from his visit in January. This time, rather than the anti-social hour of 2 a.m., it was held at 11 a.m. Two officials greeted them: General Said Zacki, the ministry's director of public relations; and General Ali Rashid, deputy director of the security department.

Speaking through an interpreter, Rashid addressed the questions they had submitted. One was potentially embarrassing, as it concerned a statement made by President Sadat at a press conference that Holden's killers had been arrested – was this the Mantovani group? Rashid gave a diplomatic reply: Sadat had only said that this group *may* have killed Holden. Rashid added that they suspected that this group was linked to a second crime or terrorist action. When Gillman asked what that was, Rashid declined to go any further. He did, however, say that the Egyptians were certain that Holden's murder was 'a political crime'.

Gillman raised the three stolen cars – a clear indication, the Insight team felt, that the killing had been prepared meticulously and long in advance. Rashid replied that the first theft, on 18 November, had been conducted as preparation for a crime that would be directed against the Sadat–Begin peace initiative but not specifically against Holden. 'There's no direct relationship between the three cars and Holden,' Rashid said. 'They planned to commit any crime and Holden was an opportunity.'

'Can you explain that?' Gillman asked.

'They planned to demonstrate the lack of security here during the visit,' Rashid replied.

Hilton intervened: 'They wanted to embarrass the security services?'

'Yes,' Rashid replied. 'They were well trained and it was well planned.'

'Why do you say that?' Hilton asked.

'Because they left no trace.'

Rashid elaborated on his argument. As Holden had met numerous Palestinians on the West Bank, this had given the terrorist group the opportunity to set up the murder. What was more, Holden had collected some documents in the West Bank which he was bringing to Cairo.

'What's your evidence for that?' Gillman asked.

'That information was collected from officials on the West Bank,' Rashid replied. He acknowledged that no documents had been found in any of the three cars but added that the woman sitting behind Holden on the Cairo flight had seen him writing in a notebook – and his notebook had not been found either.

Gillman and Hilton glanced at each other, an acknowledgement that Rashid's arguments were making little sense. At this point, a third official entered the room. He was introduced as Major General Mohammed Abdul Fatah and was carrying a folder containing a typewritten document some thirty pages long. Fatah explained that it was the security department's official summary of its inquiry into Holden's killing.

For Rashid, this seemed to offer a welcome digression, as he took the report from Fatah and began to recite details of the three stolen cars. Gillman noted down the details where they added to what the Insight team already knew. There was one startling new item, concerning 'Car Two', the one in which Holden had been killed. Previously, the Insight team had been told this contained a cartridge case matching the fatal 9mm bullet. Now, Rashid revealed that another twelve bullets had been found in the boot of the car, all of the same calibre and capable of being fired from the same gun.

'They were made in Israel,' Rashid added.

'How do you know that?' Gillman asked.

'They had "Made in Israel" on them.'

'In what language?'

Rashid said he did not know. But he added that this did not mean that Holden was killed by Israelis. 'These bullets are commonly available, including to Palestinians.'

Gillman returned to the three cars, two of which had been resprayed after they were stolen. Rashid had previously said that although car thefts were rare in Cairo, they were not difficult to carry out. In all three cases, the thieves had broken open the quarter light on the driver's side, opened the bonnet and connected the ignition wires. But the respraying meant that the thieves must have had access to a workshop or other premises. So had the police searched for these? From Rashid's answer, it appeared that they had only done so in the suburb of Dokki, where one of the cars had been stolen. But he added that the cars could have been resprayed 'anywhere in Egypt – maybe Alexandria'.

Gillman pressed Rashid again. The spacing of the car thefts – the first was stolen on 18 November, the second and third on 5 or 6 December – indicated that the terrorist group had been active in Cairo for some time. Rashid agreed but added that this confirmed that the group was a combination of residents and visitors. It was most likely, he repeated, that the group was directed from abroad. 'They were planning to commit any crime and they were waiting for orders.'

'Any *political* crime?' Gillman queried.

'Yes,' Rashid replied.

'Are you optimistic about solving this?'

'No.'

It was clear from Rashid's terse answers that he considered the interview was nearing its close. Gillman and Hilton observed the courtesies, thanking the three officials for their help. They mulled over the interview in the taxi that took them back to their hotel, the Sheraton, where they decided to take a light lunch.

'What did you make of that?' Gillman asked.

'Not much,' Hilton replied. 'None of it made any sense.'

From almost any angle, they agreed, the 'terrorist group' argument was quite implausible. It assumed that a motley terrorist group, composed of Egyptians and foreigners, had been operating with impunity in Cairo for at least a month. The contention that Holden had been murdered to embarrass Egypt's security services was quite arcane. If anything, it spoke of a paranoia on the part of those selfsame security services. And of the supposed terrorists who had been arrested, around half had been released while the remaining half languished in jail without being charged.

In meeting the Cairo police for one final time, Gillman and Hilton had hoped for information which would help shape the conclusion to the first question the *Sunday Times* had long hoped to answer: who killed Holden? The Cairo authorities had initially appeared as committed as the newspaper to identifying the killers. Now this. Instead of engaging in an open discussion, the Egyptians had proposed an improbable theory which had failed to survive the most basic of questions.

The thought crystallising was one which Gillman and his colleagues had considered as plausible, at least, among a range of options. Barry had floated it in a telex to London during the first week's inquiries, referring to 'our hosts' as possible participants in a joint operation. In short, it was the Egyptians themselves who had killed Holden. Of the possible candidates, they were the best placed to conduct it, from stealing the three cars they used to meeting Holden at Cairo Airport. They were also best placed to conduct a bogus investigation or to divert those who were doing so. And they had done their utmost to deflect attention from themselves with their fanciful arguments about who had killed Holden. There were other implications too, which Gillman and Hilton felt reluctant to voice. Far better to complete their work in Cairo and discuss matters further at home.

Before doing so, they had one final task to perform. The Cairo police had released Holden's red Samsonite suitcase into the custody of the British consul. Gillman and Hilton visited the British consulate where the consul, Muriel Hankin, opened the suitcase. Someone had clearly attempted to fold Holden's clothes, presumably to maintain an air of propriety. Among the visible items, Hilton was struck that Holden favoured silk underwear. Hankin closed the suitcase and formally consigned it to Hilton, on the understanding that once back in London, she would ensure that it was delivered to Holden's widow, Ruth. Gillman and Hilton returned to London, with the suitcase, the next day.

• • •

On 17 October, at the *Sunday Times* office, Eddy told Gillman that Evans had once again urged them to write everything they had learned about Holden and the murder. They agreed to divide the work: Eddy would write the introduction; Gillman would undertake the bulk of the report. For Gillman, it felt like a moment of reckoning, when the work undertaken by a group of journalists for the best part of a year would be judged. The team had done its best to crack the mystery of Holden's killing. Had their labours been in vain? That task of evaluation now fell to Gillman, who had spent more time than any other member on the quest. In short, it was a moment of truth.

THE REPORT

It took Gillman two weeks to write the report, which covered more than 100 pages. It began with an introduction by Eddy which opened: 'The one certainty is, Holden's death was no random act of murder.' Eddy laid out the evidence for that confident assertion. The killers used three cars in the murder; all had been stolen for the purpose, one of them a month before Holden travelled to Cairo. The killers knew his travel plans, most likely by stealing telexes from the *Sunday Times* office. They abducted Holden at Cairo Airport and held him for at least three hours before killing him with a single shot. He was stripped of all means of identification before his body was dumped. Eddy considered the Egyptians' claim that Holden had been murdered by a terrorist group. This was highly unlikely in light of the intense security operation conducted in Cairo from the moment Sadat's peace move was announced and of the fact that no terrorist group had claimed the kill. There were far better candidates among national intelligence agencies, including the Egyptians themselves. 'The problem here is defining a motive,' Eddy concluded, 'and most of this year has therefore been spent in search of one.'

Gillman then embarked upon a summary of everything the investigation had discovered about Holden's last trip and then about his life. In respect of the final trip, there were conspicuous gaps in Holden's itinerary that the Insight team had been unable to fill. The largest and most enigmatic concerned Tuesday 6 December – Holden's last day alive. Put simply, what had he done that afternoon? The team had found no one who had seen Holden between his arrival in Amman around 2 p.m. and his frantic departure for the airport around 6.30 p.m.

Here, however, the waters were muddied in terms of who had made the sightings. There was Mr Bisharat, owner of the travel agency, who said he had seen Holden going into the coffee bar of the Intercontinental Hotel with the Fisteres around 2 p.m. And there were the Fisteres themselves, who said they had only seen Holden for a few minutes around 6.30 p.m., in a 'desperate hurry' to catch his 7 p.m. flight.

Bisharat could have misremembered, but there was a problem with the statements of the Fisteres too. They claimed to have seen Holden trying to send a last-minute telex to secure his hotel booking in Cairo for that night. But no one at the telex desk could remember Holden trying to send a telex – and if he had done so, he would have found one from the Hilton dated 4 December confirming that he had a room. By then, the Insight team had learned enough about the Fisteres to make them wary.

Gillman now knew that the Fisteres were in Beirut throughout the period Philby was there, and Phil Knightley, *Sunday Times* journalist and co-author of the first book about Philby, firmly believed that John Fistere was working for the CIA. The ex-CIA official Miles Copeland, who was also there at the time, had gone even further, telling Knightley that Fistere was specifically assigned by the CIA 'to keep an eye on Philby'. It was a mystery that the Insight team could not unravel. Was Fistere keeping an eye on Holden too?

There was a similar mystery over what Holden had done in Damascus on the afternoon of Monday 28 November – deepened by the fact that Holden had made a point of telling the British press attaché that he intended to visit the souk and later that he had done so. Then there was the puzzle of the conflicting accounts of his time in Jerusalem and the West Bank, when he appeared to have been in two places at once on the afternoon of 5 December: in the Old City, where he sent the mysterious postcard to Jan Morris, and in the occupied Palestinian territories with the Palestinian academic Ahmed Rahman. Was someone impersonating Holden, Gillman wondered? Or was this a case of an alibi that had gone wrong? Was Holden engaging in clandestine meetings on all or any of those three afternoons?

Gillman next canvassed the question of how Holden had been

intercepted at Cairo Airport, concluding that he had most likely met people he knew and had gone with them willingly. As the Cairo police had revealed, there was a crucial detail which appeared to confirm this. When he applied for his visitor visa at Cairo Airport, he had stated his profession as 'writer'. If he had entered the word 'journalist' instead, he would have been intercepted by immigration officials who would have insisted on escorting him to his hotel, but Holden had avoided that.

As for who knew he was going to Cairo, and when, Gillman covered the ground of the original inquiries in considerable detail, focusing on the French journalist Kenizé Mourad. But here Gillman addressed the problem the investigation repeatedly raised: on one hand, it could be suggested that Mourad had been following Holden with a view to learning his travel plans; on the other, there could be an entirely innocent explanation for what she did. Time and again the investigation had to accept that the behaviour it was examining was subject to differing interpretations, lacking proof either way. These speculations were overridden by the thefts of the telexes from the *Sunday Times* office. This appeared to trump all previous explanations – and to reveal the formidable nature of the investigators' quarry. The familiar doubts surfaced. 'It did not necessarily mean that the people taking such a close interest in our activities were those who killed Holden,' Gillman wrote. 'Once again, it was the ambiguity of the evidence facing us that proved most disconcerting of all.'

Similar doubts marked the team's extensive chronicling of Holden's life and career. They had unearthed exhaustive amounts of detail during their research. Much of it appeared unexceptional, typical of a hard-working foreign correspondent touching as many bases as possible as he prepared his reports. But they felt they had encountered several different Holdens, skilled as he was at presenting versions of himself to suit where he was and who he was meeting. At conspicuous points in their chronology, suggestive questions arose where they could only guess at the answers, leaving them troubled and dissatisfied that so much seemed inconclusive. It was as if they had been traversing shifting sands, unable to find anywhere solid to rest. And the more they had found out, the more their unease had increased.

The story of Holden's early life and his childhood illnesses was one of a struggle against adversity that may have prepared him for his career. His wartime experiences were not different from most of his age group but still gave steel to many of that generation. He performed well at school and at Cambridge, displaying a range of talents – which included acting. Then came the curious episode of his proposed visit to Czechoslovakia, which matched a ploy used by British intelligence.

Holden's three-year career as a teacher was marked by frustration and dissatisfaction, culminating in his decision to go to Northwestern University in 1950. By then, he had started his ten-year relationship with Leo Silberman. Silberman was unquestionably Holden's lover; but was he also working for the Soviet intelligence agency, the KGB? Did he recruit Holden to the cause? That possibility was buttressed by Holden's suspicious silence over his knowledge of Philby. Those theories had to be set alongside the mystery of Holden's hiring and promotion at *The Times*, conducted at breakneck speed – and indicating a possible link with British intelligence which had perhaps placed another agent-cum-journalist in a position where he could be of immense use. During Holden's six years at *The Times*, he displayed multiple personas: the accomplished foreign correspondent on the surface, seething with alienation underneath, an indication perhaps of the stresses involved in leading one or more double lives.

Holden's four years at *The Guardian* brought the enigma of his marriage and the dinner-table guest lists that would look impressive on a spy's CV. Then came his twelve years at the *Sunday Times*, where he did his utmost to balance the competing demands on his time, a feat that brought into play the dissimulation at which he was so practised. The *Sunday Times* spell was also marked by his vituperative condemnation of the left-wing regimes in Cuba and Chile, remarkable for a correspondent who had customarily written balanced reports leavened with a wry scepticism and disinclined to think the worst of people. Gillman contended that those reports could have been scripted by the CIA as it contested global influence and hegemony with the USSR. Or were they so blatant in their bias as to suggest a contrived counterplay by Holden, keen to make a show of his supposed pro-US credentials?

Gillman also looked into Holden's interactions with Patrick Seale, his literary agent for his unfinished book on Saudi Arabia. Seale's name had occurred on a number of occasions throughout Gillman's investigation, in strange and disconcerting ways. Seale had been at Oxford's Balliol College at the same time as Silberman claimed he was there. When he was working in Paris for Reuters in the 1950s, Seale told the woman he lived with that he had worked for British intelligence, and he had replaced Philby as *The Observer*'s Middle East correspondent in Beirut after Philby's defection to Moscow.

Gillman had talked to Knightley, the former member of the Insight team who drew on his knowledge of the Philby case, which he had cracked a decade earlier. Knightley reported that Seale had worked for British intelligence but added that his career was ended by strong but unprovable suspicions that he worked for the KGB. Richard Johns, the *Financial Times* journalist who, at Seale's request, had taken over the writing of Holden's unfinished book, told Gillman: 'If you really want to do some digging, you should look into the background of Patrick Seale.' When pressed, Johns said that he knew from a contact in British intelligence that Seale was strongly suspected of having a 'KGB connection'.

Gillman found the intersections in the lives of Seale, Holden and Silberman disturbing. But he was only too aware that all that could be dismissed as rumour and malicious gossip and he simply let the suspicions lie.

In his concluding summary, Gillman considered both the who of the killing and the why in parallel. For the who, he was strongly drawn to Egypt, citing no fewer than eleven reasons why it stood out from other candidates, which included Israel and Saudi Arabia. Many of those reasons stemmed from Eddy's opening analysis of the logistics of the killing, so elaborate and meticulous that anyone but Egypt would have faced immense difficulties in carrying it out. In addition, the Egyptians were best placed to follow Holden's travel plans, irrespective of the theft of the telexes from the *Sunday Times*. And it was easiest for them to intercept him at Cairo Airport.

The police inquiry into Holden's death was flawed in many respects. Their supposed liaison with the Jordan and British police was a farce. Despite heavy hints, they had refused to allow the two Scotland Yard detectives to visit Cairo. And they had refused to show Scotland Yard their progress report, written in June. Scotland Yard had sent several formal requests to see it, which had been echoed by Gillman and Hilton in their October meeting, but the Egyptians continued to insist that it was for their eyes only. There was another possible scenario, namely that Holden had been killed by a private security force answerable directly to President Sadat. That had led in turn to the official inquiry being blocked at a later stage – hence the stonewalling responses Gillman and Hilton had encountered in October.

It looked like a powerful case. But it was still short of certainty, particularly as Gillman cited a list of counterarguments. If Sadat's private security force had killed Holden, that entailed a risk that the domestic police would uncover the killers, and one of them might reveal the truth. The killing would have violated a common security service tenet, namely not to carry out such an operation on your own patch. And it was a very delicate moment in Egypt's history to undertake such a risky operation. Gillman also considered whether the killing was a case of mistaken identity, namely that the Egyptians had wanted to kill David Hirst, a *Guardian* correspondent who had enraged Sadat with his articles about corruption in Egypt. Hirst's name in Arabic looked similar to Holden and the two vaguely looked like each other. The theory had been suggested by some Egyptian sources and had even appeared in a Lebanese newspaper. But Gillman ruled that out on the grounds that Holden had been held for several hours before he was killed, giving the killers ample time to be sure they had the right man.

To Gillman, it felt disconcerting to be simultaneously arguing both for and against a potential solution. But that ambiguity lay at the very heart of the inquiry. When considering the 'why', Gillman's arguments were more diffuse. He concluded that Holden was at least peripherally and perhaps deeply involved in espionage or other covert activity for an intelligence agency. And he had most likely been recruited through his relationship with Leo Silberman.

So whose intelligence agency was Holden working for? Gillman mentioned the three most plausible countries: Britain, the US and the Soviet Union. Gillman initially felt it probable that Holden had been working for the CIA – although he hedged that by adding that at the very least, the CIA knew more about this than it was letting on. He added that Holden's newspaper career provided cover for his spying, and some of those who assisted in his career knew of 'his other activities'. He contended that Holden had been killed because he had committed an act of betrayal or an act which inspired revenge.

That argument led to one further consideration. Gillman had selected the agency that he felt Holden had worked for, namely the CIA. But what if he had worked for more than one? Maybe he worked openly for one and clandestinely for another; maybe he was a true double agent, where one side – or even both – is aware of his dual roles but calculates that it is gaining more from the relationship than the other. If one of the two were the USSR, that made the best sense of Holden's relationship with Silberman. In this milieu – known poetically as 'the wilderness of mirrors' – notions of betrayal and revenge became a fact of life. For his final sentence, Gillman added a chilling rider: 'The killing was an execution and was intended to be recognisable as such to others in the profession – perhaps as a warning.'

Gillman's first feeling on completing the report was a familiar one of relief. But it did not bring the satisfaction journalists feel, when a deadline looms, of riding a wave of adrenaline to bring the story home. As Gillman remarked in the concluding section, the team's beliefs about Holden's life and death fell far short of proof. None of the journalists involved had ever worked on a story as baffling and unsettling before. They were accustomed to trusting their instincts or intuition and at times had felt there was a truth within their grasp. But that truth had eluded them. Gillman's culminating sense was one of frustration. So much time spent; so much detail unearthed; yet so little, in terms of a conclusive story, to show for it.

Gillman added a foreword to the report, together with the names of the four journalists who had contributed most: John Barry, Isabel Hilton, Paul Eddy and himself. There was now yet another irony to confront. Evans had urged the Insight team to wind up its inquiry so that he could publish the outcome, 'come what may'. As he completed the report, Gillman had considered what kind of story it could yield. At best, it might run as follows: 'David Holden was most likely killed by the Egyptian secret service. He had been working for one or more intelligence agencies and was killed for his betrayal and/or as an act of revenge.' It looked hard to phrase it more definitively than that.

But now that the report was ready, those thoughts were superfluous. Nothing from it could be published, as the *Sunday Times* had closed down just two weeks before.

CHAPTER 12

'JERUSALEM 1500'

The closure of both the *Sunday Times* and *The Times* in November 1978 was the outcome of a long-running titanic battle between the newspaper's owner, Lord Thomson, and the print unions which, in many respects, controlled Britain's national newspapers. Thomson wanted to introduce computers to streamline the previous labour-intensive production process but was opposed by the unions, which saw this as a threat to both their power and their livelihoods. After lengthy attempts to negotiate a solution failed, Thomson responded by closing the newspapers, a move known as a lockout. The *Sunday Times* issue of 25 November 1978 was the last to be printed for almost a year.

The journalists, however frustrated, were left in a comfortable position, as the National Union of Journalists had accepted the management's proposals and their salaries were guaranteed throughout the lockout. But one immediate consequence was that nothing from the Insight report would be made public. At least Evans and the Insight team were spared having to decide in what form its conclusions should be published. It also meant that they did not have to factor in a response which Evans had obtained after showing the report to Frank Giles, who dictated a reply bristling with indignation. 'I realise all the difficulties,' Giles began. 'By their own admission, the authors, despite a lot of leg-work, have failed to come up with any sustainable theory, let alone certainty, about who killed David or why.' Instead, they had made deductions which Giles 'found highly speculative and at times founded upon a naive or ignorant interpretation of the facts'.

What was curious about the response from Giles, it struck Gillman, was how much effort he devoted to clearing himself from suspicion or blame. Giles first focused on Holden's rapid hiring and promotion at *The Times*. Giles said he had followed an equally swift career path, having been taken on as a probationer in 1964, made assistant diplomatic correspondent within twelve months and promoted to chief correspondent in Rome within four years: 'I can swear on oath that neither then nor at any subsequent time have I worked for, or been in the pay of, the intelligence services. So it is no good suggesting that my fairly rapid promotion ... was due to the fact that I was an agent.'

Gillman had in fact suggested no such thing. Giles went on to contest the description of Holden and Leo Silberman as lovers, since it 'depended entirely' on what Freddy Silberman and his wife had said. There was 'no corroborating evidence', Giles complained, adding that even if it were true, 'it throws no light on David's murder or his alleged CIA connections'. Giles devoted a further paragraph to 'the CIA connection', saying that it would have been 'quite natural' for Holden to talk to CIA station officers. Giles conceded that if Holden was meeting CIA officers, it was possible that this relationship could be 'misunderstood'. He went on to make a more substantive point: 'This was exactly the same point made to me by my very senior [Foreign Office] source (who confirmed, after checking, that David never had any connection with the [Secret Intelligence Service]).'

Having revealed that he had a high-level intelligence contact, Giles used that to rebut any further suspicions towards him. Any suggestion that he had known that Holden was a 'spy/agent/undercover man' and had recruited him as such for the *Sunday Times* was 'pernicious rubbish'. It was the second time Giles had responded to an allegation Gillman had not made. Giles attacked other straw targets, as when he dismissed as 'far-fetched' the theory that Holden could have been working for Israeli intelligence. Gillman had in fact raised the theory in order to dismiss it, just as he did the theory that Israel could have carried out the kill. Giles concluded by asking that his memo should be attached to the report, whatever 'its final resting place'. He concluded: 'In their opening lines, the authors of the report say they hope its contents will remain confidential. It is up to them to ensure that this hope is realised.'

Giles was now contesting the insistence of Evans that the *Sunday Times* should publish its finding, 'come what may'. And Gillman had not argued that the entire report should remain confidential, only that information relying on 'insinuation and innuendo' should not be made public. Giles promptly broke his own requirement by showing the report to Holden's widow, Ruth, who delivered her own brief handwritten riposte: 'It certainly made interesting reading and some of the allegations are so preposterous they even border upon the funny!' She went on: 'I had not realised before how much the authors (or some of them at least) must have disliked David but on reflection I suppose I am not really surprised.'

Gillman felt uncomfortable that Ruth had read the report, as he had described his dealings with her during the investigation in 1978. She initially said that she was keen that the newspaper should try to find out who had murdered Holden. Later, she advanced a series of explanations for wanting the inquiry stopped. She told Evans that it was too dangerous and Gillman that it was 'morbid'. At one point, she said she would ask the newspaper's editor-in-chief, Sir Denis Hamilton, to have the inquiry dropped. The most substantive encounter came when Gillman visited her house in St Paul's Road. She had previously cancelled the meeting several times; and when

Gillman arrived, she spent most of the time sitting at a desk with her back to him, writing letters as she answered Gillman's questions.

'Was David a spy?' he asked her.

'If he was, I didn't know about it.'

• • •

By the time Giles delivered his reply to the report, Gillman was occupied with a new series of events which at first made the lack of a newspaper a matter of enormous regret but also led to remarkable developments in the Holden case.

During the first week of the closure, a telex arrived in the Insight office asking it to call a telephone number in Amman on 3 or 4 December. By the time anyone saw the telex, those dates had passed. The telex was sent by Diana Macrae, the Quaker charity worker who had smuggled Insight's torture recordings out of Israel a year before. Having missed the deadline, Gillman called the *Sunday Times* Jerusalem correspondent Eric Marsden, who knew Macrae. The upshot was that Macrae flew into London on 15 December and stayed the night at a modest rooming house near King's Cross Station. Gillman met her there the following morning.

Macrae, a woman in her thirties with an understandably anxious manner, had an extraordinary tale to relate. Macrae had a contact in the US consulate in East Jerusalem who had been conducting research into the interrogation methods used by Israel's security forces – the very subject Gillman and Eddy had covered the previous year. The source, who was in no doubt that these methods amounted to torture, had written numerous documents setting out this case. Macrae showed Gillman a set of handwritten notes she had made from the documents that appeared to confirm what she was saying.

For Gillman, the potential implications were astounding. The battle that had followed the Insight torture report had been intense. The *Sunday Times* was still alone in the national British media in covering the worst excesses of the Israeli occupation. Now, a US diplomat was offering to provide reports that would authenticate what Insight had reported. Doing his best to contain his excitement, he advised Macrae that he would need to see the diplomat's original reports or – failing that – photocopies. Macrae said she would do her best to bring that about.

Macrae returned to Jerusalem the following day. After meeting the US diplomat, she flew to London on 20 December. Gillman met her that evening and Macrae handed him a set of photocopies of the diplomat's reports. The diplomat, Macrae explained, handled visa applications made by Palestinians who had previously been interrogated by Israeli security officials, using brutal methods to force them to confess to crimes for which they could be imprisoned. The reports set out the Palestinians' accounts which the official believed to be true, sending reports to that effect to the State Department in Washington. Gillman was subject to a mix of emotions: here was powerful confirmation from a senior US diplomatic source of the June 1977 Insight report; yet, to his immense frustration, the newspaper was not in a position to publish it.

The following morning, Gillman went to the office and showed the photocopies to Evans. He immediately realised their significance and agreed that Gillman should meet the diplomat. As for publication, that was a matter of hoping for the best: maybe the dispute with the print unions would be resolved before too long. Gillman met Macrae again and asked her to arrange a meeting with the source. Macrae returned to Jerusalem that evening and soon afterwards contacted Gillman to tell him that the source, who now bore the codename Fedway, could meet him in Amman.

Gillman flew to Amman on 7 January, accompanied by Isabel Hilton. The following morning, Fedway came to meet them at the Intercontinental Hotel.

Fedway proved to be a woman in her early thirties, with neat, dark hair, glasses and a slow, methodical way of talking. Her real name was Alexandra Johnson and she was a vice-consul at the US consulate in East Jerusalem, where her principal role was to handle applications from Palestinians who wanted to emigrate to the US. She was a member of the Russian Orthodox Church, was unmarried and grew up with her mother and grandmother at their home in Sacramento, California. Johnson graduated from the University of California in 1967 and took a three-year MA course in political science. She joined the foreign service in 1972 as a political adviser, the only woman from among 10,000 applicants to secure such a role. As a Russian speaker and a specialist in Soviet relations with Arab countries at the time when the US was trying to supplant the USSR in the Middle East, she wrote reports which went directly to Henry Kissinger, the Secretary of State. Johnson had been slated to transfer to the US Embassy in Cairo, but after she had learned Arabic, the US ambassador in Cairo declined to accept her, for reasons that remained unclear. Instead, she was posted to the East Jerusalem consulate in February 1977.

To Gillman and Hilton, these were impressive credentials and, with their tape recorder running, they listened attentively as Johnson explained the procedures governing her visa work. Some visa applications were straightforward. But if the applicant had been convicted by an Israeli military court of belonging to the PLO or an affiliated group, their application had to be forwarded to Washington, where it was likely to be rejected. Washington usually based its decision on the Israeli court judgment.

As a visa officer, however, Johnson was permitted to interview the applicants, and in March 1977, she decided to meet a Palestinian who had been convicted of belonging to the PLO. Like a number of similar cases, the man had signed a confession which was used to secure his conviction, but Johnson wanted to hear this man's account for herself. He told her that he had only signed a confession because he had been beaten during his interrogation. Johnson telegrammed Washington to say it was 'conceivable that the confession was obtained under duress'. She felt gratified when the man's visa was granted.

Johnson told Gillman and Hilton that she had been apprehensive over challenging the findings of the Israeli military courts. But her resolve had been strengthened when she read the *Sunday Times* report on Israeli torture in June 1977. She handled several more cases where the evidence of belonging to the PLO or a similar group was tenuous and the applicants described being beaten to force them to confess. In April 1978 came a case which Johnson regarded as a watershed. It concerned a young man from Ramallah who had been convicted of belonging to another resistance group, of recruiting other members and of collecting funds to buy arms. He denied these charges to Johnson and said he had been stripped, beaten, held under a cold shower, placed next to a hot stove, shut outside in the cold wind and finally held for two days in a cage measuring one metre square. When the State Department in Washington granted his visa, Johnson realised that it must have accepted that the man had been tortured.

By now, Johnson was uneasily aware that she was entering a political minefield, as the State Department contained a faction who were strong defenders of Israel. She nonetheless decided to produce a report summarising fifteen cases she had handled. She wrote of 'beating with sticks and whips, prolonged immersion in cold water, hanging by the hands and sexual sadism'. The State Department had previously issued a report on human rights which gave Israel a clean bill of health. With noted understatement, Johnson wrote that her report, dispatched in early June and coded 'Jerusalem 1500', 'raised serious doubts' about that judgment and urged that her evidence be taken into account 'in any future evaluation'.

The report caused convulsions at the State Department and Johnson was warned to rein in her activities. In November, however, she submitted a second report, 'Jerusalem 3239', which was more sweeping in its judgments. She wrote that there was a clear pattern to Israeli torture methods. The interrogators graded their techniques according to the severity of the charges their suspects were facing, leading Johnson to conclude that the interrogators were trained personnel, not occasional rogue cops. The torture methods had clearly been purpose-built, including refrigerated cells, rooms where high-pitched noises were piped, rooms installed with meat hooks and equipment for electric torture. These installations were to be found in interrogation centres in Jerusalem, Ramallah, Hebron and Nablus – suggesting a central apparatus which approved and funded their construction. In an echo of the findings of the *Sunday Times* eighteen months before, Johnson concluded that the torture by Israelis of Palestinian prisoners was authorised and systematic.

Johnson's second report led to further intensive debates and manoeuvres within the State Department. The US Embassy in Tel Aviv channelled Israel's arguments against her report: the cases were old, the report was out of date, Israel's Defence Minister said that torture 'no longer took place'. A former Red Cross Jerusalem delegate was quoted to the effect that Arabs would try to disown their confessions with claims of being tortured. Johnson contested these arguments, but when the State Department produced its latest Human Rights Reports, it dismissed the claim that torture was systematic, conceding only that 'some instances of mistreatment' had occurred.

Johnson related her story over a period of two days, going into immense detail and responding to questions calmly and methodically. Gillman and Hilton said they believed her and asked what would be the consequences for her career if a newspaper published her findings. 'I have no career,' Johnson told them. Her second report, Jerusalem 3239, had proved even more contentious and her position in the foreign service had been terminated on the technical grounds that she had been in the same post for too long. She expected to leave Jerusalem at the end of the month.

Johnson had hoped that the *Sunday Times* would print an article based on her reports. Gillman now had to explain that, for the time being at least, there was no *Sunday Times*. He told Johnson that their best alternative was to find an American newspaper prepared to take on the story: the contenders included the *Washington Post*, the *New York Times* and the *Chicago Tribune*. When he and Hilton returned to London the following day, they would discuss this with the editor and let her know as soon as possible. Johnson was clearly disappointed but said she would trust them to make the best decision.

Gillman and Hilton returned to London on 11 January. The next day, Gillman sent Evans a memo telling him that their source, still referred to as Fedway, had a remarkable story. He also said that he and his Insight colleagues felt that Evans should offer it to the *Washington Post*. It had an unrivalled reputation for handling challenging stories, and Evans had a good personal relationship with its legendary editor, Ben Bradlee.

Evans called Gillman into his office that afternoon.

'You're on,' he told Gillman. 'Ben says he'll look at the story. And when you go to the *Post*, you're not to show the material to anyone except him.'

CHAPTER 13

THE WILDERNESS OF MIRRORS

In Jerusalem, Alexandra Johnson received a message from Gillman giving her the news and asking her to be ready to travel to Washington. As she continued with her arrangements to leave the foreign service, she was told that the consulate would hold a 'farewell brunch' for her on Sunday 21 January at the home of Donald Kruse, the deputy principal officer. Johnson was puzzled, as she had already been invited to what she believed to be her leaving party, to be hosted by Norman Singer, the head consul, the following day.

The brunch was scheduled to run from 10 a.m. to 4 p.m. When Johnson arrived at Kruse's house, which sat in a well-tended garden, she found there was a formal seating plan. Kruse was placed to her right. To her left was a man named Jean de Muralt, who was introduced to her as a friend of Jim Fine, a humanitarian worker and representative of the American Friends Service Committee, the Quaker peace organisation, who was also at the brunch but left after briefly discussing a visa matter with Johnson. Johnson already knew that de Muralt was an ICRC delegate who had intervened in the political rows inside the State Department over her torture reports. Seemingly on his own initiative, de Muralt had flown to Washington to tell State Department human rights officials that the ICRC backed her torture reports. In doing so, de Muralt had violated ICRC protocols which insisted their delegates must remain politically neutral, and he was sacked. He had since started working for the Quaker group with Fine.

Facing Johnson across the table on the plan was a Palestinian named Ahmed Rahman, an academic at Birzeit University in the West Bank. (Johnson did not know, of course, that Rahman had been interviewed by the *Sunday Times* team when he recounted meeting Holden on the afternoon of 5 December 1977.) When she saw Rahman, Johnson realised she had bumped into him in a florist's shop an hour before. Johnson was observing the Arab custom of taking flowers for your host – and Rahman was buying flowers too. Unaware who Johnson was, he remarked that his bunch was intended for a friend in hospital. It was a minor subterfuge that left her puzzled. She was surprised on a second account: diplomatic leaving parties were normally reserved for insiders, yet here were at least two outsiders who had been invited – and placed close to her at the table.

Among the consulate staff, Johnson recognised two CIA officials and a political officer, John Battle, on secondment from a post in Bahrain. Johnson deduced that she was going to be closely observed during the brunch, and she wondered if the consulate knew she was in contact with the *Sunday Times*. She had already been asked several times by the political officer, Edmund Hull, whether she knew anything about Holden's murder. Johnson, who had no idea why she was being asked, said she had no inside information but added that she suspected that Israel had carried out the killing. Hull quizzed her about Holden several more times, leaving her to speculate why he thought she might know anything. She had not yet been in contact with the *Sunday Times*, and when she met Gillman and Isabel Hilton in Amman, she did not mention Hull's repeated questioning as she did not want any distraction from the torture reports. Now she asked herself if the subject of Holden was going to arise again.

Before the brunch was served, Johnson spotted the host, Kruse, talking to de Muralt in the garden. When she sat down at the dining table, it was de Muralt who opened the conversation. After minor pleasantries, he told Johnson about his visit to the State Department to support her reports. He also said that he felt the ICRC did not do enough to protect prisoners and told her about his work with the Quaker group assisting Palestinians in Jerusalem and the West Bank. Johnson agreed that working in the West Bank must be depressing but, aware that Kruse was listening, was mostly non-committal in her answers. Then de Muralt made clear that he knew she was in contact with the *Sunday Times* and that she was due to travel to Washington shortly. He questioned her about her flight plans, but Johnson refused to answer. She left the brunch feeling confident that she had said nothing that could be held against her. But the exchanges with de Muralt were deeply unsettling.

The following morning, Gillman took a telephone call at home. It was from de Muralt, who was now in London. Gillman already knew of de Muralt from Diana Macrae and thought he could help reinforce Johnson's torture story. De Muralt suggested that they meet over dinner and when Gillman asked if had anywhere in mind, he replied: 'I prefer the Dorchester.'

The Dorchester had long been one of London's most upmarket hotels, renowned for the quality of its restaurant, with its menu written in French and its choreographed table service. Gillman thought this an unlikely venue at which to discuss the ill-treatment of Palestinians at the hands of Israel's security forces, but he did not demur. At 7.30 p.m., the two met in the dining room, with its immaculate table settings and pink decor.

De Muralt proved to be a tall, sturdy figure with sandy hair and a suave, confident manner. After some opening pleasantries, Gillman asked de Muralt about the torture allegations and was taken aback when he said that they had been vastly exaggerated. When Gillman contested this, de Muralt switched the conversation to the Holden inquiry, asking what the *Sunday Times* had found out. Now thoroughly alarmed, Gillman stalled his questions.

Then de Muralt asked: 'When are you planning to fly to Washington?'

Gillman had a ticket for the following day, 23 January. Even more alarmed, he told de Muralt he had not yet decided.

After settling the restaurant bill, Gillman hurried home and postponed his flight by a day. He wondered whether he was being over-cautious; but, once again, someone had shown a close interest in his travel plans, just as they had done during his Middle East trip the previous year and just as someone had done in respect of Holden's trip in December 1977. Who was de Muralt working for? His best guess, at that stage, was the CIA. But in the wilderness of mirrors, all things were possible. Gillman was not aware that de Muralt had met Johnson the previous day and asked her a similar set of questions. Had he known that, his concerns would only have deepened.

That evening, Gillman told Leni that he was flying to Washington a day later than planned. She was both pleased at this 24-hour reprieve and curious to know why. This time, Gillman did not express the worst of his fears. He gave Leni a sanitised summary of his encounter with de Muralt, though adding that he felt it was safer to delay his departure for a day. She did not press him to explain more.

Gillman arrived in Washington on 24 January and, after checking in at the Jefferson Hotel, made the five-minute walk to the *Washington Post*'s angular building on 15th Street. He was directed to the fourth floor, where he had a thrill of recognition as he walked through the newsroom, as it had been precisely replicated for *All the President's Men*, the movie about the Watergate scandal exposed by the newspaper's reporters Bob Woodward and Carl Bernstein.

Ben Bradlee occupied a surprisingly modest office and when

David Holden, photographed after joining *The Times* in 1954, was rapidly promoted to Washington correspondent, raising questions about 'friends' in high places. After a four-year stint at *The Guardian*, he moved to the *Sunday Times* in 1965, eventually becoming the newspaper's chief foreign correspondent.
Courtesy of Peter Holden

On 5 December 1977, the day before he was murdered, Holden sent a postcard from Jerusalem to his friend, the writer Jan Morris. 'In the Middle East, citadels still have their uses,' Holden wrote. Decoding his enigmatic note provided a vital clue in the inquiry into his death.
Courtesy of Peter Holden

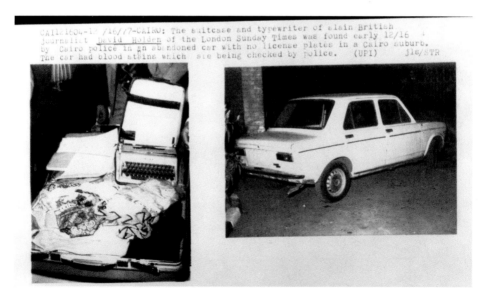

Holden flew to Cairo on the evening of 6 December 1977, then disappeared. His body, with a single bullet wound to the heart, was found dumped in the dirt by a roadside. The following week, Cairo police found a stolen car containing Holden's Samsonite suitcase and typewriter.
Courtesy of the *Sunday Times*

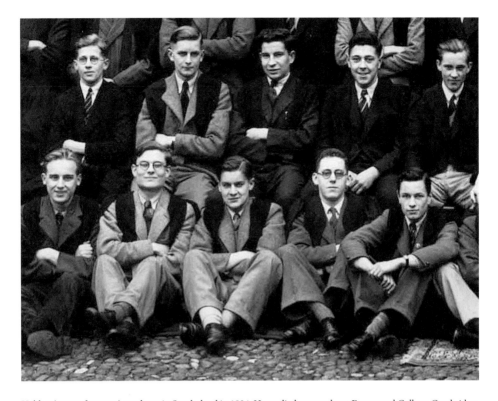

Holden (*centre, front row*) was born in Sunderland in 1924. He studied geography at Emmanuel College, Cambridge, where he was photographed with fellow members of the 1943 intake. He was a keen musician and actor who performed with a university drama group. After leaving Cambridge in 1947, he became a teacher in Scotland.
Courtesy of the master and fellows of Emmanuel College, Cambridge

By 1950, Holden had met Leo Silberman (*centre, with his brothers Gordon, left, and Freddy*). Silberman was an academic, a writer, a chancer and an impostor with intelligence connections. Holden's secret ten-year relationship with Silberman proved key to both his life and his death.
Courtesy of Freddy Silberman

Holden married Ruth Lynam, a fellow journalist, in 1962, two years after Silberman's death. They are pictured here at Beirut Airport soon after Holden joined the *Sunday Times* in 1965. Guests at their glamorous dinner parties in Islington included Princess Margaret and Lord Snowdon. Ruth died in 2016.
Courtesy of the *Sunday Times*

Peter Gillman (*right*) first wrote for the *Sunday Times* in 1965. He spent a year investigating Holden's death and wrote a 110-page report on the inquiry's findings. This photograph, taken in the late 1960s, shows him with his wife Leni, a teacher and writer, who helped in the investigation.
Private collection of Peter and Leni Gillman

Harold Evans, *Sunday Times* editor in 1977, was distraught on hearing of Holden's killing and immediately dispatched a team of journalists to the Middle East. Evans, who is considered the greatest British newspaper editor ever, remained obsessed with the case until his death in 2020.
Sally Soames / Courtesy of the *Sunday Times*

The *Sunday Times* team soon found two people who had met Holden during his final trip. John Fistere (*left*), an American, said that he and his wife saw Holden in Amman shortly before he left for Cairo. Kenizé Mourad (*right*), a French journalist who spent time with Holden in Damascus and Amman, said he was 'a wonderful man'. Both were later revealed to have links to the CIA.
Courtesy of Susan Griggs; © Louis Monier / Bridgeman Images

The *Sunday Times* team included some of its most experienced and talented journalists. John Barry (*top left*) and Cal McCrystal (*top right*) spent a week in Cairo following Holden's death and saw his body in the Cairo mortuary. Paul Eddy (*bottom left*) joined Gillman in Amman and later helped set up a sting in a bid to find out who was stealing vital documents at the *Sunday Times*. Isabel Hilton (*bottom right*) took part in the inquiry when it was broadened to encompass Holden's whole life.

Courtesy of the *Sunday Times*

Four key figures in the mystery. Alexandra Johnson (*top left*) was a US diplomat who was a secret source for Gillman as he continued to pursue the mystery long after leaving the *Sunday Times* staff. David Halton (*top right*) is a top Canadian journalist whose experiences at Cairo Airport in 1974 foreshadowed what happened to Holden three years later. Jan Morris (*bottom left*), who received Holden's puzzling 'citadels' postcard, considered Holden an enigma. Michael Adams (*bottom right*), a close friend of Holden, heard a dramatic confession twenty years after Holden's death.

Courtesy of Alexandra Johnson; courtesy of David Halton; courtesy of the *Sunday Times*; courtesy of Celia Adams

Three spooks who featured in the inquiry. Geoffrey Tantum (*top left*), MI6 intelligence chief in the Middle East, was rebuffed in an attempt to read Gillman's final report. He was later interviewed for this book. John Slade-Baker (*top right, right in picture*) was both a *Sunday Times* Middle East correspondent and an MI6 spy. He was interned with Holden in Cairo in 1956. Jim Fees (*bottom*) was the CIA's station chief in Cairo when Holden was killed. His greatest coup was to hijack a Soviet fighter jet in Egypt, shown in this photo, and ship it back to the US.

Courtesy of Geoffrey Tantum's family; courtesy of the Middle East Centre at St Antony's College, Oxford; courtesy of Paula Fees

Solving the puzzle. Mohamed Heikal (*top left*), a newspaper editor, served as a minister in the Egyptian government and was later imprisoned by President Anwar Sadat. In the 1990s, he made an astonishing admission to Michael Adams. Fred Halliday (*top right*), an academic and writer on the Middle East, told of another revelatory encounter with Holden. Gillman (*bottom left*), photographed on assignment for the *Sunday Times* in Jordan in 1977, teamed up with a journalist from today's *Sunday Times*, Emanuele Midolo (*bottom right*), in a bid to solve the Holden mystery forty-five years on. Midolo visited Cairo in October 2023 on the centenary of Heikal's birth.

Courtesy of Hassan Heikal; © Andy Paradise / Alamy Stock Photo; Leni Gillman / Private collection of Peter and Leni Gillman; Michael Binyon / Private collection of Emanuele Midolo

Gillman was ushered in, he felt that Bradlee looked uncannily like Jason Robards, who had played him in the movie. In his trademark gravelly voice, Bradlee told Gillman that from what Evans had said, it sounded like a great story and he would like it to be handled by Larry Stern, his vastly respected senior lieutenant on the paper. Remembering Evans's edict, Gillman said that Evans had told him he could only show it to Bradlee. Bradlee grunted and settled down to read the ten-page brief Gillman had prepared. When he finished, Bradlee grunted again and called in Stern. He told Gillman that he wanted Stern to take charge of the story and Gillman could be sure of Stern's absolute discretion.

It took the *Post* two weeks to prepare its story for publication. Johnson had arrived in Washington on 24 January and was staying with friends. Gillman was asked to take her to Bradlee's home in Georgetown, where he and Stern questioned her at length. They appeared convinced by what she told them; Bradlee remarked that he felt as if he was playing a part in a movie, and Stern added that the movie's title should be '*Jerusalem 1500*'.

Two *Post* reporters, both news-desk veterans, were assigned to the story: Tom Reed, who covered Washington politics, and Ed Cody, an overseas specialist who could speak Arabic. On 27 January, they interviewed Johnson over a marathon day-long session. At times, other editors took part. The foreign editor, Peter Osnos, argued that if Israel did torture Palestinians, this could be justified to combat the threat from terrorists. Johnson considered this a 'stupid' point but refrained from saying so. Reed and Cody told Johnson they found her account convincing but would need to talk to Bradlee and Stern.

Two days later, Cody called Johnson to say that the *Post* wanted to go ahead, but Bradlee was insisting that the reporters talk to some of her witnesses themselves. Johnson tracked down three to Chicago, where she and Cody met them over the next two days. Cody found their accounts convincing and they returned to Washington, where Cody told her the *Post* had all it needed from her for the moment.

It was a difficult time for Johnson as she waited for the outcome of the *Post*'s inquiries. A State Department friend warned her that if the *Post* went ahead, she faced up to twelve years in jail for leaking confidential documents. By then, Cody and Reed had approached the State Department to corroborate Johnson's story; hearing about the threat to Johnson, they found an attorney who told her that it was unlikely she would go to prison and if there were any court proceedings, he would defend her for free.

Cody and Reed also approached the Israeli Embassy. It provided a routine denial, composed after discussions with the Israeli government: allegations of systematic mistreatment or torture 'are baseless and have been refuted over and over again'. All suspects were treated 'with due process of law' and were allowed to meet ICRC delegates within fourteen days of being arrested. 'Israel respects human rights, does not engage in torture and cannot but therefore come to the conclusion that the dissemination of such allegations to the media stem from anti-Israeli political motivations.' The Israeli Embassy attempted to smear Johnson, telling the *Post* that she had had several Arab lovers and it had tape recordings to prove it. When Cody and Reed told Bradlee about that, he responded: 'Are they saying we can hear her groans?'

During the waiting period, Johnson met Gillman several times in Washington. They were joined by Isabel Hilton, the Mandarin-speaker and China expert, who had come to Washington, in part, to cover the groundbreaking visit by Deng Xiaoping, the first by a Chinese leader to the US. Gillman and Hilton broached the Holden killing with Johnson, keen to hear her views. She told them she had initially suspected Israel but was now less sure. She was impressed when they described the elaborate method of the killing and told her they were convinced that Egypt had provided the killers. But whether Egypt did so on behalf of another country, and who that might be, was an open question. They decided not to tell her about the theft of the telexes and the failure to identify the thief or thieves, as that remained a closely guarded secret. They did compare notes on de Muralt, having learned that he had met Johnson and Gillman on successive days. Johnson was convinced he was reporting on her to the State Department, and they agreed that he was not to be trusted.

On 6 February, Gillman called Johnson to say that he and Hilton had been asked to go to Stern's office at the *Post* to discuss the story. Johnson went too and was shown a proof of the report. Her initial response was one of disappointment: she felt the story 'dragged', gave too many personal details about her and portrayed her in an unflattering light. Nor had it said enough about her second cable, Jerusalem 3239, and its conclusions that Israeli torture was systematic. She spotted what she felt were some factual errors which Stern agreed to correct. Gillman and Hilton, by contrast, felt that the report was thorough and authoritative, providing convincing details from the Palestinians' accounts. It did not include the same resounding endorsement that the *Sunday Times* would have given, instead maintaining a distance that was a hallmark of American reporting. But it allowed Johnson a strong airing and had a prominent position on the front page, with a turn to a full-page inside.

Johnson met Gillman and Hilton that evening at the Jefferson Hotel. It was to be their farewell, as they had been called to New York to assist with another story. There was no time for a meal, only for a swift round of drinks, as they were due to catch a plane that night. Journalists are accustomed to relationships that are intense but finite. When Gillman said goodbye to Johnson with a handshake and a brief hug, he did so in the belief that they might never meet again.

• • •

Back in London, the *Sunday Times* remained closed. With Leni, Gillman started researching a book about the internment of so-called enemy aliens in Britain during the Second World War. Many were refugees from Germany and Austria, most of them Jewish, who were rounded up at the height of the invasion scare in the summer of 1940. Some were deported to Canada or Australia and when one of the deportation ships, the *Arandora Star*, was torpedoed by a German U-boat, hundreds were drowned. The book was titled *Collar the Lot!*, the order supposedly given by Winston Churchill to carry out the round-up, and was published in early 1980.

By then, the *Sunday Times* was being printed again, after Lord Thomson realised that the lockout had failed and he was losing too much money. The printers returned on the same pay and conditions as before, but in February 1981, Thomson sold the newspaper to the Australian press magnate Rupert Murdoch, who was likely to be more ruthless in a fight to the death with the print unions. Murdoch moved Evans from the *Sunday Times*, appointing him editor of *The Times*. Evans was replaced by Frank Giles, fulfilling the ambition he had nurtured since joining the newspaper in 1960. Gillman was part of a group of journalists who tried to oppose Murdoch's takeover, but they were outvoted in a crucial union meeting.

At first, Gillman remained part of the Insight team. Paul Eddy was now the editor, Gillman the deputy editor and principal writer, assisted by a new team of three. They continued to produce stories about scandals and disasters. In 1982, after five years with the team, Gillman felt he had been anonymous for long enough, since Insight never gave its team members bylines, and became a feature writer in his own right. When the Falklands War broke out in April 1982, he spent three weeks in Washington covering the international politics of the conflict. In September 1982, he was back in Beirut, writing about the massacre of Palestinian refugees by the Falangist regime while occupying Israeli forces stood by. In 1983, he returned to Northern Ireland, covering the transition being made by the IRA to conventional politics.

Meanwhile, there were further changes of personnel at the *Sunday Times* and *The Times*. There were bitter internal feuds at *The Times*, where a faction was determined to bring down Evans. With Murdoch's backing, they succeeded, and Evans was replaced by Charles Douglas-Home, one of the most militant of Evans's opponents. At the *Sunday Times*, Giles presided over a disaster, when it published a set of diaries purporting to have been written by Hitler but which were in fact the work of a notorious German forger and conman. Giles was replaced as editor by Andrew Neil, a journalist with political views closely aligned with Murdoch's. This meant that Murdoch had no need to violate the stipulation that he should not influence the newspaper's political views. Following a dispute over the way Neil edited one of his stories, Gillman took up the redundancy terms the *Sunday Times* was offering its most experienced journalists and left the newspaper to embark on a freelance career.

Gillman continued working on assignments for the *Sunday Times Magazine*, writing long-form features that often required extensive investigations. He undertook some in partnership with Leni, who had moved from teaching to a writing career of her own. Yet Gillman remained troubled and preoccupied by the Holden inquiry. He had never devoted so much time to a single investigation, let alone one which had failed to reach its objectives. He tried to put it to one side; but somehow it remained with him, a story that awaited its final chapter.

After the *Washington Post* story was published, Johnson remained in Washington for almost three months. She was interviewed by numerous news outlets, some sympathetic, others determined to undermine her claims. The two major US weekly news magazines, *Newsweek* and *Time*, published stories about her. *Newsweek* interviewed her first and she considered the story factual and professional. *Time*, by contrast, did not interview her and published further attacks on her integrity. Israel, it claimed, had obtained permission from the FBI to tape her telephone in Jerusalem and had learned that she had both personal and political connections with terrorist organisations. Johnson consulted a lawyer to see if *Time* would publish a retraction, but he warned her that it would be a waste of time. The *Time* story set an agenda for other newspapers and magazines, and Johnson found herself having to deny that she was linked to the PLO. By the end of March, she had had enough. She returned to her mother's home in Sacramento, where she embarked on a new career as a court stenographer and family history specialist, a pursuit for which her research skills were an ideal qualification.

Throughout this period, Gillman remained in touch with Johnson. During a telephone call in November 1983, she touched on her farewell brunch at the home of Donald Kruse. It was then that Gillman pieced together the movements of de Muralt: talking to Johnson at her brunch one day, flying to London to meet him the next. Gillman felt that Johnson had more to say.

Two years later, Gillman saw an opportunity to meet Johnson. The *Sunday Times Magazine* asked him to go to Washington and New York to report on the crisis created by the spread of crack cocaine. Gillman agreed but also suggested a second story, namely to interview the actor Ed Asner about his role as a newspaper editor in the television series *Lou Grant*, which would require him to travel to Los Angeles, California. When the magazine accepted his idea, Gillman arranged to meet Johnson at her home in Sacramento, also in California. He began the trip by flying to San Francisco where he hired a car and, reeling from jet lag, drove the seventy-five miles to Sacramento. He spent the night in a motel and met Johnson the next morning in the ground-floor apartment where she was living with her mother.

Johnson's greeting was friendly enough, but Gillman suspected she was holding something back. He had the same feeling when they began to talk about Holden. Gillman decided that it was time to be bold. He had brought a copy of the Holden report with him and offered it to Johnson. The next hour passed in silence. When she finished reading, Johnson told Gillman: 'I had come to suspect that you were spying on me, maybe for MI6 or, perhaps indirectly, for the FBI or CIA.' She concluded: 'I don't believe that any more.'

Over the rest of the day, Johnson laid out what she knew, and what she believed, that could be connected with Holden's killing. She returned to the brunch, adding details of which Gillman had been unaware. She described her conversation with de Muralt, and how he had tried to prise information out of her, with Kruse listening intently at her side. She also identified the Palestinian academic who had been sitting opposite her: Ahmed Rahman, who was named in the Holden report and was at the heart of a mystery that Insight had been unable to resolve.

As Gillman had related in his report, Rahman told the *Sunday Times* reporter Tony Terry that he had met Holden on the afternoon of 5 December, the day before Holden flew to Cairo from Amman. Rahman said he had spent two hours with Holden, walking around Birzeit and a nearby village where the Israelis were harassing the local inhabitants. But this conflicted with Holden's account that he visited Jerusalem's Old City, as he had told Edward Mortimer of *The Times* and as indicated by his postcard to Jan Morris. He did not tell Mortimer at any point that he would see Rahman, either before or after, even though he knew Mortimer planned to meet Rahman himself. But when Rahman did meet Mortimer, he made a point of telling Mortimer that he had seen Holden two days before.

Johnson next told Gillman about some other guests at the brunch. One was a man who she knew to be the CIA's station officer in East Jerusalem. She was now delving into very dark matters, as this CIA officer was not supposed to exist. There was a CIA station chief at the US Embassy in Tel Aviv who was known as such to the Israeli government. But the US had promised Israel that it would not install a CIA station in Jerusalem, yet it had done precisely that.

Johnson had liked the previous CIA station boss, who was in post until mid-1977, a man with unorthodox views and methods. She found his replacement, who was at the brunch, cold and distant. He was accompanied by one of his two communications officers, whom Johnson knew by virtue of the fact that for a time she had lived in an apartment below his in the district of Beit Hanina and could hear him making his transmissions.

The CIA chief operated under the cover of being the US economic and commercial officer, whose overt role was to deliver US aid and charity funds to Palestinian individuals and organisations on the West Bank – Johnson had attended meetings where the allocations were decided. Among those who had received funds were a West Bank mayor, a lawyer in Ramallah – Aziz Shehadeh, who the US was backing as a potential political leader but was later murdered in mysterious circumstances – and Ahmed Rahman.

In his covert CIA role, the officer pursued the full gamut of clandestine activities. These included acquiring and developing informants and agents and channelling payments to those who were giving it secret assistance. Where Palestinians had helped the CIA, the director would recommend that they were given US residential visas, and his recommendations were invariably accepted. Rahman was also one of those.

From all of this, Johnson now believed that Holden had met the CIA agent at a secret location in the Old City, which he referred to as the 'citadel', on the afternoon of 5 December. That helped to explain the postcard that had so puzzled Jan Morris, with its message: 'In the Middle East, citadels still have their uses.' As for Rahman, he had been primed to provide Holden with an alibi for his secret meeting. Johnson amplified her theory by telling Gillman about the British journalists who had been paid by the CIA to supply reports about the Middle East. She knew there were four or five in all, their reports varying from 'trite' to 'absolutely brilliant'. Their authors were referred to through titles such as 'British journalist Cairo' and 'London journalist', and many had been recruited following Senate hearings into the CIA's activities in the 1970s, which led to the CIA being banned from enlisting US journalists. Although Johnson had once been told the names of the British journalists, she said she could not remember those now, nor whether Holden was among them. However, she suspected that if Holden had been supplying reports, particularly if they fell into the 'trite' category, this provided cover for more substantial dealings with him.

Johnson also considered who had stolen telexes from the *Sunday Times* office. Of possible suspects, she said that the KGB had no need to do so, as the Soviets had devised a means of intercepting telexes sent in 'clear' (uncoded) language. The CIA, by contrast, had no direct means of doing so. Instead, it would have had to make a request, via the US National Security Agency (NSA) to Britain's GCHQ, the UK's government communications agency. But that was risky because it would leave a paper trail and so the CIA would more likely commission the thefts from freelance operators.

The disconcerting implication, which Johnson now confronted, was that the CIA had been involved in Holden's death in some way. In theory, that was impossible, because the CIA had been instructed not to engage in assassinations following the 1970s Senate hearings. In 1976, President Gerald Ford had signed an executive order stating that US government employees were specifically forbidden 'to engage in, or conspire to engage in, political assassinations'. Johnson had, however, heard CIA operatives discussing precisely those circumstances and how they might circumvent the ban. One way was to find a local partner to carry out a killing: and a CIA/Egyptian combination looked ideal.

Gillman sat back in his chair. With the calm logic Johnson had employed when handling Palestinians' visa applications, she had laid out the evidence from the Holden report and then combined it with her own knowledge. He sensed that she had held one element back when she claimed not to remember some key names, perhaps because that was too much of a violation of secrecy. Otherwise, she had been entirely open in what she had told him.

To mark the break in her discourse, Johnson brought in a simple lunch of bread and cheese. Then, as Gillman attempted to assemble the pieces she had presented into a coherent picture, she did the job for him. Holden, she said, did have a relationship with the CIA; and he had met a CIA official in the Old City of Jerusalem on the afternoon of 5 December, with a cover story that had somehow gone wrong. The CIA had helped to track his movements during his trip, in partnership with Egypt. She believed he had been met at Cairo Airport by agents of Egyptian intelligence – although here Gillman added that he felt sure that someone who knew Holden, probably from the CIA, had confirmed his identity during the three hours before he was killed. As for why he was killed, Johnson argued that it resulted from a betrayal, the CIA having discovered that he was working for another intelligence agency, most likely the KGB.

For Gillman, it was an extraordinary moment. Eight years after he wrote the Holden report, many of the ambiguities were dispelled and so much of it made sense. Among the theories he had examined, Johnson had selected the one he had long considered the most plausible. Perhaps concerned in case she had said too much, Johnson asked him to be cautious in how he used her information. 'Please check back with me before using anything I have told you,' she asked him. 'And please try to find alternative sources.'

Gillman of course agreed, even if that raised important questions about how he might proceed. Once again, they said goodbye, not knowing where and if they would meet again. Night was closing in as Gillman drove out of Sacramento and took the highway for San Francisco, his headlights slicing into the dusk. He felt a swell of affection for Johnson, his guide in the wilderness of mirrors, who had allowed him to see past the reflections to the reality beyond.

PART TWO

'Those who become obsessed with a puzzle
are not the most likely to solve it.'
CYRIL CONNOLLY

CHAPTER 14

THE STRANGE CASE OF MR HALTON

David Halton was used to this. His evening flight from London to Cairo had arrived late, but he was in no hurry. He knew the routine: the bus ride from the plane to the arrivals building; the echoing stone corridors leading to the hall; the traveller's cheques and temporary visitor's visa form, which he compiled listing his profession: 'journalist'.

Halton, aged thirty-four, was the foreign affairs correspondent for the Canadian Broadcasting Corporation (CBC), the country's public radio and TV station. CBC had no Middle East correspondent at the time, so it was common for Halton to be dispatched to Egypt – even at short notice. He had covered the Six-Day War in 1967, his first of many wars to follow, and had been there again three years later when the Egyptian President, Nasser, had died of a heart attack. This was his fourth or fifth visit to Cairo in just a few years and Halton had almost become fond of the caravanserai of the airport.

With receding brown hair parted to the right and dark-blue eyes, Halton looked much like his father, the veteran war correspondent Matthew Halton, who in the 1930s had covered for the *Toronto Star* and CBC everything from the rise of Nazism in Germany to the Spanish Civil War and the Second World War. Matthew had died suddenly when David was sixteen and it was to honour his father's legacy that he had become a foreign correspondent himself.

Despite the late hour, the airport that night was chaotic – even more than usual, Halton thought. What he did not know was that repairs were being carried out on the runways after a passenger airliner, a brand new Tupolev Tu-154, had crashed after take-off during a training flight, killing all its six passengers. The Egyptians had bought the airliner from the USSR only a few weeks before and they were furious: they were now in the process of returning the entire fleet to the Soviets and demanding a refund.

Halton started queuing along with the other passengers for visa and passport controls. After he had his documents checked and stamped and was heading towards the baggage reclaim area, he was stopped by two men wearing scruffy suits. They asked him if he was David Halton – or so he thought. 'Yes, I'm David Halton,' he replied.

The two men introduced themselves as Egyptian officials from the Ministry of Information (or the Cairo Press Centre – later, Halton could not be sure) and said that they had come to take him to his hotel. Halton was bemused: it was late at night and he had not notified the Egyptian authorities that he was coming. How could they possibly know? But it had been a long day and he could have certainly used a lift. 'Well, that's very kind of you,' Halton said and followed them into the baggage area.

The two officials retrieved his luggage then escorted him past customs and through the swing doors that separated them from the humid Cairo night. It must have been a hot day as even now the temperature outside was almost twenty-five degrees. Instead of going to the left, to the line of official taxis, Halton noticed that the two led him to the right, to the car park occupied by the cheap pirate cabs. There, a rather old saloon car was waiting, its driver already behind the wheel. Halton climbed into the front passenger seat, with the two officials sitting behind him, and the rumbling car set off for the city.

During the ride, one of the officials asked Halton about his travel plans and how long he intended to stay in Egypt. The official mentioned names that Halton did not recognise, leaving him puzzled.

'I'm sorry, but I'm not sure what you are talking about,' Halton said.

The official flashed a cryptic smile and replied that they had set up some of the meetings he had 'requested'. Halton was perplexed and told the officials he had not asked for any interviews to be arranged. Then he turned in his seat to face the two men and asked the question that had been puzzling him since they approached him at the airport.

'How did you know I was coming?'

'You are David Holden of the *Sunday Times*?' the official asked him, giving him a strange look.

'Actually, it's David Hal-ton, not David Hol-den. I'm sorry, but I think you got the wrong person. I'm David Hal-ton from CBC.'

The two officials looked at each other in disbelief. They murmured something in Arabic. 'Well,' one said after a pause, 'we're almost at the hotel, so we'll drop you off.' Both officials remained silent for the rest of the journey.

It was August 1974 and Halton thought little more of the strange encounter. He would have likely erased it from his memory altogether had he not heard the news, more than three years later, that David Holden of the *Sunday Times* had been taken by someone at Cairo Airport, driven around in a battered car and murdered.

CHAPTER 15

THE LAST OF HIS KIND

The message that lit up the phone's screen at 7.45 a.m. on 24 September 2020 showed a link to *The Times*'s website, along with a comment: 'The last of his kind.' The piece, sent by a colleague, was an obituary. 'Sir Harold Evans, esteemed newspaper editor, dies aged 92.' As Emanuele Midolo read the headline, he felt a wave of regret. He had been at *The Times* and the *Sunday Times* as a reporter for around nine months and had always hoped he would meet Evans. He had been an inspiration for generations of investigative journalists, and Midolo, like many of his colleagues, idolised him.

An Italian with a beard and a mass of unruly brown hair, Midolo had been a journalist for about ten years, mostly in France, and had moved to London in 2015 with the aim of becoming an investigative reporter. He had enrolled in a master's course in investigative journalism at City University and Evans's manual *Essential English for Journalists, Editors and Writers* was one of the first books he had read, followed by his memoir *Good Times, Bad Times*. The latter was an inspiring read, in which Evans recounted the glory days of the Insight team in the 1960s and '70s. It was widely considered a golden age of investigative journalism and one that still acted as a reminder of the heights journalism could achieve.

That morning, Midolo was back in the office for the first time in more than six months, as the Covid pandemic had forced most of the newspaper's hundreds of staff to work from home. For Midolo, this was a hard blow: he had joined the paper only a couple of months earlier and already loved the office. He was one of the first staff journalists hired to work across both *The Times* and the *Sunday Times*, having been recruited as a reporter on the property desk – or 'home and garden', as a former colleague mockingly described it. Midolo didn't mind. He loved property because it was one of the most diverse patches and he could write about almost anything: from money launderers to corruption scandals involving powerful property developers and unscrupulous politicians. He kept wandering off his beat to conduct investigations on more general subjects and already had a few front pages to his name, both on the daily and on the *Sunday Times*.

The *Sunday Times* newsroom was a sweeping open space on the ninth floor of the News Building in London Bridge, a seventeen-storey glass behemoth overlooking the Thames. The office was deserted and eerily quiet. Two monitors stood on each desk, paired with old mechanical keyboards that looked as if they had been there since the 1980s and made a rattling sound similar to that of a typewriter. All desk phones had just been replaced with an Internet-connected system that rarely worked and most journalists hated.

Midolo grabbed a copy of the newspaper and walked to his desk, on the south side of the building, overlooking Big Ben and the London Eye. He was alone as he opened the paper and began to read the long obituary, spread over two full pages, which celebrated 'a journalistic phenomenon' and 'the most outstanding journalist of his day'. While reading about the newspaper's prowess under Evans, Midolo's thoughts went to Peter Gillman, whom he had met during a training session on investigative reporting at his previous job. Gillman knew Evans well; he was part of the Insight team when

Evans was the editor in the 1970s and they had worked on many groundbreaking investigations together. Midolo emailed him to express his condolences. To his surprise, Gillman, who was then in his late seventies, replied within a few minutes.

'Yes, Harry: the family had warned the *Sunday Times* diaspora that he was nearing the end, so we had some warning, but it was no less of a shock or a sense of loss,' Gillman wrote. 'I have so many standout memories, starting with the time we squeezed into the sixth-floor lift at the *Sunday Times* offices in Gray's Inn Road and he told me he wanted me to join the Insight team.'

The email went on to describe how Evans was 'invariably charming' and 'a great editor for lots of reasons', who trusted his writers and backed them to be responsible and have integrity in what they wrote. He was 'a great figure and I feel privileged to have been part of a wonderful adventure in journalism'.

Gillman also mentioned David Holden. 'Now there's a story. The one that got away.' The last two occasions he had seen Evans, Gillman recalled, his old editor had expressed regret for not having cracked the Holden mystery. '"We must solve the case," Harry told me.' The words gave Midolo the chills. He vaguely remembered the affair: it was a tale that Gillman used in his courses to illustrate the crucial point that not all investigations are successful. In fact, despite months or even years of hard work, some prove to go nowhere. 'I told you about our successes,' Gillman would say. 'Now let me tell you about the time we failed.'

A quick Google search gave Midolo the fundamentals of Holden's story. 'Neither the motive or murderers have been conclusively identified,' read his entry in the paper's archives website. A year earlier, Gillman had written a piece for the magazine *Byline Times*. A large black and white picture of Holden in a suit and tie, looking straight into the camera with a hint of a smile on his lips, towered over the article, which detailed how Evans had dispatched Gillman and his fellow reporters to the Middle East to find out who had killed Holden and why. The team had spent a long time on the case and found plenty of evidence, but the investigation was inconclusive, their suspicions not solid enough for them to publish their results. They were eventually assigned to other duties but, Gillman wrote, 'some of us did not give up'.

Evans was one of them. He wrote a long chapter about Holden in his second memoir, *My Paper Chase*, in 2009. The *Sunday Times* serialised the book, using that very chapter as the first extract, which the newspaper ran along with an interview with Evans titled: 'The mystery that consumes Sir Harold Evans'. Midolo read the interview and ordered the book online; when it arrived a couple of days later, he went straight to the chapter, 'Death in Cairo'. 'We were plunged into many mysteries in my fourteen years as editor of the *Sunday Times*,' Evans wrote. 'The most profound was right there in our own office.'

If Midolo had already been hooked by Gillman's account of the case, Evans's words, with their chilling precision, now haunted him. He did a more thorough Internet search and, after that bore fruit, he called Gillman.

'So, you found something,' Gillman said. Midolo could hear the enthusiasm in his voice.

'I don't want to raise your hopes,' Midolo replied. 'Nothing major but an interesting detail nonetheless, I think.'

'Go on,' Gillman said.

Midolo recounted how, years before, WikiLeaks had published more than 250,000 confidential diplomatic cables written by the US Department of State and US Embassies around the world. Midolo had developed a habit, each time he was working on an investigation, to search through the 'cablegate' site and see what came up. That was how he had found precious information about an arms dealer from Belarus who had amassed a property portfolio of luxury homes in London. 'We always find something interesting in there,' Midolo told Gillman. 'So I searched David Holden's name.' Three cables were specifically about Holden's murder and were all sent on 13 December 1977, three days after Holden's body had been identified: two were from the US Embassy in Cairo to the Secretary of State in Washington and the third one from the Secretary of State to the White House.

The first cable, titled 'Murder of London Times correspondent', said that the US Embassy had been informed by a 'reliable [Egyptian] police official' that the 'official' motive for the murder was a robbery. This was based on: A) the fact the weapon used was of 'ancient vintage'; B) Holden was shot from behind and above as if from the 'back seat' of a car; C) his body was found immediately beside the road 'as if it had been pulled out of front seat and left quickly on the roadside'. The cable went on to say that Holden's wallet and other valuables had been taken, including his luggage. 'If it had been political murder, police assume perpetrators would have claimed credit or given some public signals by this time,' the cable, which was signed by the then US ambassador to Egypt, Hermann Eilts, concluded. None of the 'facts' mentioned in the cable to support the robbery theory made sense to Midolo.

'Now, here's where it gets interesting,' he told Gillman. The other two cables, he explained, both titled 'David Holden murder', were redacted. They were completely empty.

'Oh!' Gillman cried.

'There's a card for these cables that were not declassified, with some metadata, scraps of info about what the cable is about,' Midolo went on. 'Essentially, it said that it was not released because it was sensitive. "This item contains information which may violate the privacy of an individual and has been removed from the record." I don't know what the cable would contain to violate the privacy of an individual in 2011, thirty-five years after the fact, but if anything, this shows the White House took an interest in the case.'

There was nothing strange about the US Embassy in Cairo examining the murder of a British correspondent, he reasoned. But the White House?

'That is interesting,' Gillman agreed. He speculated that the privacy reason could be bogus and told Midolo the story of how the CIA had stonewalled the *Sunday Times*, first saying it did not have any files on Holden, then admitting it had some but refusing to disclose them.

Sixteen months after filing their Freedom of Information request, in February 1980, Evans took the extreme step of suing the CIA. The court action led to the agency providing the newspaper with an index of thirty-three documents it had assembled, four about Holden and the rest about Leo Silberman. The contents, however, were almost completely redacted, so the *Sunday Times* took the CIA back to court. The agency's counsel said that the files were kept secret 'in the interest of defense and foreign policy'. The newspaper offered a compromise: a judge would check the documents *in camera* and see if the CIA was justified in keeping them secret. But the agency rejected the proposal. The newspaper appealed and the court ordered the CIA to comply. The judge, who was known to be liberal and to have ruled in favour of the press before, went in, looked at the documents, came out and said that nothing would be released. Disclosure, he ruled, would constitute 'a national security risk'.

Midolo intended to send a request to the National Archives and Records Administration, the agency in charge of releasing government records, to obtain the redacted cables. He would also file new FOI requests to the CIA and the FBI. Maybe now, four decades later, they would comply at last.

Midolo and Gillman stayed on the phone for an hour, discussing the case, from Holden's personality to the mysterious encounters during his last fateful trip to the Middle East.

Then Gillman asked Midolo a question: 'Do you want to see this through? I feel strongly about it because, like Harry, I spent years of my life trying to crack it, so it obviously stayed with me. But you have come to it more than forty years later and it's intriguing to you. Your investigative instincts were clearly stirred by this because it's an unsolved murder mystery. Have you got a nagging feeling that you would like to solve it?'

Midolo let out a long sigh. He would have been lying if he said he had not thought about it. It was a sensational story, the kind of story for which he had got into journalism in the first place. He was proud of the investigations he had done so far at *The Times* and the *Sunday Times*, but this one felt different. It was a cold case in the same league as the Zodiac Killer or the Boston Strangler. Gillman was right. It was a mystery. There were not that many reporters who had been killed in such a manner. It was not a war correspondent blown up by a landmine. This was a cold-blooded assassination.

'I think so,' he replied. 'I mean, it sounds like a Graham Greene novel. I think we could write a book about this.' He returned the question to Gillman. 'You know much more about this than me. At the end of the day this is your story, so what's *your* feeling? Do you want to see this through?'

'Well, yes,' Gillman said. 'But first I think we should meet. There are some things I'd like to tell you in person and something I'd like to show you. When we do, you'll understand my reluctance to talk about this over the phone.'

CHAPTER 16

BACK ON THE CASE

It was bad timing. The day after Midolo and Gillman spoke on the phone and agreed to meet, the Prime Minister, Boris Johnson, announced a second lockdown in England to prevent the spread of the Covid virus. It would be months before Midolo and Gillman could see each other in the flesh and when they eventually did, it was a cloudy Friday afternoon in mid-May 2021.

Gillman's house was a two-storey, semi-detached property tucked at the end of a cul-de-sac. He and his wife, Leni, met Midolo at the door. When they closed it behind him, Midolo noticed a large black and white picture of young Peter and Leni, all smiles, at what he presumed was their wedding. The photograph had been taken almost sixty years before, but time did not seem to have changed the couple too much. Gillman was now standing straight with hands in his pockets, wearing a Patagonia fleece jacket which reminded Midolo that he was a keen mountaineer. Gillman had a hearing aid but looked energetic and moved quickly despite his age. Leni was slower and helped herself with a walking stick, but her grey-green eyes were clear and alert behind her spectacles and she was affable in the way she questioned him.

'So, Manu, you're helping Pete with the David Holden case?' she asked.

'That's right,' he replied.

She seemed sceptical. 'Let's hope something comes from it this time.'

Gillman took Midolo into a living room, where coffee and biscuits were waiting. Midolo's eye caught a large, white envelope on a low glass table by the sofa. 'Have a seat,' Gillman said, and he handed Midolo the envelope; it was thick and heavy. Midolo peeked inside and saw that it was a long typewritten report entitled 'Who killed David Holden?' He read the first line: 'This report contains a summary of what we know, and most of what we believe, about David Holden and his murder.' So this was what Gillman wanted to show him and did not want to discuss over the phone.

Gillman explained that it was the report he had written in November 1978, after a year spent investigating Holden's murder. 'It was not intended for publication,' he added. 'It was meant to be read by the editor only, so I could be more frank than I would have been had I written an article. Later, a condensed version of it served as the basis for Harry's chapter in his memoir. But there's stuff in here that he didn't include.'

Midolo had told Gillman he could only stay for coffee, half an hour max, as he was working on a complicated investigation that was slated for that weekend's front page. He ended up staying two hours, discussing the many discrepancies in the Holden case. At some point after 4 p.m., Midolo started getting messages and calls from his editor, as the deadline for his story was fast approaching. It was an important investigation, the last in a back-to-back series about one of the most powerful men in Boris Johnson's Cabinet. Yet, all he could think about on the train back to London Bridge was Holden.

'The report is confidential between us,' Gillman had warned him. 'There are lots of people I have refused to show it to before, including an MI6 man. I was invited to have dinner with him without knowing his role. He was introduced as someone from the Foreign Office. During the dinner, which I now think was a set-up, he asked if he could see the Holden report. I said he couldn't and provided some excuse. That it wasn't really finished, or something like that. Only much, much later did I read what his real role is supposed to have been. This whole story has a number of unsettling occasions of people trying to find out what we knew and believed. I can tell you more the next time we meet.'

Once again, Gillman was holding something back. Was it because he did not trust him? Or was there something else? On his way back to the office, Midolo could feel the weight of the report in the backpack pressing on his shoulder. He did not want to go back to the office; all he wanted was to sit down and read it all. He wondered what details Evans had left out of the memoir and why. Did they name any suspect? Had they found out who did it but they could not prove it?

It was almost 9 p.m. when Midolo came home to his one-bedroom flat in south London. He had moved in only a few months before. The apartment was tiny, noisy, with paper-thin walls and a neighbour who had a tiresome passion for blasting electronic music late at night. Midolo threw his suit on a chair, jumped on his bed and opened the report. It was 110 pages long, but he read it in one sitting, making notes, Googling names and dates, tugging at his hair as he learned about the inconsistencies and mind-blowing twists of Holden's life. It was 2 a.m. when he finished reading it. He was wrong; it was not a Graham Greene novel, as he had told Gillman. It was a John le Carré one.

The following morning, Midolo sat at his desk and went through his notes. As Gillman had admitted in the first pages of the report, the team may not have been able to answer the major questions (who killed him and why?), but they had amassed an astounding amount of detail about the death and, more importantly, the life of

Holden. Granted, some of the clues could be dismissed as insinuations and innuendos, which was precisely one of the reasons why the report had never seen the light of day. The people named could have sued the *Sunday Times* for libel, for starters, and without hard evidence to support Insight's claims, the paper could have ended up paying huge defamation costs.

Four decades later, many of the people mentioned in the report were long dead – and, as journalists know well, you can't defame the dead. That was where Midolo intended to start reinvestigating the original inquiry: check all the names mentioned in the report, establish who was still alive and who was not, find out if they had written memoirs, if their diaries or correspondence had been donated to a library, if there were declassified government files about them and so on. More crucially, verify if any of them had been exposed as belonging to an intelligence agency.

He was good at this. Finding people was his speciality at *The Times* and the *Sunday Times*. He would spend hours sifting through online databases and piecing together fragments from what is known in the jargon as 'open-source intelligence' (OSINT); painstakingly checking and cross-referencing anything from Land Registry deeds to company filings, from electoral roll data to phone numbers, email addresses and social media posts. Everything left a digital trace: a house move, an online purchase, a career change. Over days that became weeks and then months, Midolo trawled the web, retracing Gillman's steps and confirming many of his suspicions about the people who had last seen Holden alive.

Midolo hung the first Insight article about the murder in the library in front of his desk. 'Who killed David Holden?' read the headline. Alongside it, there was a picture of Holden smoking a cigarette, his piercing blue eyes staring at him, as if nudging him to answer the question.

• • •

'Talk to everybody' was Gillman's mantra, and he was going to follow it zealously. Possibly the person who knew Holden best was Jan Morris, but she had died a few months earlier, at the venerable age of ninety-four. In her autobiography, *Pleasures of a Tangled Life*, she had dedicated a chapter to Holden. Titled 'A colleague', it was not very long, not even three pages, but opened with a startling remark: 'When I heard one day in the 1970s that David Holden was dead, his body having been found murdered on the road between Cairo airport and the city, it came as a great sadness but not exactly a shock.'

Holden might have been the only journalist of his generation assassinated in such mysterious circumstances, but Morris didn't think that was shocking? Why?

'Our friendship was that of colleagues,' Morris went on, 'and it had been enjoyed always against an esoteric background, a background somewhat romantic and adventurous, and not without a string of intrigue – the background through which foreign correspondents in murkier parts of the world habitually moved.'

Morris described how, for years, their ways crossed 'frequently and often exotically', in Jordan or Cuba, Muscat or Rhodesia:

> Wherever I went he seemed lately to have been, and vice versa. In Britain he sometimes breezed in upon us unexpected, and when I needed enlivenment I occasionally knocked unannounced upon the door of his house in Islington – if he was not there his wife Ruth might be, and she was just as welcoming.

Morris said that the two frequently exchanged picture postcards, and Holden had posted a card to her from Jerusalem on the day before his death, with its inscription: 'In the Middle East, citadels still have their uses.'

Morris repeated what she had told the Insight team, namely that the postcard was the most mysterious she had received from him. She wrote that it 'bore a message that seemed to me puzzling – not a mere frivolous greeting such as we usually exchanged, but one that tantalisingly seemed to convey something between its lines, if only I could read it'. She added that when the news of the murder reached her, she had sent the card to Scotland Yard, hoping it might shed some light on the murder.

'It was a friendship, for me at least, peculiarly opaque and elusive,' Morris wrote. 'We did not know each other intimately, or even very well.' Midolo was bemused. Morris had been described by many as one of Holden's closest friends and yet here she was, saying they did not know each other very well.

They were, she wrote, very different sorts of people, adding that, although Holden's father had been a highly respected journalist in the north, David had first hoped to become an actor:

> There was to him a certain aura of The Player. He stood and moved rather as he might on stage, bearing himself consciously, and his attitude to his profession was not quite that of reporter, but more impresarial, as though he had a managing interest in the events he described.

It was another telling detail, which indicated a degree of dissimulation in Holden's personality. Holden, Morris wrote, never cared much about scoops or petty deadlines. 'By general consent he was the most brilliant British correspondent of his generation, wise, witty and accurate, but in fact he always seemed to me *hors concours*, approaching the business in a different way from everyone else.'

Morris added the caveat that this was how Holden seemed to her but that the portrait could be erroneous. She could write about him only in a slight way, because she knew him no more deeply, but she was peculiarly affected by his personality. She remained 'haunted' by the memory of his presence. Had Morris been in love with Holden? She seemed conflicted. 'I cannot account for the strength of the pull that I always felt between us, like the force of some magnetic field. Perhaps it was partly physical, but it was mostly an airy kind of fascination; and I dare say it was only I who sensed it.'

The page ended on a mysterious note, with Morris relating how Holden's wife, Ruth, once called to ask her views on his death:

> When I ventured to suggest that it might be best to abandon her quest for an explanation she thought, I suspect, that I was conveying some kind of warning, from the intelligence community perhaps; but I meant only that if I were her I would leave his life as it stood, ending in tragic mystery. A certain enigma had surrounded him always, for me anyway, showing itself in those pale blue eyes, that meditative stance, and aesthetically at least it seemed to me right that his story should find no conclusion.

The enigma, Morris wrote, had proved real:

> None of us know to this day why David died. The police in Egypt and in England failed to arrest a murderer, all the legions of investigative journalism failed to find the truth. The terrible conclusion to a charismatic life will probably be dispersed for ever in legend, surmise, half-truth and footnote.

Midolo did not know what to think. It was an utterly enigmatic note of remembrance from what many believed one of the best journalists of her generation. He shared the find with Gillman, who was equally perplexed. He had interviewed Morris twice about the successful 1953 British expedition to Everest, which Morris had reported for *The Times*, but never asked about Holden. Of his omissions over the Holden case, this one troubled him the most. It was crucial not to repeat the same mistake and to try to speak to all the people still alive who had known Holden.

The first person on their list of people to call was David Hirst, the veteran *Guardian* journalist who, according to one theory, Holden had been mistaken for. 'How could I forget?' said the 85-year-old Hirst when Midolo reached him by phone at his house in a village near Carcassonne, in France. Hirst had met Holden in Beirut and had had a few dinners with him. 'I was in awe of him,' Hirst recalled, 'because I was a rookie in the business and felt somehow privileged to be in his company.'

Hirst did not know Holden well and could not think of any specific trait of Holden's personality; nothing remarkable, except perhaps the same 'elusiveness' that Morris described in her autobiography. 'But he was courteous and pleasant company,' he said. 'He wasn't ostentatious or commanding. A regular guy really.'

Midolo asked him if he believed in the mistaken identity scenario, whether that was a credible explanation for him. 'I do believe that is very likely,' Hirst said. 'Sadat hated me and used to mention me in most of his speeches. Frothing at the mouth, he cited me as the Western journalist who says that there's going to be a putsch and he's going to be overthrown by the Egyptian people. I don't know what Egyptian peasants thought of this "man from *The Guardian*" that he referred to in every speech.'

Midolo asked why Sadat hated him so much. Hirst replied it was because of his articles, but he could not remember exactly when Sadat's attacks started. 'Then, in 1977, he threw me out of Egypt during the mass bread riots,' Hirst said. 'Some people think that these pushed him to make peace with the Israelis. The war with

Israel had badly damaged the Egyptian economy. Anyway, they deported me for what I had written. Four armed men came to my hotel, broke into my room, one of them pointed a pistol to my head and frogmarched me out of the hotel, luckily not to an Egyptian torture chamber but to the airport.'

That was not the only close encounter that Hirst had with the Egyptian police. A few months later, he went to the Egyptian Embassy in Rome and applied for a tourist visa to go back to the country. He succeeded in being admitted into Egypt and went to say hi to some colleagues at the local *Al-Ahram* newspaper.

'"My God, David, what the hell are you doing here?" they said as soon as they saw me, as if it was a really stupid thing to have done,' Hirst recalled. 'I joined the British Foreign Secretary and Robert Fisk to go to Damascus, but when I got to the airport, I was immediately accosted and taken aside. They were bent on keeping me there. They wouldn't let me get on the plane. Fisk was there and said, "If you're not letting him on that plane, I'm not getting on either." Finally, they relented and I went on board. If I had been on my own, I'm sure the Egyptians would have thrown me in jail, if not worse.'

Hirst never went to Egypt again, but as soon as he heard that Holden had been assassinated, he thought that that could have been him.

'I thought they had made a mistake,' Hirst told Midolo. 'I actually looked a little bit like Holden and the D. H., David Hirst, David Holden. I thought it was a legitimate mistake and so did a lot of other people.'

Hirst remembered something else about the assassination. 'A prevalent theory was that it had been an Israeli job, because Holden had been very instrumental in a dramatic, first-time ever grand exposé of torture of Israeli prisoners in Israeli jails,' he said. 'I don't believe myself that the Israelis would assassinate a journalist for a bad story, but that was one of the theories at the time. Have you come across that?'

Yes, except Holden, Midolo told him, was not the author of the report. Gillman was one of them and to his dismay had been revealed as such a few days after Holden had been erroneously fingered in the Israeli press. Midolo went on to explain to Hirst how he had become involved in the case and described the Insight team's effort and their findings as they had been related in the Holden report.

After an hour discussing the intricacies of the investigation, Hirst sounded shocked. 'That seems to suggest that Holden himself was an agent,' he said after a long silence. 'CIA or MI6?'

'Or both,' Midolo said. 'There was more. Insight speculated that he might have been recruited by the KGB too. Either at Cambridge or later, by a male lover. There was also the tantalising detail that Holden had been *The Times* correspondent from Beirut at the same time as Kim Philby and he was later coy about it.'

Hirst did not know the detail about Philby. He added that Philby's defection was the first story that he covered for *The Guardian* when he was a stringer in Beirut in 1963. Midolo asked him if he knew Patrick Seale, who was at *The Observer* at the same time and later wrote a book about Philby – and who was suspected of being KGB himself.

'Well, that doesn't surprise me,' Hirst said of Seale. 'I don't have any evidence whatsoever. It's just his character somehow, something in his personality. He wasn't straightforward. I didn't trust him. But he was very well connected. Particularly with the Syrians and Assad. He could have been a useful informant for the Soviets.'

Hirst was not aware that Seale had been Holden's agent for his book on Saudi Arabia.

'In light of what you told me, I now feel that it wasn't me that they were looking for, after all,' Hirst said. 'That they were effectively after him.' He expressed regret. 'Well, I'm still sure it was the Egyptians. But I suppose I should have looked harder into this.'

There were others who had briefly crossed paths with Holden, like Don McCullin, possibly the greatest photographer alive. Then in his late eighties, McCullin, a stocky man with silver hair and intense, penetrating ice-blue eyes, lived in the Somerset countryside and rarely came to London. 'I fucking hate coming down here,' McCullin told Midolo and Gillman when they met at an event in Marylebone. Born in a poor family in north London, McCullin had started taking photographs after his National Service, and it was a picture of a local north London gang that got him a freelance job with *The Observer*. In 1966, he went to work for Evans's *Sunday Times*, travelling all over the world, from the Congo to Vietnam and Cambodia, where he was hit by a mortar. But of all his dangerous assignments, McCullin said, it was in Uganda that he thought he would not make it out alive.

'David Holden was there and on Sunday night he fled,' McCullin recalled. 'Everybody thought it was very weird. He went unannounced: gone. That same night, I was yanked out of the swimming pool of the hotel and taken to Makindye military prison. A notorious killing spot and with terrible hygiene. It was me, a guy from Reuters and a fixer who could speak Swahili. We had a harrowing time. We could have died. A Tanzanian border guard was captured and brought to that prison. They beat him to death right in our cell, in front of us. It was the most dangerous moment of my life. I suppose I have to thank David Holden for that.'

McCullin recounted that the same night, twenty men were sledgehammered to death and their bodies were dumped in the Nile. 'We saw these trucks full of bodies leaving the next morning and we thought we'd never get out of there.' McCullin spent four days in prison before the British high commissioner secured his release.

'It's amazing that Holden broke his cover in a way,' he said. 'Holden knew that Milton Obote was coming across the border from Tanzania, and he buggered off and didn't tell the rest of us.'

Midolo told McCullin that he had done it before and afterwards, as in the Congo in 1960 or in Chile a few months later, in 1973.

'What was he like?' Midolo asked McCullin.

'Oh, Holden was very secretive. He was a mysterious person. I can honestly say I didn't know him. But in Uganda, I bet he was more in the British Embassy than he was with us. The embassy was a spy nest.'

'You were working with him on a story?' Gillman asked.

'No, I wasn't. He was the kind of man who wouldn't work with anybody. He was never in the office and he was someone who kept people away, as if he had something to hide. Like Philby, he used the office, he used the profession. Did he go to Cambridge?'

'He did!'

'That's another hallmark. A silver hallmark. It was a breeding ground. I never gave it another thought until you just sat me down and asked about it,' McCullin said.

'You never talked to him about it?'

'No, I never saw him again. He could have told us, he could have been generous, but he obviously was a man of coldness. He was ice cold. He couldn't risk any generosity because he had this other identity. He wasn't one of us. He was a spy. What that does, the spying, it dishonours our business. It dishonours all of us because he is hiding under an umbrella to which he doesn't belong. And he puts us in danger. We could have died in that prison. In the end, he was the one who got a bullet.'

McCullin said that he was at the *Sunday Times* office when he heard that Holden had been killed. 'In a way, there was no other rumour because no one knew him. He kept away, he was slippery, he was like the Scarlet Pimpernel really. He was very elusive.'

That word again, 'elusive'. The same word both Jan Morris and David Hirst had used to describe Holden. A number of Middle Eastern correspondents had bumped into him at a bar or in the lobby of a hotel and saw him as an evanescent, dapperly dressed man who always seemed off to his next assignment.

Tim Llewellyn, a BBC Middle East correspondent for sixteen years, saw him at the bar of the Intercontinental Hotel in Amman, in December 1977. 'I was very much in awe of him because I was a very junior, upcoming and naive Middle Eastern correspondent in the making, while he was some fifteen years older than me,' Llewellyn said. 'He was a pretty remote and respected figure. Very pleasant and very charming man. Everybody knew him. Older correspondents were friends of his and respected him.'

Roger Matthews, former Middle East editor for the *Financial Times*, was based in Madrid until 1977, when he was transferred to Cairo. 'David came through Madrid a couple of times and we had lunch together. He was a very engaging and interesting man and we talked about politics,' Matthews recalled. 'I hadn't been there that long when I had a telex from him saying that he was coming to Cairo "and can we have lunch?" and that was just prior to his death.' The lunch, of course, never happened.

Matthews described him as a very serious and capable journalist. 'He was a good foreign correspondent; he was not a sensationalist in any way. I think he would have made a jolly good diplomat. I was impressed by and liked David. He had a very high reputation and lots of people held him in high esteem. Now, whether he was anything else other than a journalist, I have no idea. You are swimming in very murky waters.'

The frontline correspondent Bernd Debusmann, who had worked for Reuters for half a century and who himself had been shot in the back by a Syrian assassin with a silenced gun in Beirut in 1980 (the bullet was still lodged near his spine), had met Holden briefly at a reception in the Lebanese capital. 'It didn't go beyond small talk and gossip,' Debusmann told Midolo. 'The most widely believed theory among Middle East correspondents at the time was that either Mossad or the CIA outsourced the operation to the Egyptians. Why is anyone's guess. If Holden did work for a spy agency, I always thought MI6 was the most probable.'

Debusmann added that he sat next to Harold Evans a few years earlier at the annual gala of the Committee to Protect Journalists in New York and tried to raise the subject. Evans didn't want to go into it. 'Good luck with getting to the bottom of that murder,' Debusmann concluded. 'So many theories, so much chit-chat, so little documentary proof. Plus, many of the people who might point you to the right (or yet another) direction are dead.'

A dozen interviews later, Midolo felt none the wiser as to what Holden was like. It reminded him of the opening scene of Peter O'Toole's 1962 film *Lawrence of Arabia*, where everyone talks about T. E. Lawrence at his memorial service in St Paul's Cathedral – he was 'a poet, a scholar and a mighty warrior' but, admittedly, no one knew him. It was ironic, considering how much Holden had done to dispel the myth of Arabia's romantic image popularised by Lawrence. Midolo was now convinced that the opacity and elusiveness that so many felt in his presence were a deliberate choice – that Holden was indeed playing a part. But of what kind? Perhaps the people who had last seen him alive could shed a light on that. Maybe, with the passage of time, they would be willing to speak, at last, about what Holden was really up to?

Five individuals, among the many that had met Holden during his perilous last journey through the Middle East, had caught Midolo's eye. They were: Robert Pelletreau, the political officer of the US Embassy in Damascus, Syria, who had been peculiarly unhelpful with the Insight team and only seemed to be interested in knowing what *they* had found out; Ahmed Rahman, a Palestinian academic, who claimed Holden was with him in the West Bank while in fact he was most likely meeting someone in Jerusalem; John Fistere, an American who lived in Beirut with his wife, Isobel, who saw Holden on the day he flew to Cairo but whose account was contradicted by another source; Michael Elkins, the American journalist who wanted to know when Holden was going to Cairo; and Kenizé Mourad, the enigmatic French journalist who seemed to follow Holden around the Middle East.

Pelletreau, who was still alive and in his mid-eighties, was a career diplomat who in the 1980s and '90s went on to become US ambassador to a string of Middle Eastern countries, including Tunisia and Egypt. He had told *The Times*'s correspondent, Edward Mortimer, that he had met Holden in Yemen in 1967 when he was researching *Farewell to Arabia*. But by then, the book had already come out, courtesy of the US publisher bankrolled by the CIA. Was Pelletreau simply misremembering? Or was this something else? Gillman suspected Pelletreau was CIA. Midolo decided to check if that was the case and got lucky with his very first phone call. The veteran *New York Times* reporter Seymour Hersh, whom Midolo cold-called on his Washington landline, straight from the phone book, told him that Pelletreau had been his neighbour for many years. 'Bob lived around the corner,' Hersh said. 'Many people in those days confused competence with spookdom. I have no reason to think Pelletreau was CIA, but I also assure you that, like most competent ambassadors, he had a trust relationship with his station chief.' Hersh went on to say that he could not guess what 'the agency guy' in Damascus in 1977 would have thought of Pelletreau. 'Very different animals,' he added. The snippet was fascinating: Pelletreau might not have been CIA himself, but he was working closely with the agency.

Rahman was also alive. Although not naming him and referring to him as 'an academic at Birzeit University', Harold Evans had written in his book that he had discovered that Rahman was 'a paid agent of the CIA'. Rahman had studied in the US and had later obtained a PhD in Washington DC. The most telling detail was that

Rahman was then living in the US, so he was likely to have obtained US citizenship. Midolo wondered whether that was the payback for his services – not knowing, yet, that Gillman's source at the State Department had told him exactly that. Midolo made a note to try to contact Rahman in due course.

Fistere was dead, but Midolo was excited to discover that he had been a member of the Office of Strategic Services (OSS), the American wartime intelligence agency and forerunner of the CIA. During the war, as head of the OSS 'Morale Operation' branch based in Bari, southern Italy, Fistere had been in charge of secret anti-Nazi propaganda and psychological warfare operations in Europe. After the war, he popped up in the Middle East. He was in Beirut in the mid-1950s and early 1960s, where he befriended Kim Philby. The Holden report mentioned that he was rumoured to have been sent there by the CIA 'to keep an eye on Philby'. An article written by the journalist and author Said Aburish in the early 2000s seemed to confirm that Fistere was a CIA operative. In the CIA archives, which were available online, Midolo found the clippings of an article of *CounterSpy* magazine from 1978. The article alleged that the Jordanian Information Bureau, which published the English-language *Jordan* newspaper, of which Fistere had been editor, was in fact a CIA front. Later, reading the memoir of the CIA station chief in Amman, Midolo could confirm that the allegation was correct.

Elkins, who had died in 2001, had also served in the OSS during the war and was sent on clandestine missions behind enemy lines in Europe, details of which were still classified. The insistent questions he asked Holden about his trip to Cairo, which puzzled Mortimer, assumed a new, more sinister significance

The last in Midolo's list of five was Mourad, perhaps the most mysterious of them all, certainly the most intriguing to Midolo. She was in her early eighties and lived in Paris. She had left *Le Nouvel Observateur* in 1983 and had become a successful novelist. Her

1987 book *Regards from the Dead Princess*, which was based on her family, had become an international bestseller, selling millions of copies. She was active on Facebook, where she often posted articles about the Middle East along with pictures of her cats. Midolo sent her a message in French. No response. A month later, he followed up. Again, no reply. He did that four or five times, but he wasn't sure she had even seen his messages. Inquiries through her publisher bore no fruit, either. Later, Midolo found out why she was perhaps not thrilled that a *Sunday Times* journalist was trying to approach her about the Holden case. After the paper had serialised Evans's memoir, she had threatened to sue it for libel. In a letter to the newspaper, her lawyer said that Mourad travelled regularly to the Middle East and that 'any association with the CIA is potentially very dangerous'. In light of what Midolo found out shortly afterwards, the lawyer's words bore a dramatic irony.

• • •

In the early hours of the morning on 4 November 1979, a mob of Iranian students stormed the US Embassy in Tehran. They were loyal to Ayatollah Khomeini, the cleric who headed the opposition to the US-backed ruler of Iran, the Shah Mohammad Reza Pahlavi. Chanting '*Marg bar Âmrikâ*' ('Death to America'), some 500 students gathered outside the gates of the compound, which Khomeini had described as 'an American spy den in Tehran'. A female student who had hidden a pair of metal cutters under her chador used them to break the chain locking the gates, then the demonstrators broke through.

Khomeini was not lying; the embassy indeed hosted an important CIA station. Realising that the takeover of the embassy was imminent, CIA officers started shredding documents which were then supposed to be burnt in a furnace. Secret cables, reports, memos, correspondence, all sorts of highly classified documents and, most importantly, crucial evidence of the CIA meddling in the country. But the furnace malfunctioned and the shredded documents were retrieved by the Iranians, who hired a team of carpet weavers to painstakingly reassemble them piece by piece. They worked for six years, recombining 2,300 files from the tangled strips of papers from the shredders. The recovered papers would later be published by the Iranian government in eighty-five volumes called *Documents from the US Espionage Den*.

Most of these were now online. Among them, Midolo found a series of top-secret memos relating to a CIA asset codenamed UNPOLO/1. It was Kenizé Mourad. Midolo could not believe his eyes. The documents related how Mourad had been recruited by the CIA in Paris in the autumn of 1973, to spy on Chinese diplomats 'and [Near East] targets'. But a month later, she had a change of heart: 'The idea seemed exciting,' she wrote to her case officer. 'But I finally realised it was going deeply against my feelings ... It would be a constant struggle in my mind.' The memo specified that Mourad was then 'aware that she was in contact with RTACTION' – one of the cryptonyms CIA officers used to describe the agency itself – 'in Paris and Islamabad' and had agreed to being on its payroll. It continued, intriguingly saying that 'operational approval was cancelled in April 1979'. Midolo learned that 'operational approval' was a type of approval granted for covert and clandestine operations. But if Mourad had changed her mind after just a few weeks, why had the approval lasted almost six years?

In September 1979, after reviewing her 'operations background', the CIA attempted to re-establish contact with Mourad. On 13 September, a Paris station officer named Ernest Timken took her out for lunch and talked with her at length about the political situation in Iran. Mourad was due to depart for Tehran the next day and volunteered to brief him upon her return. This time, it was unclear from the documents if she was aware that the diplomat was a CIA officer. 'We are anxious to learn what may be available from operational and restricted [counter-intelligence] folders on UNPOLO/1,' Timken wrote, adding that this could lead to 'her operational exploitation as potential unwitting conduit' for information on Iran and the Middle East. There was one more memo, almost entirely illegible, which mentioned that Timken and Mourad had had at least one other encounter, 'a drink at her place'.

The consequences of Midolo's findings were devastating. There appeared to be evidence suggesting that all five 'witnesses' who were among the last to see Holden alive had at some point either worked directly for the CIA or had been close to the agency. It was now more than just coincidences, as Gillman and his colleagues had suspected but could not prove. Of course, there was no evidence or suggestion that Pelletreau, Ahmed or Mourad were in any way complicit in the murder, but it could be argued that the CIA had at least appeared interested in Holden during his last trip.

Then there was the case of Mustafa Amin, an Egyptian newspaper editor and friend of Holden since the 1950s who was supposed to meet him in Cairo but never managed to do so. The Insight report mentioned in passing that Amin was one of the first people Holden had contacted after accepting his last assignment, so Midolo decided to check his background, looking for clues.

Amin, who had died aged eighty-three in 1997, was one of the most renowned journalists in Egypt, alongside his twin brother, Ali. Together, in the 1940s, they founded the daily newspaper *Akhbar el-Yom* and its weekly magazine, which were still published, although now tightly controlled by the Egyptian government. Mustafa Amin's obituary in the *New York Times* celebrated him as 'a pioneer of Arab journalism and an advocate of Western-style democracy', but there were other aspects of his past that made him more important than Gillman had realised.

In July 1965, Amin was having lunch at his villa in Alexandria with an American diplomat, Bruce Taylor Odell, a political officer at the US Embassy, when the police raided the house. They arrested both men, but Odell, who had diplomatic immunity, was released shortly after. On the same day, the Middle East News Agency (MENA), which was controlled by the Egyptian government, reported that Amin 'was arrested while passing political and military information to the US Central Intelligence Agency'. The agency wrote that Amin had been recruited 'a long time ago' by the CIA and was in the process of giving a weekly report to Odell. It said that the police confiscated a paper that contained handwritten questions by Odell along with Amin's answers, described as 'harmful to the security and the safety of the nation'.

Official Egyptian sources told the *New York Times* that the authorities had been unwittingly led to Amin by Odell, who had been expelled from Iraq because of suspicious activities there. He had been put under surveillance as soon as he had arrived in Cairo the previous summer and was seen meeting repeatedly with Amin at a rented apartment in Heliopolis. The authorities had bugged the flat, which had been rented under Amin's name, and the tapes had disclosed that he was passing sensitive information to the American. Odell was expelled from the country and returned to the US. Later, he talked openly about his secret mission to provide tanks, ammunition and guns to the military officers who had overthrown and assassinated the Prime Minister of Iraq, Abd al-Karim Qasim, in 1963. Odell told a *Boston Globe* reporter in 1976 that he had been involved in CIA clandestine operations for nearly twenty years.

Mustafa Amin was jailed and, after being gruesomely tortured by the secret police, confessed he had been spying for the CIA for over a decade. He had also implicated his brother, Ali, who was in London at the time and did not return to Egypt, saying he was sharing with him half of what he was paid for his intelligence work.

Shortly before his arrest, Mustafa had wired Ali $46,000, or almost four times the editor's annual salary. The evidence was incontrovertible and, although under duress, Amin himself had confessed. The public prosecutor at the trial asked for the death penalty, but Amin was sentenced to life with hard labour instead. He would spend nine years behind bars and was only released by Sadat in 1974, ostensibly on the grounds of poor health. Midolo noticed the date: 1974 was the year Egypt and the US had re-established diplomatic relations after Sadat's predecessor, Nasser, had severed them in 1967.

Sadat allowed the two brothers to resume writing. When Ali died, aged sixty-two, in 1976, Mustafa took over his daily column, which was published in Cairo and London. He later wrote a memoir, in which he proclaimed his innocence and said the Egyptian secret service, the mukhabarat, had extracted his confession by torture. It was Nasser himself, he claimed, who had asked him to keep secret channels open with the CIA. There might have been an element of truth to it.

According to the Cairo station chief in the 1950s, James Eichelberger, it was the CIA that had informed Nasser that MI6 intended to 'do a Mosaddegh' on Egypt, i.e. removing Nasser either by assassination or by an army coup. Eichelberger said that the Amin brothers were one of the channels by which the CIA and the State Department passed valuable intelligence to the Egyptians. Eichelberger also warned Nasser that, given the apparent mental instability of the British Prime Minister, Anthony Eden, the UK's behaviour was becoming unpredictable even for CIA analysts. The American academic Owen Sirrs, who had written a history of the Egyptian secret services, argued that the CIA did not pass intelligence to Egypt out of altruism. 'There were some in Langley who still believed Nasser was the best alternative to communism and that an Egyptian defeat would only pave the way for Moscow's dominance of the Middle East,' Sirrs wrote. 'Moreover, Mustafa Amin later claimed the CIA wanted one of Egypt's new Soviet-made MiGs in return for the information it provided.'

In the Middle East, diplomacy was one thing – covert intelligence, or the 'third option', was another. On a whim, Midolo decided to check if there was any public information about who was the station chief in Cairo in 1977, the year of Holden's murder. By sheer luck, he found a *Daily Mirror* story published only a couple of months earlier. 'Secrets of the Cold War spy and CIA mastermind who bagged advanced Soviet MiG-23 jet', read the headline. The story reported that the Cairo station chief in the mid- to late 1970s 'lived his life in the shadows and had to hide his medals behind a picture at his home'. Midolo felt his heart quickening. He called Gillman.

'I think I've found the name of the CIA station chief in Cairo in 1977,' he told him over the phone.

'Go on,' Gillman said.

'A man named James Fees. Jim Fees.'

'Ah! You just hit the jackpot!'

CHAPTER 17

THE NAME'S FEES, JAMES FEES

Gillman had asked Midolo to meet again. This time, the living room in Gillman's house was cluttered with boxes, folders and piles of documents. 'These are my Holden files,' Gillman explained. 'I was going through them when you called the other day and told me about Jim Fees. You see, I've been looking for this man for almost forty years.'

Gillman told him that he already knew that Fees was the CIA station chief in Cairo at the time. The person who had revealed that to him was the diplomatic source that Harold Evans had hinted at in his memoir. Now, Gillman was ready to hand Midolo information that he had not shared with anyone, not even Evans himself. The source nicknamed 'Fedway', he told him, was Alexandra Johnson, an American diplomat in Jerusalem in the late 1970s.

Gillman told Midolo how the Insight torture story and the Holden investigation had become entangled, with Johnson at the heart of it. Midolo was especially captivated by the tale of the 'farewell brunch' and the fact that the former Red Cross delegate, Jean de Muralt, had questioned Johnson about her dealings with the *Sunday Times*. Even more remarkably, de Muralt had shown up in London twenty-four hours later to invite himself to dinner with Gillman at the Dorchester and inquire about Holden. Gillman suspected him of working for the CIA but, once again, could not prove it.

A trained lawyer, de Muralt was the scion of an important Swiss family. There was scant information available on the web about him, only a few clippings from old newspaper articles. According to the Italian daily *La Stampa*, in May 1969 de Muralt was president of the Investors Overseas Service, an investment company based in Geneva that 'targeted American expatriates and US servicemen who sought to avoid paying income tax'. The company went bust in a major financial scandal in the early 1970s and during the unravelling, James Roosevelt, Franklin D. Roosevelt's son and one of the company's executives, was stabbed by his wife at a chalet in Geneva.

Clearly, de Muralt was already in touch with wealthy and important Americans in the 1960s. In the aftermath of the financial scandal, he fled to Israel. Midolo wondered if he cut a deal with the CIA to avoid prosecution in the US.

There were a few references to de Muralt in the diplomatic cables published by WikiLeaks. A cable marked confidential from July 1978 sent from the US consulate in Jerusalem to the Secretary of State was titled 'Possible Press Revelation of de Muralt Firing'. It warned the US State Department that an American journalist (and de Muralt's girlfriend) 'has been in Jerusalem recently and obtained from de Muralt full details of his firing by ICRC [the Red Cross]'. The cable stated that the journalist was also aware of Johnson's report, Jerusalem 1500, and concluded, cryptically, that it was unclear what the journalist would write but 'expect it would attack ICRC for its handling of de Muralt which would inevitably bring in fact of his talks in Washington'.

Midolo and Gillman were puzzled by the cable. They speculated why American diplomats in Jerusalem were so worried about the tale of de Muralt's firing from the Red Cross becoming public. Midolo could not find any articles written by the journalist about the matter; nor could he find de Muralt to ask him. But Gillman was able to find and talk to Jim Fine, the former representative of the American Friends Service Committee, the Quaker-funded organisation that de Muralt went to work for after being fired from the Red Cross.

'He was a strange character,' Fine said, on a call with his wife Debbie, who had also known de Muralt. 'Very strange.'

Gillman asked him to elaborate.

'He just seemed to us to be someone who didn't quite fit the mould of a Quaker service,' Fine went on. 'I remember he had a fairly hefty bit of alimony to pay, and he somehow managed to get the organisation to pay his alimony for him. Shortly after that, he was gone.'

Gillman asked Fine if he knew anything about what de Muralt did after leaving the Quaker organisation.

'No idea. He went off our radar when he left.'

Gillman told the story of the brunch and the dinner at the Dorchester the next day and how he suspected de Muralt was working for the CIA and trying to find out what the *Sunday Times* knew.

'Very interesting,' Fine said. He added that in January 1979, when the brunch happened, de Muralt must have left the Quaker organisation. 'You know, for what it's worth, I would see him wanting to cosy up to authorities like that. I wouldn't put it past him. He liked to deal at the top.'

Midolo managed to track down another one of de Muralt's ex-girlfriends in Jerusalem who told him that de Muralt had recently died, aged ninety-two, in Geneva. As she was about to end the phone call, Midolo asked the woman if de Muralt had been working for the CIA. 'Well, sir, if he did, I don't know,' she said. 'And he's dead. Whatever he did before, he's dead now.' She hung up.

Alexandra Johnson had also died, of brain cancer, in Oklahoma in 2002. She was only fifty-six years old. Gillman said that after reading the Holden report during their last meeting in 1986, she had become convinced that the killing had been ordered by the CIA and had decided to tell him the name of the man who must have sanctioned it: Jim Fees, CIA station chief in Cairo. Now that Johnson had died, Gillman could share what he knew with Midolo.

After meeting Johnson, Gillman had wanted to have another shot at Holden. He remembered her request that he find alternative sources for what she had told him, leading to her conclusion that Egypt conducted the killing for the CIA, but felt it was well worth a try. 'To my surprise and disappointment, the *Sunday Times Magazine* turned me down,' Gillman said. 'So I wrote an article for the *Independent Magazine*, which did not have the resources to back a new investigation.' Gillman hoped that the article would lead people to contact him. A number did, providing him with new evidence, including fresh details about Leo Silberman's life.

Gillman discussed his findings with his former partner, Paul Eddy, and the two agreed to write a book and secured an advance from an American publisher. Gillman and Leni embarked on interviews and felt they were getting useful material. 'But Paul did almost nothing,' Gillman said.

The crunch came over Tony Terry, the *Sunday Times* colleague who had been dispatched to Jerusalem during the first week of the investigation. Terry was a strong contact, a good friend of Eddy and was also rumoured to have been working for MI6 before becoming a journalist. 'Paul kept prevaricating, saying he wanted to talk to him near the end of the research process,' Gillman told Midolo. 'That struck me as 100 per cent wrong, as Terry could have given us the key to the whole story.'

Then came news that Terry was ill in New Zealand. 'We discussed whether Paul should try to see him, but the flights were expensive and he did not go. Terry died soon afterwards, on 2 October 1992. Leni and I decided to do no further work until Paul started to do so. He never did, and the project died.' (After becoming a successful thriller writer in the 1990s, Eddy died of an aneurysm, aged sixty-four, in 2009.)

At the top of the list of people Gillman wanted to track down was Fees. Johnson had followed Fees's career with enormous admiration throughout her time with the US foreign service. Documents based on Fees's reports reached Johnson at the time when she was writing memos on Soviet activity in the Middle East for Henry Kissinger. With attributions such as 'National security adviser close to Sadat', they were clearly from what Johnson considered 'stellar sources' and provided a high-grade flow of intelligence from Cairo. They included detailed information about Soviet spying operations in Egypt and specifics of Soviet weapon transfers.

In 1974, Johnson was dispatched to Cairo, where she asked if she could meet Fees. She found him a compelling, charismatic figure: tall, good-looking and inspiring high personal loyalty among his colleagues. Fees told Johnson that he had recommended using Egypt's economic problems as a lever to induce Sadat to agree to the Camp David Accords with Egypt in 1978. Egypt was given aid valued at 90 per cent of Israel's allocation in return for agreeing to the talks. Johnson also learned that Sadat had been personally bribed, to the tune of millions of dollars. In 1975, Fees became head of CIA clandestine operations for the entire Middle East, still based in Cairo. He was still in that role in December 1977, when Holden was murdered.

From time to time, Gillman would try to search for Fees. Now, decades later, he realised he had the wrong spelling of his name, 'Feis' or 'Fies'. But even with the correct spelling, Gillman would have likely found nothing. The first open reference to Fees was in February 2021, in the article about the Soviet MiG jet that Midolo had stumbled across during one of his searches. Fees died in 2017 and although he appeared only once in official CIA archive material, Midolo managed to reconstruct most of his life and career as a master spy.

• • •

Born in Nebraska in 1931, James Hans Fees grew up in Montana and Washington State. His first encounter with the CIA came by chance. While he was in the army at Camp Gordon in Georgia in the mid-1950s, he became engaged to a young woman who lived nearby. Her sister was a CIA recruiter who suggested he might like to apply for a job at the agency. Fees started working for the agency in 1957 and his first notable post abroad, in the early 1960s, could not have been more different to his native Nebraska. After a brief stint in Khartoum, Sudan, he was sent to Yemen.

A quadrilateral of yellow sand, green plateaux and granite mountains lying at the bottom of the Arabian Peninsula, sandwiched between Saudi Arabia to the north and Oman to the east, the country was once rich and powerful. The Romans called it Arabia Felix. The Bedouin believed that the 'Arab Al Araba', the purest strain of their race, originated in the region and T. E. Lawrence described it in his memoirs as the cradle of the Semitic tribes. Here 'the last autumnal whisper of the monsoon against the peaks brought a steady, refreshing rain and made the Yemen the most verdant and populous corner in all Arabia', as Holden described it in *Farewell to Arabia*.

The Yemen that Fees found upon his arrival was a torn country. On its north-western side, between the cities of Sanaa and Taiz, was the Kingdom of Yemen, a mediaeval theocracy ruled by an imam. To the east, Aden, the historic capital of the ancient kingdom and a strategic port between the Red Sea and the Indian Ocean, was occupied by the British. When the imam died in September 1962, Egyptian-trained military forces, inspired by the revolution of

Nasser's free officers a decade earlier, launched a coup, deposed the newly crowned imam and proclaimed the Yemen Arab Republic.

The Egyptians had been plotting for some time. A year earlier, the CIA intercepted a phone call between a cleaning woman tasked with placing a bomb under the imam's bed and her Egyptian case officer. She had difficulty reading the bomb's instructions and the exasperated officer was trying to guide her through them. The assassination plot failed and the imam died of natural causes, but his son's rule lasted only a week. When tanks surrounded the new imam's palace and the pro-Nasser government was formed, the Brits next door in Aden started panicking. They were caught by surprise by the coup and had no intelligence capability on the ground, relying almost entirely on the CIA. The agency assessed that Nasser would send some 12,000 troops to the region and that there would be a stable government within a week. They were bang on with their first assessment but spectacularly wrong with their second. Nasser indeed sent troops, but what was intended to be a swift, decisive coup turned into a long deadly civil war.

Soon, Cairo's radio Voice of the Arabs, with its 'venomous propaganda' as Holden put it, was calling for a revolution in the occupied south and 'vengeance' against the southern tribal chiefs, who now sought British protection. Riots broke out in Aden and even King Saud, in neighbouring Saudi Arabia, became alarmed. He told his US allies that Nasser's move was part of a broader plot to undermine the security of the Arabian Peninsula with the aim of handing it to the Soviets. The king built a convincing case because at the end of November, the director of the CIA's Middle East division, James Critchfield, met the head of MI6, Dick White, in London. 'The Russians are waging war across Arabia,' he told White. 'We've got to stop them.'

It was into this mighty mess that Fees parachuted himself. Using the cover of a humanitarian aid officer, he set up a one-man clandestine CIA station in Taiz. Energetic, intelligent and aggressively anti-Soviet, as White later described him, Fees became a knowledgeable Arabist. Also a skilled pilot, Fees was enabled by his cover to fly his lightweight plane throughout the newly formed Yemen Republic, meeting sources and setting up a network of agents.

Fees charmed and bribed his way into the citadels of both the republican and Egyptian military headquarters. In exchange for gold coins, he obtained and dispatched to Washington a copy of the enemy's war-room map displaying the disposition of its military units, its order of battle, targets, the after-battle reports and intended political initiatives. The CIA passed on some of this intel to the British and from there to the Yemeni royalists, fighting on the other side.

Fees was also delivering intelligence that exposed flaws in MI6 operations. He would later say that White, MI6's chief, took 'a lively interest' in his dispatches. 'After all, we [the US and the UK] were spending lots of money.' That was an understatement. Astronomical sums were being wasted and bribes paid 'to the wrong people'. An estimated £30 million, or £535 million in today's money, was laundered in England, then handed out to tribal rulers on both sides of the border. The Yemeni royalist fighters committed unspeakable atrocities and the Egyptian troops, according to Fees, were 'terrified' of them. The royalists decapitated some of their victims and, per one of Fees's reports, had a habit of 'sending back captured troops with their lips cut off in a ghastly grin'. The fighters were trained by British mercenaries led by an ex-SAS colonel, Henry 'Jim' Johnson, with the unofficial blessing of MI6.

It soon became clear to Nasser's men in Cairo that the Egyptian Army and the Yemeni republicans were not just fighting the royalists; they were battling the CIA, MI6 and the SAS, Israel's Mossad, the Saudis, the Jordanians and the Iranians, all operating on or near the front line. Among the spies on the ground, Midolo encountered a name that popped up regularly, like a jack-in-the-box, in his research: Kamal Adham. Head of Saudi intelligence, the brother-in-law of the new Saudi king, Faisal, and whispered to be his *éminence grise*, Adham was working closely with the SAS's founder, David Stirling. Using Saudi money, Stirling set up a radio station in Aden that employed a number of British mercenaries with close links to the SAS, including Jim Johnson.

Side by side with the spies – and at times indistinguishable from them – were troops of British journalists. Kim Philby, on his last assignment for *The Observer* and *The Economist*, was one of the first to arrive, undoubtedly busy between his pro-royalist dispatches for his editors and MI6 on one side and his pro-republican ones for the KGB on the other.

Holden was there, working for *The Guardian* and writing dispatches from Aden from November 1962 onwards. He had visited Yemen for the first time five years earlier, when he was thought to be the first European to enter certain towns; one was Jibla, 'a place still genuinely inviolate, in spite of my own incongruous presence – a virgin community amid the twentieth-century's world-wide rape'. Holden's reporting served as the basis for *Farewell to Arabia*. It was unclear if Holden had met Fees in Yemen, but it was almost certain that Fees had his first encounter there with Adham, who became a long-lasting associate.

Journalism provided excellent concealment for spooks. The foreign editor of the *Daily Telegraph*, S. R. 'Pop' Pawley, a 'friend' of MI6, sent on assignment Colonel David Smiley, the ex-Special Operations Executive (SOE) Second World War agent who had commanded SAS men running covert operations in Muscat and Oman. Smiley, who toured the royalist areas for three months and wrote a report calling for the use of European mercenaries, noted in his memoir that his journalist cover – and *Daily Telegraph* press card – gave him 'respectability' for his secret mission.

The *Telegraph* and Fees were also at the centre of a mini-scandal that swept through MI6 a few months later. Among the material obtained by Fees was a report that royalist tribesmen were being attacked by Egyptian bombs containing poison gas. MI6 delivered the casing of one of the bombs to London and leaked the information to the *Telegraph*. The story sparked outrage and was picked up by the United Nations, but it was soon revealed that the bomb contained tear gas, much to the embarrassment of the British spies. 'We are all agreed that it would be best to let the matter die a natural death,' wrote a British diplomat at the UN.

Yemen turned out to be Nasser's Vietnam, lasting five years, costing Egypt dear and proving a humbling experience for both the country and its leader. As for Fees, his daring missions won him his first honours on the field: an intelligence medal of merit awarded to him in 1964. 'For outstanding performance of duty under hazardous physical and operational conditions,' the citation read. 'As chief of a one-man station in a country torn by continuous guerrilla warfare and despite the massive presence of unfriendly forces, Mr Fees single-handedly provided excellent coverage of priority intelligence targets and recruited important intelligence assets.'

At the end of the 1960s, Fees left Yemen for Iraq, where he provided covert paramilitary assistance to the Kurds engaged in an armed insurgency against both Iraq and Iran. He moved on to Jordan, then on the verge of civil war. Known as Black September, the conflict saw the King of Jordan opposing Yasser Arafat's Palestine Liberation Organization (PLO).

Fees was not alone in Jordan, where he was part of a much larger station. The CIA contingency in Amman provided principal liaison with King Hussein in exchange for a multi-million-dollar subsidy of CIA funds, to the point that Washington once had to recall an ambassador who was unwilling to continue the custom.

But the country during Black September was just as risky as

Yemen, if not more. One day, Fees's wife opened the door of their house to find a Palestinian *fedayeen*, a Kalashnikov in his hand and a keffiyeh on his face, asking her to donate money to the PLO cause. 'My husband gives at the office,' Fees's wife told him with a broad smile. The man thanked her profusely and left. She and her young daughter were soon evacuated, leaving Fees lonely and anxious to be posted somewhere else.

The occasion came in late 1973, when Secretary of State Kissinger asked him to open a new CIA station in Cairo. Kissinger was trying to convince Sadat to move Egypt out of the Soviet camp and into the American sphere of influence, hopefully making it the cornerstone of the US's Middle East policy.

Fees arrived in Cairo in early 1974. He and his family lived in a large detached house in the upscale suburb of Dokki. They had a full household staff, with a cook, maids, a gardener and a chauffeur who carried a gun at all times. 'I think I was very aware very young of danger and that we had to be careful, that we didn't talk to strangers, that we had guards and that kind of thing,' said Fees's daughter, Paula, who was then aged five. Her father was absent, working all the time – out in the field during the day, hosting dinners and cocktail parties most nights. 'There were a lot of American dignitaries, the senators, the congressmen, whoever, and they'd regularly come out on visits,' Paula said. 'That James Bond element of martinis and cocktail parties was very actual.'

Fees's official cover was 'special assistant to the ambassador' and his first assignment was to lay the groundwork for President Richard Nixon's official visit to Egypt in June 1974, dealing directly with the Egyptian head of intelligence (and Mossad double agent), Ashraf Marwan. Secretly, it was Yemen all over again: Fees was bribing and charming his way through. The CIA had agreed to provide Egypt with special assistance on sensitive matters, namely Sadat's private security. Back in 1986, Alexandra Johnson had told Gillman that the CIA was bribing Sadat to the tune of several million dollars. She was right: just for Sadat's personal security, the CIA was spending some $20 million a year and had contracted American anti-terrorism experts to train the President's 100 bodyguards. In charge of the programme was William 'Bill' Buckley, a close friend of Fees and his subordinate at the Cairo station, who later became CIA station chief in Beirut.

As well as flushing the Egyptian President with cash, the Americans had committed to giving Sadat everything he wanted. Marwan provided Fees with a long shopping list, which included encrypted car phones, special communications antennae that were installed on the high cliffs around Cairo, three brand-new Westland helicopters and, lastly, the most extravagant of requests: a Boeing 707, a perfect copy of the US President's Air Force One aircraft. Officially, Egypt was paying the US back. Unofficially, the money was coming from the CIA's main ally in the Middle East: Saudi Arabia. Kamal Adham, the enormously wealthy head of Saudi intelligence, had been bankrolling Sadat since before he became leader, while he was still Nasser's Vice-President. As Bob Woodward put it: 'It was impossible to determine where Saudi interests in these arrangements ended and American CIA interests began.'

When Gillman's source, Johnson, visited Egypt in 1974, she learned that Fees had recruited Sadat's national security adviser and presidential chief of staff, Mohammed Hafez Ismail. Fees also told her that he had detailed information about Soviet intelligence operations in Egypt.

Sadat had become worried that his villa in Giza had been bugged by the Soviets, who had their embassy nearby. The Egyptian security services lacked the latest technology to debug the residence, so Marwan asked for the CIA's help. Fees was reluctant at first: he worried that the Egyptians would suspect the CIA had used the opportunity to bug the villa themselves. But Marwan insisted, and the

CIA flew in a technician with all the necessary equipment, on the condition that he would be escorted at all times by officers of the Presidential Guard, so that there would be no room for accusations. Shortly after he started working, however, the Egyptian guards left the CIA's technician unattended, so he returned to the American Embassy. Marwan pleaded to have him back, but when he resumed work, the guards left him alone again. This time, the technician packed up and left the country for good. Marwan, who was not someone who easily admitted his own failures, told Sadat that the mission had been completed and no bugs had been found.

Marwan was just as fervent an anti-communist as his new American friend and the two met on an almost daily basis. Marwan showed his admiration for US culture by obtaining suitcases full of pirate American TV videotapes, impossible to find in Egypt, that he would put on during his meetings 'to fabricate a modern American atmosphere' for his guests. Fees reciprocated by bringing Marwan expensive Hermès neckties. (Years later, after his role as a double agent for Mossad was uncovered, Marwan died in mysterious circumstances in London, most likely assassinated by Egyptian spies.)

The Egyptians welcomed the gift-bearing Fees into their inner circles and he soon developed an excellent personal relationship with Sadat himself as well as with his Vice-President, Hosni Mubarak. 'Leaders like Sadat used the operations as a kind of wedge, as if the operations gave them a back door to the United States government, a way of skirting normal diplomatic channels and calling upon the CIA, seeking special information, favours, even money,' was how Bob Woodward described the arrangement. 'Broadly speaking, Sadat was an intelligence asset, not directly in the pay of the CIA, not in any sense under its control, but he had opened himself and his country, in his definition of their mutual self-interest, to the CIA. It was very much a two-way street. But it was dangerous, for both sides.'

It was not only cocktail parties and tuxedos. Some wanted Fees dead. In 1977, the CIA station chief in Tripoli, Libya, had come across detailed information showing that the Libyan dictator Muammar Gaddafi wanted to kill either the US ambassador in Cairo, Hermann Eilts, or chief-of-station Fees. 'They'd provided the names of the assassins and a lot of details,' Fees's daughter recalled. 'It was considered a valid threat.' Two bodyguards were sent to Cairo, one for Fees and one for his daughter. 'They were concerned that he might be difficult to get to and that they might decide to kidnap me instead,' she explained. Fees himself started carrying a gun.

'After some renewed practice at the Egyptian presidential guard shooting range, I carried a 9mm, sixteen-shot Browning automatic with me, 24/7, for six months, while worrying about the safety of my wife and my young daughter, who was in the French elementary school in Cairo,' Fees later wrote.

'Finally the Egyptians wanted this threat to end, lest it turned into a gunfight at the OK Corral, where a lot of innocent people could be killed in Cairo.' President Jimmy Carter, new in office, was told about it and he sent a letter to Gaddafi, hand-carried to the Libyan ambassador to the UN,

> with our basic intel about the plot, including the names and photos of the assassins. The letter said that if such a plot were executed the USA would be at war with Libya. Of course, in his response, Gaddafi rejected the whole matter as nonsense. And that was the end of it, thanks to good intelligence and the president's actions.

The most daring covert operation Fees was responsible for during his post in Egypt was the smuggling of a MiG-23. It was not the first time the CIA had tried to obtain a Soviet fighter jet. Two decades earlier, Fees's predecessor, Cairo station chief Eichelberger, had traded vital information with the newspaperman Mustafa Amin about MI6 plotting to assassinate Nasser. In exchange, according to Amin, the CIA wanted a MiG, but Nasser refused. During the late 1950s, Mossad had tried to pull the same trick. The Israelis recruited a Cairo-based Armenian named Jacques Leon Thomas, who set up a spy ring that included an agent in the Egyptian military. At one point, his paymasters asked him if he could recruit an Egyptian pilot to fly a MiG out of the country. The mission failed and in 1961, the Egyptians arrested Thomas along with his spies, seizing thousands of microfilm documents.

In the mid-1970s, the MiG-23 was one of the most sophisticated and arguably most mysterious fighter jets around. The Americans' information about the jet was almost non-existent. Fees, a keen aviator, started asking about the MiG shortly after he arrived in Cairo but received a flat no. Eventually, he managed to get into the graces of Mubarak, the Vice-President and a fellow keen pilot, and came up with a compromise: rather than the plane itself, perhaps they could get the aircraft's manual. Mubarak agreed and the CIA photographed the 1,000-page manual, shipping the photos to Langley. Then, Fees was able to convince the Egyptians to allow a US pilot to test-fly the jet. Chosen for the job was reportedly Richard Secord, a brigadier general stationed in Iran who was later implicated in the Iran–Contra scandal.

Ultimately, in September 1977, Sadat gave the green light for the 'extraction' mission. The man in charge of the operation was an air attaché in Cairo named Leroy 'Swede' Svendsen, who would become a lifelong friend of Fees.

'My first three years in Cairo, they told me it was impossible, but I never gave up,' Fees later said. Fees's daughter said that the MiG was smuggled out of the country on the day of her father's birthday, 21 September – a birthday gift to himself and so that he 'wouldn't forget it'.

Fees stayed in Egypt for nine months after the MiG operation, until June 1978, and as a reward for his achievements, he was offered the prestigious post of station chief in Tehran, Iran. 'He turned them down,' his daughter recalled. 'He said, "I'm too tired, my family has been through enough these last four years, I need an easy posting where I'd need not to worry about security and things, just for a couple of years." They said, "How about Geneva, Switzerland?"'

Having dodged the bullet of the Iranian Revolution in 1979, Fees was installed as chief of the sleepy CIA station in Geneva. Although they were positioned next to the United Nations headquarters, all the CIA officers cared about was when and where they would next go skiing. Fees, who did not ski, was more interested in producing intelligence and recruiting double agents, so he put his officers to work. But the agency, under the direction of Admiral Stansfield Turner, was changing and when it refused to approve the recruitment of a German woman with a close relationship to a senior KGB official, a 'disgusted' Fees thought it was time to quit. It was easier said than done. 'Being an ex-CIA officer is like being a hooker,' he later said. 'No one believes you stopped.'

After his retirement, Fees and his family decided to stay on in Geneva, but he and his wife separated. Fees became an associate of Kamal Adham, the former Saudi head of intelligence, who had a penchant for employing CIA veterans, like Raymond Close, a former chief of station in Jeddah, Saudi Arabia, and even, at one point, Sadat's wife, Jehan. Fees set up a 'consulting company' in Switzerland called Tradeco, through which he provided undisclosed advice to businesses in the Middle East and facilitated arms deals with a number of nations, including Egypt, now under the rule of his friend Mubarak. Not everyone was happy with Fees's successful business ventures. Some within the CIA resented the fact that he would use his agency contacts to enrich himself. 'We were supposed to be fighting communism, serving our country, not to become rich through the intelligence we'd gathered,' one retired CIA agent told Midolo years later.

In the 1980s, Fees's name and that of his firm, Tradeco, were thrown around in connection with the Iran–Contra scandal that was souring US President Ronald Reagan's second term. Curiously, the only reference to Fees that Midolo could find in the CIA archives was in a newspaper article published by the *New York Times* in February 1987. Fees, described as 'a former State Department official' and 'head of a Geneva consulting company, Tradeco', said that in 1983 he had been introduced by his old friend, now general, Swede Svendsen, to two French arms dealers who wanted to buy F-4 planes from Egypt, ostensibly for Paraguay but in reality intended for Iran. Fees told the *New York Times* that he had become 'suspicious and had broken off further contacts'. Svendsen, then a consultant to the Washington lobbying group Alcalde, Henderson, O'Bannon & Rousselot and head of a military consulting company in San Antonio, also told the newspaper that he had bailed out of a deal to sell the French arms dealers' tanks. 'I found out it was an Iranian thing, and I left.' (Svendsen died in 2022, aged ninety-three.)

Fees was destined to play another minor part in the Iran–Contra affair. In 1984, he was summoned to the White House in an effort to find where the terrorist organisation Hezbollah was holding a group of American hostages captured in Lebanon. Among them was Fees's deputy from Cairo, Bill Buckley. Fees asked one of his best Middle East sources to check whether the hostages were still in Lebanon or, as some officials believed, in Iran. Shortly after the kidnapping, the US government initiated a clandestine operation to sell weapons to Iran, which had been subject to an international embargo since the 1979 Tehran hostage crisis. The proceeds of the arms sale were used to fund the Contras, a right-wing paramilitary rebel group in Nicaragua. US officials thought the arms sales would convince Iran to plead with Hezbollah to release the American hostages in Lebanon.

The plan did not work: Buckley, among others, was tortured and eventually killed after more than a year of captivity.

Midolo could find very little information about what Fees had done in the 1990s. Perhaps, he speculated, after seeing his name and that of his company splashed in the *New York Times*, Fees had chosen to lie low for a while? What was certain was that he and his second wife did a lot of travelling, mainly between Brussels, where they were based for a time, and Hong Kong, where Tradeco had a subsidiary.

In 2000, Fees published his first novel, *Operation Hebron*, under the nom de plume Eric Jordan. Midolo found a hardcover copy of the book on Amazon for a few dollars. On the cover, he was surprised to find a drawing by a renowned Italian film poster artist, Renato Casaro. It was a retake of his poster for Luc Besson's *La Femme Nikita* from 1990: a woman garbed in a skimpy pink dress and black stockings holding a gun with a silencer, with a spot of red blood dripping over the White House and FBI insignia in the background. In the acknowledgements of the book, Fees thanked his 'good friend' Casaro.

Thanks to Quentin Tarantino, who had used him for his latest film, Casaro, then in his late eighties, was having something of a renaissance. Still living in his native town, Treviso, in north-east Italy, he told Midolo that he had met Fees at one of his poster exhibitions in Cannes in the late 1990s. 'He came to the exhibition and invited me over to dinner,' he recalled. The two became good friends, despite Fees's predilection for putting ketchup everywhere, including on pasta, which left the Italian artist horrified. 'He convinced me and my wife to move to Estepona, near Mallorca, and we were his neighbours for thirteen years.'

In Spain, Fees had somehow become associated with unsavoury characters. Two articles from the 1990s in *El País* linked him and his companies, including Tradeco and a company in Bermuda, Sierra

Nevada Holding, to the entrepreneur Javier de la Rosa. A self-made millionaire and financier, de la Rosa was arrested and charged with fraud and embezzlement in relation to a $400 million amusement park near Barcelona in 1994. He was later sentenced to three years in prison. Fees had been suspected of laundering money abroad for de la Rosa and, in late 1997, he was summoned by a Spanish judge but never charged with any crime.

There was one last whiff of the Cold War in Fees's biography during his book launch at the Cosmos Club in Washington in June 2000. Among the guests was the retired KGB general Oleg Kalugin, once chief of the Soviets' counter-intelligence directorate.

'He's not a friend of mine, but he's a friend of a friend,' Fees told the *Washington Post*. Fees must have been in a convivial mood that night. Introducing himself as 'the American James Bond', he said cheerfully that he was 'very happy that I'm finally going to meet General Kalugin'.

He was echoed by Kalugin: 'I am familiar with him and I'll be honoured to meet him.' The *Post*'s journalist then asked the two how they liked their martinis. Both answered that they liked them with gin, rather than vodka, and stirred, not shaken. 'My goodness,' Fees exclaimed, 'how times have changed!'

Times had changed to the point where mortal enemies like Fees and Kalugin could mingle merrily over cocktails in Washington. But certain things were not dead and buried and it would not be long before someone started posing Fees awkward questions about his time in Cairo. A couple of years later, the new editor of the *Sunday Times* Insight team knocked on the door of his villa in Spain and asked him what he knew about the murder of David Holden.

CHAPTER 18

RED AND LAVENDER

A concrete monolith overlooking a pond, the National Archives building in Kew, south-west London, makes for a striking contrast with the Royal Botanic Gardens and its colourful plants and flowers. The brutalist building, which serves as the official archives of the UK government, houses 11 million documents, including original copies of everything from Magna Carta to the Domesday Book, and the index can be searched online.

Midolo discovered that three folders from the Foreign Office regarding Holden's murder had recently been declassified. After passing airport-like security, he was handed the three folders, each with a different secrecy classification. The first, with a bright red jacket and marked 'secret', was titled: 'Death of David Holden (*Sunday Times* correspondent)'.

Midolo opened the thick dossier. The first page contained a note, also marked 'secret', written by a C. D. Powell from the Near East and North Africa Department at the Foreign and Commonwealth Office (FCO) on 21 December 1977. A quick internet search told Midolo that Charles Powell, later Lord Powell, had been first secretary to Washington before becoming private secretary to Margaret Thatcher in 1983. In the note, Powell asked 'to make a distinction between assistance to the *Sunday Times* in winding up Holden's affairs and help in putting together a journalistic story on the circumstances of his death'. Powell recommended that the FCO's press office speak to the *Sunday Times* 'at a high level to make sure they understand the distinction'.

Midolo was stunned by such a recommendation. Surely, he thought, they shared the same goal? Finding out who had committed the murder and why?

The following page detailed what had happened: John Barry had tried to send a message to the *Sunday Times* through the FCO, but one of the diplomats, a man named Morris, had refused to comply. Barry's message was that 'a past senior member of the Egyptian state security department had told Barry that, according to friends still in the department, the story was circulating among senior echelons of state security that Holden had been killed by the Egyptian police in the mistaken belief that he was David Hirst'.

In his note accompanying the story, Morris stated that passing messages to assist the Egyptian authorities in their investigation was one thing, but this was 'quite different' and 'that we do not wish to be involved'.

Morris continued:

> However, the story has now currency which will probably ensure its publication sooner or later. I do not think we should expose ourselves to the accusation by the *Sunday Times* that we tried to cover it up, but equally I think we should disengage ourselves from inquiries of their representatives if they are going to pursue this kind of line.

The remaining declassified dossiers contained bureaucratic exchanges regarding Holden's body and speculation about the motive behind his killing. The British police, a junior diplomat reported, seemed to have given up. 'To put it bluntly, Scotland Yard have no idea who killed Holden,' the diplomat wrote. Detective 'Small remarked rather thankfully that this was an Egyptian investigation'.

The diplomat's blunt verdict reflected the conclusions reached by the Yard team, Ray Small and his partner Tony Comben, in their final report. Their best bet was that the killing was 'a robbery that went wrong', arguing that Holden was the victim of a criminal group who both stole cars and carried out robberies. They felt that there was nothing in his activities during the preceding week that had contributed to his death – but, unlike the *Sunday Times*, they had not broadened their inquiries to encompass his whole life. Along the way, Comben later related, they had inquired whether Holden had been involved with British intelligence, and they believed the answer they received, namely 'No.'

In the dossiers Midolo was examining, there were renewed calls for the Foreign Office to distance itself from the *Sunday Times* inquiry, which sounded increasingly odd, given that the journalists were the only British investigators who were in Egypt. 'While you should continue to give their staff all appropriate help in winding up Holden's affairs,' one telegram from Jerusalem read, 'care should be taken to avoid associating [Her Majesty's government] with any speculation about the background to his death.'

The pink slip of paper included another interesting detail: it mentioned 'the line taken by Terry as reported in Jerusalem telegram', which would indicate 'the sort of conclusions' the Insight team may reach. That meant that Tony Terry, whom the newspaper had dispatched to Jerusalem during the initial week of Insight investigations in December 1977, was either letting the FCO know of the investigation's progress or his telegrams to the paper had been intercepted by MI6. In any case, the actions of Gillman and the rest of the team were closely monitored.

There was also a note which revealed that Evans's deputy, Frank Giles, had phoned the Foreign Office on 12 December to report that he had received a call from Arnaud de Borchgrave of *Newsweek* who was passing through London. De Borchgrave had been staying with King Hussein of Jordan, who had mentioned to him that he had received an intelligence report that 'a European terrorist group' was heading for the Middle East. Their purpose was to acquire journalists' credentials in order to get into press conferences to assassinate Sadat or one of his ministers. 'Hussein had taken the report sufficiently seriously to apply unusually strict security precautions when he himself gave a press conference in Amman a few days ago,' the cable read. 'De Borchgrave thought the *Sunday Times* should be aware of this, since it was just possibly the explanation for the murder of Holden.'

The cable said that Giles had commented that this 'seemed far-fetched' but 'anything was possible'. He thought it should be passed back to Cairo by secure means. So the Foreign Office was not inclined to help the *Sunday Times* with its investigation but the *Sunday Times*, through Giles, on the other hand seemed eager to provide assistance to the Foreign Office.

Arnaud de Borchgrave. Midolo remembered the name because he had read about him in one of the US diplomatic cables: de Borchgrave had told the same story to the US ambassador in Cairo, Hermann Eilts, just days after Holden's body had been identified. It was de Borchgrave, Midolo had found out, whose privacy the US Department of State was protecting in 2011, when it had decided to not declassify the cables about Holden's murder. De Borchgrave was still alive then; he had died, aged eighty-eight, in 2015.

The son of a Belgian count who was head of military intelligence for the Belgian government in exile during the Second World War, de Borchgrave had become a foreign correspondent for *Newsweek* and was close to the CIA – some believed he was on the agency payroll. Among them was the Egyptian President, Sadat. 'Kissinger told me that Sadat gave him a smile and said, "our mutual friend,

Arnaud de Borchgrave, works for the agency"', de Borchgrave related in an interview with the *Washington Post* in 1984. 'Kissinger said he had heard the story so many times that he investigated and he gave Sadat his word of honor that it wasn't true.'

De Borchgrave was also a 'close friend' of the former head of counter-intelligence at the CIA, James Angleton, with whom he had boozy lunches and, according to a confidential assessment Midolo found within the CIA archives, shared outlandish conspiracy theories about communist plots.

Was the terrorist scenario a deliberate attempt to put the inquiry off track? Gillman and Midolo agreed that it was highly likely that de Borchgrave was misleading the British authorities and his fellow journalists by pushing the terrorist theory.

As he walked out of the National Archives and into the summer sun still blazing in Kew Gardens, Midolo's head was awash with possibilities. Why was the Foreign Office determined not to help the *Sunday Times*? Was it afraid of what Insight might find, as had happened with Kim Philby ten years before?

Midolo decided to ask Roger Boyes, a veteran foreign correspondent at *The Times* who was now the paper's diplomatic editor. Midolo ambushed him by the vending machine in the office kitchen and Boyes, an affable, bespectacled man, always slightly dishevelled with his khaki shirts and beige trousers, told him he had been hired by Evans during his brief stint as editor of *The Times* in 1980, before Evans was sacked by Rupert Murdoch.

By then, Boyes had performed stints in Moscow and Bonn for Reuters and had avoided a Soviet 'honeytrap' with a woman in a hotel in Poland a couple of years earlier. Evans wanted to hire him as his Eastern Europe correspondent, but first he had an important question to ask: 'He got me into a room and asked me if I was "a friend"', Boyes recalled. 'I didn't understand him at first. Then he explained that he could not afford to have another foreign correspondent connected to the secret service after what had happened to Holden.'

Boyes gave Midolo a few names of older foreign correspondents who might help. 'Have you talked to Binyon?' he asked.

• • •

Michael Binyon was a legend at *The Times*. He had joined the paper more than half a century earlier, in 1971, and had become one of the most respected foreign correspondents in Britain, reporting first from the Middle East and then Moscow at the end of the Cold War. He had never met Holden, but he had been the first journalist to win the David Holden Award, in 1980, which the *Press Gazette* awarded to foreign reporters who wrote with flair. A tall, slender man in his late seventies, with youthful blue eyes and a cavernous voice, Binyon was now mostly writing leaders and obituaries. He was also rumoured in the office to be a spy. Over lunch, Midolo put the rumour to him. 'Oh no, I was never tapped on the shoulder,' Binyon replied, bursting into a roaring laughter. 'I think they just thought I talked too much.'

Yet Binyon, in his own words, seemed to have done 'everything right' for MI6 to recruit him. Cambridge-educated, he had moved to Lebanon as a young student in the early 1960s to learn Arabic. He enrolled in the Middle East Centre for Arab Studies (MECAS), a school nestled in the hills outside Beirut, in the village of Shemlan. The school, which had been set up in Jerusalem during the Second World War, had been relocated to Lebanon after the conflict and quickly nicknamed 'the British spy school' by locals.

When Binyon attended, it was routinely described in the Lebanese press as 'the biggest espionage centre in the Near East' and even as, rather poetically, 'a poisonous dagger in the heart of this beloved homeland'. George Blake was studying there in 1961 when he fell under suspicion of being a KGB mole, was summoned to London and arrested. Two years later, after Kim Philby's defection, the UK Embassy in Beirut had to issue a statement saying that Philby had never set foot in the school. 'It had regular Foreign Office people,' Binyon conceded, recalling that the director, Sir John Wilton, was a diplomat and later UK ambassador to Saudi Arabia. Binyon said the Lebanese 'were thinking that the school was training Brits to be spies in the Arab world, but in fact, quite a lot of people who were spying against Britain went there'. Binyon omitted to say that, of course, Blake was MI6 to begin with. 'I was in Beirut when Philby vanished,' Binyon recalled. 'I was only eighteen at the time and I couldn't understand what all the fuss was about, reading the newspapers about this journalist who had disappeared. There was immediate suspicion and it did seem very odd until he showed up in Moscow.'

After Lebanon, Binyon went to work for the British Council in Minsk, now capital of Belarus but then part of the USSR, where he learned Russian. 'I spent a year in Minsk, which is pretty grim. I was the first teacher they had.'

Upon his return, he was debriefed by what he thought was MI5. 'They never said exactly who they were,' Binyon said, 'but they sent me this letter, marked "private and confidential", saying, "You've been invited to come and have a talk, we think it would be very useful to hear your experiences in the Soviet Union." They wanted to know about the various people in Minsk, my Russian contacts, the other Western teachers and so on.'

One of his colleagues, a fellow teacher, was later compromised by the KGB. They took pictures of him sleeping with a male lover and he was expelled. Binyon said that the Soviets tried the *kompromat* on as many people as they could and gay individuals were the easiest of all, 'because a very large number of senior diplomats had messed around from time to time and you only needed one photograph'.

He continued: 'In those days, you'd be instantly dismissed from the Foreign Office if you were thought to be gay. That made them all very, very vulnerable. That's why the Russians particularly focused on them.'

Binyon left Minsk in 1968 and first applied for a job with the Foreign Office. 'I got through the exams and then asked myself, actually, do I really want to do that?' he said. 'I bumped into someone at a party who told me there was an opening at the *Times Educational Supplement*, the *TES*. I wrote to the editor out of the blue, putting the bait at the top: "Would you possibly have an opening for a Cambridge graduate who's just spent a year in the Soviet Union?"'

Binyon would go on to work for the paper for fifty years. Over long lunches near the office, Midolo used him as a sounding board for what he had found out about Holden, specifically his rapid rise within the ranks of *The Times*. Binyon agreed it was odd, as the rule was to spend at least two years working for regional newspapers or specialists' supplements, like the *TES*, before going to a national newspaper, as Holden had done. 'It was a closed shop,' Binyon said, and he told the story of another correspondent in Washington who had been recalled to London. 'The junior guy got into trouble. He was gay at a time when in Washington that was also big trouble.'

'Do you remember the guy's name?' Midolo asked.

'Oh yes, Woolley. Geoffrey Woolley. He was a wonderful man, fantastic guy, very suave. But he left Washington under a cloud and became an extremely good and long-serving letters editor for something like thirty years.'

Woolley had died in 2010, but his obituary in *The Times* reported that he was sent in 1948 by the foreign editor, Ralph Deakin, to Washington, where he covered Harry Truman's White House and the 1948 presidential election. In late 1952, Woolley returned to London, but the obit did not say why. 'He was withdrawn,' Binyon had said. 'He was not sacked. But he was caught with somebody in some place. It was very taboo and illegal back then.' It was only a couple of years before Holden had become *The Times*'s junior guy in Washington himself. Binyon was aware that Holden was gay or bisexual and asked Midolo: 'Was your chap, Holden, ever caught in flagrante?'

It was a good question. This was at the height of what historians dubbed the Lavender Scare, which led to a wide purge of gay employees across the US. Midolo knew about the Red Scare but was not aware of this persecution, which he learned was especially severe in the government and in the CIA in particular. 'Homosexuals must not be handling top-secret material,' Senator Joseph McCarthy, already behind the Red Scare, roared. 'The pervert is easy prey to the blackmailer.'

Since 1950, McCarthy, until then an obscure junior senator from Wisconsin, had launched a number of investigations of the State Department and the CIA, which he had accused of harbouring hundreds of communists in their ranks. A number of public hearings were set up, during one of which a government official testified that ninety-one gay State Department employees had been fired. In McCarthy's view, communism and homosexuality were interchangeable sins.

In January 1953, shortly after Woolley had left Washington, Allen W. Dulles was appointed head of the CIA. During one of the very first meetings he attended, the agency's head of security told him they had 'a serious problem'.

'Sir, six of the men you have brought over from OSS into the CIA are serious security risks,' the chief said. Dulles asked what made them security risks.

'Jesus, Allen, they are homosexuals,' a third intelligence adviser shouted. 'Just like goddamned Carmel Offie. I can assure you that if we know, the Soviets know. What the President is concerned about is, does McCarthy know? Because if he finds out, we have serious problems.'

Carmel Offie, an Italian-American from a humble family, was a brilliant CIA operative during the early days of the agency. He was the deputy to the head of clandestine service, Frank Wisner, and was in charge of a number of highly sensitive and secretive operations, including Operation Paperclip, which recruited and smuggled into the US thousands of German scientists and engineers, many of whom ended up working for the NASA space programmes.

'Offie was a world-class sophisticate who could put a stiletto in an opponent and offer him a treatise on the cognac he was serving him at the same time,' the CIA's counter-intelligence chief, Angleton, would later say of him. 'He was a master intriguer.'

Offie was also flamboyant and made no secret of his sexual orientation. He would boast that his bed was 'the playing fields of Eton'. In 1943, Offie was arrested for propositioning an undercover cop in Lafayette Park, across the street from the White House, but somehow managed to keep his job at the State Department. Six years later, while he was Wisner's deputy at the CIA, Offie got in trouble again: he hit on a US Army officer who immediately filed a complaint. An investigation was opened and Offie was forced to leave the agency, 'never to be rehired again'.

But Angleton, the counter-intelligence chief, went against the CIA director's orders and offered him a job. He told a friend that he wanted to use Offie 'in homo circles in Europe'. Offie knew that Angleton hated him and was surprised by the offer. Why would he do that? 'That's just the reason,' Angleton replied. 'No one would ever suspect.' (Offie refused the offer.)

Angleton himself was suspected of being gay. In December 1949, he had welcomed his old wartime friend – and mentor in the dark arts of counter-espionage – Kim Philby in Washington. Officially, Philby was first secretary at the British Embassy. Covertly, he was the MI6 man in charge of liaison with the American intelligence agencies, with Angleton as his chief point of contact within the CIA.

The two started having long lunches every week, eating lobsters and drinking heavily. A few months later, in the summer of 1950, Philby's old Cambridge friend and fellow KGB mole Guy Burgess arrived in Washington. Burgess, who had been recruited by MI6 while he was a BBC journalist, was even more flamboyant than Offie. He was staying, as a temporary guest, in Philby's house at 5100 Nebraska Avenue. One morning, one of their embassy colleagues showed up at the house unannounced and found Philby and Burgess in bed, dressed in bathrobes and drinking champagne. Philby introduced Burgess to Angleton and soon the three would play drunken games at the CIA spymaster's house. Angleton's daughter later recalled them 'chasing each other through the house in this little choo-choo train', screaming and laughing.

While Angleton was drinking with Philby and Burgess, the FBI was keeping a close eye on the Cambridge spies. Midolo had found top-secret memos to the FBI director, J. Edgar Hoover, now declassified, which noted that Burgess was 'homosexual', Donald Maclean 'reportedly homosexual' and Anthony Blunt 'notoriously homosexual'.

When, in May 1951, Burgess and Maclean defected to Moscow, tipped off by Philby, Angleton tried to cover for his friend, writing in a memo for the CIA heads that Philby was only guilty of being too fond of Burgess. But many within the CIA did not buy that. Bill Harvey, a former FBI agent then in charge of the CIA's electronic surveillance department, scrawled across Angleton's report: 'Where's the rest of the story?' Harvey confided to a colleague that he suspected that either Angleton and Philby were in a relationship or the two were such good friends that Angleton could not face the possibility that Philby was a Soviet double agent – which, of course, he was.

Philby was sent back to London where, over five months, he was interrogated and, according to some, admitted that he and Burgess were occasional lovers. He was fired from MI6 and returned to journalism, becoming the Middle Eastern correspondent for *The Observer* and *The Economist*.

Midolo realised that Holden was appointed to Washington at a time when, after the Burgess and Maclean defection, both the Red and Lavender Scares were at their height. The man who had recruited Holden was Donald Tyerman, the same editor who, only a year later, would hire Philby at *The Economist*. Tyerman, who had died aged seventy-three in 1981, had been affected by polio as a child and was forced to walk with sticks. He had started working at *The Economist* in 1936 and was effectively the magazine's editor during the war. His obit in *The Times* mentioned that he was also deputy editor at *The Observer* in 1943 and 1944, a detail that Midolo found odd. *The Observer* was the other newspaper that had hired Philby after his dismissal from MI6. Tyerman had joined *The Times* in 1944 as assistant editor and de facto deputy editor of the paper and stayed on for twelve years before returning to *The Economist* as its editor in 1956.

Midolo remembered that Tyerman had told the Insight team that he had recruited Holden on a whim, after the latter had written to him unannounced, saying that they had gone to the same school. It sounded far-fetched. In a column in 2004, the late journalist and editor Peregrine Worsthorne wrote that Tyerman had given him a very different response. 'In 1947, when I was out of the army, I wrote out of the blue to Donald Tyerman, deputy editor of *The Times*, saying that I was anxious to be a journalist,' Worsthorne wrote. 'He asked me to come in and we spoke about my ambitions; he said *The Times* wouldn't take me on until I'd spent at least two years in the provinces. So off I went to the *Glasgow Herald*. I made a note to write to him two years later, to the day, and he was impressed when I did, and gave me a job on the paper.'

Worsthorne described the late Tyerman as his 'mentor', but the column concluded with an unfortunate coda: 'Donald became editor of *The Economist* but it all ended in tears when he became an alcoholic.' Worsthorne wrote: 'He was asked to go on a [television] programme, but he arrived drunk and had to be faded out by the cameras. One of the newspapers the next day ran a cartoon saying "Econopissed".'

Worsthorne went on to serve as the newspaper's correspondent from Washington between 1950 and 1952 – Geoffrey Woolley was in fact his deputy. In 1953, Worsthorne left *The Times*, whose coverage jarred with his open support for Senator McCarthy's witch-hunt, for the more sympathetic *Telegraph*. The uber-conservative Worsthorne, like Holden, would end up writing for *Encounter*, the magazine bankrolled by the CIA and, Midolo was now not surprised to learn, directly controlled by its counter-intelligence chief, Angleton. Tellingly, Worsthorne held comparable views to Holden on Allende's government in Chile – at one point, he supported Pinochet's coup and called for a similar one in Britain. Tyerman himself was also writing regularly for *Encounter*. 'The latest issue of *Encounter* is quite like old times,' read a diary piece from *The Times* in 1972. 'No fewer than four of [Tyerman's] former protégés on *The Times*' appeared in the issue: Worsthorne, Holden, Morris and Henry Fairlie. Tyerman himself was quoted saying that Worsthorne had applied to join the paper 'but we told him to go away for a couple of years and get some experience on a provincial paper'. Yet Holden was not. Why? Because of his intelligence connections?

Who had plucked Holden out of the supplements and sent him to the US was the foreign editor, Iverach McDonald. A former MI6 officer had told Gillman that McDonald was 'an MI6 man' or 'at least did what MI6 wanted'. McDonald had died, aged ninety-eight, in 2006. His obituary in *The Times* revealed that in 1939, after the war broke out, he joined the Directorate of Military Intelligence, which both MI5 and MI6 were part of, where he worked for two years before returning to *The Times*.

McDonald was a Russian speaker and had visited the Soviet

Union many times in the 1930s. 'He came to know most of the Soviet and other communist leaders,' the obituary read. 'As a result, he had a deeper insight than most commentators on communist affairs.' McDonald appeared in the acknowledgements of a book, *Forty Thousand Against the Arctic: Russia's Polar Empire*, by Hans Peter Smolka, aka Peter Smollett, a former central Europe correspondent for *The Times* who went on to become head of the Russian section at Britain's Ministry of Information. Smolka was both a close friend of Philby and a Soviet double agent who had been recruited at the same time as Philby in Vienna in the 1930s. Smolka's identity as a KGB mole was not revealed until the 1990s. His book was a crass piece of propaganda that described Stalin's gulags as 'an idealistic experiment in social reform'. In the acknowledgements, he thanked 'Mr Iverach McDonald of *The Times* for acting as physician and surgeon to this book in its infancy'. Some suspected McDonald of being a KGB agent himself. Was this the reason he chose Holden, of all people, for the Washington correspondent job?

In 1955, as Holden arrived in Washington, Senator McCarthy's star was fading but McCarthyism would long outlive the senator, who died aged forty-eight in 1957, most likely due to alcoholism. The FBI, led by J. Edgar Hoover, continued the senator's witch-hunt of communists and gay individuals even after McCarthy had been shunned. Midolo found this a dark irony, as Hoover was gay and McCarthy himself probably was too. The FBI had a thick dossier of sexual assaults of young male soldiers allegedly perpetrated by McCarthy in the early 1950s.

Seven months after arriving in the US, Holden was mentioned in an FBI report dated 12 October 1955. The report was shared with the *Sunday Times* when the newspaper sued the bureau and the CIA for refusing to disclose files related to Holden. Other than the header ('Federal Bureau of Investigation'), the classification ('Confidential'), where the report originated from ('Washington DC') and the date, the entire file was blacked out. The only thing that was discernible was a handwritten note, 'DC VA Hungary', at the bottom of the page.

As noted previously, a source had told the Insight team that the report was the description of an 'observed meeting' between Holden and a 'known Soviet-bloc agent'. The same source had also revealed that Leo Silberman, Holden's lover, had an FBI file as well. It contained a visa application to visit the US, along with a recommendation from an FBI field officer that Silberman be 'investigated'. The file contained a note of Silberman's death in 1960, a detail which puzzled the source. He could not understand why the Bureau 'should know or care' that Silberman had died. One thing was certain: if Holden and Silberman had met during Holden's stay in Washington, the bureau would have known about it.

Normally, the files declassified by the FBI were published on the bureau's website in a section called 'The Vault'. Midolo searched for both Holden and Silberman but found no records. That meant that the files were still classified, almost seventy years after the facts. But there were a number of files relating to Silberman within the online CIA archive that had been declassified in 2015.

The first file, marked 'secret' and 'US officials only', was dated 9 December 1954. It was written by the deputy director of plans and addressed to the Secretary of State and marked for the attention of the director of the agency's office of security:

SUBJECT: SILBERMAN, LEO.
1. Reference is made to your BY memorandum VO/172, dated 18 November 1954, subject as above, whose name you desired checked against the files of this office.
2. The files of this office reflect the following information concerning the subject of your request.
3. A report dated 30 June 1952...

The rest of the file was still redacted and blanked out, while the original 1952 report mentioned was, for some reason, not included in the batch of declassified files.

Midolo noticed the date: 1952. This was at the time when Silberman was a lecturer at Northwestern University, Illinois, where he claimed he had met Holden. But Gillman knew from Silberman's brother that that was not true: they had met in London at least two years earlier. Somehow, they did not want to let people know that. In the summer of 1952, Holden was still a student at Northwestern, but in early 1953, he would leave the university to go on his Mexico trip with Silberman.

By the time the follow-up report had been written, in December 1954, Silberman had left Northwestern. He and Holden had been to Mexico together in the spring of 1953. Holden had joined *The Times* the following year and within three months was in Washington, while Silberman was applying to the University of Chicago.

There was a four-year gap in the CIA files. The remaining ones were from 1958. One memorandum was titled: 'Activities of Dr Leo Silberman in Somalia'. Once again, the files were heavily redacted, but Midolo could read between the lines. At some point in the spring of 1958, a CIA field officer in East Africa had asked his superiors at the agency for information on Silberman. Langley had sent back a dossier patched together through 'sources, State Department files and [REDACTED]...' – most likely FBI files.

The file included a physical description of Silberman: 'short, dark complexion, black hair, fast talker, and is regarded as a "smooth operator"'. He was also described by another source as 'glib, slick, quick-tongued, fast talker, and creates impressions which are not true'. The memo went on to note that Silberman's mailing address was at Balliol College in Oxford, England. The CIA had even made the effort to confirm whether he was indeed associated with Oxford – he was not:

[REDACTED] serious doubts of his alleged connection with Oxford. [REDACTED] Silberman notified [REDACTED] that he had been awarded a grant by the Carnegie Endowment for International Peace. He said that this grant was in the amount of eleven thousand dollars and was for the purpose of making a study of the Somali–Ethiopia Border Dispute. [REDACTED].

The memo specified that the Carnegie Foundation did not award grants, 'since it is a pension organization for teachers'. The innuendo was that Silberman must have got that sum through other means. It was not pocket money. Adjusted for today's inflation, it amounted to more than $117,000. Quite a sum to write an academic paper on 'the Somali–Ethiopia border dispute'.

Other miscellaneous information on Silberman listed that 'he was associated with the Free French during World War II; he has connections in the British Airline Industry; that he is a pilot, a sociologist, and a statistician.' Another report stated that there was 'reason to believe he is an impostor'.

'Because subject's source of funds and true mission are unclear,' the last dispatch read, 'we are forwarding the information as received without attempting to distil or analyse it. We felt that any conclusions we might draw would be misleading. We do know that Subject is "slick" – probably to the point of misrepresenting himself, and we do not discount [REDACTED].'

They did not discount that Silberman was in fact a KGB spy?

Midolo shared his findings with Gillman, who, in the meantime, had received a tantalising message from an old contact of his. Dominic Hipkins, a journalist with whom he had worked on a project years and years earlier, had emailed him out of the blue.

Dear Peter,
    I hope this finds you well. I'm getting in touch regarding the

David Holden case as I remember your interest during our conversations in the Czech Republic.

I've been doing research the last few years in the archives of the Czech Security Services in Prague and quite by chance I came across this reference to a 'David Holden' which mentions MI6. I understand there was some speculation he was involved in that area prior to his unfortunate death.

This page is dated 1979 which I'm aware is two years following his assassination. I did conduct a detailed search for Holden with his name and date of birth after coming across this reference, but I'm afraid this did not yield any further trace. I know you've invested a lot of time investigating this case so wanted to share this information in confidence, however slight it may appear.

The timing of the message was remarkable, even more so considering the fact that the two had not been in touch for years and Hipkins did not know that Gillman was back on the case. Attached to the email was a single-page document marked London, 16 October 1979. The document, in Czech, was a list of names, the first of which was 'Holden, David'. Next to it, two words that did not open up to interpretation: 'agent MI6'.

CHAPTER 19

THE MOCKINGBIRDS

The voice had a nasal intonation, a light twang of a mid-Atlantic accent and a slight lisp. At times, it would pause, and the reporter on the other side of the receiver could hear the hiss of a cigarette being furiously drawn in. The plummy voice introduced itself as James Jesus Angleton.

Upon hearing the name, the reporter, Joseph Trento, tried not to gasp. He knew it well. Angleton had been the former head of counter-espionage at the CIA for more than twenty-five years. Nicknamed 'the ghost', he was a living legend in espionage circles. A man of many talents, Angleton was a poet, a fly-fisherman, an orchid-grower, a lover of exotic teas and a complete paranoid whose decades-long hunt for a KGB mole within the CIA had devastated the agency. It was Angleton who first used the expression 'wilderness of mirrors' to describe the world of espionage and counter-espionage and, in particular, of KGB deception operations, taking a line from his favourite poem, 'Gerontion' by T. S. Eliot.

After his retirement, Angleton had become a public figure. His black and white portrait by the photographer Richard Avedon had appeared in *Rolling Stone* magazine a year earlier and a profile in *Newsweek* noted, aptly, that 'if John le Carré and Graham Greene had collaborated on a superspy, the result might have been James Jesus Angleton'.

Angleton said he wanted to discuss an article Trento had written a few weeks before. The piece, published by the magazine *Penthouse* in September 1977, was titled 'The spies who came in from the newsroom' and reported how an American news organisation named Copley Press, which published some nine local newspapers in California and Illinois, had at least twenty-three intelligence agents from the CIA masquerading as reporters on its payroll. 'The agency's involvement with the Copley organisation is so extensive that it's almost impossible to sort out,' a CIA official had told Trento. In his piece, Trento revealed that almost 200 American journalists had CIA connections.

'My holes in that article were what prompted Angleton to contact me,' Trento told Midolo over the phone, when he reached him at his home in Florida in April 2022. 'He wanted to know what I knew.' It was the beginning of a relationship that lasted until Angleton's death in 1987.

'He was out of the CIA at that point; he'd been fired by Colby,' Trento explained. 'There was an investigation on Angleton and his activities as head of counter-intelligence that had been going on for some time. The molehunt, the use of defectors et cetera.'

A second-generation Italian-American, Trento was born in Los Angeles in 1947. His father, Tom Adamo Trento, was from Midolo's hometown, Messina, Sicily. In 1968, aged twenty-one, Joe Trento started his career working with the renowned investigative reporter Jack Anderson. In 1972, Anderson was the target of an assassination plot by the White House and the CIA, but the plot was aborted when the conspirators were arrested for the Watergate break-in. Trento went on to work for CNN's investigative unit and as a consultant for *60 Minutes* and *Nightline*. He later authored several books on the CIA.

What Trento did not know at the time of that phone call was

that after Angleton's retirement, he had started 'running' journalists just as he had once run agents in the field. 'To paraphrase Mark Twain, listening to Angleton for a half-hour could make you dizzy,' Loch Johnson, a professor of intelligence history at the University of Georgia who also used to have lunch with Angleton, later said. 'Listening to him for a whole hour could make you drunk.'

Midolo asked Trento why, if Angleton was so eager to talk to reporters back then, he had refused to talk to the Insight team investigating Holden's murder in 1978. Trento speculated that there could have been two reasons why Angleton had decided to keep shtum.

The first was that Angleton had just been embroiled in the investigation over the death of a CIA employee named John Arthur Paisley. In September 1978, an unmanned sailboat had run aground on the shore of the Chesapeake Bay with, in its cabin, a trove of papers marked 'top secret' and a phone directory of the CIA. The boat's owner turned out to be Paisley, later described by the agency as a 'low-level analyst'. A week later, a corpse was discovered floating in the bay, with a gunshot wound to his head and a weighted dive belt around his waist. It was identified by the agency's chief medical examiner as Paisley. Cause of death: suicide.

Trento was one of the first reporters to find out that Paisley was not a 'low-level analyst', as the CIA had claimed, but rather a top strategic expert for the agency. What's more, the body that had been recovered did not match Paisley's physical description, but it was cremated before his family could see it. The incident, however, occurred in September 1978 and Midolo told Trento that Angleton had been contacted by Insight before then, at some point in the spring of that year.

The second explanation was that Angleton, who had been in charge of recruiting both foreign journalists and gay men as CIA assets and was controlling *Encounter* magazine, probably knew a lot about the Holden affair and did not want to talk about it.

By a freak coincidence, at the time Holden was killed in Cairo, the US press was being rocked by allegations about the ultra-secret relationships between the CIA and journalists. Trento's article in 1977 had been the first of a series that year exposing how much the lines were blurred between the two professions. It was followed up, less than two months later, by a piece in *Rolling Stone* magazine by Carl Bernstein.

Titled 'The CIA and the Media', the 25,000-word cover story detailed how media organisations worked 'hand in glove' with the CIA. 'The use of journalists was among the CIA's most sensitive undertakings,' Bernstein wrote, 'with full knowledge restricted to the Director of Central Intelligence and a few of his chosen deputies.' Journalists had been among the most productive means of intelligence-gathering employed by the CIA.

The relationship dated from the early days of the agency in the early 1950s, when Allen Dulles was CIA director. Dulles sought to establish a recruiting-and-cover capability within America's most prestigious institutions, where journalism was used as a cover for spying activities. 'By operating under the guise of accredited news correspondents, Dulles believed, CIA operatives abroad would be accorded a degree of access and freedom of movement unobtainable under almost any other type of cover,' Bernstein wrote. The inquisitive nature of a reporter's job, their access and their ability to ask questions without arousing suspicion made journalistic cover ideal. In the 1950s, the CIA ran a formal training programme to teach its agents to work as journalists, even telling them how to 'make noises like reporters'.

Bernstein revealed how many American and European publishers were willing to commit resources to the struggle against the communist threat. The idea was devastating: contrary to the common notion that the CIA insidiously infiltrated the journalistic community, there was ample evidence that publishers and news executives allowed themselves and their organisations 'to become handmaidens to the intelligence services'. Some twenty-five media organisations in the US were known to have provided cover for the agency, including the *New York Times*, *Time*, *Life* and *Newsweek* magazines and the CBS.

The secrecy was essential. Dulles was fearful of what would have happened if a journalist/agent's cover was blown. As a result, contacts with the heads of the news services were initiated in person by Dulles and his successors or by the deputy directors and division chiefs in charge of covert operations. All work by journalists fell under that category, covert or black ops, rather than foreign intelligence. One senator described it as 'the highest, most sensitive covert program of all' for the agency.

Few American agents were 'spies' in the popular sense of the term. '"Spying" – the acquisition of secrets from a foreign government – is almost always done by foreign nationals who have been recruited by the CIA and are under CIA control in their own countries,' Bernstein wrote, adding that the primary role of an American working undercover abroad is often to aid in the recruitment and 'handling' of foreign nationals who are channels for secret information to reach American intelligence. Journalists – foreign journalists in particular – were therefore invaluable to CIA agents posted abroad and Bernstein's sources said that some of them had 'the reputation of being among the best' in the business.

An unnamed CIA official quoted in the article said: 'After a foreigner is recruited, a case officer often has to stay in the background. So you use a journalist to carry messages to and from both parties.' A journalist, the CIA official noted, had the opportunity to form long-term personal relationships with sources and 'is in a position to make correct judgments about the susceptibility and availability of foreign nationals for recruitment as spies'.

Bernstein wrote that the tasks they performed sometimes

consisted of little more than serving as 'eyes and ears' for the CIA; reporting on what they had seen or overheard in an Eastern European factory, at a diplomatic reception in Bonn, on the perimeter of a military base in Portugal.

On other occasions, their assignments were more complex: planting subtly concocted pieces of misinformation; hosting parties or receptions designed to bring together American agents and foreign spies; serving up "black" propaganda to leading foreign journalists at lunch or dinner; providing their hotel rooms or bureau offices as "drops" for highly sensitive information moving to and from foreign agents; conveying instructions and dollars to CIA-controlled members of foreign governments.

Midolo was intrigued to see so many parallels between Insight's findings on Holden and Bernstein's investigation. From Holden's famous dinner parties to his uncanny ability to find himself in the right place at the right time, to the pieces of crass anti-Soviet propaganda he'd written for the CIA-controlled *Encounter* magazine. In his article, Bernstein described how reporters were used extensively in the CIA offensive against Salvador Allende in Chile: 'They provided funds to Allende's opponents and wrote anti-Allende propaganda for CIA proprietary publications.' Holden, of course, had done that both for the *Sunday Times* and, in much more vicious terms, for *Encounter*.

Bernstein provided only a few names in his piece. 'It was not something American publishers and journalists wanted to hear, for obvious reasons,' Bernstein told Midolo more than forty-five years later. The Pulitzer Prize winner wrote that the CIA considered C. L. Sulzberger, the *New York Times* leading foreign correspondent in the 1940s and '50s, 'an asset'. Bernstein reported that on one occasion, the agency gave him a briefing paper that ran 'almost verbatim' under the correspondent's byline in the *New York Times* (Sulzberger denied it).

Around the same time, another of America's best-known reporters, Joseph Alsop, went to cover a local election in the Philippines at the request of the CIA. Bernstein argued that, if many CIA officials regarded these helpful journalists as actual operatives, the journalists often tended to see themselves as mere 'friends' of the agency who performed occasional favours in the national interest. 'I'm proud they asked me and proud to have done it,' Alsop told Bernstein. Others, like Alsop's brother Stewart, also a journalist, were flatly 'CIA agents' formally recruited by the agency. They would prove particularly helpful to the CIA in discussions with foreign governments, 'asking questions to which the CIA was seeking answers, planting misinformation advantageous to American policy, assessing opportunities for CIA recruitment of well-placed foreigners.'

In his 1978 memoir, *Honourable Men: My Life in the CIA*, the agency's director William Colby described how he had hired a journalist on the staff of a technical publication 'whose management was patriotic enough to allow the use of their name by CIA'.

'As an inquiring reporter, he could go into circles and ask questions that would certainly not be appropriate for an embassy officer such as myself to do, and in the process he could "spot" likely candidates to help CIA's operations,' Colby explained.

According to Bernstein, Colby did all he could to prevent the truth about these journalist 'helpers' from coming out. In 1976, during the investigation of the CIA clandestine operations by the Senate Intelligence Committee led by Frank Church, 'the dimensions of the Agency's involvement with the press became apparent', Bernstein wrote. But Colby first and, later, his successor as CIA director, George H. W. Bush, managed to persuade the committee 'to restrict its inquiry into the matter and to deliberately misrepresent the actual scope of the activities in its final report'. Colby was quoted telling the Church committee's investigators: 'Let's not pick on some poor reporters, for God's sake! Let's go to the managements. They were witting.'

The Church committee final report, however, did include nine pages on the agency's use of journalists. The committee concluded: 'The CIA currently maintains a network of several hundred foreign individuals around the world who provide intelligence for the CIA and at times attempt to influence opinion through the use of covert propaganda.'

The CIA's use of journalists continued virtually unabated until 1973, when information about such practices started to leak, and Colby scaled down the programme. Publicly, the CIA director was trying to minimise the whole affair. But behind the scenes, Colby was throwing a protective cloak around his journalistic assets. 'He ordered his deputies to maintain Agency ties with its best journalist contacts while severing formal relationships with many regarded as inactive, relatively unproductive or only marginally important,' Bernstein wrote. 'In reviewing Agency files to comply with Colby's directive, officials found that many journalists had not performed useful functions for the CIA in years. Such relationships, perhaps as many as a hundred, were terminated between 1973 and 1976.'

Was this the reason why Holden was so keen to report from the Middle East for the *New York Times*? To resume his contacts with the CIA? On the face of it, the *Sunday Times* did not have a formal relationship with the CIA, but the *New York Times* did. Were the meetings Holden had with so many people close to the agency in Syria, Jerusalem and Jordan to that effect?

Bernstein's investigation contained one last chilling detail: 'James Angleton, who was recently removed as the Agency's head of counter-intelligence operations, ran a completely independent group of journalist-operatives who performed sensitive and frequently dangerous assignments,' Bernstein wrote. 'Little is known about this group for the simple reason that Angleton deliberately kept only the vaguest of files.' Upon reading that, Midolo sat bolt upright in his chair. This was Angleton, who had been in control of *Encounter* magazine and as such most likely knew Holden; Angleton, who was inviting dozens of reporters to lunch but would shut the Insight team down completely when they asked him if he knew anything about Holden.

The scandal of the CIA's relationship with the press raged for months. Bernstein's reportage was followed by a three-part series by the *New York Times*, published only two weeks after Holden's death, in December 1977. In some regards, the series went even further than the stories by Trento and Bernstein, detailing how the CIA had been using news organisations and book publishers for three decades in an effort to shape public opinion, including through the use of 'black propaganda'.

One CIA official told the *New York Times* that such relationships were entered into with promises of 'eternal confidentiality' and that the agency would continue to refuse to discuss them 'in perpetuity'. Bernstein had also written that CIA officials almost always refused to divulge the names of journalists who had cooperated with the agency. That was still true forty-five years later.

On a dark November evening, Midolo received an email from a CIA employee asking him to call them back. A month earlier, he had emailed the CIA press office inquiring if they could help him find the answer to an old Freedom of Information (FOI) request that had been filed in 2002. The CIA FOI log, which listed all requests sent to the agency, showed that someone had asked the CIA for 'information held about David Shipley Holden and Leo Silberman' – and the log said that the request had been partly granted. Midolo did not know who had sent the request, but his idea was that it would have been easier to obtain the information that way, rather than file a fresh request that the CIA could have taken years to respond to.

When Midolo called back, the employee, who introduced themselves with their first name only, said that they had been able to do some research on the matter but wanted to discuss it 'off the record'.

'Sure,' Midolo said.

'I would really steer you off the idea that the CIA had anything to do with David Holden.'

Midolo was thunderstruck. It was an answer to a question he had not asked. It made him think of a Latin expression: *'Excusatio non petita, accusatio manifesta.'* An excuse that has not been sought is an obvious self-accusation. What did they mean by that? That the agency had nothing to do with Holden's murder? For a second, he did not know what to say. There was an awkward silence.

'What do you mean "anything to do" with Holden?' he asked.

'I... I mean...' Silence. They were weighing their words. 'I have no reason to believe there is anything in our holdings about David Holden.'

Now that was a different matter and Midolo knew that it was simply not true. What's more, it did not make any sense: in 1978, the CIA had initially denied it had a file on Holden. Eventually, however, it had admitted a file existed, but the contents would not be shared. The *Sunday Times* had sued the CIA and a judge had gone to inspect the files but had opted not to release them. Midolo explained all that to the agency employee.

'What you are telling me now is at odds with the history of this case,' Midolo said, trying to be diplomatic.

'I'm afraid I don't have any guidance to offer you.'

Another non-answer. The conversation was more and more absurd – and spooky, too. After some pushing, Midolo managed to get another statement off them.

'You found the press clippings, which were just that, just press clippings of current events,' the employee said. 'But I have no reason to believe you would find anything else.'

That was something else entirely. Midolo knew that there was nothing else to find in the CIA archive available on the web, which was precisely why he had asked the CIA for assistance for files that were *not* on the website. He had asked for files that had been declassified or released after a FOI request two decades before.

'Sometimes there is declassified material or resources that we can point people to, but not in this case, unfortunately,' the employee added.

What about Silberman? They had ignored him completely. The employee replied that they had focused on Holden because Midolo had said in his email that he had found some information about Silberman on the CIA's website. There was nothing else. Yet the employee was saying that there was nothing at all about Holden, which was impossible.

'I'm steering you off the idea that Holden had an association with the CIA,' they repeated. 'And that is off the record.'

But what did they mean by 'association'?

'If you think about all of the different people who have relationships of different types with your news outlet, with *The Times*,' they said, at last opening up slightly. 'You've got people who are employees, you've got people who are contractors, people who are contacts, right? People have all sorts of different relationships with an organisation. And lots of those relationships leave paper trails behind them. So... any sort of affiliation would leave a paper trail behind. That's the only way we have to trace something like this going back to the 1970s.'

'The 1970s? What about the 1950s?' Midolo asked, adding that the suspicion, after the original *Sunday Times* investigation, was that Holden had been recruited much earlier, when he was a student at Northwestern University.

The employee let out a long sigh. 'Let's see.' Midolo could hear them typing for a few seconds, but the typing soon stopped. 'I'm afraid... I have no reason to believe... And I can provide you with no guidance.'

If the idea, as the employee had said, was to steer him away from the CIA, they had failed spectacularly. Midolo kept searching for clues that could connect Holden to the agency. When it came to the works of the CIA, it was hard to separate fact from fiction and a lot could be dismissed as rumours and conspiracy theories.

Midolo learned that, over the years, the CIA's use of reporters had erroneously become known as 'Operation Mockingbird' and the journalists who had helped the agency were dubbed 'the mockingbirds'. The confusion was likely due to a reference within the 'Family Jewels', a report detailing illegal activities conducted by the CIA that was revealed on the *New York Times*'s front page by Seymour Hersh in December 1974. The article, which came just four months after Nixon had resigned in the wake of the Watergate scandal, detailed how Kissinger had authorised the CIA to conduct a massive, illegal domestic surveillance operation of dissidents and war activists that also included the wiretapping of journalists.

Dubbed by Colby 'the skeletons in the CIA's closet' and considered one of the agency's darkest secrets, the Family Jewels list had been commissioned by the CIA's director when Watergate was raging. The complete list, detailing operations from 1959 to 1973, included assassination plots and the use of psychoactive drugs on unwitting subjects. Totalling almost 700 pages, it was eventually released in 2007.

The second entry on the sanitised list was titled 'Project Mockingbird'. It read: 'During the period from 12 March 1963 to 15 June 1963, this Office installed telephone taps on two Washington-based newsmen who were suspected of disclosing classified information obtained from a variety of governmental and congressional sources.'

The two journalists were later revealed to be Robert S. Allen and Paul Scott. Other journalists who had been targeted by the CIA included the national security reporter for the *New York Times*, Hanson Baldwin. A secretly recorded conversation in the Oval Office in 1962 revealed that the President, J. F. Kennedy, had asked the CIA to spy on Baldwin to find out about his sources. The latter had angered the President with an article in the *New York Times* that summer that divulged classified information.

Project Mockingbird, the CIA's illegal wiretapping of journalists, and Operation Mockingbird, the use of journalists by the CIA, were conflated. The result, the erroneous idea that the CIA bribed thousands of journalists to deliberately publish fake news, festered on online forums and went on to add fuel to the explosive – and completely bogus – QAnon conspiracy theory and far-right political movement. The reality was sinister enough and put the lives of countless journalists abroad in danger.

It was not confined to the US. Midolo was about to learn that the UK, too, had had its fair share of mockingbirds, including the father of the most famous spy in the world.

CHAPTER 20

ON HER MAJESTY'S SECRET SERVICE

The living room in Midolo's flat was looking increasingly like Gillman's. Gillman had warned him that the Holden case would consume him, if he allowed it to, just as it had consumed him and Harold Evans for so long. Now, Midolo understood what he meant. His apartment was scattered with tall piles of books about the Cold War, memoirs and biographies of journalists and spies, and photocopies of documents from the archives of intelligence agencies in the UK or the US, marked 'top secret', 'confidential' and 'for your eyes only'. But the biggest pile was of printouts of old articles, clippings that had been lost in the haze of the past and that historians had overlooked.

One of them related how, on 18 December 1968, the Soviet news agency TASS held a press conference for foreign correspondents in Moscow. Among them were British correspondents from *The Times* and the *Daily Telegraph*. TASS told them that Soviet newspapers would start publishing articles detailing the 'carefully masked connections' between MI6 and British journalists. Three days later, *The Times* relayed the story under the headline: 'Russia accuses Fleet Street'. The Soviets, the article read, were releasing documents 'to demonstrate the existence of sinister links between Fleet Street and the British secret service and to establish that Britain's free press is a myth'.

Izvestia, the Russian daily that published the documents, claimed that 'secret service men are to be found in the sedate *Sunday Times* and the brash *People*. They control scientific publications in London as well as provincial newspapers.' The Soviet newspaper published a list of 'Special Operational' journalists/agents, each with their own codename, alongside their 'handlers' from MI6. Some of the names included: Arthur 'Lord Arran' Gore from the *Daily Mail*, aka BIN-1153, tasked to recruit 'foreign representatives of the newspaper'; Michael Berry, the owner of the *Daily Telegraph*, aka BIN-943; Lord David Astor, Mark Arnold-Forster, Wayland Young and Edward Crankshaw at *The Observer*; Henry Brandon from the *Sunday Times*; and Brian Crozier of *The Economist*.

The Times's report was fundamentally a long list of denials from the people mentioned and their associates, the most tongue in cheek of which was Lord Arran's: 'Of course I am a secret agent, a triple agent. I am delighted at this recognition at long last.' In a more serious (and boasting) tone, the *Sunday Times*'s Washington correspondent, Brandon, elaborated that the Soviet press had always 'found it difficult to understand' that the British press or British foreign correspondents work independently of their government. 'It simply assumes that what applies to Soviet foreign correspondents must also be true of British foreign correspondents.'

The 'absurd story', as *The Guardian* labelled it, caused a 'great deal of amusement in Fleet Street and the Foreign Office' and was quickly dismissed as Red propaganda. It would take forty-five years for the truth to come out. In 2013, an investigation by the BBC's Radio 4 found that the top-secret documents were genuine. They had likely been passed on to the Soviets by George Blake, who in the late 1950s was recruiting journalists on MI6's behalf.

Radio 4 had found a redacted memo in the BBC archives from

1969, which expressed sympathy for '"friends" caught up in the scandal'. Those kinds of friends. 'It doesn't surprise me,' Phillip Knightley told the BBC. 'I had heard these names before bandied around on Fleet Street. I don't think [the memos] are forged, what would be the point? They are just telling the truth.' Knightley added that it was well known in the *Sunday Times* office that Brandon worked for MI6 and that before the foreign editor of the *Daily Mail* sent a correspondent abroad, he would 'arrange a briefing for him, or her, by MI6'.

A *Sunday Times* veteran and member of the Insight team for many years – as well as the man who had cracked the Philby case – Knightley knew a thing or two about hacks and spooks. In 2006, he was one of the first to expose the collusion between journalists and the British intelligence services. His direct experience was that MI5 and MI6 had penetrated the media extensively and had 'agents in most newspaper offices'. (Knightley died, aged eighty-seven, in 2016.)

One of the most important links between the British press and the Secret Intelligence Service (SIS) after the Second World War was Kemsley Newspapers, which owned the *Sunday Times*, among other titles. Founded by the press baron James Gomer Berry, later Viscount Kemsley, the group's international news agency, the Kemsley Imperial and Foreign Service, provided journalistic cover to MI6 officers working abroad. Best known by its cable address, Mercury, the network was run by Ian Fleming and hired many 'former' intelligence officers and dispatched them across the world.

Anthony Cavendish, a former MI6 officer whose memoir *Inside Intelligence* the British secret services tried to prevent from being published, wrote in 1987 that at the end of the war, a number of MI6 agents were sent abroad under the cover of newspaper men. 'Indeed the Kemsley Press allowed many of their foreign correspondents to cooperate with MI6 and even took on MI6 operatives as foreign correspondents.' Cavendish had elaborated on that in an interview with Gillman in 1989. 'Kemsley was very keen on this because it gave him unrivalled foreign coverage and made the coverage very cheap.' At its height, Cavendish estimated, MI6 agents accounted for 40 per cent of the *Sunday Times* foreign staff.

Fleming, who himself was a former naval intelligence officer, ran the correspondents as agents in the field, instructing them to produce 'situation reports' ('sitreps') about their activities in their part of the world. Unusually for a group of foreign correspondents, the sitreps were not for publication.

'Fleming sent Cedric Salter of Special Operations Executive (Second World War secret army) to Barcelona, Ian Colvin (who had close links to the SIS) to Berlin and Henry Brandon, an "SIS asset" from central Europe to Washington,' Knightley wrote. 'Donald McCormick, formerly of Naval Intelligence, became Mercury's stringer in Tangier and later foreign manager of the *Sunday Times*. The link between journalism and spying was largely "old boy" and informal but sometimes Mercury produced important "scoops" for British intelligence.'

Two other spooks in Mercury were Richard Hughes, the *Sunday Times* correspondent in the Far East (the journalist behind the idea of organising a press conference in Moscow with the defectors Burgess and Maclean in 1956); and Tony Terry, later the *Sunday Times* correspondent in Vienna, Berlin and Bonn, who had worked for Fleming as a roving 'correspondent' in Europe.

Terry was the man Evans had sent to Jerusalem during the original Holden investigation and who was likely sharing his findings with the Foreign Office. A quick search confirmed that Terry had died some thirty years earlier, in 1992, but his stepdaughter, Judith Lenart, had published a book about him back in 2007. The book, with the peculiar title *Berlin to Bond and Beyond: The Story of a Fleming Man*, told an incredible story.

Terry had been Lenart's mother's third husband. When he died, aged seventy-nine, at his home in Wellington, New Zealand, Lenart sat at his desk to make funeral arrangements and noticed a file marked 'Fleming'. Curious, she opened the folder and found a thick collection of letters between Ian Fleming and Terry, from 1949 until the former's death in 1964.

'Reading through this', she wrote, 'was the beginning of a journey into Antony's past and persona, a journey made difficult by the secret nature of that past, the fact he had no children or close relatives, and by Antony's determination to leave no trace or trail to follow.'

To Midolo, now deep into the intrigues of Holden's double life, it all sounded wearily familiar.

• • •

Antony Terry was born in north London in 1913. His father had been a captain in the 7th Hussars who served in the Boer Wars and later worked in the British Embassy in Berlin (most likely, according to Lenart, as a spy) in the 1920s. Terry grew up trilingual in English, German and French.

Lenart believed that Terry had been recruited by the British intelligence service in 1932, given a PR front and sent undercover, thanks to his fluency in German. He joined the Intelligence Centre as a junior officer in 1940 and started training in the interrogation of German soldiers. The following year, he assumed a fake German identity and was planted among high-ranking German prisoners. In March 1942, he took part in Operation Chariot, an attack by British commandos on a German/French U-boat submarine base in Normandy. He was captured by the Nazis and spent three years in a prison camp. After being released in 1945, he worked in the war crimes investigation unit of the War Office until 1947.

Terry's early life and career, Lenart observed, was 'very consistent' with what she knew from later on, the notion of a man who 'stayed out in the cold'. In Terry's case,

> a man intimate with his surroundings but with no sense of belonging; a man of more use away than at home; a man apart from others, often above, occasionally below, or apparently on their level; a man completely at ease in three languages and cultures yet truly identifying with none; a man whose natural state involved observation, investigation, exposing, reporting and being driven by the act as much as the cause.

The parallels with Holden's life were striking. Midolo wondered if Terry had known Holden personally and what he had thought of him. Lenart said that Terry had strong beliefs, notably against fascism and communism. She also mentioned one MI6 deputy director who had said that Terry 'had green fingers for intelligence work'. Lenart wrote: 'It seems he kept those fingers quite busy for most of his life.'

It was after the war, upon leaving the War Office in 1947, that Terry met Ian Fleming.

Fleming's biographer, Andrew Lycett, wrote:

> Ian liked to imagine Mercury/Kemsley as an adjunct to the secret service ... Many journalists with intelligence connections gravitated towards him. Antony Terry ... was a typical example. After the war he doubled as Ian's correspondent and an agent of the Secret Intelligence Service in Vienna and later Berlin. Before going to Vienna in 1947, the German-speaking Terry married his girlfriend Rachel Stainer because, she recalled, the SIS would not employ a single man there. She was informed that her husband was a spy and Ian "arranged the cover" for them both to go to Vienna.

Rachel, a beautiful young divorcee, later wrote bestselling spy novels under the pen name Sarah Gainham, partly fictionalising her own spying career. At one point, Fleming himself commissioned her to produce a study of how to gain access to West Berlin from East Berlin.

There were more parallels between Terry and Holden. Terry's head of station in Vienna was George Kennedy Young, also a former journalist, who was appointed head of Middle East operations during the Suez Canal Crisis – and would therefore have certainly dealt with Holden. Young later rose to become deputy director of MI6 and was allegedly one of the conspirators who tried to undermine the Labour Prime Minister Harold Wilson in the 1960s.

In Vienna, Terry kept busy, working for both Young and Fleming. In his own words, he was 'actually doing two rather exciting jobs'. In a 1949 letter, Fleming gave him guidance to cover his dual role as journalist and agent. About journalism, Fleming advised: 'I hope you will start establishing the very best contacts throughout Germany and also reading up industriously contemporary German history. Try to cultivate a light touch for the *Sunday Times*.' As for the spying, Fleming told Terry: 'I attach particulars of a man who has been well recommended to me as being particularly well informed especially regarding Russian manoeuvres in Germany, and I think that from time to time you may get useful material from him.'

Terry was even arrested by the Russians 'while engaged in my *journalistic* duties – but they let me go', as he wrote to a friend almost forty years later. 'Obviously a case of the right hand not knowing what the left hand was doing...'

In 1949, he was posted to Berlin and instructed to tell everyone, including his wife Rachel, that his spying days were over. 'I shall simply be a newspaper correspondent from now on. Nothing behind it any more. The post-war job is over ... The past is a sealed book, as they say, and don't forget it.'

It was a lie. But Rachel was too smart not to notice Terry's 'second job' and he soon came clean; he even decided to use her for his missions, delivering parcels that turned out to contain guns and acting as a watcher when he suspected someone of treason within his own station. Rachel would end up writing about it all, with minor variations, in her novel *The Tiger, Life*.

Terry continued working for his two masters. In 1951, Fleming wrote to him:

> I personally regard your assignment as the most important politically of any of our correspondents ... and I want you to make your service to the *Sunday Times* your first priority ... I hope you had a fine holiday and that your shoulders now feel strong enough to assume the mantle which I am intent on thrusting upon them.

Terry and Fleming became friends and when Fleming published the first Bond novel, *Casino Royale*, two years later, he sent a copy to Terry and Rachel. Upon reading it, Terry would have certainly found it amusing that Bond's controller was a journalist – 'a taciturn man who was head of the picture desk on the *Daily Gleaner*, the famous newspaper of the Caribbean'. Over the years, Fleming would occasionally ask Terry for details about the spying business in Germany that invariably ended up in his 007 novels. When Fleming visited Berlin, in 1959, Terry gave him a spook's tour of the city. After going to the cinema together and over dinner, Fleming asked Rachel to sleep with him. 'In a disengaged, slightly drowsy manner, he begged her, "It would be wonderful to relax for a moment."' She refused. But the marriage did not last and soon Terry divorced her, citing in the papers her adultery with Kenneth Ames, a *Daily Mail* journalist whom Rachel later married.

Terry kept on working for the *Sunday Times* for the following three decades, occasionally delivering proper scoops, like interviewing

Elvis Presley in 1960, but more often intelligence coups. In a letter to a friend in 1987, referring to his double role of journalist and spy, Terry said of his editors at the *Sunday Times*: 'Although naturally they've always known, they like to be able to pretend ignorance.'

Midolo remembered that during one of his visits to Gillman's house, Peter's wife, Leni, told him about a conversation she had had with Terry in Paris. 'He told me, never believe a word the secret services say. They all lie.' Terry even lied to his stepdaughter. 'I knew that Fleming had been a foreign manager for Kemsley Newspapers when Antony started his career as a newspaperman,' Lenart told Midolo over the phone from Australia. 'But I was completely unaware of all the subtext. Totally unaware of that.'

'Do you think your mother knew?' Midolo asked her.

'I'm absolutely certain that she did.'

'Was your mother a secretive figure who kept things to herself?'

'Very secretive. *Very*. And before she died, she was burning a lot of stuff. I wonder what all that was. Antony was very careful about what he kept and most of it looked innocuous. It was only when you started to put one scrap of paper with another one that you could piece things together. It was very difficult.'

There was another detail in the letters between Fleming and Terry that caught Midolo's attention. In October 1960, after he had left the *Sunday Times* to write the Bond novels full-time, Fleming told Terry: 'I think you are going to have much more fun in your job when Frank Giles takes over as Foreign Editor. I know him very well personally and I shall be giving him a full briefing before he gets going.'

A briefing on foreign correspondents or on spies?

Giles, of course, was the man who had poached Holden from *The Guardian* to become the *Sunday Times*' chief foreign correspondent. He had died, aged 100, in 2019. Midolo had read his memoir, *Sundry Times*, looking for clues. He thought it was painfully boring and found very little, other than references to the fact that Giles's lifestyle was too expensive for his journalist's salary – allegedly because his wife, Lady Katherine 'Kitty' Sackville, came from a noble family and had been brought up in luxury. Yet Giles had an interesting background. During the war, he was in the directorate of military operations at the War Office and in 1945 moved to the Foreign Office as a temporary civil servant, working in the private office of the Secretary of State, Ernest Bevin.

The following year, Giles failed the permanent Foreign Office exam and, according to his obit in the paper, 'for the rest of his life displayed traces of the diplomat manqué'. He became a journalist instead, working as a foreign correspondent for *The Times* in Paris and Rome in the 1940s and '50s – a period he was defensive about in his scathing response to Gillman's Holden report. In Paris, Giles and Kitty were friends and regular guests of Joseph Alsop, the CIA 'friend', and his wife Mary. In the obit of Giles's wife, Mary was quoted saying: 'The Gileses do more and give more pleasure with less money than any couple in Paris.'

Giles mentioned in his autobiography that it was Fleming who had recommended him for the foreign editor's job at the *Sunday Times*. 'Ian Fleming, who despite his growing absorption with James Bond was still connected with the *Sunday Times*, told me in confidence that that paper was looking for a new foreign editor,' Giles wrote, quickly dismissing the whole affair as if it was unimportant. It was the only reference to Fleming in the entire book.

Giles got the job and seven years later, in 1967, became Evans's deputy, missing the chance of becoming the editor because, in Denis Hamilton's words, although he had 'a safe pair of hands, he was not likely to run investigative journalism and take chances'. Giles eventually became editor of the *Sunday Times* in 1981, after Evans left to head *The Times*, but was fired only a couple of years later after the fiasco of the fake Hitler diaries.

One former foreign correspondent whom Gillman had contacted had described Giles as 'a pompous ass' who used to interview prospective news recruits in French. James Fox, another ex-*Sunday Times* reporter and bestseller writer, author of *White Mischief* and co-author of Keith Richards's memoir, had a more intriguing tale to relate.

In late 1974, through his contacts with some prominent Saudi businessmen, including henchmen of the arms dealer Adnan Khashoggi, Fox was invited to Riyadh, along with Don McCullin, to interview the then crown prince. A few months later, in March 1975, the Saudi king, Faisal, was shot and killed by one of his nephews. Thanks to his contacts, Fox was able to get a rare visa to cover the king's funeral.

'The fact is, it was almost impossible to get a visa to go to Saudi Arabia then,' Fox explained. 'I don't think many journalists had actually been. When I interviewed the crown prince the previous year, I was locked up in a guest house for three days and I was taken straight to the airport after the interview. There was no hanging about. No tourism. Just that.'

Fox managed to obtain the visa and was due to fly off the next day when the telephone rang: it was Giles. 'Could you come up to my office for a second?' he said. 'I want to ask you something.' Fox did not know Giles very well, but he and the other reporters 'were all very suspicious' of him. 'We didn't rate him. And he was always going on about the Foreign Office in a very pompous kind of way. I told myself, "Do not trust this fucker."'

Fox went into Giles's office and Holden was there. 'I remember Holden was looking very sheepish,' Fox recalled. 'They were both standing up and Giles said to me, "I know you're going to Saudi Arabia. We want David to go instead because he's a more experienced reporter and he knows the Middle East very well. This is a very big event and the newspaper really wants him to go."' Fox said no. 'I said I couldn't possibly do that. I had been invited by my contacts. It was all very awkward. It was an extraordinary request. Unbelievable and unprofessional of Giles.'

It was a short meeting and it was the first and last time that Fox would see Holden. 'Why couldn't Holden get his own visa and go?' Fox wondered. 'He's been travelling these parts for many years, right? Had he fallen out with the Saudis?' Holden had indeed been to Saudi Arabia a dozen times in just a few years and was writing his last book, about the Saudi royal family, which in theory had the Saud dynasty's blessing. But the anecdote was important because it indicated that at some point, Holden had become *persona non grata* in Saudi Arabia. Had the Saudis found out about his 'other' activities? And what was Giles's role in all that? Did he know what Holden was up to?

'Frank Giles had all sorts of spooky connections,' Michael Binyon had told Midolo. Maybe the key, he suggested, was in the people he had hired during his stint as foreign editor. Holden had been hired in 1965, before Evans had joined the paper, but who else was there?

Holden's predecessor as chief foreign correspondent at the *Sunday Times* had been Tom Stacey. A swashbuckling figure, always away from the office looking for near-extinct tribes in the Malaysian jungle or getting himself arrested in India, Stacey had been hired by Giles in 1960, as soon as the latter had joined the paper. He was the main shareholder of the mysterious company Correspondents Worldwide, which was suspected of being a front for British intelligence operations and of which Holden had also been a shareholder. Other shareholders included Sir Alastair Buchan, the son of the famous writer and MI6 spy and recruiter John Buchan, author of *The Thirty-Nine Steps*, who was rumoured to be MI6 like his old man; and Edward Crankshaw, *Observer* journalist and MI6 agent reporting from Soviet Russia. In the 1980s, Stacey sold Correspondents Worldwide to Robert Maxwell, who had his own fair share of intelligence connections, from MI6 to Mossad and even the KGB.

Sadly, Stacey was another one Midolo and Gillman had just missed, in what had become a recurring theme. He had died aged ninety-two in December 2022, before they could contact him. His *Times* obit, written by Binyon, of course, made no reference to his presumed intelligence activities but related a curious episode involving Lord Thomson:

> [Stacey] went on to secure interviews with figures such as Chiang Kai-shek, Indira Gandhi and, through cunning tactics, Nikita Khrushchev when he joined his proprietor, Lord Thomson of Fleet, on a 1963 trip to Moscow. Thomson, unexpectedly, received an invitation to meet the Soviet leader; Stacey accompanied him and led the conversation while secretly recording it on a machine controlled through his wristwatch.

A secret recorder controlled from a wristwatch? In 1963? Binyon was right, there was a pattern in Giles's hires at the *Sunday Times*, just like for Fleming before him. As another former colleague of Gillman had put it: 'Giles was bringing in useless establishment boys and they were all spies too.'

There was one overriding and unsolved question underlying the continuing speculation. It concerned one of the most disturbing episodes in the entire original investigation, the theft of the telexes from inside the *Sunday Times*. It was all the more troubling because it compelled the team to suspect a group of colleagues from the newspaper staff, taking it into paranoia territory. One candidate had to be Terry, who his stepdaughter revealed had never severed his post-war connections with the intelligence world. But it turned out he had been in Vienna at the time of the first theft, ruling him out unless he had somehow enlisted a proxy. Could it have been Giles?

It may have seemed far-fetched: but later, a close friend of Evans told Gillman and Midolo that Evans himself had become convinced that Giles had been obstructing the investigation of Holden and even suspected him of being the telexes thief. There seemed at least a plausible case. Inside, Giles had access to the foreign department where the telexes were kept. Outside, he had intelligence connections and was, after all, the man who had hired Holden; he was cooperating with the Foreign Office during the investigation while the FCO, on the other hand, was openly telling its men not to help the *Sunday Times* journalists; he had dismissed Gillman's report and had refused to share some of his files about Holden with Scotland Yard.

At a late stage in their research, Gillman and Midolo learned the name of a new suspect: Donald McCormick, another of the wartime intelligence men hired by Fleming as both journalist and spy. McCormick, previously the *Sunday Times* foreign department manager, was still working there part-time in 1977 and 1978. A former telex operator related how he had been grilled by an MI6 officer about Holden's last telexes. Later, McCormick told him some telexes relating to Holden were missing. 'Christ! Is there a spy in the department?' the operator asked. McCormick laughed, adding that 'half the foreign desk' were spies. McCormick asked him to hand over copies of future telexes. The operator concluded that he was the 'mole' who was tracking the movements of the inquiry team.

As for Terry, even if he were ruled out as the thief, his stepdaughter continued to believe that he might have helped MI6 to cover up what had happened to Holden. 'The interesting angle about Antony in this particular case is not necessarily what he did but what he didn't do and why,' Lenart told Midolo. 'Given Antony's connections in intelligence circles, he would have probably known quite quickly what had happened. The fact that he didn't come up with anything, at least publicly, suggests to me that it wasn't convenient or appropriate for the truth to surface.' Lenart was convinced that

Terry would have been able to solve the murder mystery. Unless, of course, Holden was a double agent. In which case, Terry would have covered it up to protect British interests.

The document from the archives of the StB, the Czech security services, said, unequivocally, that Holden was an MI6 'agent' too. Was that the key to the mystery? Midolo was determined to find out more about the Czech security services' sources. Dominic Hipkins, the researcher who had been in touch with Gillman and had delivered this message in the bottle from 1979, had said that he had searched for further references to Holden in the archives but without luck.

The StB, like every other secret service, was also active abroad and from the archives' registries, which were available online, Midolo could see that the number handwritten next to Holden's name, 12339, was the reference for a bundle containing information about British intelligence during the 1960s and 1970s. He emailed the archives, asking if they could send him the file via email. They could not, they replied, because the bundle contained more than 4,000 files. But they could send a DVD. For Midolo, the hardest part was trying to find a DVD player.

The files, which he received a few days later, looked promising: neat colour photographs of every yellowed page of the folder. The first few ones of the batch were a handwritten index of names and locations. He went to H, but Holden's name was not there. The reference must have been somewhere else. But there were simply too many files in the folder and because these were photos of the actual pages, he could not search through them. It would take him days to spot Holden's name. But maybe there was no need to.

A new computer program designed for journalists, Google Pinpoint, could detect the text within photos – even handwritten notes – and digitise it. Midolo started uploading each one of the 4,341 files in the collection. The program would then convert the files into PDFs and make them searchable. Eventually, he could search through the entire dataset. There were only four hits: two from the indexes; a typed letter; and the photocopy of an article in a British newspaper. The typed letter, in Czech, was headed '16 October 1979, London'. It read:

Dispatch BK c.9/79
<u>HOLDEN, DAVID, British agent special services MI6 – information</u>
By monitoring and evaluating the British press it was discovered that on 14/10/1979 an article was published in the *Sunday Mirror* about former MI6 agent David HOLDEN.

That was it. Midolo was baffled. The article attached, by David Knight, was titled 'Was Holden one of Smiley's men?' Knight wrote: 'It is now clear that David Holden, the British journalist mysteriously murdered in Cairo, died for his country. He was working for MI6, which controls our Secret Service Agents abroad, and it was as a British agent that Holden was slain in the line of duty.'

Knight, who had died in 2019, went on to say that Holden's role had been revealed to him by an unnamed 'senior British intelligence source' who explained that Holden 'worked for Six. He was a collector of information.'

The article also quoted Evans, who said that the idea that Holden had been MI6 was news to him and also mentioned, indirectly, Gillman's report. 'We have a long report, but it does not say what we want to know: who killed him and why.'

Later that night, Midolo showed the findings to Gillman. 'That's all?' he replied, visibly frustrated.

'I'm afraid so.'

There was a moment of silence. Numerous people over the

decades had said that Holden was working for MI6. But in the absence of hard evidence, the information was just another rumour.

What about speaking with someone who was MI6 at the time? Midolo asked Gillman. There was the spook who had cornered him at the dinner. What was his name?

'Geoffrey Tantum,' Gillman replied.

There was a fair bit about Tantum on the web. A 1997 article in *The Independent* mentioned Tantum, former MI6 controller for the Middle East, in relation to a secret group known as Le Cercle, an exclusive think tank said to be funded by the CIA.

Formed in the 1950s, the group was 'advocating right-wing causes round the world and growing into a confidential talking shop for about seventy politicians, businessmen, polemicists and personnel from the diplomatic and security services'. One of the members stood out: Brian Crozier, a journalist and author who had self-professedly worked for the CIA and MI6 for decades. In 1965, Crozier, then a correspondent for *The Economist*, was appointed chairman of a London-based CIA propaganda operation called Forum World Features. Crozier was the editor of *The Economist*'s 'insider' news sheet Foreign Report but, as he later recorded in his memoirs, kept some of his best stories for the CIA.

Other members included Anthony Cavendish and Nicholas Elliott, both former MI6. Kissinger and the ex-CIA directors Bill Casey and William Colby were also reported to be senior members. Tantum was named as the group's British secretary.

There were other titbits about Tantum from over the years and an amusing anecdote too. 'His daughter, Laura, operates Universal Exports, G3's charitable foundation which is also the name of the fictional company used as cover by James Bond,' a 2011 article in the *Telegraph* noted.

In the 1990s, Tantum had become an adviser to the Emir of Bahrain, a tiny island-country east of Saudi Arabia. In 2018, Tantum was knighted 'for his outstanding service and contributions' in the development of relations between Bahrain and the UK.

Midolo traced Tantum to an address in Bath, Somerset, but he could not find a number or an email address. Gillman decided to try through his colleague who had organised the dinner in the 1980s where Tantum asked Gillman if he could read the Holden report. The colleague gave him Tantum's number but added a mysterious caveat: 'Peter, don't forget that these men are putting their lives on the line to defend our country.'

Gillman called Tantum right away. To his relief, he was still alive. 'I'm very happy to help you,' Tantum said. 'But I have to warn you. I'm starting to have dementia.'

• • •

On a bright April morning, Gillman and Midolo boarded a train to Bath. During the journey, they reviewed what they knew about the former spy and what they wanted to know from him. By then, Gillman had realised he first met Tantum in Amman during the original Insight inquiry, when he was told that Tantum was merely a British Embassy 'official'. The first question now, of course, was whether Tantum knew why Holden was killed. Midolo had a hunch that Tantum (and so MI6) did not know what had happened to Holden and wanted to find out. Which would explain why Tantum, even years later, was asking Gillman to read his report. Gillman was open to the possibility, but he remembered well how much the encounter with Tantum had spooked him and warned that they should not underestimate the spy, even in old age.

A tall man in a high-collared pile jacket with blue eyes and thick grey eyebrows opened the front door. He looked younger than his eighty-three years. 'Welcome,' Tantum said, leading them inside. Gillman had decided to play 'good cop' and introduced himself by saying they had both been at Oxford. He also mentioned that they had met, which Tantum could not remember. He said he was struggling with his memory and found it easier to recall things from a long time ago.

'Can you tell us whether you can remember anything at all about David Holden?' Gillman asked.

'I remember the event, and the difficulty of finding out what was going on,' Tantum said. 'Not knowing who did it and why. I assumed he had some kind of problems with some of these people that wasn't public knowledge. Why were they pursuing him otherwise?'

'Well, that's the key,' Gillman said. 'That's what we haven't got to. Do you remember at all thinking about who did it at the time?'

'This really does take me back,' Tantum said, struggling to remember.

'Did you personally know the man?' Midolo asked.

'David Holden? Yes, I did.'

'We understand he was… "helping" MI6,' Midolo said. He was partly bluffing, but he was hoping Tantum would not notice.

'Yes,' Tantum said.

Midolo and Gillman looked at each other. They were not sure he had understood the question.

'I mean he was part of the group of press people who were always in the Middle East and active there,' Tantum added. 'I wouldn't say I knew him well, but I certainly did know him and I was stunned and horrified when the news came through.'

Tantum went on, saying that they, the 'friends', had all been surprised and wanted to know what could have been the reason Holden was assassinated.

'In the end, I think we felt this was something specific to David Holden – he must have had some kind of problem with somebody,' Tantum explained. 'There was nothing going on at that time we'd been aware of that would have justified him being murdered in that way.'

Tantum's wife arrived with coffee and biscuits. 'So, you are journalists investigating the murder of this man?' she asked.

'He was a very nice man and a quite eminent chap who worked for the *Sunday Times*, and we didn't know why and we don't know why,' Tantum told his wife. Who is 'we', Midolo thought? Us three? MI6?

Tantum said he did not see Holden during his last visit to Amman before he boarded the plane to Cairo. Tantum was then station chief in Amman, under the cover of first secretary at the British Embassy, which made the two reporters wonder how he'd met Holden and where. It could have been in Aden, Yemen, where Tantum was posted before Jordan. Or it could have been at Le Cercle, the secretive think tank that sprouted with journalists, politicians and spies. Tantum could not – or would not? – remember.

Gillman told him that Insight's original investigation had concluded that the only people who could have mounted the operation to kill Holden were the Egyptians themselves.

'Well, knowing the Egyptians, it doesn't surprise me,' Tantum replied. 'They're pretty dubious people. Especially the Egyptian intelligence service – they are not people you'd want to mix with. But the question is why would they? Why would they go to the trouble of killing a British journalist? What was the motive?'

'Well, we have a theory about that,' Midolo said. He asked Tantum about the relationship between MI6 and the CIA in Jordan.

'In general, it's regarded as a necessary relationship, but on the ground, it depended entirely on the individuals on both sides,' Tantum replied. 'The CIA station chief in Amman was someone I cordially disliked. And I don't think I had many dealings with the guy.' He could not remember the name.

'There were one or two good CIA people that I had worked with, but you had to be very careful with them; I never really had extreme dealings. The last time I dealt with them I was involved with the Syrians, which was not something I wanted the Americans to know about.'

'Why would you not want the Americans to know about that?' Midolo asked him.

'Whatever you do, they'll steal whatever your assets and resources are, everything. And they had no links with the Syrians at all. You had to be very cautious when you were running your intelligence via them, the Americans,' Tantum noted. 'They're very good at being full of bonhomie and friendship and some of them are good. But on the whole, they're very focused on their own interest and their interest would come first. I have a rather jaundiced view of operating with the CIA.'

Tantum added that there was a fair bit of competition between intelligence agencies in the Middle East, even allies like the British and the Americans. Then he asked if Holden had any dealings with the CIA. Gillman told him about the original investigation and the details that they had now managed to confirm.

'Did you have a working relationship with journalists?'

'There's always been an interest between the two sides, but the relationship with MI6 and journalists has always been tricky,' Tantum said. 'We were not encouraged to deal with journalists at that time. I can assure you that there wasn't a relationship when I was in Jordan. I didn't have dealings with David Holden there.'

Yet Tantum could still not remember how he had met Holden.

'He was good and very engaging,' Tantum recalled, looking into the distance, as if he was trying to remember more about what Holden was like as a man. Then he asked an unexpected question: 'I don't suppose there were any reasons for the Russians to be involved in that incident in Cairo?'

CHAPTER 21

RUNNING SANDS

It was an extremely good question, which Gillman and Midolo had been asking themselves many times. Ever since Gillman had written the Holden report, the most plausible theory had been that Holden had betrayed some sort of cause and, for this reason, he had to die.

Which side Holden had betrayed and for which he had given his life was still subject to speculation, but the most likely scenario was that Holden was also working for the Soviet Union. However, the two journalists had found no evidence to confirm this theory and were left wondering whether it was yet another red herring.

All they had were Holden's personal and professional connections, the most damning of which were with Leo Silberman, Patrick Seale and Kim Philby. Silberman, his lover with communist connections, who, they knew now, had been kept under surveillance by the CIA as a potential suspect; Seale, his literary agent who had long been suspected of being KGB; and Philby, his double at *The Observer* and *The Economist* in Beirut whom Holden had recommended for a job at *The Times* even though he had been fingered as the third man of the Cambridge spy ring.

Seale had died, aged eighty-three, of brain cancer, in 2014. His second wife, Rana, to whom he had been married for twenty-nine years, was living in London's Holland Park. Rana was Syrian royalty, the niece of the Syrian poet Nizar Qabbani and the ex-wife of the renowned Palestinian poet Mahmoud Darwish. Seale and Rana had a stormy relationship and after he died, she became locked in a court battle with Seale's sons and daughters over the family house, worth millions of pounds, and the author's vast art collection.

Seale was the correspondent who succeeded Philby in Beirut for *The Observer*, but in the 1970s and 1980s he had somehow become a multi-millionaire moonlighting both as an art dealer and as a literary agent. He also worked for at least one intelligence agency: in 1989, Anthony Cavendish told Gillman he had recruited Seale to MI6. Seale was alleged to have worked for the KGB as well, after being enlisted by Philby, a rumour which led to his sacking from MI6. Seale had also been at Balliol College in Oxford at the same time as Silberman, which could perhaps explain the mystery of how Holden and Silberman had met in 1950.

'For a long time, some people thought he was the fifth man in Philby's spy ring,' Seale's wife, Rana, told Midolo. 'I know for a fact that he desperately wanted to join MI6 and they interviewed him,' she said, adding that later, 'they didn't feel he was trustworthy enough. If he was a spy for anybody, he was a spy for the Russians. I'm convinced of that.'

Rana certainly had a grudge against her late husband, but to Midolo she sounded rational and informed about Cold War matters. They spoke for over an hour. She explained that the British establishment 'disliked Patrick' and 'did not trust him', which might have pushed him to go work for the other side, as he always had left-leaning ideas. He had also started travelling to strange places in Russia and the other Soviet republics. 'Whether this was out of inclination, because, you know, he was one of those Oxbridge lefties who thought communism and the Soviet Union were this great utopian dream and all that rubbish; or whether he actually worked actively for them I can't tell you because I don't know,' Rana added. 'I knew nothing about his finances.'

Midolo told her that he was finding that many of these journalists were strapped for cash.

'They were always strapped for cash because they all lived above their means!' Rana exploded. 'They all hung out with heads of intelligence or businessmen, quote unquote, who are very rich and corrupt.' She continued: 'They liked boozing and they liked smoking and they liked going out and either womanising or being gay or whatever they like. So that cost money. And journalism, as you must know yourself, doesn't pay. They tried other routes to make some pocket money.'

Rama concluded with a remark that sounded particularly true: 'It was a very, very strange group of journalists. A lot of them with pretty dubious sources and connections. That world… I don't know. I don't think it exists anymore.'

Among this very strange group, Philby's life was undoubtedly the most scrutinised. Since the *Sunday Times*' Insight team had first revealed, in 1967, that Philby had been one of the most important double agents in the history of espionage, there had been endless books on the matter, and the last of them had come out just as Gillman and Midolo were back on the case. Written by the former deputy editor of the *Independent on Sunday*, James Hanning, *Love and Deception: Philby in Beirut* gave a meticulous account of the spy's life in Lebanon in the 1950s and until his defection to the USSR in 1963. And yet there was not a single reference, in the 400-odd pages of the book, to Holden. Contacted by Gillman, Hanning said that he knew nothing of Holden, 'whose death must conceal a really good story'. But he suggested getting in touch with Celia Adams, the widow of the late Middle East correspondent for *The Guardian*, Michael Adams, who must have known Holden. Gillman said he would try to talk to her.

The other authority on Philby was Ben Macintyre, *The Times* journalist turned author of bestselling non-fiction spy novels. His 2014 book *A Spy Among Friends* told the story of the friendship between Nicholas Elliott and Philby and was being adapted into a TV series with Guy Pearce as Kim and Damian Lewis as Elliott.

Macintyre had a vague recollection of the Holden case. 'I knew Harry Evans and he was obsessed with it,' he said. 'But I always felt that he was motivated partly by guilt over what had happened to Holden. I also knew David Blundy, who was a close friend of mine and was killed in El Salvador. I'm pretty sure he knew Holden and he too was obsessed by it. They would both talk about him all the time.'

Macintyre told Midolo that he would never get anything out of MI6, no documents, no confirmation, nothing. 'To be honest, it's not even worth trying; you're never going to get any documentary evidence,' Macintyre said. 'I never did. People seem to think that I have access to MI6, but I really don't. What I had access to, and this was hard enough, was officers who had been directly involved in that particular case and it took me three years to persuade them to talk to me and they wouldn't have done so without the permission of their bosses. It's a depressing thought but nonetheless true that MI6 will not release the files, particularly if it's controversial.'

What he suggested was to find people, either from MI6 or other journalists, who knew Holden. 'I think it's a really fascinating story, but alas I don't think I can be of much use to you,' Macintyre concluded. 'Besides, I'm always very surprised by journalists who are also operating as intelligence agents because I think they're very rare. I don't think it happens very often because the two things are fundamentally very different activities: spies are good at keeping secrets and journalists are good at exposing them.'

It was true. The lines between the two professions were much clearer now, but Midolo and Gillman had found endless examples of spies posing as journalists and vice versa during the Cold War. In a 2018 article for *The Times* titled 'The spy who came in from the newsroom', Macintyre himself had written that 'history is littered with examples of journalists who turned out to be spies' and that journalism provided a convenient disguise for espionage. 'This newspaper, and its sister Sunday paper, are no exceptions,' Macintyre wrote, mentioning Ian Fleming at the *Sunday Times*. He also named three journalists from *The Times*: its correspondent in pre-war Bucharest, Archie Gibson, who was in reality the city's MI6 station chief and ran a highly successful network of agents; the British officer Dudley Wrangel Clarke, who was arrested by the Spanish police during the Second World War while dressed as a woman and told a baffled police officer that he was the Madrid correspondent of *The Times*; and Guy Burgess of Cambridge Five fame, who lasted exactly twenty-six days at the paper, as he was too loud and too drunk to operate efficiently.

What about Philby himself? Midolo asked Macintyre. He was the most prominent example of both journalist and spy.

'Holden didn't come up in my research about Philby,' Macintyre said, admitting that, like Hanning, he did not know that Holden was in Beirut at the same time as Philby. Possibly because *The Times* had no bylines at that point, no one seemed to have noticed. Macintyre speculated if Philby would have 'burnt' Holden after his defection. 'Philby went out of his way to embarrass everyone he'd worked with at that point. But if Holden was KGB, as you suspect, then maybe he would have covered him. It's possible.'

Philby was known to play games with his former colleagues and friends, even after he defected to Moscow. At the Bolshoi Theatre in 1978, he chanced to meet the newly appointed correspondent for the *Telegraph*, Richard 'Dick' Beeston. 'As I live and breathe, Dick Beeston!' Philby roared with a broad smile on his face. 'I heard you were in Moscow. I hope the Soviet authorities are looking after you well.' Philby seemed delighted to see his old friend and asked plenty of questions about England. He was particularly interested to learn that Beeston's son, who himself would go on to become a foreign correspondent and foreign editor at *The Times*, had been at his old school, Westminster. 'Ah Westminster,' Philby said. 'You should be careful. Sometimes they produce some, some...' he began to stutter. 'Bad hats?' Beeston suggested. Philby grinned.

The two men also talked about James Angleton, the CIA counter-intelligence chief, then retired. Beeston, who had been the Washington correspondent for the paper, was also a close friend of Angleton and told Philby that he had spent his final days in the US at Angleton's fishing lodge in Wisconsin. 'Oh, really, I remember it well,' said Philby. 'How's Jim? Does he still make his own flies?'

Beeston wrote in his memoir that Angleton had been 'devastated' when the news of Philby's defection reached him. 'He had fallen under Philby's spell when Kim was the SIS representative in Washington in the 1950s.'

What did Beeston, who himself was rumoured to have been close to MI6, mean by that? Did he know about the rumours of an affair between Angleton and Philby? Midolo and Gillman could not ask him to clarify. The veteran foreign correspondent had died, aged eighty-eight, in 2015. His son, *The Times* foreign editor, had preceded him two years earlier, dying of cancer when he was only fifty.

Beeston senior knew Holden well and, just like him, had started his journalistic career in strange circumstances. After the war, during which he served with the RAF and then the Royal Berkshire Regiment, he worked at a public relations firm in Mayfair. While there, he was recruited, bizarrely, as an assistant editor with the Near East Arab Broadcasting Service in Cyprus. 'Bizarrely' because he knew nothing about radio and spoke no Arabic. He was interviewed at the Junior Carlton Club by a Foreign Office official whose chief concern was that Beeston and his wife had good table manners. The radio station, it turned out, was owned by MI6, which used it as a clandestine propaganda outfit. After a few years in Cyprus, he was sent to Amman and, three years later, to Beirut, where he met both Holden and Philby.

Beeston and his wife Moyra, who was also a writer, had a rambling house in the hills above Beirut. The couple threw memorable parties, during which arak, the Lebanese liquor, flowed freely. One night, Moyra turned to Philby, who looked dead drunk, and asked him if he was really 'the Third Man' in the spy ring with Guy Burgess and Donald Maclean. Suddenly sobering himself, Philby grasped her by the wrist and replied: 'You know, Moyra, I always believe that loyalty to your friends is more important than anything.'

In his 1997 memoir *Looking for Trouble*, Beeston declared that he never suspected Philby of being a KGB agent. 'Kim certainly fooled me, and probably his other press colleagues too,' he wrote. The book, alongside black and white shots of Beeston and Philby having picnics, included a photograph of Holden sitting at a cafe in Cairo in 1958. Always the dandy, his hair was slicked back meticulously and he was wearing a grey tweed jacket and a lightly coloured necktie. Sitting next to him, with penetrating brown eyes and a dignified profile in a black turtleneck jumper, was an Egyptian journalist named Hariya Khairy.

Beeston dedicated only one line to the 'ill-fated' Holden, mentioning him among other correspondents based in Beirut during the turbulent years of the Suez Crisis and its aftermath, among them Joe Alex Morris Jr of the *Los Angeles Times*, shot dead by a sniper in 1979 during the Iranian Revolution. 'Lebanon was the only Arab country without censorship and with good communications,' Beeston wrote, 'so inevitably Beirut became the listening post for the region, with the St George and its bar its epicentre – a bar for the trading of information between diplomats, politicians, journalists and spies.'

Here was a corps of foreign British correspondents, all in some shape or form connected to MI6, mingling over martinis at the St George Hotel Bar in Beirut. The bar was so famous that the Palestinian journalist and writer Said Aburish had written a whole book about it. It was the place you went 'if you wanted to know the news before it appeared in the media'.

According to Aburish, Holden was among a 'very small group of bar regulars who should have known better, but who maintained a disdainful, neo-colonial attitude which totally ignored local peoples' feelings and aspirations'. Aburish asked, rhetorically: 'How could anyone who hates the Middle East and the Arabs possibly ever be a good correspondent there?'

Aburish added that most of these 'neo-colonialists' were Britons unable to abandon the ways of the empire. 'David Holden of *The Times* did not hate the Arabs, but he always behaved as if he was bored with them and talked down to them, which helped neither his cause nor that of *The Times*.'

Unfortunately, once again, there was no way to ask the author what he meant by that, since Aburish had died in 2012.

The second member of this 'very small group' was a certain John Slade-Baker, then the *Sunday Times* correspondent in Beirut. 'Colonel John Slade-Baker of the *Sunday Times* offensively addressed bar waiters as "boy". When the *Sunday Times* recalled him, he told bar visitors how he visited the various Arab heads of state and, totally misunderstanding Arab hospitality, asked each for something to remember them by,' Aburish wrote. 'He returned home with a collection of gold watches, but missed the looks of wonder on the faces of his hosts.'

Among the people whom Slade-Baker racistly called 'boy' was the head barman (and suspected spy working for Nasser), Ali Bitar, who Aburish said still reddened at the memory, some thirty years later. Aburish delivered a brutal verdict on the lot: 'If one accepts the premise that sensitivity to the world around serves a correspondent well, then these people were bad reporters.'

It was not the only scathing portrait Aburish drew in the book. Western journalists and spies were often depicted as greedy, drunks and womanisers (when they were not gay). But there was also space for affection, even admiration, especially for certain habitués of the bar. One of them was Philby, whom Aburish clearly liked. 'Everyone loved Kim,' Said's brother, Afif, who lived in England and once dated Philby's eldest daughter, told Midolo. 'He was a charming man.'

Philby belonged to a 'third group', separate from the other correspondents: 'The journalist-spies, those who used journalism as cover for their espionage activity.' Some of them, Aburish wrote, carried out their spying activity undetected and thus remained unknown. Some journalists spied with their employers' knowledge, while others did not have the consent of their news organisations to be used for cover.

Aburish wrote that this confirmed 'the commonly held belief that journalism is a good cover for spying'. But he warned that to confuse journalism with spying was harmful 'in practical, everyday ways', if anything because it endangered colleagues' lives. It was the same mantra Evans repeated each time he talked about Holden.

Among the journalist spies mentioned in Aburish's book was a familiar name: John Fistere, the ex-OSS man who had seen Holden in Amman on the last day of his life, only a few hours before he boarded the flight to Cairo. 'A handsome, grey-haired American with Eastern establishment manners doing public relations for King Hussein of Jordan,' Fistere would rock up at the bar with a demeanour and behaviour that, according to Aburish, were more appropriate to Madison Avenue than Beirut. 'He exhibited no real understanding of the Middle East and often led Hussein into troublesome, uncharted territory through sheer, pretentious ignorance,' Aburish wrote. 'Fistere is now known to have been a CIA agent.'

Fistere went out of his way to befriend Kim and Eleanor Philby; even if he had very little in common with the Philbys, Fistere often drank with them at the bar and invited them to his frequent cocktail parties. But he went even further: he hired Kim's daughter, Josephine, to work for him at a time when, Aburish wrote, 'her main interest in life seemed to be her teenage crush on her boyfriend, my younger brother Afif'. A trained, Arabic-speaking Lebanese girl, Aburish argued, would have done a better job than the inexperienced, eighteen-year-old Philby girl. Yet she got the job – more indication that Fistere had a professional interest in Philby. Aburish interviewed nine friends of Philby who explicitly accused Fistere of heading a cabal to get Philby. 'Two went so far as to insist that Fistere's efforts and the American determination to trap Philby had as much as anything or anyone to do with his defection.'

In November 2022, Gillman met Fistere's stepdaughter, Susan Griggs. He first knew her in the 1960s, when they were both on the staff of the *Weekend Telegraph* magazine, where she was the picture editor. Over coffee in her ground-floor apartment in west London, she explained that her mother Isobel had married John after having her in a previous marriage. 'Papa', as she called him, certainly had a colourful CV, including his wartime service with the OSS. After working in New York for Henry Luce, founder of *Time* magazine, he and the family moved to Beirut in the mid-1950s, where he first had a spell with the United Nations refugee agency, then took up another job for Luce. Griggs described life in Beirut as 'heady times, so glamorous, dancing, eating out at the most divine restaurants and all the women wore Dior'. Following an introduction from a journalist, Fistere became an aide and adviser to Jordan's King Hussein, commuting between Beirut and Amman. It was a close relationship, Griggs testified: the king 'was such a wonderful man'. Griggs was aware of Aburish's assertion that John had worked for the CIA, which she disputed. However, her alternative explanation was intriguing. She related a conversation with Ed Applewhite, the former CIA station chief in Beirut, who told her that the CIA had indeed considered enlisting Fistere, 'a good American who has had OSS training and will tell us anything that he thinks we ought to know'. But Applewhite said that if the CIA employed him formally and his cover were revealed, 'then he stops being useful to us, he stops being useful to Hussein, he stops being useful to everybody'.

That decision, Griggs told Gillman, was a matter of regret to her mother, Isobel, who said, after hearing the rumour that John was a CIA operative: 'Chance would be a fine thing.' Griggs elaborated: 'We could have done with the extra income from being employed by the CIA.' To Gillman, it all added up to something close to a non-denial denial: no need for the CIA to employ Fistere as he was entirely willing to work for the agency unpaid.

It was not just Fistere who was interested in Philby. Angleton also had him followed by Miles Copeland, then working undercover as an oil company executive roaming around the Middle East. Copeland's sources reported that Philby habitually shook off anyone who was following him. But he was not meeting with his KGB handler. Instead, he was sneaking off for some regular rendezvous with the wife of a friend, the *New York Times* journalist Sam Pope Brewer, who would become Philby's third wife. Angleton and Copeland were satisfied: Kim was a rogue, not a Red.

Angleton's life changed in January 1963 when Philby disappeared from Beirut and showed up in Moscow. His wife later said that the news came 'as a terrible shock' and affected Angleton 'terribly, deeply'. She added: 'It was a bitter blow he never forgot.' Nicholas Elliott, Philby's friend who let him slip away, told John le Carré that Philby's defection 'had a cataclysmic effect on [Angleton's] personality ... He had trusted him and confided in him far beyond any routine relationship between the colleagues of two friendly countries.' Elliott added: 'Jim henceforth found it difficult to trust anybody, to make two and two add up to four. Over-suspicion can sometimes have more tragic results than over-credulity. His tragedy was that he was so often deceived by his own ingenuity, and the consequences were often disastrous.'

As a result, Angleton threw himself into the molehunt, something that would devour him for the rest of his career – and the rest of his life, too. Angleton investigated at least forty agency employees, effectively ending the careers of many of them, yet he ostensibly never found a mole. As the CIA's own historian Benjamin Fischer put it, the Great Mole Hunt or Great Mole Scare of the late 1960s turned the CIA inside out, ruining careers and reputations in search of Soviet penetration that may not have existed.

In March 1968, Angleton retrieved his copy of the *Washington Post* from his doorstep to read that Philby had published a memoir. The article named Angleton as one of Philby's chief contacts within the CIA. Furious, Angleton called the *Post*'s editor and his longtime friend, Ben Bradlee, demanding an explanation. 'You've blown my cover,' Angleton shouted. Bradlee rebuffed him by saying that the book was 'news'. By the time the conversation ended, the two were no longer friends. Trying not to take Philby's book personally, Angleton concluded that Philby was targeting him in public in order to protect ongoing KGB operations. As Angleton's biographer Jefferson Morley put it: 'Just as he had protected Burgess and Maclean back in 1951, so Philby was seeking to protect other moles now.' Could Angleton have been right this time? Was it possible that, as Macintyre had speculated, Philby was indeed 'protecting other moles', including Holden?

As for Angleton's personal relationship with Philby, which the CIA spymaster Bill Harvey thought was more than a friendship, even towards the end of his life Angleton kept his mouth shut. Before he retired, his CIA colleagues threw him a farewell party, where he was asked if he wanted to say anything that he had previously never disclosed about the Philby case. 'There are some matters I shall have to take to the grave with me,' he replied, 'and Kim is one of them.'

He would open up a bit more with his confidant, the journalist Joe Trento. 'Sometimes you can find the real enemy right in the mirror,' Angleton, then dying of lung cancer, told him during one of their last conversations. 'Fundamentally, the founding fathers of US intelligence were liars,' he continued. 'The better you lied and the more you betrayed, the more likely you would be promoted. These people attracted and promoted each other. Outside of their duplicity, the only thing they had in common was a desire for absolute power. I did things that, in looking back on my life, I regret. But I was part of it and loved being in it. Allen Dulles, Richard Helms, Carmel Offie and Frank Wisner were the grand masters. If you were in a room with them, you were in a room full of people that you had to believe would deservedly end up in hell. I guess I will see them there soon.'

Angleton died shortly after, on 11 May 1987. Philby followed him a year later to the day, on 11 May 1988.

• • •

There were so many coincidences and connections between Philby and Holden, the two lives of the spy and the journalist echoing each other, that Midolo's head was spinning. The more he knew, the more he felt lost within the wilderness of mirrors. He remembered what Gillman had told him when the two had just embarked on the quest: either you dismissed them as coincidences or you believed they were something more.

The most chilling parallels yet were to be found in the biography of one of the 'small group' of journalists who regularly attended the St George Hotel's bar: John Slade-Baker, the retired army colonel and *Sunday Times* foreign correspondent who, to Midolo and Gillman's excitement, had recently been exposed as being an MI6 spy, too. James Barr, a historian and author of three acclaimed books on the Middle East, had found Slade-Baker's diaries, in which the latter wrote candidly – and in colourful detail – about his spying activities.

A slender, owlish figure in a dark suit and knit tie, Barr told Midolo over coffee at *The Times* office that the diary was a gold mine for his 2018 book, *Lords of the Desert*, about the struggle between Britain and America in the Middle East. 'A spy who could write!' Barr told Midolo, failing to contain his excitement. Barr had found a brief reference to Slade-Baker's diary in a previous book about the Suez Canal Crisis by the historian Michael T. Thornhill. 'Although Thornhill had a feeling that there was something interesting about Slade-Baker, that perhaps he wasn't like other journalists, he had not realised what and had not read the diaries from the start,' Barr said. 'Because of their size, I don't think anyone had ever read them before.'

A reflective steel tunnel suspended between two venerable Victorian brick buildings, the archive of the Middle East Centre at St Antony's College in Oxford was a remarkable sight. It held Oxford University's primary collection on the modern Middle East, including the John Slade-Baker papers, which totalled thirty boxes and were donated to the archive by Slade-Baker's widow after her husband's death in 1966. The most interesting documents were his Middle East diaries: sixteen volumes spanning almost 3,000 pages, some typed, some handwritten.

Born in 1896, the son of a professional soldier, John Bigelow Slade-Baker was educated at Marlborough College and then at the Royal Military Academy Sandhurst. As an army officer like his father, Slade-Baker had had a long and eventful career, serving in the British Army for thirty-two years, from 1915 to 1947, surviving two world wars. His twin brother, Robert, was also a soldier, who won the Military Cross for leading daylight raids on German positions during the First World War and was killed in France by a German sniper in 1917.

A couple of years after retiring from the army with the rank of colonel, Slade-Baker was approached by Lord Kemsley, owner of the *Sunday Times*, who asked him if he wanted to become the newspaper's Middle Eastern correspondent. The year, 1949, was when Kemsley and Ian Fleming had hired Tony Terry to be their Vienna correspondent. Like many of his colleagues within Kemsley newspapers, Slade-Baker had no journalistic experience, but he had a very good eye for detail – and his diaries were much more interesting than the reports he produced for the newspaper. Tellingly, he would write far more diary entries than articles.

What had struck Barr, and would strike Gillman and Midolo too, was that the diaries were a contemporaneous account of what Slade-Baker had been doing, described in page after page that he wrote every day. Barr had realised this upon reading Slade-Baker's description of Philby, whom the colonel had called 'a gentleman'. 'I found it pretty hard to believe that someone like the patriotic Slade-Baker would say nice things about Philby, the notorious Soviet double agent who had betrayed Britain,' Barr told Midolo. This made Barr think that the diary must have been written *before* Philby's defection to Moscow in 1963. The sheer volume of the diaries themselves and the number of details contained in their pages also made it improbable that they could have been written after the events.

After reading a few pages, it became clear to Gillman that Slade-Baker had two paymasters: on one hand, he was reporting to Harry Hodson, assistant editor at the *Sunday Times* from 1945, then editor from 1950 to 1961; on the other, he had regular meetings with 'HOS', which stood for 'head of station', the MI6 man in Cairo, as well as a case officer codenamed 'H'. 'H', Slade-Baker's handler, was sometimes called 'Harry', in inverted commas, perhaps to differentiate him from the editor.

Gillman and Midolo found it remarkable that Slade-Baker clearly felt no embarrassment about playing these twin roles – and neither did the *Sunday Times*, which was fully aware of them too. There were others who suspected that the colonel was more than a journalist: like the Egyptian secret service, the mukhabarat. A week after arriving in Cairo in August 1952, Slade-Baker, who in a photograph of the time looked like a gangly man with furry eyebrows over bulgy eyes, dark hair and a bravura moustache, discovered that he was being 'shadowed', i.e. followed everywhere, by members of the secret police in a black Chevrolet.

It was the secretary of the Turf Club, a gentlemen's club in downtown Cairo that had once been frequented by T. E. Lawrence, who alerted him to his tail, saying that it was embarrassing the other members. Spooked, Slade-Baker tried to call 'H' and arrange for a meeting the next morning, but the men in the black car, the secretary warned him, were now waiting for him outside. Slade-Baker was very concerned. 'I was not certain whether they had been instructed to kidnap me or murder me,' he wrote in his diary. What's more, he had some papers with him that he had intended to burn back at the hotel.

He decided to risk it, stepping out of the club whereupon the black car started following him. Suddenly, he had an idea: he walked into a nearby restaurant and exited via a back door, finally losing his 'shadow'. The next day, after discussing the incident with 'H', he appealed his case to the Egyptian general who was head of the secret police, playing the card of the innocent and naive British reporter on assignment. 'My heart was in my mouth – everything depended on the general's reaction,' Slade-Baker wrote. 'If he was convinced I deserved to be watched, my number was up.' Luckily for him, the general apologised and said that the watchers would be called off. The next morning, the black car had vanished.

A few days later, in a diary entry that perfectly illustrated his journalistic cover for his spying activities, Slade-Baker reported a conversation with 'H' after the incident with the secret police. '"H" was very good about it and said that what had happened was due to sheer bad luck,' Slade-Baker wrote:

> The whole episode was due to a most unfortunate chain of accidents, helped by my own inexperience. As to the future, he thinks that while the [head of station] will not refuse to have me out again, he will refuse to my working in direct contact with 'H' or with anyone else, for six months or even a year, until I have completely established myself as a working journalist and have been accepted as such.

It was unclear if Slade-Baker would ever become 'established' as a journalist. After meeting him in 1955, the Israeli politician Moshe Sharett was perplexed. 'Quite a strange type of a journalist is he,' Sharett wrote in his diary:

> Seemed to me as rather limited and even a moron. He asked highly simplistic questions and slowly took down [everything] word by word. In the end, his meticulousness and carefulness outweighed his slowness and dumbness. Who knows whether his obtuse visage and cumbersome behavior were indeed a true mirror of his wisdom?

What Barr had found bizarre, and could not understand, was why a spy like Slade-Baker was keeping such a meticulously detailed diary. But buried within tightly handwritten notes, Gillman and Midolo found references to the fact that copies of the pages were hand delivered 'to our people in London'. That was what the diary was for: to give MI6 a complete debrief of everything Slade-Baker was doing. It made Gillman and Midolo wonder: how many such diaries populate MI6's archives? And how much of history would be rewritten if just a fraction of those was to be revealed to the public? Holden himself had been known to keep meticulous, handwritten notes in his notebooks, which Ruth had refused to give to the Insight team. Richard Johns, the *Financial Times* journalist who had finished Holden's book on Saudi Arabia, had told Gillman that it seemed that 'she feared something might be uncovered'.

Slade-Baker returned to Egypt in May 1956 during the gathering storm of the nationalisation of the Suez Canal Company, which would lead to the Suez Crisis and the invasion of Egypt by British, French and Israeli troops in October that year. Slade-Baker became an unofficial intermediary between the British government of Anthony Eden and the Egyptian President Nasser. One of the Egyptian officials Slade-Baker was regularly meeting said that he was 'something more' than a mere correspondent. In Slade-Baker's paraphrase: 'I am a colonel, a gentleman and a patriot and I should do something more to help my country than write articles for the *Sunday Times!*'

Unknown to the Egyptians, Slade-Baker was doing much more than just writing articles for the Sunday paper: he was busy recruiting agents, including 'B', a Jordanian journalist paid £200 a month – almost £4,500 in today's money – a sum that the agent was dissatisfied with. Slade-Baker had also managed to convince Philby's father, St John Philby, to write two articles detailing corruption in Saudi Arabia that Slade-Baker (and MI6) would use to win a propaganda war against the kingdom and protect British interests in the region – an episode Barr included in his book *Lords of the Desert*. Apparently unaware of being used by MI6, Philby senior filed the two pieces in August 1955, but the publication, which was carefully coordinated between the *Sunday Times* and the Foreign Office, was delayed until the end of October for maximum effect.

As for Holden, the first reference in Slade-Baker's diary was from late August 1956. He had just arrived in Cairo as *The Times* correspondent, succeeding James Morris, and on a hot summer evening, he went for a drink at Joe's Bar within the Semiramis Hotel with Douglas Stuart of the BBC, later presenter of *The World Tonight*, and Slade-Baker – who mistakenly called Holden 'James'.

Within days, events spiralled out of control. On 3 September, the Egyptian police arrested some thirty foreigners on espionage charges, including an Englishman. 'The sands were running out fast and I was conscious of unaccustomed tension between us,' Slade-Baker wrote after meeting Nasser. The spy had caught Nasser's eye at a reception and had asked to have a word with him before going to London, where he had been summoned by Hodson, his editor. The Egyptian President agreed and, in private, he told Slade-Baker that if war broke out, his country would most certainly lose in the 'conventional' sense of the term. But the struggle would be continued on the ground by a 'highly organised' resistance movement that would cause huge losses to the British. Nasser also hinted that they would wreak as much damage as possible to British interests in the Gulf, from oil installations to diplomatic premises and businesses. Slade-Baker listened carefully, then said that he would pass all this on in London. Nasser replied that he wanted to see him when he returned.

The colonel flew to London on 17 September, briefed the Foreign Office about his conversation with Nasser and then went back to Cairo on 26 September. Less than three days later, Israel invaded Egypt. Slade-Baker went to the British Embassy, where staffers were busy burning confidential papers in twelve braziers in the embassy's court. 'One of the saddest things I have ever seen,' he wrote. At first, foreign correspondents were allowed to work, although they were watched closely by armed police. But after a few days, they were all interned in the Semiramis Hotel. A Swiss delegate told Slade-Baker he could go home, but he said he was not going to abandon the other British journalists.

'On arrival, I asked David Holden of *The Times* if he would like to share a room with me, as we were told there were no single rooms,' Slade-Baker wrote. 'He agreed and we moved into a good sized room on the second floor in a wing of the hotel.' Holden played the clarinet during the long, empty days at the hotel. '[Holden] kept me awake in the afternoons by playing music and what he described as "excerpts from Mozart",' Slade-Baker wrote. 'In the evenings he attempted to teach the *Manchester Guardian* in the person of Michael Adams how to play the guitar.' Eventually, on 23 November, the British journalists were escorted out of the hotel and taken to the airport, where they were placed on planes home.

Slade-Baker crossed paths with Holden in Beirut the following year, where the two had drinks, luncheons and dinners together with Philby, often at the St George Hotel's bar. Beeston and Adams were also part of the bar's regulars. Holden and Slade-Baker met again in Amman in April 1957, at the time of an alleged military coup attempt by the Jordanian Army in the city of Zarqa and the countercoup by King Hussein. Once again, the three musketeers – Holden, Philby and Slade-Baker – had 'liquid' lunches together while the world around them was going up in flames.

If Slade-Baker had nice words for Philby ('I shall be glad to have him here,' he wrote. 'He is a gentleman and we see eye to eye over the Middle East'), he seemed to dislike Holden, describing him as 'much too temperamental for a job like this, and [he] always seems to be acting a part – as though he is not sure of himself. I have found that he is not a very popular person.' What 'job' of the two was that, Gillman and Midolo speculated? Journalism or spying? In December 1957, Slade-Baker met a British diplomat in Baghdad who commented on a piece by Holden in *The Times*. 'It was a typical piece of

David's writing – bitter, cruel, insulting and needlessly offensive and damaging to the Embassy staff,' Slade-Baker wrote.

Intriguing as they were, the references to Holden seemed trivial compared with the tale Gillman and Midolo found on the back of a speech given by the political scientist Richard Löwenthal in 1953. It was an interview with Nasser's Vice-President, Anwar Sadat, from later that year. While they were travelling on the presidential train to Alexandria, Sadat and Slade-Baker were discussing the motives behind various political murders of the past, including that of a judge and former Finance Minister, who had been shot dead a few years earlier in front of the Old Victorian Club in Cairo.

'Sadat suddenly grinned and I can remember the thrill of horror I felt as he told me that [he] had been personally responsible for the murder,' Slade-Baker wrote:

'You?' I exclaimed incredulously.

He nodded unconcernedly and said that he and his accomplice had tossed up a five-piaster piece to decide who should fire the fatal shot.

'Did you win?' I asked, concealing my disgust.

He lifted his head back and clicked his tongue in the negative gesture. 'My friend won the toss,' he replied, and for a moment the recollection of failure seemed to depress him. A moment later, however, he rallied and, as if to indicate that I should not underrate him, exclaimed: 'It is I who make the assassinations!' and throwing back his head and revealing a very pink tongue and very white teeth, he shouted with laughter.

CHAPTER 22

THE WRONG MAN

David Halton had a warm, low voice that had become raspy with age. A tall man with soft eyes and thick eyebrows, Halton, eighty-two, was journalism royalty in Canada. He lived in a two-storey stone house with a thatched roof near Rockcliffe Park, a leafy neighbourhood just outside Ottawa city centre. Midolo had found him through his publisher.

'David Holden was the chief correspondent for the *Sunday Times* and he was assassinated in Cairo in 1977—' Midolo had just started to explain when Halton cut him off.

'Yes, I know. I know it well,' he said, laughing rather uneasily. 'I was called in by MI6 when I got back to London, talked to them about it.'

Midolo stopped in his tracks. 'I'm sorry, you were called in by MI6?'

'Yeah, well, I'll start from the beginning if you like,' Halton replied. 'But why don't you go ahead and just fill me in with what *you* know and I can tell you everything I know.'

Midolo went through the many twists and turns of the original investigation as well as what he and Gillman had uncovered since Evans's death in September 2020. Then Halton related how he had narrowly escaped being killed back in 1974. The arrival at Cairo

Airport late at night; the two Egyptians in scruffy suits who had approached him after the passport controls; the battered car; the strange questions the men had asked him; and, finally, the telling remark: 'You are David Holden of the *Sunday Times*?'

'I've covered a lot of wars, as most foreign correspondents do,' Halton said, after he had finished his tale, 'and yet possibly the most dangerous and most memorable moment in my career was this near miss on a drive from Cairo Airport to downtown Cairo.'

Halton also told Midolo how, once he had got back to London, then his base, from Egypt, he was contacted by the British secret services.

'I automatically thought it was MI6,' Halton said. 'They called me without really saying who they were and we had a chat and I recounted everything that I could about why I was in Cairo, my visit and this mistaken identity situation.' Halton could not recall whether the debriefing with MI6 was in 1974, when the mistaken identity incident occurred, or in 1977, after Holden's death – which to Midolo sounded more likely.

Halton explained that he was back in Israel in November '77 when Sadat made his historical – and unexpected – visit to the country. 'I'd previously applied for some time for an interview with Sadat,' Halton explained. 'There were some faint rumours of a possible visit to Jerusalem, so I'd got a call from my office in London saying that Sadat was willing to give me an interview, but I had to get to Cairo as soon as I could and stand by there and wait. So I made haste over the Allenby Bridge to Amman either on the same day or the next day and booked a flight from Amman to Cairo.'

The next day at noon, Sadat called him in for the interview. When he entered the presidential palace, an aide told him: 'Make sure you ask him about his plans to visit Israel.' Halton did so and Sadat announced that he was planning to visit Israel within that very week. It was the first official admission of the unprecedented step and a sensational scoop for Halton. He travelled back and forth from Israel to Egypt and vice versa a few more times that year to cover the visit and then the peace conference; and it was while he was in Cairo that he heard that Holden had been assassinated.

'It was a shocking revelation that it could have been me and an enormous relief,' Halton recalled. 'And it came home rather graphically because some Canadian private radio station in Western Canada, where part of my family come from, had heard the news and made the same mistake as the mukhabarat. They put out a broadcast saying that CBC correspondent David Halton had been assassinated.'

Halton's relatives reached out to his wife to express their condolences. Fortunately, Halton called his wife and reassured her that he was not dead. 'I said, "Darling, it's not me" and I could use the Mark Twain line, that the news of my death was greatly exaggerated.'

Midolo and Gillman were flabbergasted. That was the third mistaken identity incident, if they included the David Hirst scenario. Halton was not aware of that theory and was surprised to hear it. 'I knew Hirst, he was our stringer in Beirut for a time,' he said. 'Lovely guy. I had never heard that story before. Totally fascinating.'

There was more. Halton relayed the story of a junior Canadian diplomat, named David Malone, who went to the Cairo morgue to identify a Canadian soldier who had drowned in the Nile and was asked if he was there 'to see the body of David Holden'. Malone, who knew Halton, thought they meant him and was bemused when they showed him the body of a Western man he did not know.

Midolo remembered the incident as it was buried towards the end of the Holden report, but the Insight team had not, it seemed, paid too much attention to it. If true, it proved that the Egyptian authorities knew from the beginning that the 'unknown European male' who lay at the morgue was in fact Holden.

Halton remembered that he was shocked to hear the news about

Holden – and not just because of his own narrow escape in 1974. 'I didn't know Holden personally,' Halton said, 'but he had a fairly giant reputation. He had been the chief foreign correspondent for a considerable amount of time and was very well regarded.' Halton said he recalled that there was 'a rash of speculation' that the Egyptian secret service had been involved in the murder. 'There were sections of the mukhabarat who did not want Sadat to go to Jerusalem. How Holden fitted into that I'm not sure. I think there was some hostility or suspicion about Holden as well in Egyptian circles, but all of this is very much hearsay.'

Midolo asked him what he meant. What kind of suspicions?

'Even that, and this is total hearsay, he might have been involved in MI6 à la Philby.'

Midolo was intrigued by the rumour, and also by the fact that Halton had mentioned Kim Philby of all people, and told him about the connections between the two 'journalists'.

'Ah, that's interesting,' Halton said. 'I was actually in Moscow when Philby was there and one day a colleague of mine went to the Bolshoi. In the interval, he went to the restroom and standing at the urinals, he casually glanced at the person next to him and there was Philby. Unfortunately, Philby had started peeing well before him and so he had disappeared by the time he had finished!'

For Midolo and Gillman, the Halton story was decisive for a number of reasons, the main one being that it confirmed their growing suspicion that Holden had been targeted for years before he was eventually killed. A second key element to understanding the whole affair was that Holden had not been to Egypt since 1972 and that the next time he went, in 1977, he was immediately picked up and shot. The incident also put to rest, once and for all, the speculation that Holden had been mistaken for someone else. Lastly, it was yet another indication that the Egyptians were behind the murder. What still remained to be answered was why the mukhabarat had him in its crosshairs.

The two reporters felt that the year the first attempt on Holden had been made, 1974, was crucial. It was the year Jim Fees took up his post as CIA station chief in Cairo and it was also when the Egyptian President, Sadat, officially switched sides, from being close to the USSR to becoming dependent on the US. Midolo and Gillman learned that the bond between Egypt and the Soviet Union dated back to the Second World War when, in 1943, the USSR established formal diplomatic relations with Egypt and opened its embassy in Cairo and a consulate in Alexandria, the important port city on the Mediterranean. It was a decade later, after the 1952 revolution led by Nasser, that the relationship intensified. In 1955, Egypt struck a huge arms deal with the USSR, after which Egyptian Army officers were trained in Eastern bloc countries. The relationship was a troubled one and had to encompass the Suez invasion of 1956 and the Six-Day War of 1967. During that period, the USSR sent some 10,000 servicemen to operate Egypt's air defence against Israeli attacks.

Events took an unexpected turn in September 1970, when Nasser died of a heart attack and was succeeded by his Vice-President, Sadat. Sadat had never been a fan of the Soviets and within a matter of months, he effectively severed the country's long-standing relationship with the USSR. A power struggle within the Egyptian government ensued between the Vice-President and other powerful political figures, such as the former Vice-President and former head of the mukhabarat, Ali Sabri, who was regarded as Nasser's likely heir. As for Sadat, he was widely believed, both in Egypt and abroad, to lack the clout and ruthlessness of his rivals to take on Nasser's mantle, his rivals judging him a weak transitional figure.

But Sadat's rivals underestimated his past. Born in 1918 in what was then the British-occupied Sultanate of Egypt, the young Sadat graduated from the Royal Military Academy in Cairo and was posted to the Sudan, where he met Nasser. Sadat was suspected by the British authorities of having pro-Nazi and pro-fascist sympathies – like many Egyptians, the junior officer hoped that the Axis forces would defeat the British, their main enemy, and give Egypt its independence – so he was transferred to an outpost in the desert. Undeterred, he joined a German spy ring, later immortalised in the Ken Follett novel *The Key to Rebecca*. But the Nazi spies were spending more time in Cairo's nightclubs than plotting and were soon captured by the British authorities.

Sadat was arrested and sent to a prison in the desert. Soon after, however, he managed to escape and took part in several assassination attempts, including the minister he later boasted about to John Slade-Baker, which were aimed at terrorising Egyptians collaborating with the British. On another occasion, Sadat and an accomplice threw grenades at the car of the Prime Minister, but the driver accelerated to avoid a tram and their target survived.

Upon becoming President, 'the veteran conspirator' and ex-spy Sadat shrewdly surrounded himself with capable military and intelligence people. There were also hints that Sadat's links with the CIA helped bolster his hold on the presidency. The mukhabarat's bugs had captured clandestine conversations between Sadat's men and US diplomats regarding a possible peace deal with Israel. At first, however, the agency did not believe that Sadat would last. In one of its earliest assessments of his rule, the CIA commented that Sadat did not 'carry much political weight' and that it was 'doubtful' that he could retain the presidency 'for more than an interim period'. It was a conspiracy to remove him as interim President that, against all odds, consolidated Sadat's power.

There is an old Arabic saying: he devoured them for lunch before they could eat him for dinner. Sadat followed that rule when, in April 1971, he defused what came to be known as the 'Ali Sabri plot'. A number of military units around Cairo were mobilised for a possible coup while the mukhabarat secretly took control of the state radio and television to prevent Sadat from appealing to the people. But Sadat had been tipped off and was ready to strike back. He neutralised Sabri and arrested the other conspirators, who were charged with treason and received death sentences – later commuted to life with hard labour.

Among the ninety-one conspirators was Sami Sharaf, the Minister of State for Presidential Affairs and de facto head of the Egyptian intelligence services. With stooped, round shoulders, a bald head, bulging stomach and dark moony eyes, Sharaf had been a shadowy and powerful figure during the Nasser era, in the early days of the 'mukhabarat state'. Nasser was innately conspiratorial and pathologically suspicious, as one UN diplomat described him. The President himself once confided to a British diplomat that he 'had been a conspirator for so long' that he thought like one and was 'suspicious of everyone'. As the man in charge of filtering information for the President (thus shaping his thinking on key issues), Sharaf was 'Iago to Nasser's Othello'.

But there was more to Sharaf's character. A number of Soviet defectors, including Oleg Gordievsky, later said that Sharaf had been recruited by the KGB in the mid-1950s with the unlikely codename of Asad, 'the lion'. Following Nasser's trip to the USSR in 1958, the Egyptian mukhabarat and the KGB established a strong partnership, which included sharing intelligence, obtaining surveillance equipment from the Soviets, training in interrogation and counter-intelligence and even joint secret operations. The man behind the KGB–mukhabarat alliance was Sharaf. Cairo was then, in the words of a young KGB officer, 'a big, murky pond' where 'everyone', as in every intelligence agency, was trying to fish.

It was as if, after Nasser's death, the colour of the pond had suddenly started to change. But the Soviets were desperate to retain control of the pond and, at Nasser's funeral, Soviet Prime Minister Alexei Kosygin urged Sadat to preserve the relationship. 'Let me tell you how we used to deal with things when Nasser was alive,' he told the President. 'We never had any secrets from him, and he never had any secrets from us. It is essential that each of us tell the other everything.'

How Sadat learned about the Sabri and Sharaf plot, six months later, was disputed. According to the official narrative, a major from military intelligence approached Sadat with secret tapes of the conspirators discussing the moves against the President; Sadat struck back before the coup could be carried out. But buried within old memoirs of ex-CIA and KGB spooks, Midolo found another version of these events.

Sharaf's efforts to transform the mukhabarat into a wing of the KGB had made it exceptionally difficult for the CIA to operate in Cairo. The agency's officers had nicknamed the country 'the Soviet Republic of Egypt'. To complicate matters, after the Six-Day War in 1967, Nasser had cut diplomatic relations with the US, forcing the CIA to run a small clandestine operation from the American interests section of the Spanish Embassy. In 1971, a young CIA case officer received a 'flash' cable from the agency headquarters in Langley that warned of a KGB plot to overthrow Sadat. Details were scant, but the officer managed to gather enough evidence to realise that the threat was a serious one.

The most precious information came from a KGB officer, Vladimir Sakharov, who had worked in Egypt for years and was in reality a double agent who had been spying for the CIA since the early 1960s. Among the intel gathered by the young CIA officer were recordings and transcripts of telephone conversations between the plotters. The officer was determined to pass on the information to Ashraf Marwan, Nasser's son-in-law, who used to sit next to Sadat during Cabinet meetings and shared the Egyptian President's distrust of the Soviets. But first, the CIA officer had to 'shake the tail' that the KGB had put on him. After three hours of wandering randomly around under the implacable Cairo sun, he managed to lose his pursuers, met Marwan and outlined the plot against Sadat. Within days, Sadat broke the back of the coup and arrested the plotters.

Was the KGB behind the plot to oust Sadat? Certainly, no country stood to lose more during the Sadat era than the USSR. Overthrowing Sadat would have locked Egypt into the Soviet camp, redeeming the billions of roubles that the Soviet Union had 'invested' in the country. The unofficial version could also explain why Sadat turned so decisively to the US – and the CIA – in the years after what was called the Corrective Revolution of 1971. In the aftermath of the coup, Sadat appointed Marwan to replace Sharaf as head of the intelligence services. (Sharaf, who died in January 2023 aged ninety-three, was released from prison after Sadat's assassination in 1981. He claimed that Sadat had been 'bribed' by the CIA since 1966.) As for Sakharov, the KGB–CIA double agent, he defected to the US and later wrote a memoir, *High Treason*, telling his story. His help was invaluable. 'Thanks to Sakharov's information, the CIA was able to identify every known Soviet intelligence asset in Egypt, in effect turning the former Soviet Egyptian republic into a KGB gulag,' wrote the CIA historian Mark Perry.

Soviet intelligence was thrown off stride when Sadat crushed his opponents and the KGB lost many of its best double agents in the purges of Egyptian officials and security personnel that followed. 'Hitherto routine clandestine contacts between Soviet case officers and their spy networks were broken and several agents refused to continue spying for the USSR,' the Egyptian intelligence historian Owen Sirrs wrote. 'Moreover, Egyptian counter-intelligence stepped up its harassment of Soviet intelligence officers and disrupted their meetings with agents and contacts.'

Unofficially at first, Sadat reopened contacts with the Americans. At one point, the Egyptian military secret services were conducting radio security checks in Cairo when they came across a series of suspicious signals exchanged with the American diplomatic mission at the Spanish Embassy; eventually, they determined that they were coming from Sadat's villa in Giza.

In July 1972, Sadat terminated the Soviet military mission in Egypt, expelling thousands of Russian military advisers. It was the end of the Soviet Republic of Egypt. Free from Soviet interference, Sadat could go to war with Israel and in October 1973, he launched a flash offensive, crossing the Suez Canal in what became the Yom Kippur War. He could also, officially this time, talk to the Americans, who in 1974 had reopened their embassy – and CIA station under its new chief Jim Fees – in Cairo.

One man was crucial in the decision to switch sides: Kamal Adham. Turkish-born, with blond hair and blue eyes, Adham was the head of Saudi intelligence and the brother-in-law of the Saudi king, Faisal. Adham had been personally bankrolling Sadat long before he became President. The relationship between the two men dated back to the early 1950s, when Sadat was approached by the wealthy Adham and began accepting his 'gifts'. By 1955, they were so close that Sadat was a witness at Adham's marriage.

Adham was in Cairo when Sadat announced the decision to expel the Soviet advisers and, according to multiple sources, it was he who had convinced Sadat to make the shift. Adham was also mediating between Cairo and Washington, smoothing the talks with plenty of cash for Egypt – some say up to $200 million a year. He made it clear to Sadat that he would have the full backing of the Saudi royal family if he leaned towards the US. As a result, Sadat became 'as staunchly anti-communist as the Shah and the Saudis'.

Adham's name kept popping up in Midolo's research like a jack-in-the-box. Adham was the man who would hire Sadat's wife, Jehan, and Fees as consultants. Even the CIA station chief in Riyadh, Saudi Arabia, would get on Adham's payroll in 1977.

Adham was also the brains behind the creation of the so-called Safari Club, a coalition of foreign intelligence services based in

Cairo that would run anti-Soviet operations in Africa. Established in 1974, this ultra-secretive 'anti-communist' alliance was composed of France, Iran, Saudi Arabia, Egypt and Morocco, with the blessing and backing of the US. Henry Kissinger was delighted to see his aims in Africa implemented by proxy, as his hands were tied by Congress after the Watergate scandal.

The alliance was named after the Mount Kenya Safari Club, an exclusive resort of ninety-one acres owned by the Saudi arms dealer and Adham associate Adnan Khashoggi.

From providing the dictator of Zaire, Mobutu Sese Seko, with funds and weapons to fight separatists in his country to supplying arms to the dictator of Somalia, Siad Barre, and so luring him away from the USSR, the Safari Club ran a spectacular number of successful missions. In 1979, it was responsible for the delivery of old Soviet ammunition and military technology to the Afghan rebels. The mujahidin fought the Soviets using Soviet weapons that the USSR had gifted to its old ally, Egypt, and that Sadat was now shipping to the rebels via Saudi Arabia and Iraq. Adham was in charge of the shipping through a bank, the Bank of Credit and Commerce International (BCCI), which would be at the centre of a major financial scandal in the 1990s. In 1992, Adham pleaded guilty in the US, paid a $105 million fine and cooperated with the investigators in return for a reduced sentence. The BCCI was also implicated in the Iran–Contra affair, for which Fees came back from his retirement.

The Safari Club could even claim responsibility for Sadat's visit to Israel in November 1977, which prompted Holden's final trip to the Middle East. A letter suggesting the meeting came from the Israeli Prime Minister, Yitzhak Rabin, and was carried to Sadat by the Moroccan representative of the club.

As head of Saudi intelligence, Adham had contact with Holden when he was writing *The House of Saud*. Adham made sure that Holden, during his time in Saudi Arabia, was being taken care of and he passed him on to his nephew, and son of King Faisal, Prince Turki bin Faisal, who helped him with his research.

Turki eventually succeeded Adham as head of Saudi intelligence at the end of December 1977, only weeks after Holden was assassinated. Turki would later boast about his role in the Safari Club. In a 2002 speech at Georgetown University, he told the audience:

> In 1976, after the Watergate matters took place here, your intelligence community was literally tied up by Congress. It could not do anything. It could not send spies, it could not write reports and it could not pay money. In order to compensate for that, a group of countries got together in the hope of fighting Communism and established what was called the Safari Club. The principal aim of this club was that we would share information with each other and help each other in countering Soviet influence worldwide, and especially in Africa.

Adham died of a heart attack in Cairo in 1999. The department for television and digital journalism of the American University in Cairo was named after him. Turki, who resigned as head of the Saudi secret service ten days before the 9/11 attacks, later became Saudi ambassador to the US and the UK. Jamal Khashoggi, the nephew of the arms dealer Adnan Khashoggi and *Washington Post* journalist who was assassinated and dismembered by Saudi spies at the Saudi consulate in Istanbul, was his press officer.

Turki was often in London and Midolo had heard that he could sometimes be found at 5 Hertford Street, a private members' club in Mayfair known as 'London's most secretive club', where visitors have since included George Clooney, Leonardo DiCaprio, Mick Jagger and Meghan Markle.

As Midolo walked into the club, Turki had just finished dinner and was retiring to a private room for drinks with some friends. Midolo introduced himself. Turki, seventy-nine, was impeccably dressed, with a pinstripe grey suit and red tie, sporting a tightly clipped goatee. He looked tired, but his blue eyes, like his uncle's, were alert and intense. He spoke with a slight accent and was very courteous.

As they stepped into the room, with large armchairs and logs cracking in a fireplace, champagne was served but the prince did not drink.

'How come no one has written a book about the Safari Club?' Midolo asked. He didn't want to spook him by asking about Holden straight away.

'Oh, bits and pieces have come out in various books,' Turki replied with a smile. 'The Egyptian journalist Mohamed Heikal has written about it in his book about Iran.'

Still, Midolo said, there was not much information available about the club's activities. 'In your speech at Princeton, you referred to it as "a secret" that you "never told to anybody before", and that was in 2002.'

Turki explained that the club was established in 1974 to fight off the Soviets in Africa and lasted until the Soviet invasion of Afghanistan in December 1979, when the CIA could resume its covert operations. He added that the revolution in Iran and the change in government in France was another reason the Safari Club 'lapsed'.

'Why was it based in Cairo?'

'Because Egypt is in Africa,' Turki replied simply, adding that it wasn't convenient solely from a geographical point of view but also because Egypt had the capability to deliver weapons in places like the Congo or Ethiopia. He seemed proud of what they had achieved, stopping the Soviets from expanding their influence in Africa.

Midolo asked why Sadat shifted from the Soviets to the Americans. Turki said that Sadat had never been as close to the Russians as Nasser. 'They didn't think he would last,' Turki said. 'Nobody did! Not us, not even the Americans.' But Sadat managed to survive and to outflank the other Vice-Presidents who were in the Russians' pocket.

In a book he had written about Afghanistan, Turki had argued that his late uncle, Adham, had been sacked as head of intelligence because he did not predict Sadat's visit to Israel. Given how close Adham was to Sadat, Midolo told him that that struck him as unlikely. Turki admitted that in fact Adham was fired because he was 'too close to Sadat'. There were other reasons, Turki said, which had to do with Adham's relationship with the king and the crown prince. Adham was closer to King Faisal – Turki's father, who had been assassinated in 1975 – than to his successor, King Khalid.

Midolo's precise questions must have made the prince suspicious. 'Remind me, do you work for *The Times*?' he asked. Midolo told him he worked for *The Times* and the *Sunday Times*. 'In the '70s you had met another *Sunday Times* journalist,' he said. 'His name was David Holden.'

'The name rings a bell,' Turki said, but he couldn't remember how he had known him or why. Midolo explained who Holden was, how Turki had met him several times while Holden was writing *The House of Saud* and how he died.

'Once he arrived in Cairo, Holden was picked up at the airport and shot.'

'By the Egyptians?' Turki asked.

'Yes, we think so,' Midolo replied. He laid all his cards on the table and told him that he thought Holden was a spy, that the Egyptians most likely knew it and that that was the reason he was murdered. He also related the Halton incident and the fact that the Egyptians by all accounts had targeted Holden since at least 1974. Turki laughed at that, for some reason.

It was noisy in the room and Turki was very quiet, but Midolo heard him saying something along the lines that if Sadat had Holden assassinated, 'he must have had his reasons'. But Turki couldn't speculate any further because he said he didn't know.

'There are many mysteries in the Middle East that would remain unexplained,' Turki said. 'It's a place of intrigue.' He was suggesting that the journalists would never find the solution to the murder.

Midolo asked about the CIA and the KGB killing each other's agents. 'What could get you killed in those days?'

'Oh, there's plenty of literature out there about the subject and about their justifications for doing so,' Turki replied.

What about other intelligence agencies, Midolo asked, like the Egyptians, for example? 'Would they take on jobs on behalf of, say, the CIA?'

'Well, they were, and still are, allies. Those things happened, yes. Is this an interview?'

'Maybe,' Midolo said with a smile.

Turki apologised, saying that he needed to go and stood up. Midolo followed him and thanked him for his time. 'Are you going to be in London over the next few days, to continue the conversation?'

'I will be in London, but I need to check if I have time,' Turki said and walked out.

Midolo was left with the impression that Turki knew more than he was letting on and that he was deflecting his questions. He also had the feeling that Turki wanted to know how much *he* knew. Turki had revealed that he had taken on the mantle of head of intelligence from his uncle at the end of December 1977. The murder could have happened during his uncle's tenure, who was too close to Sadat not to know, but maybe Turki genuinely did not know about it. It was a possibility.

Turki's reference to 'the Egyptian journalist Mohamed Heikal' contained more undertones that Midolo could have expected, arising from a visit which Gillman and Leni paid to Celia Adams, widow of Michael Adams, the long-standing BBC Middle Eastern correspondent. They saw her at her house in Devon where, over a generous afternoon tea, Celia talked about Michael's friendship with Holden, which dated from the time they were both interned during the Suez Crisis in 1956. After they had left Cairo for Beirut, Michael and Holden would meet every Saturday morning to talk through the latest turn of events.

'You know, journalists talking,' Celia recalled. 'They were very serious, getting as near to the truth as they possibly could. I would take a back seat, obviously.' Celia nurtured some familiar doubts about Holden: 'He had a slight touch of artificiality about him, to tell you the truth. He was perfectly civil to me but never particularly warmed to me, I don't think.' Celia had memories of Philby from Beirut too, 'getting drunk and throwing himself about and behaving stupidly'. Her key memory, however, was of Michael's obsession with Holden's fate, to the point where each time he interviewed someone about Egypt, he would ask what they knew about him. During Michael's final visit to Cairo, which she dated to the late 1990s, he had a crucial encounter. He called into a hotel where he saw Heikal in the lobby. They had known each other since the 1950s. Now, Celia related, 'they greeted each other, but Heikal was in a great hurry'. He was about to get into a lift when Michael approached him.

'Look, I do want to talk to you,' Michael told him.

'I'm late, sorry, I can't talk,' Heikal said.

'OK, just tell me, who killed David?' Michael asked.

'We did,' Heikal replied and looked down, as the doors of the lift closed. Michael never saw him again.

CHAPTER 23

THE SCRIBE

Mohamed Heikal was no ordinary journalist. He was widely considered the most influential journalist in his country, and during his two decades as editor of *Al-Ahram*, the Egyptian daily had become one of the most read and quoted newspapers in the entire Middle East. He had been the author of a dozen bestselling books, most written in fluent, elegant English, which had won him recognition as a leading Arab intellectual and an authority on current affairs. It was Heikal who had first revealed the existence of the Safari Club, having found a copy of the coalition's charter in the archives of the Iranian secret service after the revolution.

Heikal had also been an important member of Nasser's Egyptian Revolution and a member of the Revolutionary Command Council. Heikal was Nasser's *éminence grise*, his confidant and, some would even whisper, his Richelieu.

When Nasser died in 1970, Heikal resigned as Minister of Information but kept his role as a member of Egypt's National Security Council and played an important part in the ensuing political struggle from which Sadat emerged as Nasser's unlikely successor. Heikal was also very close to Sadat – at least for a while. For the first four years of Sadat's presidency, Heikal was, in Sadat's own words, closer to him than anyone else.

'I was very fond of Sadat as a man,' Heikal wrote. 'While fully conscious of his shortcomings, I hoped that the responsibilities of office would strengthen the positive elements of his character and enable him to overcome the weak ones.'

Heikal managed Sadat's campaign to confirm him in the presidency and remained in almost daily contact with him until they fell out over the policies the President pursued in the aftermath of the 1973 war. Namely, it was the decision to take sides with the Americans and sign the peace treaty with Israel that had been the straw that broke the camel's back.

'Sadat turned his back on the Arabs whose help he needed, staking all on the friendship of the Americans,' Heikal wrote of Sadat's 1977 visit to Israel and the peace initiative, using a tale about a Turkish officer on manoeuvres to illustrate his point. 'Who do you want to get your medals from?' the officer was asked. 'From your own people or from the other side?' Heikal continued: 'It is always important to watch where the medals are coming from. It is not the mark of a good general to capture a new position at the cost of losing his own base.'

Michael Adams had been aghast at Heikal's response but he could not ask any more questions. Adams never saw him again and died not too long after, aged eighty-four, in 2005. Heikal passed away in 2016, aged ninety-two. The tale carried weight because of Heikal's influence at the heart of Egyptian politics. Those two words – 'we did' – reminded Gillman of a conversation with an academic and expert on the Middle East, Fred Halliday, in 1990. Halliday had known Holden and told Gillman that he had discussed his murder case with P. J. Vatikiotis, known as Taki, a writer and journalist who had grown up in Egypt and had written a modern history of the country.

Taki had told Halliday, who then in turn told Gillman, that the head of Egyptian police had confessed that the Egyptians had carried out the assassination. 'We did it,' the police chief said. 'They asked us to do it. Holden was working for the KGB.' As for *who* had asked the Egyptians to kill Holden, Halliday was not sure. The British? The Americans? Halliday remembered Taki had mentioned both MI6 and the CIA, but it was a long time ago and he could not recall any more details. At the time, Gillman had dismissed the episode as second-hand hearsay, but in light of the Heikal story it had taken on a new significance.

There was more: in the early 1990s, Gillman had learned that Heikal had unburdened himself to a young American journalist who was based in Cairo. The journalist, Rachel, had been asked by her newspaper to 'rake over the coals' of the Holden case and see if anything new could be written to coincide with the fifteenth anniversary of the assassination. Rachel had gone straight to Heikal, who had taken her under his wing. He raised a finger, intimating her to stay silent, then turned the radio on at high volume. 'Rachel, I liked David very much, but the trouble is, he was much more than a journalist,' Heikal told her. 'This is a case that is closed and can never be reopened. There will never be a solution. It is too important.' Heikal told her that he could not reveal anything about the killing except that it was 'a state matter'. He added that there would never be a time when the story was safe to pursue. Undaunted, Rachel decided to make some calls, but she hit a brick wall. No one would talk. When she went back to Heikal, he turned on the radio again and whispered: 'I beg you, do *not* pursue this case.'

In 2023, Rachel, then in her sixties, was still based in Cairo. When Midolo reached her, he had barely mentioned the word 'murder' when she cut him short.

'All right, you've gotta stop,' she said, her voice trembling. 'Stop talking. You're gonna call me back on Signal or Viber. You're gonna have a very quick education, partly given by me, about how to stay safe and—'

The line was cut and he couldn't hear the rest. When he called her back using an encrypted app, she sounded very concerned.

'Listen,' she said, 'I need to ask you a couple more questions because our line was cut. Do you know why it was cut? Because of the subject matter that you started to talk about on the phone.'

She went on to say that, as a foreigner who had lived in that country for a long time, she assumed that her phone, like most journalists', was not secure.

'Have you ever been to Egypt?' she asked him.

Midolo had, once, for work in 2019. He was there to write about the country's new capital that Egypt's strongman, General Sisi, was building in the desert east of Cairo. He had been officially invited by the British contractor responsible for the construction as well as by the Egyptian government itself. He had met the Minister of Infrastructure, and even though his article was critical and mentioned the real reason Sisi was building his mirage city in the desert – to isolate himself and his government from protests like the ones that had led to the ousting of Mubarak in 2011 – the Egyptian government officials seemed to have loved the publicity. They had purchased thousands of copies of the magazine, *Property Week*, in which the article had appeared as its cover story, and handed it to whoever walked past their stand at a real estate conference in Cannes, in the south of France. There was no way they would love *this* story, Midolo thought.

He explained all this to Rachel, who did not sound impressed. Midolo was apologetic: 'Sorry I called you on your phone, I stupidly thought mobile phones would be OK...'

'That was a goof!' she cut him short again, 'that was such a goof. All right, listen, that one subject in this country will bring you a lot of grief. I know I cut you off, but I'm assuming it's about the Italian student.'

She was talking about Giulio Regeni, the journalist and Cambridge

PhD student who had been abducted, horribly tortured and then killed in January 2016. There were chilling echoes of Holden's case in the murder of Regeni, almost forty years later. Somehow the latter felt closer to the bone – and not just because the victim was also Italian. Regeni was only a few months younger than Midolo – he was born in 1987, Regeni in 1988 – and the two even had a couple of friends in common. They were both left wing; they both spoke five languages proficiently. Regeni was only twenty-eight when he was murdered, as he was studying for a PhD in development studies at Girton College, Cambridge, while Midolo was doing his MA in investigative journalism at City University in London. Regeni had arrived in Cairo a few months earlier to conduct ground research on Egypt's independent unions, which he saw as a fragile hope for democracy in the country after General Sisi's coup three years earlier. He was focusing, in particular, on street vendors. 'Regeni plunged into their world, hoping to assess their union's potential to drive political and social change,' the *New York Times* wrote in 2017.

In December 2015, Regeni attended a meeting of trade union activists in central Cairo and wrote about it, under a pseudonym, for an Italian newspaper. He noticed a veiled young woman taking a picture of him with her mobile. Two weeks later, he was on his way to a birthday party when he disappeared. His friends tried to call him, then launched an online search campaign with the hashtag #whereisgiulio. His parents flew in from Italy, while the Italian ambassador in Cairo frantically tried to obtain any information from the Egyptian authorities, who claimed to know nothing about it. Regeni's friends were interviewed by Egyptian police detectives, who repeatedly asked them if he was gay. 'I told them he has a girlfriend,' one of his friends remembered. 'Then the next guy goes: "Are you sure he is straight? Maybe he's one of these bisexuals."'

Days later, a body was found. A bus driver noticed something on the side of the busy Alexandria Desert Highway in western Cairo.

The body was half naked and covered in dry blood. When the Italian ambassador arrived at the Zeinhom morgue that night, after midnight, he was refused entry. 'Open the door!' the ambassador yelled, and he was allowed in. Regeni's body lay on a metal tray. His hair was smeared with blood, his right earlobe sliced off, his mouth open, one of his front teeth was missing and many others were chipped or broken. He had cigarette burns on his skin, deep wounds on his back and the bones on his wrists, shoulders and feet were broken. Regeni had been tortured, possibly for four days on end. The autopsy confirmed that he had been beaten, burnt, stabbed and, eventually, killed after his neck had been snapped.

Absurdly, the chief Egyptian detective assigned to the case said that Regeni had died in a car crash. Egyptian TV and newspapers claimed that Regeni was gay and had been murdered by a jealous lover; that he was a drug addict; that he was a spy. Regeni had been working for Oxford Analytica, a business research firm founded by an ex-Nixon administration official, and some suggested this meant that he was working for the CIA or MI6. A breakthrough came after the US government passed on explosive information to Italy revealing that the Egyptian security forces were behind the kidnapping, torture and murder. 'We had incontrovertible evidence of official Egyptian responsibility,' an Obama administration official who had confirmed the intelligence told the *New York Times*. 'There was no doubt.'

In June 2024, four Egyptian intelligence officials were on trial *in absentia* in Rome for Regeni's murder. One was overheard telling another officer: 'We kidnapped Regeni, we thought he was a British spy.' The day the four officers were indicted in Italy, Egypt's public prosecution officially closed its own investigation, blaming the murder on unknown 'enemy parties'. An Italian senator, speaking with the *New York Times*, used a Latin expression to describe Regeni's case: '*Arcana imperii.*' The secrets of power.

Midolo told Rachel that he did not mean to ask about Regeni but about Holden. He added that he understood that some thirty years before, she had looked into the matter.

'Did I?' she asked. She couldn't remember. She knew the case, but she did not recall talking to Heikal about it.

'This is so sweet, it goes back to the mists of time,' she said. 'I was super young. I was meant to be this super stringer. It was a different era.' She didn't know if she ever wrote about Holden, she doubted it, but she remembered the story.

'Emanuele, forgive me, but I was short with you because a very good friend of mine wrote about the Italian student and for the following four years, she could not get a year-long visa,' she explained. 'She had to renew the visa every three months, six months, it was ridiculous. It's the one story that, if you touch it, as a foreigner, when you leave and go back to Egypt you might not be allowed back in.'

That's why she had been so jumpy over the phone and apologised again. 'You have to know something,' she warned him. 'If you're coming to Cairo or talking to people in Cairo, do not have these conversations on the phone. This stuff can get dangerous and I don't want you to have problems. Are you British, if I may ask?'

'I'm not,' he replied, 'I'm Italian, actually.'

'Even better,' she said sarcastically. 'You have to take your security considerations seriously. And the fact that you're Italian, even though you're living in England, would also make them suspicious. Because of this whole thing about the dead Italian student, the security services here are extremely sensitive. Do you follow me?'

Midolo decided to ask Roger Boyes, the veteran *Times* foreign correspondent and diplomatic editor, what he made of Rachel's warnings. Could a murder from forty-five years ago generate so much paranoia? Boyes remembered Rachel from when she was a young woman. He agreed that she sounded very paranoid. He also argued that maybe Sisi was trying to distance himself from his predecessors – Nasser, Sadat and Mubarak. Maybe it was in his interest to help Midolo solve the cold case and prove that Egypt under his rule was a different country than in the past? Midolo was not convinced, but Boyes slipped a detail into the conversation, something that he did not expect.

'You know, John is going to Egypt in September to speak at some conference about freedom of the press,' Boyes said.

'John?' Midolo asked.

'Witherow.'

It turned out that John Witherow, the long-time editor of both *The Times* and the *Sunday Times*, who had just stepped down to become chairman of Times Newspapers, had been invited as the main speaker at an event marking the centenary of none other than Mohamed Heikal. The conference was being organised by Heikal's son, Hassan.

Midolo emailed Hassan Heikal straight away. Over Zoom, a few days later, he filled him in about the Holden investigation. Hassan seemed enthusiastic and told him that he should be able to find some 'old-timers' from the government or the security services who should be willing to help. He also said he would ask his mother, Heikal's widow, Hedayat, if she remembered Holden. By the end of that week, Hassan had invited him to the conference. Michael Binyon would also come, along with Witherow. Midolo, a property reporter, would go to Egypt with two of the most senior and respected journalists at *The Times*. The thing was so far-fetched that he could still not quite believe it. It looked like a heaven-sent opportunity.

• • •

The days before his Cairo trip were clouded by ill omens. The weather itself seemed to conjure darkness, as southern England's hottest

Indian summer came to a close, with thunder clouds coalescing in a blackening sky. The second warning came from Richard Spencer, the long-time Middle East correspondent for *The Times*, who had just been given the role of Beijing correspondent. Spencer was in London for a few days while he was waiting for his visa and he met Midolo for coffee at the office canteen on the fourteenth floor. Outside the large windows, London was crushed by a wall of clouds.

Spencer listened carefully as Midolo explained the Holden case and why he was determined to go to Egypt. After a moment of silence, Spencer said that it all sounded very plausible. For the Egyptians to kill him was 'certainly in line with what they had been doing for the past seventy years', he said. 'Killing, torturing, jailing and making people disappear.' The situation in Egypt was dire. Spencer himself had been banned in 2019 after writing about President Sisi's three children – all in positions of power and one a colonel in Egyptian intelligence – who had been linked in the press to the Regeni case. 'I had tried to dissuade John Witherow from going to the Heikal memorial,' Spencer said.

'Why?' Midolo asked.

'Because Heikal was Nasser's main propagandist,' he replied. '*Al-Ahram* prides itself as *The Times* of Egypt, but they're just a propaganda machine. We might not be perfect, but we're not a dictator's rag!' Spencer went on to say that after Nasser's death and Sadat opened up to Israel, Heikal started criticising Sadat and ended up in jail, 'becoming a martyr' of press freedom. 'He kept doing the same under Mubarak, whose fault was to be less of a fascist, antisemitic dictator than Nasser.'

Spencer added that Heikal's stance as an outspoken political commentator for *Al Jazeera* in his later years was ironic considering he had been 'a dictator's puppet' and because of this he had discouraged Witherow from going. But it would be a good opportunity for Midolo, who would be much safer with a contingent of

British journalists than snooping around on his own. He warned Midolo that no fixer in Cairo would likely help him: 'People there are scared and don't want to work with Western journalists.' The Egyptian government was going to assume that he, as a British journalist, was MI6 and so he was going to be watched and followed around.

'I'm Italian. I have an Italian passport,' Midolo told him.

'Well, that's another problem altogether,' Spencer said darkly while taking a sip of his coffee. He recommended that Midolo should approach his sources from London, as contacting them while he was in Cairo would be 'risky'.

'What do you mean?'

'The Egyptians might pick you up and ask you, "What the fuck do you think you're doing?" Instead, if you contact them just before you go there, you can show them the emails and tell them you had permission.' Spencer added that there was a risk that Midolo would not be allowed into the country if he contacted sources beforehand, but he reckoned the risk was quite low. 'And it's certainly better than being picked up while you're there and being taken to a police station for questioning,' he added. The Holden matter was less sensitive because it was a cold case. Asking questions about the current regime or Regeni's murder would be much more dangerous. 'Once you're in a room with an ex-government official or a general, it's unlikely they would call the police to arrest you,' Spencer said. 'That would be very bad form.'

Hassan Heikal had seemed expansive and helpful. Midolo followed up with an email thanking him for the invitation and checking if he had asked his mother if she remembered anything about Holden. He also asked if he could see a list of invitees to the conference, so that he could arrange his interviews in advance, following Spencer's advice.

Hassan replied with a single sentence, telling him that he was not aware that his mother had 'any recollection of such events' and that he would not share the list of invitees. In short, Midolo was on his own. He discussed Hassan's change of tune with Gillman. On one reading, he had over-promised. On another, Gillman speculated, he had made approaches to officials about Holden and had been abruptly warned off. If so, that accorded with another warning Midolo had received from Binyon, who had called him on the suggestion of his 'friend' from MI6 who had run operations in Egypt.

'Manu!' Binyon exclaimed in his deep, loud voice. 'I told this friend we're going to Egypt together and he told me to be very, very careful.' He went on to give his warning about not snooping around or asking questions. 'It's still a police state, don't ever forget that.' Binyon added that he did not want the Egyptians to think that the trip was some kind of intelligence operation – the irony of that was not lost on them. 'I just don't want us, all of us, to be put in jeopardy,' Binyon said. 'And I certainly don't want you to get the three of us blown up in a car!' They both laughed, but Midolo's mind went to Daphne Caruana Galizia, the Maltese investigative journalist killed by a car bomb in 2017. It was a troubling reminder of the paranoia that had tinged the original Holden investigation.

At the top of Midolo's depressingly short list of people to seek out in Cairo was an Egyptian general who had been head of intelligence between 1966 and 1978. He had found his number through a friend and called and called for days but the general never picked up. Midolo was not even sure he was still alive.

The second person was Safia Amin, the daughter of Mustafa Amin, the Egyptian journalist who had been jailed by Nasser for his contacts with the CIA and freed by Sadat in 1974. Mustafa Amin was one of the few people who knew Holden was coming to Cairo. Midolo had come to suspect that Amin had been the person who had alerted the Egyptians that Holden was coming that evening – and, possibly, that he was even there to identify Holden when he landed and to convince him to get into the stolen car.

Midolo rang Safia and she sounded very worried. At first, she seemed to doubt Midolo was a journalist. Eventually, she told him it was better if he emailed her with his request so that she could check whether he was legitimate. Midolo said he would be in Cairo the following week and asked if they could meet face to face. 'I'm not in Cairo and I'm not sure I will be back next week,' she said. But after he emailed her, a tracking software that Midolo used to check if people had opened his emails proved what he suspected: she was in Cairo. She just didn't want to see him.

Rachel did not want to see him, either. It was a dramatic U-turn from their first conversations. At first, she had been openly enthusiastic at the idea of helping him with his quest. 'I look forward to meeting you!' she had messaged him just a few weeks before. But as his trip approached, she had sounded less keen. 'I did make a couple of inquiries but without result. I'm afraid the trail on this story may have gone cold. Just too many years have gone by.' When he messaged her again, the day before his flight, she told him she would prefer not to meet up, after all. 'People here are not going to help you with this, sorry to say.'

CHAPTER 24

UNDER THE PYRAMIDS

Cairo International Airport was not as Midolo remembered it. An anonymous modern space filled with huge slabs of marble, it could have been anywhere but for a colossal Egyptian goddess painted in gold that greeted passengers in the arrivals hall.

A bespectacled Egyptian man in a suit that was too tight for him was waiting for Midolo, Binyon and Witherow, holding a sign with their names. He asked for their passports and told them to follow him. He handed the passports and visa forms to an officer, who stamped them right away, barely glancing at the journalists. Midolo was left for last, which prompted Witherow to joke: 'They know you're up to no good.'

The bespectacled man took back their passports and, after the baggage claim, handed them to another security officer who was standing in front of the automatic doors that read 'nothing to declare' in green and 'items to declare' in red. The officer barely looked at them and they passed through. The bespectacled man handed them back their passports, to Midolo's relief, and as the automatic doors swung open, the heat of Cairo hit him like a punch.

Outside were line after line of taxis, some clearly marked and official, many others private. Their taxi was a black, unmarked car immediately to the left. The three climbed in and soon joined Cairo's horrendous stream of traffic, just another black car among the thousands that were piling along in the five-lane-wide boulevards heading to the city centre. Mopeds and scooters were trying to pass them left and right, honking on their horns, no helmets in sight. Once in a while, the road opened up and they could see stretches of desert that the highway had yet to conquer. Midolo knew it was there that Holden's body had been found.

After half an hour's drive, they arrived at the Four Seasons Hotel in the Garden City neighbourhood, a thirty-storey fortress towering over the Nile on Cairo's fabled riverfront, the Corniche. The gates opened and two soldiers carrying semi-automatic machine guns came round the car, one of them holding a dog, checking for explosives – a practice that, the journalists were told, had become commonplace at high-end hotels after an Islamist group bombed a resort in Sharm El Sheikh in 2005, killing eighty-eight people. It was 4 p.m. when the three journalists finished checking in. They were free for the rest of the afternoon, so they agreed to regroup in an hour and to meet in Witherow's room on the fifth floor for a drink.

When 5 p.m. rolled around, they sat on the balcony perched above the spectacle of the shimmering Nile at sunset, dotted with the sails of feluccas. As soon as the waiter left with his empty tray, Witherow pointed at Midolo and asked: 'So, who killed him?'

Midolo squirmed in his chair and laughed uncomfortably. He did not expect such a direct question. Was it safe to discuss it here? The room was probably bugged, but the balcony? 'Certainly not the Egyptians!' he said loudly, looking around. 'I'm sure the Egyptian government had nothing to do with it.'

'So you think they did it?' Witherow pressed him. South-African born, educated in Britain, Witherow was tall, handsome, with longish grey hair and did not look his age – he was almost seventy-two but had the energy of a much younger man. He seemed more relaxed than he ever had been in the office, a bottle of Sakara Gold in his hand, three buttons of his shirt undone.

'I do,' Midolo said, becoming serious. He explained that this had also been the conclusion the Insight team had reached during the original investigation. 'But back then, it was more a deduction based on the evidence that they had gathered that pointed towards the Egyptians,' he explained. 'There was no smoking gun.'

This time around, the evidence was incontrovertible. First, Mohamed Heikal had told Michael Adams that the Egyptians were behind it.

'Heikal said that?' Binyon asked, looking shocked. 'Oh dear. He would have known.'

The fact that such a commanding figure as Heikal knew who had killed Holden and why was not surprising. 'Mohamed Hassanein Heikal was not an Egyptian journalist,' the American correspondent, Rachel, had told Midolo. 'He was the power behind Gamal Abdel Nasser. He created him. And for the next fifty years, he continued to be a very powerful man in Egypt.' Heikal had told her that the Holden killing was 'a state matter' – i.e. a political assassination. In a country like Egypt in 1977, which was under the ironclad rule of Sadat, the order could only have come from the top. After all, Sadat himself had boasted that he alone was in charge of assassinations, and he hated the Brits as much as he hated the Soviets – if not even more.

Then there was the near miss with David Halton in 1974. The two men who had approached him at Cairo Airport had introduced themselves as Egyptian government officials. Midolo believed that was the truth – that the two were not, say, Mossad killers in disguise. For starters, they were inside the terminal, between the passport controls and the baggage reclaim belts. It was a highly secure area and would have represented an impossibly high risk for foreign agents, let alone terrorists. The men knew Halton/Holden was coming and escorted him to a battered car (stolen, presumably). It was the same technique Holden's killers used three years later, stealing the three old Fiats in advance and repainting them. The Halton incident introduced two new elements: first, the people who had met Holden at the airport were Egyptian government officials and they had met him *inside* the airport; second, the killers had targeted Holden years before they killed him.

Besides, Holden was on the last leg of a grand tour of the Middle East. He had been to Syria, Israel and Jordan before boarding his flight to Cairo. If either Mossad or Palestinian terrorists were after him, why not kill him in Damascus? Or Jerusalem? Or the West Bank? Why wait for him to get to Cairo, which was heavily guarded ahead of the peace conference? 'Because it had to happen in Egypt,' Midolo said. 'Because the Egyptians did it. They wanted him dead. And I think Holden knew. He knew the ground had shifted since 1974, that's why he didn't want to come back here. That's why he told a colleague that he thought he was going to be "public enemy number one". And that's why he was in such a foul mood on his last flight.'

'What happened in '74?' Witherow asked him.

Midolo explained that 1974 was a crucial year because, after much mutual courting, Egypt had shifted from the Soviet to the American side. It had reopened diplomatic relations with the US and the CIA had set up shop in Cairo, with a new, energetic and staunchly anti-communist station chief named James Fees. 'Fees and his vice, Bill Buckley, trained Sadat's private guard,' Midolo said. 'The agency gave Sadat everything he wanted: money, weapons, even a replica of Air Force One. The Americans were desperate to shift Egypt and curb the Soviets' presence in the Middle East.'

In exchange for their generosity, Midolo continued, the Egyptians gave the CIA carte blanche to run covert operations throughout the Middle East from their new Cairo base. After being trained by the Americans, the Egyptian secret service started running joint black ops with them. From 1976, the Egyptian capital became the headquarters of the Safari Club, a joint-intelligence organisation that led anti-Soviet missions in Africa and was bankrolled by Saudi money. The man behind it was the head of Saudi intelligence, Kamal Adham, a close ally of Sadat. This suited the CIA nicely because, after the Watergate scandal and the election of the Democrat Jimmy Carter at the White House, the agency's covert operations had been severely curbed and put under the control of the US Congress.

'Why kill a journalist though? What was Holden writing about that made him such a threat?' Binyon asked.

'Holden wasn't killed because of his journalism,' Midolo said. 'He was shot dead because he was, or was suspected to be, a spy. We know he had been an informant to the CIA; he had written for Western propaganda publications that were bankrolled by the CIA. And we think he was helping MI6, if he was not straight on their payroll, like many of his colleagues at the *Sunday Times*. But we believe he was also working for the KGB.'

'Like Philby,' Witherow said.

'Exactly,' Midolo replied. 'We think the killing of David Holden was "a wedding gift" from the Egyptians to their newlyweds, the Americans. And, incidentally, also a big favour to their other new friends, the Saudis.'

'What you're suggesting,' Binyon interceded, 'is that after five, six or so many Cambridge spies who had escaped to Soviet Russia, the Egyptians told the Americans, "We're going to take care of this one," is that right?'

'Mmm,' Witherow murmured. 'I can see the Egyptians doing it. But I don't believe the Americans would have dared kill a British journalist. I can see the Egyptians telling them afterwards and the CIA people going, "What the hell have you done?"'

Midolo conceded that that was one of the scenarios. The other one was that the Americans or the Saudis (or both) had found out about what Holden was up to and had asked the Egyptians to rid them of this troublesome journalist. 'What I find unlikely is that the CIA didn't know that Holden was going to his death,' Midolo added. 'Whether they were actively involved or just turned a blind eye, we don't know.'

'And you're here to find out,' Witherow said. 'You need a deathbed confession. But I'll tell you why you can't go around asking questions. Because of Hassan. You can't put him in trouble.'

• • •

Mohamed Heikal's home was a grand if dated apartment on the top floor of a tall building on the other side of the river. As soon as Midolo walked out of the lift, a balding man with narrow, alert eyes and a broad smile shouted: 'Ah, you are the gentleman who's causing us so much trouble!' and gave a raucous laugh. It was Hassan Heikal. He told his other guests that he had given Midolo a hard time via email. 'You have to forgive me, but we're walking over eggshells here,' Hassan told him, explaining that there was a presidential election in a couple of months and the government was very jumpy. 'You're very welcome to talk to everyone tonight and at the event tomorrow.'

As they stepped into the apartment, which had wooden floors and oak panelling on the walls, the journalists were greeted by Hassan's mother and Mohamed's widow, Hedayat. With a full head of silver hair and penetrating eyes that were highlighted by a dark jumpsuit, Hedayat was spry for an 89-year-old.

Midolo introduced himself and revealed the reason for his visit. Hedayat remembered Holden's name, but she couldn't place him.

She told him that Heikal was a family man who distanced himself from the world of journalism – and journalists – when he was at home. Yet the two had first met in his newsroom. They were introduced by Mustafa Amin, she said – Midolo almost choked on his champagne upon hearing Amin's name but tried to act nonchalantly. She and Heikal had three children – Ali, Hassan and Ahmed – the first a doctor and the other two successful businessmen. Tellingly, none of them was a journalist.

A small squadron of butlers, who treated the Heikal family members with due reverence, announced that food had been served. The lavish buffet consisted of stuffed vine leaves, roast chicken, black rice and delicious aubergines with tomatoes that reminded Midolo of a Sicilian *parmigiana*. After dinner, the guests drank wine and mingled. There were journalists, diplomats and ex-government officials. Midolo had set his sights on a portly old man who, he had been told, had been President Hosni Mubarak's secretary for a decade during the 1980s, after Mubarak had succeeded Sadat.

The reception was almost over and Midolo decided it was not time to tiptoe around. He approached the secretary, who had also been Egypt's ambassador to a number of European countries, and asked him straight out if he remembered Holden.

'Remind me, who was he?' said the secretary, who was bald, stout and had thick glasses and sat heavily on a yellow sofa. Midolo told him the bare bones of the case: the British journalist who had been murdered in Cairo in 1977.

'This was the man who was picked up at the airport', the secretary said, 'but never reached his destination and was found dead alongside the road the next morning?'

'Exactly,' Midolo said. 'So you do remember the case.'

'No, I don't.'

'Well, it sounds like you do.' Midolo was perplexed.

'I really don't,' the secretary said, an inscrutable expression on his face. 'But I seem to remember it was a personal matter.' Then, after a pause, he asked Midolo: 'Tell me, are you related to this man?'

Midolo said he wasn't.

'No? Then why bother?'

'Because he was working for my newspaper and we're trying to find out what happened, forty-five years later. It's still a mystery.'

'I'd stay away from it,' he told Midolo, waving his hand.

'Why?'

'Egypt is a country with a very long history. Thousands of years of history. There are many mysteries in Egypt, many secrets. You'll never get to the bottom of it.'

It struck Midolo that the secretary had used exactly the same words as Prince Turki, the former head of Saudi intelligence he had met at the private members' club in London. But Midolo was determined not to be impressed by the secretary's admonition. As a Sicilian, he could recognise intimidation when he saw it, even if expressed in such a seemingly pleasant way. The word '*Mafia*', after all, originated from the Arabic language. 'Do you think I can ask the Egyptian government if they have any knowledge of the case?' he persevered. 'See if there's any information in the archives?'

The secretary replied that there was no harm in asking the government, perhaps the Ministry of Interior, through the British Embassy. 'They're probably going to say they don't know anything about it, which of course says a lot,' he said. 'It means they know, but they won't tell you.'

The secretary turned to a man in an armchair to his left and started speaking in Arabic, gesturing at Midolo. A woman sitting opposite them was staring at Midolo. 'How's your Arabic?' the woman, in heavily accented English, asked him.

'Non-existent,' Midolo replied, smiling.

'Ah, I see.'

'Can you tell what they're saying?'

'They're talking about youth,' she said, mysteriously, and stood up, leaving Midolo wondering if she had said 'youth' or 'you'.

• • •

Back at the hotel, Midolo was surprised to see that his room had been cleaned while he was at the dinner, either due to an overzealous hotel service or to something else. In any case, he was relieved he didn't have his laptop with him. He kicked off his shoes and was about to wash his hands when he noticed some dark spots in one of the two sinks of his bathroom. It looked like blood. He checked his hands to see if he had any cuts, but there weren't any. He took some photos with the burner phone that the newspaper's head of security had given him for the trip, then sent them to Gillman.

'Strange thing in hotel room,' he texted along with the photos:

Room is immaculate, has been cleaned (again) after I left at 7 – no idea how many times they got in. But there are some strange dark drops in one of the sinks. Looks like blood. Very strange as rest of the room is spanking clean. I thought of marble cleaning product but don't see why it would be dark.

Gillman was online and replied straight away. 'Do you think they are sending a message?'

The thought had occurred to him. Certainly, the general climate of paranoia did not help. But if it was a threat, it was a peculiar one. 'I'd put more blood if I was sending a message, not three or four drops around the sink,' he replied. 'Checked for a horse's head in the bed but none to be found.'

'Glad you're keeping your sense of humour,' Gillman said.

The following morning, Witherow, Binyon and Midolo took a

guided tour of the Citadel of Saladin, the residence of Egypt's rulers for 700 years that towers over central Cairo from its position on top of a hill. As soon as their guide learned that Midolo was Italian, he spoke in a surprisingly open and frank manner about the Regeni case. 'They've tried to suppress what happened,' he told them. 'The government buys arms and aircraft from Italy and lets them drill our gas, but they can't do that for ever because Regeni's family wants to know why he was killed.' The guide went on to say that the Egyptian public too wanted to know. There was nothing in Egyptian newspapers about the case, as the censors wouldn't allow it. 'But the people know because they can't close the internet,' he added.

Witherow asked the guide what would happen to him if someone had heard him saying such things. 'Would you be told off? Warned to stop? Or would they arrest you?'

'They would arrest me straight away and throw me in jail,' he said. 'There are thousands and thousands of people in prison.' The political prisoners in Egyptian jails throughout the country, according to a human rights group, numbered at least 60,000. In 2020, a 24-year-old filmmaker who had mocked President Sisi in a music video, comparing him to a date (the fruit), died in prison after two years of incarceration without trial. 'They're not political prisoners,' the guide said. 'They're just people. Our people.'

The discussion continued over lunch, after they went back to the hotel and sat at a table by the pool. Midolo spotted the man sitting opposite them almost an hour into the lunch. He had no idea how long the watcher had been there staring at him. For a moment, he considered telling the rest of the group. But then he remembered Binyon's words – 'I just don't want us, all of us, to be put in jeopardy' – and thought better of it.

Witherow announced he was going to the gym and Midolo felt a slight panic at the idea of having to leave the table. Luckily for him, Binyon was still reminiscing about what Egypt looked like in 1973, when he was reporting the Arab–Israeli War for *The Times*, exactly fifty years before. Midolo had never been so happy that Binyon talked a lot.

After leaving Binyon by the pool, and as he saw the man keeping the lift open for him, Midolo had the strangest thought. Am I going to get myself killed because I'm polite? What an idiot. '*Shukran*,' he thanked the man as he got in the lift with him. To his relief, an elderly lady with a flowery dress was also there. 'Hi, how are ya?' she asked Midolo, with a strong American accent. He smiled in reply. The terrace was on the sixth floor and the lift was about to go up. Midolo's room was on the twelfth floor, but he did not want the man to know that. The button for the fourteenth floor had already been pushed, surely by the American lady. 'Oh, you're also going to the fourteenth floor? Good,' Midolo told her. She replied: 'The view is great, right?' Midolo was pleased to be able to chat with her as the lift was approaching the fourteenth floor. Next to him, the man was staring in the void, totally silent. As the doors opened, Midolo motioned for the woman to go ahead. 'Ladies first,' he said, and she giggled. He looked at the man as the doors closed on him. He did not like the expression on his face. Midolo said goodbye to the lady and sprinted for the stairs. He walked briskly down to the twelfth floor and gently closed the door of his room behind him, his heart pounding. What the hell am I doing? he asked himself.

Heikal's centenary celebration was held that night, 23 September 2023, at the National Museum of Egyptian Civilization (NMEC), a colossal new building of over 5 million square feet that had been commissioned by General Sisi himself. In 2021, when it was inaugurated, the mummies of twenty-two kings and queens were paraded through the streets of Cairo.

The imposing white museum gleamed in the sunset as guests piled in. There were many important political figures, including Adly Mansour, the interim President of Egypt after the 2013 coup d'état that toppled the elected President, Mohamed Morsi. Morsi had died in 2019 at Tora Prison, where he was being held on espionage charges, the same prison that had become the tomb of the young filmmaker who had compared Sisi to a date. Morsi's last words were from a poem: 'My country is dear even if it oppressed me and my people are honourable even if they were unjust to me.'

Heikal's face towered over the number 100 with the figure '1' styled as a pen. Inside the auditorium hung giant photographs of Heikal with Nasser and Sadat, with Mubarak, with Sisi, as well as pictures of the covers of his books. When Hedayat Heikal opened the conference at 7 p.m., she was visibly emotional. Her speech was followed by a short documentary about Heikal's life. The interpreter from Arabic into English was hopeless and Midolo's headphones weren't working. After a while, he gave up and took them off, focusing on the images rather than the words. The keynote talk was given by John Witherow, who used the news of Rupert Murdoch stepping down from News Corp to become chairman emeritus of the company to talk about the freedom of the press. 'How I wished I had met Heikal,' he concluded. Midolo thought exactly the same, although for different reasons.

After the event, Midolo met a friend of Heikal, who had been leading fierce student protests under Sadat. The man did not remember Holden, but he recalled an episode in which Sadat told an American journalist: 'In other times, I would have had you shot.'

It was September 1981 and Sadat had just arrested thousands of 'religious dissidents' and political opponents. The Egyptian President defended his decision in a press conference with foreign journalists, but he became furious when one of the reporters asked him if he had informed the US President Reagan of his intentions. Midolo was surprised to find out that Gillman had covered the press conference. 'Sadat exploded,' Gillman wrote. 'Trembling with rage, he shouted at his questioner: "You have no right to ask this question.

No one makes decisions here except me through my institutions."' Later, Sadat apologised for his behaviour while adding candidly the 'I would have had you shot' remark. 'But this is democracy.'

Among the thousands of people arrested that week was Heikal. It was his son Ahmed who opened the door of their home at 2 a.m. and, he told Midolo, saw an entire platoon of soldiers holding automatic rifles on the small landing outside their apartment, who had come to arrest his father. Ahmed woke Heikal up and the editor spoke to the two officers, 'the visitors of the dawn', as he described them. After he packed and came out, he could hear the soldiers speaking to each other on their walkie-talkies: 'Mission number nine completed...'

'Am I mission number nine?' Heikal asked them. When they arrived at the police station, Heikal realised he was only one of hundreds of people arrested that morning. Together with him were many distinguished figures in Egyptian public life: politicians, economists, writers, intellectuals. In total, the arrests numbered more than 3,000. The prisoners were led to Tora Prison, which had just been built. Heikal described it as 'a triumph of American penal technology transplanted onto Egyptian soil and tastefully named *sijn el-salam*, "the prison of peace".'

It was the last desperate order of a President who was losing his grip; who travelled everywhere by helicopter; who was closer to Kissinger than he was to members of his own government; who was threatening to have foreign reporters shot for asking insolent questions. Three weeks later, on 6 October 1981, during the annual military parade to celebrate the crossing of the Suez Canal during the Yom Kippur War eight years earlier, a truck swerved from the parade route and halted next to the presidential stand. Sadat rose from his chair, probably because he expected a salute. Instead, a small group of army officers started shooting at him and launched grenades towards the stand. Sadat was shot in the neck, then the assassin, an army officer named Khalid al-Islambuli, emptied his machine gun into the President's body, spraying him with bullets. Sadat's CIA-trained bodyguards were nowhere to be found. As Heikal later wrote, 'For the first time, the people of Egypt had killed their pharaoh.'

• • •

On the flight back to London, Midolo was torn. On one side, it had been a wonderful trip and he had met wonderfully kind people. On the other, he had not been allowed to roam freely and had not found what he was looking for, the definitive answer to the million-dollar question: why did the Egyptians kill Holden? Midolo had a list of contacts he would try to meet in London, but he wondered whether he should go back to Egypt in the future, if it were safe to do so.

There was another Egyptian he could try to talk to: Isis Elten. She had been a close friend of Holden in Egypt in the 1950s and Celia Adams had told Gillman they ought to speak to her. Luckily for Midolo, Elten was not in Egypt but lived, of all places, in Italy. Midolo had two weeks of holidays booked that he was supposed to spend back home in Sicily. The island, however, was ravaged by fierce wildfires and the authorities were forced to close the two main airports, Catania and Palermo. Instead of booking another flight, Midolo decided to take the opportunity to pay a visit to Elten.

'Poor David,' she had told Midolo, in perfect Italian, when he first spoke to her on the phone a few days earlier. 'No one could solve the case of his murder. Many had tried.' They had chatted for almost an hour, but she admitted she had been taken aback by the call and her memory – although formidable for a nonagenarian – was patchy. She had promised to think about Holden and see what else she could remember. She had also invited him to come see her in person.

Midolo flew from London to Florence and drove about two and a half hours along the Apennine range. Outside the car's windows rolled a Tuscan landscape of red-brick country houses with terracotta tile roofs, dark green cypresses and field after field of sunflowers. This being the Chianti region, the brown hills were lined up with luscious green vineyards. After leaving the highway, the landscape changed, turning into a tortuous road between the mountains. Eventually, the road became a winding white dirt track, obscured by tall trees and haunted by the deafening sound of cicadas.

Elten, now ninety-four, owned a house in a tiny hamlet of a few dozen souls called Acqualoreto, between Orvieto and Todi in the Umbrian hills.

'I'll meet you at the bar,' she had told Midolo.

'OK, which bar?' he had replied. She seemed perplexed, then laughed.

'There is only one bar.'

Acqualoreto nestles on a yellow hill of secular olive trees, its handful of stone houses barricaded around a central piazza and a campanile. An old lady was sitting on a bench of the town's one bar, which doubled up as a pizzeria on Saturdays, but she looked far too young to be ninety-four years old. She was red-haired and wore a colourful green and turquoise shirt on a white dress, over which hung a necklace of large blue globes. She looked straight at him and her grey eyes and light olive skin betrayed her.

After introducing herself in Italian, Elten nonchalantly switched to English. She told Midolo she spoke five languages 'but I can only write in four'. Surprisingly, the one language she could not write was Arabic. A Christian Copt, she was born in 1929 Isis Al-Bashria, the eldest daughter of a doctor, and was educated in English and French – both of which she spoke with no accent. 'I was too much of a rebel to be a good Egyptian girl, marry young and settle down,' she said with a grin.

In 1956, before the Suez Canal Crisis, she went to a party at the house of a friend near the Pyramids of Giza and met a handsome German reporter named Jorg Andrees Elten. She asked 'Andy', as he introduced himself, what he was looking for.

'A wife,' came the reply.

'Well, don't look at me, I've just dumped a German boyfriend and have no intention to take another one.'

A year later, in 1957, they were married. Andy introduced her to his colleagues, a troupe of foreign correspondents – most of them British and American – who were busy filing story after story about the Franco-British debacle of the Suez Crisis. 'Those were extraordinary times, after the Suez Canal Crisis,' Elten told Midolo almost seventy years later. 'Nasser was loved very much and hated very much too.'

She found the world of journalism, and foreign correspondents in particular, captivating. 'Journalists are like priests,' she said. 'They are good with people. They know how to listen. And they hear people's secrets.'

One day, Andy brought home a young British journalist named David Holden. 'I remember that day very well, we started laughing at some joke he cracked and we couldn't stop,' Elten recalled. 'David was not necessarily a funny person, but he had been very funny on that occasion.'

She continued: 'He was a beautiful man and very smart, particularly smart. I've always cared more about intelligence than beauty.' Holden clearly left a mark on the young Egyptian woman. 'He was a great conversationalist. He saw things clearly. I loved him very much. David and Michael Adams were our best friends.' Celia Adams had told Gillman she thought Elten had been in love with Holden. 'Nonsense,' she told Midolo. 'David was like a brother to me. I was possibly the only woman who didn't have a crush on him.'

Just like the rest of the British journalists, Holden had been expelled from Egypt during the Suez Crisis. But even if he was theoretically based in Beirut, Elten said he used to come to Cairo regularly. 'Cairo was the most cosmopolitan city in the world, more than London or Paris,' she said. 'It was much more interesting than Beirut, which was only good for shopping. All the journalists were coming to Cairo to get the best stories.'

Among them was Kim Philby. Elten met him in the late 1950s through Holden and often saw him at parties and social events. She remembered his stammer. 'I didn't like him,' she said. 'I wasn't surprised when the news broke that he had escaped to Moscow.' Yet in her house in Acqualoreto, she had Philby's autobiography, *My Silent War*, as well as the Insight book on him, *Philby: The Spy Who Betrayed a Generation*. She also had Holden's *Farewell to Arabia*, with a dedication that read: 'For Andy and Isis Elten – who shared so many Middle Eastern memories with – David 14/9/67'. Elten told Midolo she had only kept 'books written by her friends' after she had downsized a year earlier. For a moment, she seemed to mistake Philby and Holden, a slip that Midolo found curious. She said Holden had been in Moscow, or at least so she thought. Midolo told her that it was unlikely; he and Gillman would have known. Maybe, he suggested, Holden said that he wanted to go to Moscow? That he wished he had visited the Soviet Union? She could not recall.

What was certain, Elten explained, was the common knowledge that journalists were also working as spies. She said the Americans in particular would try to recruit foreign journalists so that they wouldn't compromise their own American reporters. 'The CIA tried to recruit my husband, but he said no,' she explained. 'He told them he had an Egyptian wife and didn't want to have any problems, for her or himself. Most journalists we knew refused to work for American or British intelligence. It was a dangerous business.'

The Egyptian government, she added, was suspicious of all foreign journalists and assumed all of them to be spies. 'One morning, I saw our butler picking up a piece of paper Andy had written and discarded. I confronted him and he admitted he had been asked by the government to transmit Andy's drafts and carbon copies of his letters because they suspected he was a spy.'

Elten had told Midolo over the phone that she didn't have any pictures of Holden, so he brought her a few printouts. In the one taken by Richard Beeston in Cairo in 1958, Holden was sitting at a cafe table with an Egyptian woman. Elten recognised her straight away. 'Hariya Khairy, she was also a journalist. She was my best friend.' Midolo was amazed: Elten told him that Holden had once proposed to her. Elten remembered the matter well. '"I don't love him, Isis," she told me. "I don't want to hear about it." She was in love with Ali Amin and married him. Ali was such a sweetheart.'

'Lords of the press' was how Elten described Ali and his twin brother Mustafa. 'They were gigantic,' she remembered, 'two mountains of meat.' Ali died in 1976, but Holden was due to meet Mustafa during his last fateful trip a year later. What Gillman and Midolo did not know was that Holden was also due to have lunch with Elten and Khairy the day his body was identified at the morgue. 'Hariya called me and said there would be no lunch, as David had been assassinated. It came as such a shock.'

Just over a year later, another one of her journalist friends, the *Los Angeles Times* correspondent Joe Alex Morris, was shot dead by a sniper in Tehran during the Iranian Revolution. It was tragic, but Holden's death was different, Elten said, because it was such a mystery. 'I still wonder why he was killed; no one could figure it out,' she said. But she would not get into speculations about why he was murdered and by whom, saying that she could not help the two journalists on their quest.

'I miss him dearly,' Elten concluded, as she accompanied Midolo to the door. 'There's no one left from that group. They are all dead now. I often think of who I would like to bring back, if I could, of all my friends, and David is one of them.'

CHAPTER 25

AGENT OF INFLUENCE

Fred Halliday was dying. The writer, journalist and academic had been fighting cancer for almost a year, but he was losing the battle – and he knew it. For five years, he had been dividing his time between his flat in Bloomsbury and Barcelona, Spain, where he was a visiting professor at two universities. It was the spring of 2010 and, before going back to Spain, he called his good friend, Roger Hardy. Hardy was a Middle Eastern specialist and foreign correspondent who had worked at the BBC for over two decades. The two had known each other for donkey's years.

Hardy was happy to hear from Halliday and inquired about his health, but he did not want to talk about that. Listen, he told Hardy, there's something I want to tell you that I've never told anyone. Do you remember David Holden?

Hardy had met Holden a few times and remembered the mystery surrounding his death. Halliday went on to say that Holden had written a marvellous book called *Farewell to Arabia* and started to recite, from memory, its opening lines: 'Arabia. The name has always evoked an exotic image. Because it signified for so long a land so desolate, isolated and unknown, it conveys even now a ring of loneliness and a promise of escape calculated to stir in all of us some flicker of romance.'

In 1973, while Halliday was conducting his own research on the Arabian Peninsula, Holden had offered to help him and even shared some of his notebooks. Thanks to his assistance, Halliday's research became a book titled *Arabia Without Sultans*, 'a kind of left-wing version of *Farewell to Arabia*'. The title paid homage to another of Holden's books, *Greece Without Columns*, published a couple of years before.

As Halliday now related, in the 1970s Holden had turned up at his home, unannounced, and declared he had a confession to make. He said that he was secretly a Marxist and that he was working as an agent for the KGB. 'We are on the same side,' Holden told him.

Halliday was shocked. He was not sure whether to believe Holden. He was, to all appearances, a member of the establishment and had also been rumoured to have worked for British intelligence. Was this a trap? Was Holden trying to get Halliday to say that he too had been working for the KGB?

The dying Halliday confessed to Hardy that he had never told the story before but said he had mentioned the incident in a footnote to one of his books, without naming names. 'I didn't name him, but the guy in question was Holden,' Halliday said. The conversation proved to be the last the two friends would have. Halliday went back to Barcelona a few days later and died there, aged sixty-four, in April 2010.

'I think he wanted me to do something with this information,' Hardy told Gillman in September 2023. 'When I asked if he'd like to repeat what he'd told me on tape, he declined. To do so would have strongly implied that he believed what Holden had told him.'

Hardy had contacted Gillman out of the blue. 'Have some information about David Holden,' he had written in a message left on Gillman's website, along with his contact details. Astonishingly, Hardy did not know that Gillman was back on the case. He had

Googled Holden's name and found Gillman's article for *Byline Times* from 2019.

At a pub in Oxford, where Hardy, now in his seventies, lived, Gillman and Midolo asked him why he thought Halliday had been so cautious. A lean man with long, curly hair, Hardy spoke slowly in exact sentences, a consequence of his long years of working in radio. 'The sense I had got was that Fred hadn't made up his mind about whether he had believed Holden,' Hardy said. He had asked Halliday if he thought Holden's visit could shed a light on his assassination in Egypt only a few years later. Halliday wasn't sure. There were many theories about his death, but doubts remained about all of them. 'It looks as if Fred himself genuinely didn't know why Holden was killed.'

Midolo asked Hardy if Halliday was lucid, despite the illness.

'Oh yes,' Hardy said. 'His illness had made him talkative, garrulous even, but his mind was razor sharp. He had formidable brain power.'

'Did you have the feeling, during the phone call, that it could have been the last time that you were speaking with him?' Midolo asked.

'Yes, we knew he was very ill. He said to me on the phone that he was going to Spain and that's where he died.'

Hardy remembered that the subject of Holden had come up some time before, as they had both read Harold Evans's memoir, *My Paper Chase*.

'Holden was a man he admired,' Hardy said.

'The question is,' Gillman interjected, 'why would Holden tell him? Why would he give himself away? He'd had this cover for all this time and suddenly he tells Fred.'

Hardy said that Holden was telling Halliday that, ideologically, they were friends. 'It was no secret; Fred was writing a Marxist critique of the British-supported regimes in Arabia. The way Fred presented it, Holden came saying, "I am not only sympathetic to what you're doing – if I can help, I will help" and offered his very extensive notebooks to help with Fred's research. But it is odd, it's the out-of-the-blue character that is surprising.'

'It was a hell of a risk to take,' Gillman said.

'But equally, let's suppose MI6 had put Holden up to it, regardless of Holden's real loyalties, whether he was a double agent or not; that was clearly in the back of Fred's mind. I like this guy, I like his work, he's written a book I admire, but can I trust him? The oddity continued to puzzle him until his very last days.'

Gillman said that when he had met Halliday in 1990, Halliday had not told him that story. Halliday had, however, relayed another tale that also, crucially, claimed Holden had been a KGB agent. Halliday, then a professor of Middle Eastern politics at the London School of Economics (LSE), was 6ft 2in., with a receding hairline, blue eyes and glasses. He was alarmed that Leni had mentioned Holden over the phone when he called Gillman's house, after Peter had left a message for him at the LSE. 'There's nothing to be done,' Halliday said, cryptically, 'and one has to get on with living as normally as possible.' Leni didn't know what he meant. They arranged for a Chinese meal near Halliday's home in Muswell Hill, north London. He told Peter that they should be 'discreet'.

As they sat down, Halliday said two things as a preamble. First, he had made it a rule to steer clear of the field of intelligence in his writings and research. It was 'too risky, murky and a field prone to paranoia'. Secondly, he repeated his request that they should be discreet. He explained that smears against him had been planted in the media, presumably by intelligence circles. But he had managed to stay clean. He told Gillman again that mentioning Holden over the phone was not safe.

When Halliday was researching the war in Oman and British

involvement, he had been to see Holden, who had proved incredibly helpful. 'I was surprised at how forthcoming he was and was very pleased,' Halliday told Gillman. Holden had read reams from his own notebooks about the covert activities of the SAS in Yemen, for which Halliday, later, received much praise. 'How on earth had he uncovered so much?' Halliday asked.

A couple of years later, in the autumn of 1973, came the episode after Holden had returned from Chile and made crass remarks against Salvador Allende. Halliday considered that a 'grotesque performance' and could never reconcile the two Holdens he had seen. Then there was the tale of P. J. 'Taki' Vatikiotis, who had been at school with the head of Cairo police, who had allegedly told him: 'We did it. Holden was working for the KGB.' (Taki had died in 1997.)

Hardy told Gillman and Midolo that he had trawled through *Arabia Without Sultans* a dozen times but he couldn't find the footnote. Things were complicated by the fact the book had three editions. The reporters looked through all of them, but the note wasn't there. 'I can't think of any other book the footnote would have been in,' Hardy told them. 'In the mid-1970s, that was the book he was working on and Arabia was after all Holden's speciality. I've asked a couple of Fred's friends and family members if they can recall the reference. But the main thing is surely this: you now have different bits of information suggesting that Holden was spying for the Soviet Union.'

The last part was true. But without the footnote, Gillman felt, the story was weakened. Midolo was undecided. On one side, he shared Gillman's concerns about the footnote: if that detail was wrong, could the whole tale be credible? On the other side, he believed Hardy, who had proved to have a formidable memory and was convinced the footnote was to be found somewhere – perhaps in one of Halliday's articles. 'I can picture it in front of me,' Hardy told the two reporters at the pub in Oxford.

There was more that connected Halliday to the KGB and perhaps explained his circumspection in talking with the Gillmans in 1990, or the fact that he did not tell them everything he knew about Holden on that occasion. In February 1995, a front-page story in the *Sunday Times* accused a number of leading British left-wingers of being 'agents of influence' for the KGB. These included Michael Foot, the former leader of the Labour Party, and Fred Halliday.

The story originated from the manuscript of the autobiography of the KGB officer Oleg Gordievsky, who had defected to London in 1985 after secretly working as an MI6 double agent for more than a decade. Gordievsky said that Halliday was 'an unwitting agent of influence' who had been manipulated by a Soviet intelligence officer posing as a journalist in London. Yuri Kobaladze, a correspondent for the Soviet Central Radio and Television in London between 1977 and 1985 – but in reality a KGB colonel – had befriended Halliday and benefited from his extensive knowledge of geopolitics, particularly on the Middle East.

Foot and Halliday threatened to sue the *Sunday Times* for defamation. (Foot later sued and the paper settled, paying him some £25,000 in damages.) After writing about it in the *Spectator* magazine, accusing the newspaper of smearing him, Halliday sat at a round table with Gordievsky himself 'to debate the issue of alleged Soviet agents of influence in Britain during the Cold War'. The magazine ran an edited transcript of the debate, which took place in the magazine editor's office.

'First of all, I want it to be understood that I am not attacking the left or the Labour Party,' Gordievsky said as a preamble.

Halliday retorted with a curious remark: 'Is this true for Britain as well, that you think that the best information for the Russians came not from the Labour Party but from the Conservative Party?' He then listed a few names of such Conservative contacts: Brian

Beedham, Alfred Sherman and Peregrine Worsthorne. 'Yes,' Gordievsky replied. 'Some contacts were good.'

Reading the transcript, Midolo and Gillman were stunned by the mention of Worsthorne, the uber-right-wing newspaper editor who had been recruited by Donald Tyerman at *The Times* but, unlike Holden, had to work for local newspapers for two years before joining the paper. Worsthorne had later written for the CIA-backed *Encounter*, at times in the same issue as Tyerman and Holden. Halliday was now accusing him of being a 'KGB contact' in British conservative circles – and Gordievsky, the KGB chief in London, had confirmed that that was the case. '*Some contacts were good.*' Midolo and Gillman could not ask Worsthorne, who had died, aged ninety-six, in 2020. But the info added another name to the list of problematic recruits by Tyerman, alongside Holden and Philby. It left the two reporters wondering: had Tyerman just been incompetent? Or was he a KGB asset himself? It was an enigma that they could not resolve.

After a few back and forths, Gordievsky openly accused Halliday of helping the KGB and the conversation became heated.

'You think I'm lying? Let's be clear about this. I don't mind, but if you think I'm lying, say I'm lying,' Halliday said. Gordievsky replied saying that he was sure Halliday knew that his Russian friend, Kobaladze, was KGB. 'You may deny it, but I think it's impossible that a person of your background can be so naive.' He went on: 'Kobaladze was your good contact, and you were a good contact of Kobaladze. Yet you have so little here [in Halliday's article from the previous week] about Kobaladze. The information about Kobaladze is conspicuous by its absence. I find that very strange because it would have been the most interesting thing to read about. Why do you think there is such a long and thick KGB file on you? And reports of meetings? Did you influence Kobaladze, or did he influence you? Either is possible. Kobaladze liked you very much, and he liked your knowledge, but if, for example, the Foreign Office had taken you, and put you in the press department, or any department whatever, he would have been ten times happier than he was. Because really the KGB wanted not the influence as such, but the intelligence.'

Halliday protested that he wasn't a prominent person. 'I didn't even have a university post at the time.'

'It was your general knowledge he wanted,' Gordievsky said.

It struck the two reporters that Gordievsky, as the KGB station chief in London, knew firsthand about the meetings and conversations between Halliday and Kobaladze. Kobaladze was regularly asking Halliday about the Arabian Gulf area, Afghanistan, Iran, Iraq. 'What would be in the best interests of the Soviet Union? What measures or steps ought to be taken?' Halliday's answers, according to Kobaladze's reports seen by Gordievsky, were sympathetic. Halliday would even give recommendations to the Soviet leadership. Kobaladze would tell KGB analysts at the local station in London, who would write reports that would be sent on to Moscow for evaluation.

Gordievsky did say that he knew that these intelligence reports were usually exaggerated by field agents. 'The fact was that, of course, I was realistic enough to see there was nothing sinister in your relationship and it is one of those cases that you understand very well, one of those whose importance is obviously exaggerated,' he told Halliday. At this point, Halliday reached out across the table and offered his hand to Gordievsky, who shook it. But the friendliness did not last and the debate concluded with Halliday ranting against the *Sunday Times*: 'They are sleazeballs, they are muckrakers,' he said. 'Printing calumnies to make money.' Gordievsky retorted that *The Guardian* and *The Independent* had printed abusive and offensive articles about him. But Halliday was relentless. 'The *Sunday Times*, to quote Tolstoy: "*Podayut yevo kak sterlyat.*" They serve you up like a fish. They eat you up and throw away the bones. They have done it to Princess Diana, and now they will do it to you.'

In 2023, Gordievsky, then in his mid-eighties, was still living in London, although under an assumed identity. For years, he would appear on television to discuss Russian matters. Sporting fake hair and a fake beard, he was regularly seen at book launches and conferences. But since the poisoning of fellow Russian double agent Sergei Skripal by killers sent by Vladimir Putin in Salisbury in 2018, Gordievsky had disappeared from the public eye. Ben Macintyre, whose book on Gordievsky's daring escape to England had been a bestseller, had told Midolo that MI6 was keeping him under lock and key. 'Gordievsky was not in London until the early 1980s, and in any case, he's not able and unwilling to talk to anybody these days. He's completely shut up.' What's worse, Midolo had heard that he had early signs of dementia. Still, he thought it was worth trying to contact him and ask him if he knew anything about Holden. He did so through Michael Binyon, who had a 'friend' who was in regular contact with Gordievsky. The response came back negative: he didn't know anything about the case.

There was another Oleg whom Midolo could try to contact: Oleg Kalugin, the former KGB general who had met Jim Fees at his book launch in Washington in 2000. Midolo found his number in the phone book and called him up one evening. 'Wait a second, let me switch off the television,' Kalugin told him in heavily accented English. 'This is Kalugin. I'm all yours.' Kalugin had heard about Holden, but he did not know anything else. 'These things happened,' he said mysteriously, referring to the killing of double agents.

Kalugin could not remember how he had heard about the case; he apologised as his memory was fading. He was almost ninety and had been living in self-exile in Maryland for twenty years, after he had fallen out of grace with Putin. 'Putin was one of my subordinates and wanted to get rid of me,' Kalugin told Midolo. 'That's why

I asked for political asylum in the United States. He publicly called me a traitor; I called him a war criminal.' In 2002, Kalugin was tried *in absentia* in Moscow and sentenced to fifteen years in prison. He never returned to Russia.

Born in Leningrad, now St Petersburg, in 1934, the son of an NKVD officer, Kalugin was recruited by the KGB while studying at Leningrad State University. After training, in 1958, he was sent to New York, under the cover of studying journalism at the prestigious Columbia University on a Fulbright scholarship. After graduating, he went on to become the Radio Moscow correspondent from the United Nations. 'I was the only representative of Radio Moscow in the United States at that time, but of course I was already an officer in the KGB,' Kalugin told Midolo, adding that he had become the youngest general in the history of the KGB, aged thirty-six. 'Being a journalist was a good cover. Diplomatic cover would have made you feel more safe in case you were arrested, but generally speaking, diplomats had less freedom than journalists. Journalists were free to do anything.'

Shortly after his five-year spell in New York posing as a journalist, he was assigned to Washington, officially as deputy press officer for the Soviet Embassy but in reality deputy chief of the local KGB station. After becoming a general in 1974, he returned to Moscow to become head of the foreign counter-intelligence of the First Chief Directorate of the KGB, in charge of all international clandestine operations.

'I was supervising Philby when he was in Moscow, along with other defectors,' Kalugin said. 'I had a very warm relationship with Philby; he was a good man. We were friends, even outside work.'

Could Philby have told him about Holden? Kalugin could not recall. There were many Brits, he explained, who were helping. 'Many foreign recruits were primarily driven by ideology and support of the Soviet brand of socialism.'

It was a crucial point that Midolo and Gillman had discussed many times. Why had Holden chosen to spy on behalf of the Soviets? Was it ideology? Or money? Or both? Was he a paid agent or just 'a fellow traveller', as Kalugin described someone with communist beliefs but who was not a member of the party? The CIA used an acronym, MICE, to describe the motives for a spy to betray their country and become a double agent: money, ideology, coercion, ego.

At first, the two reporters thought that, due to his sexuality, Holden would have been vulnerable to blackmail. Maybe, they speculated, he had fallen victim to a Soviet honeytrap. These were not just female seductresses, known in jargon as 'swallows', like the one who had tried to seduce Midolo's colleague Roger Boyes in Poland in the late 1970s, but also male ones, 'Romeos' or 'ravens', like the one who seduced John Vassall, the clerk at the British Embassy in Moscow, or the journalists Joseph Alsop and Edward Crankshaw, who were both closeted.

Soviet ravens had claimed another illustrious journalism victim: Jeremy Wolfenden, the son of Sir John Wolfenden, who had chaired the commission – known as the Wolfenden Committee – that had led to the decriminalisation of homosexuality in the UK in 1967. Two years before Sir John was approached to become chairman of the committee, his eighteen-year-old son Jeremy had laid all his cards on the table and told him that he was gay. Jeremy was, at the time, between school and university and was doing his National Service with the naval intelligence section of the Royal Navy, where he learned Russian. 'I am not attracted by girls either physically or emotionally or aesthetically,' he wrote to a friend. But he disliked 'camp' gay men too and preferred to seduce womanisers instead.

A talented young man, dubbed 'the cleverest boy in England', Wolfenden had obtained a top scholarship at Eton College and won another at Oxford, where he was reading politics, philosophy and economics the year his father's committee began its work. His father wrote him a letter around this time asking him two things: '1) That we stay out of each other's way for the time being; 2) that you wear rather less make-up.' After a first in his final exams and a fellowship at All Souls College, Jeremy decided to become a journalist. But first he explored what he called London's 'homosexual underworld'.

His first job in journalism, in 1958, was on the foreign desk of *The Times*, where he crossed paths with Holden. In the newspaper's archives, Midolo and Gillman had found letters between the two – and even a letter Wolfenden had sent to Holden's mother to reassure her that her son was well and was coming home for his summer holidays. The tone of that letter, which referred to Holden as David and included some personal details, seemed to suggest that Wolfenden and Holden had personally known each other. Were they more than just colleagues? It was impossible to say.

Wolfenden quickly rose through the ranks of the newspaper, becoming night editor in 1959 and then Paris correspondent the following year. In 1961, only a few months after Holden had left for *The Guardian*, Wolfenden moved to the *Daily Telegraph* to become its Moscow correspondent, a suitable job for the Russian-speaking journalist. After exploring London's 'homosexual underworld', Wolfenden did the same in Moscow.

One day, as he was in bed with the barber of the Soviet Ministry of Foreign Trade in a room at the Ukraine Hotel, a KGB agent jumped out of the wardrobe and took photographs of the two men. The KGB proceeded to blackmail Wolfenden to pass on information about the Western community in Moscow. At first, Wolfenden resisted, but he was worried that the KGB would tell the *Telegraph* about the incident and he would lose his job. He chose to report the matter to the British Embassy, which alerted MI6. During his next visit to London, Wolfenden was called in and a British intelligence officer told him to cooperate with the Russians but report back to MI6.

Hooked by both services, Wolfenden, who had always been a

heavy drinker, became an alcoholic. In 1964, he wrote an article saying that British firms that had been associated with the British spy Greville Wynne were to be blacklisted by the Soviet Ministry of Foreign Trade. He knew the story to be untrue, but he had filed it because the Soviets had made him do so. During a trip to Washington, Wolfenden bumped into Martina Browne, an Englishwoman whom he had met in Moscow when she was working as a nanny for Roderick Chisholm, officially a visa officer at the British Embassy but in reality an MI6 officer. Wolfenden and Browne were soon married, but when he was due to return to Moscow, his British controller advised him not to take his wife with him.

Wolfenden asked the *Telegraph* to be transferred to Washington and told a friend that he hoped that he could forget about his intelligence misadventures. But as soon as he arrived in Washington in 1965, at the Queen's birthday party at the British Embassy, his MI6 controller came up to him, greeted him warmly and introduced himself under a new name.

A few months later, Wolfenden was dead. He was only thirty-one. It was said that, drunk, he had fainted in the bathroom, cracked his head against the washbasin and died from a cerebral haemorrhage. He was found by Martina, who after the funeral returned to London. One of Wolfenden's friends met her for a farewell drink and asked her what she planned to do: 'I don't know,' she replied, revealing that she herself was an MI6 agent. 'I can't go back to my old job. I'm getting a bit old for looking through keyholes. Anyway, I've lost all my Russian contacts.'

Wolfenden's tragic story remained a mystery for more than twenty years, sparking speculation that he had been killed by the CIA, MI6 or the KGB, until Phil Knightley revealed the truth in a book in 1986. Knightley was convinced that Wolfenden had drunk himself to death. 'Whether Wolfenden knew the extent to which SIS had gone to involve him must remain speculation,' Knightley wrote:

But some of his friends believe that, whatever the physical causes of his death, the KGB and SIS between them had driven him into a state of such desperation that he had lost the will to live. They also doubt what real use he could have been, except as part of the intelligence agencies' game between themselves, because the weakness they exploited led him to tell each side all he knew about the other.

Wolfenden's story was tragic, but there was perhaps more to it than Knightley had been aware of. According to multiple sources, Wolfenden was already working for MI6 when he arrived in Moscow. He was reportedly recruited while he was at Oxford and was moonlighting as a spy throughout his career at *The Times* and the *Telegraph*. What's more, rather than being in despair over the *kompromat* the Soviets had gained of him with his male lover, Wolfenden allegedly professed to be so delighted with the photographs that he requested enlargements. In Moscow, Wolfenden had become a close friend of Guy Burgess, one of the two 'missing diplomats' of the Cambridge Five spy ring. Both gay and Etonians, the two also shared a love for alcohol, conversation, intellectual arrogance, left-wing politics 'and a desire to *épater le bourgeois*'. Soon, Wolfenden became Burgess's confidant, perhaps his lover too, and when Burgess drank himself to death, he left Wolfenden the first pick of his library (but the KGB got there first). Wolfenden, together with Donald Maclean, was a pallbearer at Burgess's funeral in August 1963 in Moscow. Had Wolfenden been a double agent like the two missing diplomats? And was it this that had cost him his life, whether he had drunk himself to death or, as his friends suspected, had been killed? We might never know.

It was while researching Wolfenden and Burgess's relationship in Moscow that Midolo was thrilled to stumble upon the name of Leo Silberman. Holden's lover was mentioned in the autobiography of another KGB spy close to the Cambridge Five, Michael Straight. In 1934, Straight, a rich young American and a Marxist who was studying at Cambridge, attended a communist rally at Hyde Park. He had just embarrassed himself in front of the crowd after volunteering to do a simultaneous translation of a French delegate, despite having dreadful French. Unable to understand the delegate let alone to translate what he was saying, he was kicked off the stage.

'I forced my way like a fugitive through the crowd,' Straight wrote in his autobiography half a century later, in 1983:

> At its rim, I paused to regain my breath. I hoped that no one would recognize me, but a small, dark man came toward me. He smiled and stretched out his hand. 'My name is Leo Silberman,' he said. 'I am a German refugee. I cannot say that I admired your French, but I must tell you that I admire your spirit.' I wanted only to escape. I hurried away, and he trotted along beside me. He suggested that we go to his house. I was too humiliated to say no.
>
> We sat in his parlor. The conversation dwindled. Silberman excused himself and left the room. To my astonishment, he reappeared clad in a pair of tight shorts and a sleeveless shirt. He sat down beside me and took hold of my hand. Nothing at Dartington had prepared me for any such experience. I stood up and started for the door. Silberman watched me. 'I thought you were one of us,' he said.

The anecdote was illuminating for one important reason. It proved that Silberman had indeed been a communist as early as in the 1930s. He had introduced himself as 'a German refugee', surely to boost his anti-fascist credentials. As Gillman had found out, Silberman would later lie about this part of his life, telling his colleagues at Liverpool University in the 1940s that he had not been in Britain before the Second World War and pretending he didn't know the trade unionist who had called him 'Brother Silberman'.

There was another detail in Straight's book, but it muddied the waters more than it cleared them. At the end of the chapter, describing how his political ideas had carried them along in a powerful current and cast them up 'on many distant shores', Straight listed what had happened to his old comrades. One had become Foreign Minister of India, another had killed himself and a third had died of a heart attack while he was under interrogation by British intelligence officers. The most intriguing description, however, was the one dedicated to Silberman. 'Silberman was murdered in a plot in which the intelligence services of South Africa and other nations were involved,' Straight wrote. Midolo and Gillman were baffled. Silberman had died of cancer, that was a fact. Had Straight somehow confused Silberman with Holden? Yet the reference to South Africa, of which Silberman was effectively a citizen, was precise and intriguing. Midolo also remembered that the FBI source who had told Insight that the bureau had a dossier on Silberman was bewildered on seeing that the file contained a note of Silberman's death in 1960. Had Silberman not died of natural causes? Straight was another source the two could not contact – he had died in 2004.

For Straight, the 'long silence', which he had borrowed from a W. B. Yeats poem as the title of his autobiography, ended in 1981 when a correspondent from the *Daily Mail* knocked on the door of his house in Washington:

> I knew what was coming. I had been waiting for this day – and dreading it – for thirty-five years.
> 'Mr Straight, were you a student at Cambridge University in 1937?' the reporter asked.
> 'Yes, I was.'
> 'Were you acquainted at that time with Anthony Blunt?'

'Yes.'

'Mr Straight, the *Daily Mail* is running a series of articles on the Soviet spy network in Britain. They are being reprinted in the *London Times*, and indeed, throughout the world. In tomorrow's article, you are mentioned as the man who unmasked Blunt – Sir Anthony, as he was then.'

In 1963, Straight had been offered a top job at the White House in the JFK administration and, ahead of a background check, he had decided to inform the President's assistant of his communist connections at Cambridge. That had led to the unmasking of Blunt, who was not, however, publicly named as 'the fourth man' until 1979.

Philby, Burgess, Maclean, Blunt, Wolfenden and Straight. The connections between all these famous KGB spies on one side and Holden and Silberman on the other were now numerous and damning. The difference, of course, was that the first four were high-ranking MI6 or Foreign Office officials, while Holden and Silberman were not. So what use, Midolo and Gillman wondered, could Holden have been to the KGB?

In the absence of Holden's KGB file – Putin had shut the archives upon becoming President in the early 2000s – the two reporters were left speculating. But Philby himself had indirectly suggested a possible answer. The subject of greatest interest to the Soviet Union in the Middle East, Philby wrote in his autobiography, was that of American and British intentions in the area. Philby in Beirut went about this target by exploiting his journalistic access to British, American and other officials. The USSR at that time did not have diplomatic representation everywhere in the Middle East, 'the Arabian Peninsula being particularly blank' – the very place Holden specialised in for his book, *Farewell to Arabia*. 'Here, even as a straight journalist, [Philby] would have been able to fill in gaps in Moscow's knowledge. But he had one other advantage: he was British.'

Phil Knightley had written that, in the espionage game, Western intelligence agencies favoured the use of defectors such as Vladimir Sakharov and Oleg Gordievsky; the KGB, on the other hand, preferred to play the penetration card – a card that the KGB would play with infinite patience. Knightley noted that it took ten years from his KGB recruitment in the 1930s for Philby, then a simple foreign correspondent at *The Times*, to manoeuvre himself into the right place in British intelligence.

The reason Midolo was initially sceptical about the idea that Holden could have been yet another Cambridge spy was mainly down to one factor: age. Holden was much younger than the Cambridge Five. He had been just a kid when the Nazis won the 1933 German elections or when the Spanish Civil War broke out in 1936. But Silberman wasn't. Born in 1915, Silberman was only three years younger than Philby and was part of that generation who thought that communism was the only power that could overcome fascism, as Straight had put it in his autobiography. A generation shattered by the rise of Hitler, the Guernica massacre and, later, by the horror of concentration camps. Communist Russia had indeed defeated the Nazis, and according to the documents Midolo had found in the CIA archives, Silberman had even been close to the resistance in Nazi-occupied France during the Second World War. That and the references in Straight's biography were all news to Gillman, who had a strong suspicion that Silberman had been a secret communist but could not definitely prove it. They finally had proof, but they wanted more.

The only link Midolo could find between Silberman and the Maquis, the French resistance fighters, was a notice from the Bibliothèque nationale de France (BnF), the national library of France in Paris, of multiple letters Silberman had written to a French composer, Louis Saguer.

The letters, written between 1935 and 1960, the year of Silberman's death, were held at the music department of the BnF, in the original, grand eighteenth-century palace on Rue de Richelieu at the heart of Paris's second arrondissement. It was the perfect excuse for Midolo to go to Paris and, hopefully, a chance to kill two birds with one stone: Kenizé Mourad also lived in Paris. On a warm spring day in June 2024, Midolo boarded the Eurostar train headed to Gare du Nord.

• • •

The address was Rue de la Source – 'the road of the source'. Could this be a good sign? Could he persuade Mourad to speak with him and tell him, once and for all, of her CIA dealings and why she seemed to have been following Holden around? He had found her address in the archives of *The Times*'s legal department. Mourad had complained to John Witherow, then editor of the *Sunday Times*, after the paper had serialised Harold Evans's book. 'I am shocked to find my photo and the insinuation that I could be an accomplice in the assassination, in 1977, of my colleague journalist, Mr David Holden,' she had written – an insinuation that neither the newspaper nor Evans had expressed.

The address was a block of flats and to access the buzzer Midolo had to go through a door with a code, which he didn't have. Beyond that, he could see from behind the glass, was a second door. Now what? he thought. A few minutes later, a man used his key to open the door and Midolo could sneak in. Holding the door open with his foot, he spied Mourad's flat number from the letterboxes. He buzzed and buzzed. No answer.

There were no names or numbers next to the doors and the building was silent. He checked each floor, then went back to the ground floor and looked around. There was a line of books on top of the letterboxes, like a little library. Norman Mailer, Andrea Camilleri, a novel about Turkey. Something told him that these were her books. He rang again. As he did so, he realised that the ringing of the buzzer was coming from a door next to him. He stayed there, listening, holding the door open with a foot while hitting the buzzer. Not a sound. He decided to wait outside. It was sunny and he could see Mourad's windows from the road. One of them was slightly open, but the curtains were shut.

Midolo was sitting on a bench gnawing at a sandwich when he saw her, a petite woman with sandy hair and a caramel complexion. She was walking briskly towards him. For a second, he thought to run to her, but he thought better of it; he didn't want to scare her off. It was only when she was a couple of metres away that he realised it wasn't Mourad.

This was a posh residential neighbourhood, an area of Paris for the geriatric, and everyone seemed rather old: Midolo was almost the only one below the age of sixty. All of a sudden, he saw Mourad everywhere: wearing bright stabilo green trousers and a green double-breasted blazer; carrying a shopping cart or hurrying up a short alley. He followed an eighty-something woman into the florist at the corner, to make sure it wasn't her. He followed another to a pharmacy.

Midolo went back to the address the next morning. This time the windows were wide open; he could see a few plants that looked well kept. He bought some flowers from the florist and went back. The external door was shut. He stood outside, flowers in hand, for a few minutes until a man came out and he slid inside. He kept the second door open and rang the bell. No response. He knocked on the door and as he did that, he heard a toilet flush. She was in!

'Oui? What is it about?' a woman said in French from behind the door.

'Madame Mourad, I'm...'

'She's not here.'

'Ah.'
'Who are you?'
'I'm a journalist, I'm here to see madame. Who am I talking to?'
'Come back when she's there. She'll be back in a month.'
'In a month?'
'Yes!'
'Can I leave my business card with you?'
'Leave it in the letterbox.'
'Will you tell her that I came around?'
'Oui, monsieur.'

Midolo wasn't convinced it wasn't her. It was the voice of an old woman – but maybe not too old after all? Hard to tell. Why wouldn't she open the door and talk to him face to face? Why the curt replies behind the door? Midolo crossed to the far side of the road. He could see a shadow moving behind the curtains of Mourad's flat. Was she looking at him? After watching for an hour, Midolo ditched the flowers and took the Métro to the national library. The attempted doorknock had been a wasted trip. He doubted Mourad would call him back, but maybe the letters Silberman had written to Saguer would prove useful.

Many months later, Mourad responded to Midolo's questions, adding that she had never received his previous messages. She said that she had not been following Holden during his last trip or collecting any information on him: 'I just admired him as a seasoned journalist, as I was just a beginner in the job.' She insisted that she had never worked for the CIA, as the documents appeared to show. She did meet an American diplomat in 1973 and was 'stunned' he asked her to work for the CIA. She tentatively pretended to agree so that she could write about the CIA attempting to recruit a leftist journalist. But she said she became 'frightened' when he started asking questions about people she knew. 'I realised I was a fool and that I could not write about the CIA without risking a terrible revenge.' Rather than confront the man, she wrote to him 'pretending that I was sorry, that I thought I could, but I could not'. Mourad emphasised that she never discussed Holden with the CIA nor, as far as she knew, had she met any of its agents after 1973. 'That is all I can tell you. Sorry it is not so interesting, but things are often simpler than they look.'

Richelieu, as one of the main sites of the BnF is commonly known, is an imposing palace that occupies an entire city block near the Louvre. Previously the royal library, it became the national library after the French Revolution in 1789 and for centuries was the largest book depository in the world. In the 1990s, most of the books and documents were moved to a new site on the south bank of the Seine, but Richelieu retained a number of collections. The wooden floor screeched as Midolo walked towards a red seat that had been reserved for him. A library assistant brought a paper folder with a note: 'Letters of Leo Silberman to Louis Saguer 1935–1960'.

Saguer was the pseudonym of Wolfgang Simoni, a German-born composer who became a naturalised French citizen. The information on his life was scarce. Born in Berlin to an Italian father and a German Jewish mother in 1907, Simoni studied at the Stern Conservatory of Berlin. In the 1920s, he became the assistant of fellow German composer Edmund Meisel and collaborated with him on the score of several films, including the two revolutionary propaganda masterpieces by the Soviet director Sergei Eisenstein, *Battleship Potemkin* and *October: Ten Days That Shook the World*.

A Jewish communist, Simoni fled to Paris after the rise of Nazism in 1933 and used pseudonyms such as Jean Claude Simon and Louis Saguer. In 1936, he went to Spain, where he enrolled in the Soviet-backed International Brigades to fight against Franco. Back in France during the Second World War, Saguer became a resistance fighter with the Maquis. There was no information about this period, which the only biographical note described as 'obscure'. Whatever Saguer had been up to during the war, he had made sure to delete all traces. He reappeared in 1947, when he adopted French citizenship. 'Leading a mysterious life,' according to the note, he even refused to claim ownership of his musical works. He died in Paris, aged eighty-three, in 1991.

There were seventy-three letters that the notice said had been donated to the library in 2002. Midolo expected the correspondence to be in French or English and was dismayed when he saw that the first few letters were in German – a language he did not speak or read. But most were typewritten, so Midolo could scan them with his phone using the camera of the Google Translate app and obtain a simultaneous translation.

Silberman and Saguer had clearly known each other for years and the letters picked up midstream. The first letter, dated 29 May 1935, started abruptly: 'Dear friend, thank you very much etc.,' Silberman wrote, adding inexplicably: 'The prompt completion made a big impression on me and sets me apart from other people.'

The letter outlined a series of mundane points: books, money and articles the two had sent each other as well as a number of letters that Silberman asked Saguer to forward to other people. Among them was John Heartfield, a famous German artist and close friend of Bertolt Brecht who pioneered the use of photomontage for political purposes. In 1918, Heartfield was one of the first members of the German Communist Party (KPD). When the Nazis took power in 1933, the SS broke into his apartment to arrest him. Heartfield escaped by jumping from his balcony and hid in a rubbish bin, then fled Germany by walking over the mountains at the border with Czechoslovakia. In 1935, after the Gestapo put him as number five on its 'most wanted list', he was a fugitive in Paris, where he regularly met communists of the calibre of Gustav Regler, Tristan Tzara and Walter Benjamin.

Another letter was for 'Marlai'. 'Just go to see him some evening,' Silberman wrote:

> He is shy. You will be amused by his somewhat homosexual behavior, but I ask you to be very careful with comments of this kind. He fears that his innocent nature will be discovered. He's afraid, angry ... If the conversation turns to these kinds of topics, he will ask you how I am, L. S., because he is very curious to find out how and what ... You know, I surrounded myself (copying Hitler) with the veil of the unknown/with a veil of uncertainty in that Swiss school where we studied together.

So Silberman and Saguer had met at the Dr Schmidt Institute in Switzerland, where Silberman's father had sent him shortly before Hitler seized power.

'It is very important to me (!!!) that this veil is not lifted,' Silberman went on:

> So answer that I generally avoid such topics, that you are completely in the dark, and then add some mythical crap about the inscrutability of humans and my actions in particular. However, it will be good to emphasise that you know me from the movement, where you worked with me ... and that I see you as a Parisian connection and possibly for a job in London.

Silberman seemed to be speaking in code, referring to the acquisition and resale of books.

The second letter came a few weeks later and mentioned 'Wiesengrund' aka Theodor Adorno, the leading neo-Marxist philosopher of the Frankfurt School alongside Walter Benjamin, who had also escaped the Nazis and was then living in exile in Oxford. Silberman also referenced the Revolutionäre Gewerkschafts Opposition

(Revolutionary Union Opposition), the ultra-left communist union during the Weimar Republic that was created by the Comintern of the Soviet Union and went underground after the Nazis seized power but that was crushed later that year.

Enigmatically, the letter contained a drawing indicating where certain books were kept, adding more intrigue to the cryptic content of the previous letter. 'I wrote to you where the books were: in the passage room to the AEAR exhibition hall on the narrow side of the room.' The Association des Écrivains et Artistes Révolutionnaires, a French association of revolutionary artists and writers active in the 1930s, was also a Comintern-founded organisation. The letter did not specify what these books were; it only mentioned that 'the one in the middle' was by the German philosopher Feuerbach.

On the second page, Silberman switched back to the subject of 'Marlai'. It was clear that he was a young, wealthy man whom Silberman had groomed, both sexually and politically. 'In a radical turn, he looked for girls, found them in the socialist movement – and lost them there. He wanted them to be socialists because he repressed his lack of sexual experience by pretending to be financially poor.' Silberman suggested to Saguer, who was also gay, that he should make a sexual approach to Marlai and see how he responded.

'*C'est tout*,' Silberman concluded. 'The book question is urgent. Make sure that things get sorted out in the end.' Reading those lines, Midolo gained the strong impression that the books were ciphers for communicating with the underground communist movement in Germany.

The next letter strengthened his suspicion: it was dated August 1935 and Silberman talked openly and humorously of infiltrating the Labour Party in Britain.

'As you know, I am an honourable member of the Labour Party (oh no!),' he wrote. 'Should you have any idea of a reformist party, multiply it by 10,001 and you will get an idea of the totally rotten, stagnating, crazy state ... Mould, ignorance, narrow-mindedness, fear of everything that slightly smells of communism.'

Silberman declared that he got to 'play a wonderful role' in the party. 'I need to make a job out of politics – so make friends with the rich ... then I will have a concrete political mission ... I need to intrigue continuously, work for both left and right, gain trust on both sides, etc.'

This roleplaying, as Silberman described it, went so far as to use a codename:

> For the rich, I'm called 'Silb' ... for the comrades in the youth movement (in front of which now I have to do open and honest and proper politics, otherwise they'll get even more confused) – 'Molbritt'. This lovely game of hide and seek can't continue forever. I will then openly move to Molbritt, all the while having made myself indispensable.

One of the tools Silberman/Molbritt used to lure youngsters towards the communist cause was sex. It was 'the sexual revolution' or 'the sexual struggle', he wrote, that would follow a Marxist revolution. In practice, that gave him the excuse to be as promiscuous as he pleased. 'In my cell at the SAJ [the German Socialist Workers' Youth organisation] is a boy whose homosexual inclinations have created a whole ideology of fascist conclusions,' Silberman wrote. 'He is obviously afraid of me ... He is obviously only looking for pure devotion and eternal love.'

In the next paragraph, Silberman described meeting another 'boy' at a communist camp in Grenoble. 'I immediately took him with me.' Both young men were in awe of him, Silberman wrote, and he clearly intended to use them for both sexual and political purposes. 'I fascinate and create fear at the same time. Like the attitude towards a totem animal.' Another paragraph, another 'little boy', this time a sixteen-year-old from Birmingham. 'Ben is crazy about swing ... communism (since I met him) and unconventional things.'

Silberman was charming women too – although he was not (or not always) sleeping with them. 'I am very honest with the girls and have told them that my life and love is unfortunately Mme La Revolution. I belong to no one else and I can only see everything as preparation for it.'

Silberman was not just recruiting young radicals while playing the moderate with 'the bigwigs' of the Labour Party; he was playing agent provocateur in fascist organisations as well. 'I'm about to spill some highly interesting things from the Fascist Swiss camp, possibly their entire party, unravel money connections. Siegheil.'

For the extremist Silberman, who quoted Lenin and idolised Stalin ('I read through Stalin's writings once, looking for their literary and stylistic value ... it was worth 1,000 times over. The ideas and explanatory theories ... simply intoxicate me'), such masquerades must have been exhilarating. He clearly took himself very seriously, signing off his letters with the words 'greetings, revolutionary'. But Midolo felt that his arrogance betrayed his egotistical nature. 'I am too foreign, very intellectual, too intelligent, have too little time, can't sing, too self-centred, domineering, rude ... I'm not interested in people, their individual happiness and misfortune. I'm just grossly amoral.'

His faith in the revolution, however, seemed total and unshakeable: 'Nature is a network, the revolutionary Marxist stands at one of the many nodes and pulls the network together,' he wrote. 'You must feel the connection with your comrades all over the world. Faith makes me strong, the fervent and childlike belief in the party, in the leader, in me. This will enable me to do anything.'

In December 1935, Silberman announced that he had become 'a

real bigwig' in the Labour Party and had 'plenty of opportunity to practise this kind of disguise'. With the exuberant tone of the agent in the field debriefing his handler about his successes, Silberman updated Saguer on his progress in integrating radical communist recruits into the Labour Party. 'Our work is still in its early stages, although you can clearly see how it is progressing,' he wrote. 'My activity ... is of a certain importance.'

Sometimes, he told 'Wolf', in January 1936, he felt depressed:

> But luckily it only takes a little bit of Stalin to get me back on my feet. Some good news, a kind word, the thought of the revolution. In short, the awareness and belief of the strength of our class, the greatness of our comrades and the thought of the army of revolutionaries in all countries.

After the summer of 1936, as Saguer went to fight in the Spanish Civil War, the letters became sparser ('Please tell me something ... e.g. that you played for the fishermen in Malaga after the battle in the civil war'). In December, Silberman wrote that he was going to visit Paris and wanted to meet 'a few people who can tell me details about popular front propaganda', as he was organising 'an anti-fascist bureau' in London and that the British government was 'in cahoots with the fascists'.

Then came a gap of almost five years before Silberman wrote again, from Johannesburg, in May 1941. This time, the letter was in English. Silberman told Saguer he had received his letters, although months late. 'What a tale ... I marvel again and again at your enormous pluck and bravour, your sangfroid and good humour. Sitting here in a comfy flat, with plenty-plenty of food, eternal sunshine, and a jolly lot of singing natives putting up a building opposite, the contrast seems unbearable.' At this point, Saguer was fighting the Nazis in the French Resistance, a period of his life he would later keep quiet about. Yet Silberman could not resist cracking a dirty joke: 'I'm looking forward to your photos en uniforme. The soldiers here have the shortest possible trousers on, very blond and pretty. When I daydream, I imagine us together here.'

The next letter came just after the end of the war in Europe, in August 1945. 'I wrote to you at different stages during the war,' Silberman wrote. 'Have all these terrific communications lost themselves in the hurricane of the times?' At that point, Silberman had travelled widely in Africa. 'But can I tell you, even approximately, of my activities in the abysmal '40s? No, we must meet for a long while.'

This was an intriguing remark that would signal a palpable switch in the correspondence between the two comrades. Silberman, so blatantly open before the war, was now suddenly coy about his 'activities'. He was still a Marxist and the war, for him, had meant two things: 'a shift from philosophy to planning and a discovery of non-European peoples', the latter coupled with the end of imperialism in Asia, which Silberman rightly predicted would soon happen in Africa and the Middle East. The letter ended with another cryptic coda. 'PS: I haven't after all told you about my work, that must wait.'

The letters resumed again and were largely mundane and trivial, but for the unfailing descriptions of his lovers. 'I am getting through a very large number of "friends", alas the friendship lasts not long, with very few exceptions' or 'I am seeing one friend in the flesh after another. And when I say "flesh" I mean it'. Silberman himself was apologetic about the content of his correspondence: 'Forgive this idiotic way of writing, circumlocutionary and vague.'

In letter after letter, Silberman wrote of 'the so many things' he wanted to tell Saguer but, invariably, left it 'until another time' when they could speak in person. What were the many things that Silberman would not put in writing? The two finally saw each other in Paris in the summer of 1947. They continued to correspond and to meet in Paris or London over the following thirteen years – but the letters never mentioned political matters again. In an undated letter from the early 1950s, possibly from 1950 or 1951, Midolo was certain he had found a reference to Holden. 'My little pet', Silberman wrote, 'is still a bit inexperienced in the higher going-ons of L. S. and his friends. Sweet inexperience.'

The last paper was a handwritten letter by Elisabeth Russell Taylor, Freddy Silberman's ex-wife, dated 26 October 1960, announcing that Leo had died. 'He went finally to bed on Monday, fell into a coma by evening & died 3 days later.' She went on to say that because Leo was an atheist, there was no religious ceremony and Freddy delivered a moving eulogy for his brother. 'I cared; Freddy cared; his mother cared; but for the most part the people present were just those Leo would have scorned. His friends, as you know, are scattered. Of course his work was unfinished. Leo's life was a magnificent failure. How much more worthy than a "limited success".'

• • •

By the time he finished reading the letters, some four hours later, Midolo's jaw was on the floor. He had had a hunch that the correspondence with Saguer could be important, but he did not expect what was the closest thing to a full confession that Silberman had been a communist fanatic, a Comintern spy, an all-round Soviet agent of influence. Still more shocking was the tireless way Silberman had seduced and recruited young men to the cause. There could be little doubt that Holden, his 'young pet', was one of them. Gillman was right: Silberman was the most important relationship in Holden's life and the key to his murder.

If Silberman had recruited Holden in 1950 – another 'card' that the KGB had played patiently, as it had with Philby – then all of Holden's adult life needed to be reread in this light, as part of Moscow's complicated penetration game into the West. His period in Mexico, a notorious KGB training ground, which both he and Silberman lied about; his contacts, if not his secret employment, with both MI6 and the CIA; his job with *The Times* and his flash posting to Washington at the hand of an editor with KGB connections; his meetings with 'known Soviet-bloc agents', as recorded by the FBI in 1955; his sudden interest in the Middle East, where Soviet agents had limited capability while Holden could roam around undisturbed; his finding himself at the heart of pretty much every coup d'état, revolution or uprising between 1956 and 1977; his vicious writing for *Encounter* magazine and his posing as a staunch anti-communist Cold Warrior; his closeness to Kim Philby, which he wouldn't disclose to his colleagues, and the work he was doing for his 'agent', Patrick Seale; his being banned from Saudi Arabia; his reluctance to travel to Egypt, by then a hostile environment for Soviet agents and home to both Jim Fees's station and the Safari Club; his last meetings with CIA assets and, potentially, with CIA officers before his fateful flight to Cairo.

The CIA. That was one of the many loose strings of their reporting that Midolo and Gillman could not unravel, as much as they tried. Had the CIA commissioned the Egyptians to carry out the assassination of yet another Cambridge spy or did they let it happen? What did all the CIA people Holden had met during his last trip want? And if the agency had 'nothing to do with it', as the CIA employee had told Midolo in that spooky phone call, why have they not come clean and disclosed all the documents they had? Midolo's FOI requests to the CIA and the FBI were still pending, almost four years on. The agency had not even shared the documents that they had released to whoever had filed their request on Holden and Silberman in 2002.

Back at the office in London, Midolo learned by chance who had filed that FOI request. To his surprise, it was the editor of the Insight team at the time, Stephen Grey. It was an unexpected twist, because the *Sunday Times* had not published a word about the Holden murder since the 1970s. With the exception of the serialisation of

Evans's book in 2009, Midolo and Gillman thought that the newspaper had dropped the case completely.

But the request showed that Grey had not only taken an interest in the case years before *My Paper Chase*; he had done enough research to find out about Silberman too. Grey, now a special correspondent at Reuters, had conducted a number of groundbreaking investigations, from the exposure of the CIA 'extraordinary rendition flights' and torture programme to the inquiry into the murder of the Maltese journalist Daphne Caruana Galizia, for which he had just won an award.

Midolo and Gillman met him at a small, noisy cafe on Brixton Road in south London. Wearing a baggy T-shirt and shorts, Grey looked younger than his age and had a bubbling energy under his unassuming appearance. He told the two reporters that he had become the editor of Insight under John Witherow, then editor of the *Sunday Times*, in the summer of 2001.

'Hell of a time to become investigations editor,' Midolo told him.

'Yeah,' Grey agreed. 'We were consumed by 9/11, obviously.' Grey said that he had been fascinated by the story of Insight, so he posted on the office wall its big scoops of the 1960s and 1970s, the Evans era. He also pulled Insight's archives and found the Holden report.

'That's what sparked it, I was absolutely fascinated by it,' Grey explained. He felt that Insight's failure to crack the case 'challenged' the team's method of assembling facts in the belief that somehow the truth would emerge. 'You found all kinds of interesting things about David Holden but really got nowhere near actually working out why he was murdered on that airport road in 1977,' Grey said. 'That's why Harry Evans zeroed in on it in his dying days.'

Instead of replicating the previous inquiry, Grey said, his proposal was to find a key insider or insiders who could crack the case. Grey had brought a bundle of papers with him. At the top was a memo he had sent to himself, labelled: 'David Holden plan of action'. It was headed:

Re: Murder of David Holden on 6 December 1977

Objective
To solve the mystery of David Holden's death. To find out who killed him and why.

Background
The previous Insight investigation concluded that Holden was recruited by an intelligence service but found no details nor proof. We will exploit the passage of time to seek to expose anything clandestine that involved Holden. There are also certain enigmatic or reticent characters who told very little to the Insight team that we will seek to investigate.

The memo continued with a list of 'targets': access Holden's CIA file; make FOI applications; find clandestine intelligence agents operating in the Middle East in the late 1970s; and reinterview the most enigmatic characters identified by Insight, including Patrick Seale, Mustafa Amin and Kenizé Mourad. The brief was so similar to the one Midolo had done in 2020 that it could have been its carbon copy.

The next email, to Witherow, the editor, in May 2002, was stunning. It detailed what Grey had learned from his FOI request to the FBI.

We have established following new points:
- **Holden's lover – Leo Silberman – was a former Communist Party member in Germany**: therefore would have been a definite magnet for KGB recruiters. (The Insight report identified his left-wing past, but did not have his actual CP membership).
- **Holden was photographed meeting a Soviet contact in Washington**. The original Insight report had an unsubstantiated

report of this. We have documents showing how Holden himself was placed under surveillance by the FBI in Washington in 1955/56 as they tried to establish if the unidentified man who met the Soviet contact – codenamed 'UNSUB' – was indeed Holden. They concluded he was.

Then came a startling revelation, in a paragraph headed 'CIA field officers'. Grey had found none other than Jim Fees, the CIA's station chief in Cairo at the time Holden was killed, who later became the head of all clandestine operations in Arab countries. Grey had tracked him down to Spain and interviewed him at his home on the Costa del Sol, as he recounted in the email.

Fees, he wrote:

> disagreed with a number of assertions in the original Insight report, but supported much of the thrust. He did not know Holden, heard only of his death as a simple homicide at the time, and said he was certain he was not a CIA agent (unless he was part of James Angleton's [journalists] maverick counter-intelligence network).

Fees told Grey that the facts of the Holden case were 'staring us in the face'. He made two key points:

- **Holden's death bore every hallmark of an Israeli (Mossad) assassination.** The modus operandi was Israeli; they would have had no compunction of carrying it out, even during sensitive peace negotiations.
- **Holden himself was a Soviet asset.** Evidence of this is not only his closet homosexuality and secret love affair with Silberman, his disappearances to Mexico, his mysteriously rapid career track at *The Times*, his acquaintance with Philby, his

relationship with Patrick Seale (suspected of KGB involvement and of being Philby's man in Paris). Fees suspects Holden of playing some kind of double game with the Israelis and they killed him when they discovered his Soviet connections.

Midolo and Gillman looked at each other in disbelief. 'What the...' Midolo blurted out.

'I always like when people look at my findings and say, "What the fuck?"' Grey said, laughing.

Grey said that he had found Fees after searching for the local CIA chief. 'I thought, "Who might know something?" That's what led me to Fees. He was a fabulous guy, a great character. He told us a lot about his secret missions, he was quite upfront about that. And he was a door-opener, he introduced me to other people in the agency. We basically became friends.'

Grey made it clear that Fees's second key assertion, that Holden was a Soviet 'asset', was based on his reading of the original Holden report and on the new material Grey had obtained from the FBI. Gillman explained that they had come to the same conclusion: they now had Halliday's 'deathbed confession' to that effect as well as the evidence that Silberman had been a communist agent who had been recruiting young gay men to the Soviet cause.

It was Fees's first point – that Holden had been killed by Mossad – that Gillman and Midolo found hard to believe. Fees had also said that he had known nothing about Holden at the time, apart from the fact he had been murdered. Midolo and Gillman were sceptical. If the CIA had killed Holden, 'he would have known about it', Grey told them, adding that the only part of the CIA that Fees wouldn't have known about would have been the counter-intelligence department headed by James Angleton. 'He couldn't rule out that Holden had become some sort of unofficial agent for Angleton or had a relationship with him. His was such a close hold that the regular part of the Directorate of Operations, which is the real spy network, wouldn't be told much about what was going on.'

It was the same conclusion Midolo had reached. Holden had been working for *Encounter* magazine, Angleton's pet project. Angleton had been secretly running both journalists and gay men to spy 'on homo circles', as he described them, as agents. These journalist operatives 'performed sensitive and dangerous assignments', according to Carl Bernstein, and Angleton deliberately 'kept only the vaguest of files', which could explain what the CIA person had told Midolo over the phone: that there were no files proving Holden had worked for the CIA. Lastly, Angleton had refused to talk to the Insight team in 1978, after his retirement, at a time when he was spilling secrets with reporters during boozy lunches. It was interesting that Fees had suggested this after reading the Holden report. Was Fees making an educated guess or did he know for a fact that Holden had been working for Angleton?

What neither Midolo nor Gillman could believe was that Fees, who was so close to Sadat, Mubarak and Ashraf Marwan in 1977, to the point where he could 'steal' a Soviet MiG fighter jet with their blessing that very summer, would not have known what the Egyptian secret service was up to. Particularly considering they had found out that Holden had a bullet with his name on it since at least 1974, the year Fees had installed himself as station chief in Cairo.

'The Insight report concluded that the Egyptians were the most likely suspects,' Midolo said. 'We now know that for sure through a number of sources and pieces of evidence. Did you ask Fees about the Egyptians?'

'That wasn't his conclusion,' Grey said.

'What I don't understand', Midolo replied, 'is that Fees makes all these great points about Holden being KGB and potentially working for Angleton and betraying a cause but then he turns around and says, "It was Mossad." It just doesn't make any sense. Did you believe him? Did you feel he was being sincere?'

'I believed him as you believe any intelligence operatives,' Grey said. 'In the sense that if there was something *really* important that would compromise him or his government, it's very possible that he would have held it back. He was a wily old fox.'

Midolo and Gillman then listed their new findings. There was Sadat's switch to the US and the Cairo-based Safari Club; the CIA's assassinations by proxies; Saudi Arabia's Kamal Adham convincing Sadat to expel the Soviet advisers; Fees going to work for Adham after leaving the CIA; the Halton incident in 1974; and the CIA spies or contacts swirling around Holden during his last trip. The other thing to keep in mind, Midolo said, was that in 2002, Mubarak was still the President of Egypt and Fees was still close to him. After retiring from the CIA, he had sold weapons to Egypt for decades with his old friend Swede Svendsen.

Midolo reminded Grey of a line in his book about the CIA torture programme, attributed to the ex-CIA operative Bob Baer: 'If you want a serious interrogation, you send a prisoner to Jordan. If you want them to be tortured, you send them to Syria. If you want someone to disappear – never to see them again – you send them to Egypt.' By making Holden disappear, the Egyptians were doing a big favour to both the Saudis and the Americans.

'You're basically saying that the Egyptians did it, and because of Fees's position close to Egyptian intelligence, he was probably lying to us when he said he didn't know anything about it,' Grey said. 'It's a reasonable conclusion.'

Gillman and Midolo were impressed that Grey had been prepared to question the veracity of a source who had also become a friend, to the point where Fees featured in the acknowledgements to Grey's book about the CIA's secret rendition programme. They told him that whether Fees was deflecting attention from the Egyptians because he had a good working relationship with them or because, as Alexandra Johnson had come to believe, he had commissioned the murder himself and the Egyptians had carried it out, Midolo and Gillman could not tell.

'I think one thing that stands out as an injustice, if you like, is the failure of the Americans, and potentially the British, to come clean on what they knew about Holden and his relationship with the Russians,' Grey said. 'That's a key clue and would bring justice to the case. They owed that to the *Sunday Times* and Ruth, I suppose. It's possible that they felt that they were doing him and the family a favour by not revealing all that, but I think it's an evident injustice to resist all these efforts.'

Grey had met Ruth and had talked to her at great length. 'She was charming but fundamentally ignorant of Holden's secret life or lives,' Grey said. 'The meeting was partly out of fairness to her, to tell her what we'd done and what we'd found out.'

Ruth died in 2016, aged ninety-one, at her house in Islington. The two reporters had found her will, written only a few months before she passed, and they were startled to see that her estate amounted to over £3 million. Ruth had no heir and had left most of it to her school. She also had an impressive collection of art, which she had left to her friends and neighbours, plus the house, which had sold for £1.25 million.

There were only eight people mentioned in the will and it wasn't hard for Midolo to track them down. He went to knock on the door of Ronald Ward, the man Ruth had left most things to, including £20,000 in cash, only to find out that he had died a few months before. His neighbour, a ninety-year-old lady, told him that Ward was 'very gay' and 'very camp'. She remembered Ruth, who came from time to time for a drink in the garden. She thought she was gay too. 'Ron liked lesbians because he didn't have to touch them,' the old woman said dismissively.

One of Ruth's neighbours told Midolo that she and Ward had fallen out before she died. 'She was this quite cantankerous old woman and she could be so vile to people,' the neighbour said. 'She didn't have many friends. She was horrible to Ron; he used to call her Poison Ivy.' The neighbour knew that Holden was gay and thought that she 'probably' was as well. 'It was a marriage of convenience, I suppose. She was single the rest of her life. She never had another partner, a man or a woman. Things were very different for gay women of that age, weren't they?'

The daughter of a *Telegraph* journalist who had been a close friend of Ruth said that she had the most exquisite taste. 'Her house was unbelievably beautiful,' she said. 'She had been the muse for Vidal Sassoon for years and had these insanely beautiful haircuts.' She would not comment on the relationship with Holden, saying only that they did love each other deeply. 'I think his death took a real toll on her.' All the people Midolo contacted agreed that Ruth had stopped working shortly after Holden had died. They did not know how she was able to support herself. Holden had left £28,000 in his will, which adjusted for 2024 inflation was some £150,000 – a sizeable sum but far from the millions of pounds Ruth had when she died. Where was all that money coming from? Ruth's lawyer thought that she had come from a rich family, but Midolo and Gillman knew that that wasn't the case.

Michael Adams's widow, Celia, remembered something else about Ruth that she had forgotten to mention when she had met Gillman. 'Not that long ago, I rang her for some reason I can't remember and found myself asking her what she then thought had really happened to David,' Celia said. 'Who had killed him, I asked her. She replied that it had been the work of the CIA.' Celia was astonished and couldn't believe what Ruth was telling her. 'I told her that I could think of no reason why the CIA would want to kill David. But she seemed sure that it had been the CIA.'

• • •

In films or novels, murder cases are often likened to a jigsaw puzzle. But police detectives and investigative journalists know better. Real people's lives are not perfect pictures. In the game, if you lose a piece of the puzzle, or two, or three, the puzzle cannot be solved. Someone wanted to remove the pieces of the puzzle that is Holden's assassination so that no one could solve it. But find enough pieces and assemble them together and you can still tell what the image underneath looks like. What you *can* see, despite all the missing pieces and leftover ones that just won't fit, is the truth. Not the whole truth, but the best obtainable version of the truth, as Carl Bernstein calls it.

Reality is complicated. It's not linear. It doesn't follow a plot. Holden was the most complicated protagonist, one that a novelist would want to avoid at all costs. Was he the hero or the villain of this story? And what is a hero or a villain anyway? It depends on the angle from which one looks at things, like the difference between a resistance fighter and a terrorist. It's a matter of perspective. For the West, Holden was a traitor who deserved the bullet that pierced his heart. But for the Soviet Union, he might have been a hero worthy of the Order of Lenin, like Philby.

What motivated Holden to do what he did and risk his life? Most likely it wasn't because of blackmail, despite the secret of his sexuality. It wasn't for money; Holden was not a material man, although the KGB probably looked after him and may well have taken care of Ruth after he died. It wasn't for ideology either; Holden was leftwing but by all accounts not an extremist like Silberman. It could have been for love; but in 1960, the love of his life had died, so why continue? Was it power? Or simply acting a part? After all, he had wanted to become an actor and had 'a certain aura of The Player', as Jan Morris had put it. Richard Johns had told Gillman that he felt Holden was 'the sort of person for whom a bit of spookery might be rather romantic'. Was it then the 'flicker of romance' which he had described in *Farewell to Arabia* that drove him? The thrill of living dangerously? We might never know.

What was certain was that Holden had led the two reporters down very dark paths. 'Innocence is a form of insanity,' Graham Greene had written, and Midolo definitely felt that his innocence had been dented by all they had found about journalists and spies. Their quest had destroyed the tales journalists constantly tell themselves about the purity of the profession, about their *mission* – what a strange word. It was not something limited to the Cold War, as most hacks argued. On 29 March 2023, a reporter from the *Wall Street Journal*, Evan Gershkovich, was arrested in Moscow on charges of spying on behalf of the CIA – the first time a Western journalist had been tried on such charges since the Cold War.

Emma Tucker, the editor of the *Journal*, had been in her post for less than two months at the time, having joined from the *Sunday Times* (she was the editor who had hired Midolo). During a news conference, the same day, one of the managing editors told Tucker, almost as an aside, that Gershkovich had not checked in. 'Not to worry; these things sometimes happen.' It was an almost word-for-word replay of the news conference in which Cal McCrystal had told Harry Evans that they had not heard from Holden. A search party was sent out to look for Gershkovich, who the Kremlin later confirmed had been arrested. Gershkovich was eventually released in August 2024, as part of a prisoner swap. The year and four months he spent in a Russian jail was a stark reminder of the risks foreign correspondents were exposed to after decades of juxtaposition between the two professions.

Midolo and Gillman had finally found Jim Fees's daughter, Paula. Or rather, they had finally found the courage to get in touch with her and ask her, 'We're sorry to bother you, but did your father conspire to murder a British journalist in 1977?' It was a tough phone call to make and the two reporters had kept it as one of the last on their list.

Paula was forthcoming and answered all the reporters' questions over the course of two two-hour-long conversations. She was just a child at the time of Holden's murder, but they hoped her father had talked to her about it in later years. The first time she had heard about Holden, however, was when Stephen Grey had gone to see her father in Spain in 2002. She had been very close to her father in the last years of his life, but he had been very absent, she said, while she was growing up. In the 1980s, her parents divorced and her father remarried. He was living between Belgium and Spain while she stayed on with her mum.

During their second conversation, Midolo and Gillman decided to come clean and told her that they thought her father was steering Grey away from the Egyptians – and the CIA too.

'We were shocked to see that your father confirmed that Holden was KGB, based on the evidence that he'd seen,' Midolo told her. 'But then he added, "And that's why it's a Mossad job. They killed him because they found out that he was a double agent." Which just doesn't add up.'

'It's an embarrassing question to ask, but, knowing your dad, do you think he could have been...?' Gillman started asking the crucial question, but Paula interrupted him.

'Yeah, definitely,' she said. 'I have no idea, but sure, I mean, why not? You know, part of his job was also deflecting attention, unwanted attention. So it's entirely possible, but I have no idea either way. I assume you're coming down on the basis that you think that the Egyptians killed Holden.'

'Absolutely,' Gillman and Midolo answered as one.

'We know that the Egyptians did it,' Gillman went on. 'The thing that we find hard to believe is that your father didn't know. With the kind of connections he had, and with the kind of operations that he was running, literally, at the same time. That MiG operation was at the end of September 1977. Holden was killed weeks after that.'

'It's entirely possible,' Paula said. 'Now, people who've been in the

CIA for five minutes come out and write a book about all their exploits and talk about everything they did. But my dad was old school. He believed that he was sworn to secrecy and never talked about certain things. It was only much later in life, and it was only snippets. But he was definitely someone who would take secrets to the grave.'

Paula agreed that it was difficult to imagine Fees didn't know, given his close working relationship with Sadat and Egyptian intelligence. 'If he did, then he would have obviously been deflecting when that journalist came asking.'

She added that her father had opened up in the last days of his life, as he was dying of cancer and she was taking care of him. 'He told me things he had not told me before, like the frustration with [Admiral] Turner [the CIA director when Fees resigned], but I don't think he would have… I don't know.' She stopped. 'I don't think he could have taken a look of disappointment in my eyes.'

In his final days, as cancer spread to the rest of his body, Fees had become delirious, Paula explained. He was hallucinating, particularly at night, and the hallucinations were always about killers or terrorists coming to get him. '"Oh my God, I think the Israelis have found a code, and we have to know what it is,"' she said. 'Or "the terrorists are coming, quick, you have to hide". At one point, he thought the doctors were spies. One day they were Mossad, another week they were Russians. You know, fifty years of a very odd job coming to the fore.'

Jim Fees died at his home in Hasselt, Belgium, in 2017, forty years after Holden.

EPILOGUE

Peter Holden was in a jovial mood. With a full head of white hair and a beard, chequered shirt and blue jeans, he did not look much like his uncle, except for the same azure eyes. 'I look more like my mum,' Peter said with a smile when Gillman, Leni and Midolo went to see him at his house in Cirencester, in the Cotswolds, in the spring of 2024. The son of David's brother Geoffrey, Gillman had found him through a group of local bell ringers. Aged seventy-seven, short and wiry, Peter cycled sixty miles a day and went bell ringing several times a week with his wife, Joanne. The two reporters found him affable and cheerful, with a soft north-eastern accent and a gentle, almost shy, way of laughing.

Born in Sunderland, like his father and uncle, Peter was thirty when David was murdered. 'Dad rang me up when the *Sunday Times* was searching for him,' Peter recalled. 'They called us to say that he was missing and to ask if we'd heard from him. Then my dad called back and said that a body had been found.'

He said that Geoffrey, who was four years older than David, was devastated by the news.

'Dad was really cut up when he died,' Peter said. 'They played the clarinet at his funeral, the slow movement of the clarinet concerto by Mozart. And that really got my dad going. Because he'd heard that so many times being played by David. That must have been quite painful for him. I don't think he'd listen to it after that.'

Peter often closed his eyes, as if it helped him firming up the details. He was reminiscing about facts he hadn't thought about for years. He remembered Lord Snowdon and Princess Margaret at the funeral, with whom he talked briefly after the ceremony. As they were leaving, Ruth told him and his father that MI6 wouldn't leave her alone. 'They certainly interviewed her at some length,' Peter said. 'They obviously suspected something was going on. I don't know what. Whether they really knew something or just suspected, I don't know. All I remember is her saying that she had been interviewed for hours.'

It was the first time the two reporters had heard that and it perhaps explained Ruth's reluctance to discuss the murder, even years after the fact. It was clear MI6 was trying to find out what she knew. She did not stay in touch with the family, except for cards at Christmas. When Peter's father died, aged ninety-five, in 2015, Peter rang her to let her know.

He added that his father was convinced that the killing was 'a secret service job'.

'That was the sort of general consensus,' he added. 'It wasn't just a murder.'

'Did he ever think that David could have been involved with some secret service?' Gillman asked him.

'I don't know whether he did. I think we were all a bit surprised.'

The thing that shocked them the most, however, was the story of David's love affair with Silberman.

'Dad never knew about that,' Peter said. 'When he saw it in Harold Evans's book, that was the first he knew of it. It was really quite something.'

'That didn't square with what he knew about David,' Gillman said. 'Did he disbelieve it?'

EPILOGUE

'He found it hard to believe, certainly. His first reaction was "No, that wasn't David."'

David, he added, had a reputation for being rather left-wing. He reprimanded Geoffrey for using the term 'wogs' and the two argued over politics. Even though Geoffrey read *The Guardian*, David was considered more radical. Peter remembered that, after David had been at university in the US, there was a running joke in the house that he was lucky to have escaped McCarthy's witch-hunt.

'I don't know if that's because he was a bit of a communist or not; it was the sort of bit of gossip that flew around in the family.'

Midolo said that David seemed to have been quite radical during his youth but then switched. 'We now think that it was because he was building this sort of anti-communist persona.'

'He probably didn't do that with Dad, though. That's my guess,' Peter said. 'If he was trying to build something up for everyone else, when he was with Dad, he would have just been himself.'

Peter stood up and opened a sideboard, producing a knife, a short curved dagger with a black handle and a steel cover carved with an elegant Arabic inscription.

'He brought this up to me back from Egypt, when I was about seven,' Peter said. 'I managed to clip it to my belt somehow and I was walking down the street like a warrior. Can you imagine, as a kid, receiving a gift like this from a glamorous uncle?'

Seen through Peter's eyes, the intrigues of David's life and career must have felt so alien, a million miles removed from the tranquil life his family was living in the north-east of England.

'We can discuss all these things abstractly, but it must be slightly strange that this person you knew as a very nice, kind uncle is suddenly the focus of this investigation,' Gillman said apologetically.

'It was always hard,' Peter conceded. 'Obviously, over the years, I realised there was a lot more to him. Even before his death, there was quite a lot to this chap, you know. A lot more than I ever saw.'

Peter confessed he had never read Holden's books but his son Simon had. He was fascinated by the story of the murder and had read Evans's memoir too.

'Does this all sound quite implausible to you?' Gillman asked him. 'It must be a bit difficult to accommodate, doesn't it?'

'Yes,' Peter said. 'I mean God, why would anyone want to work for the Soviets? He might have been a bit left-wing and things, but the totalitarian regime that went marching into Hungary? But, of course, sometimes these people get dragged in against their will almost, don't they? And then they have to sort of play along with it.'

Peter was right. Whether Holden had been helping the Soviets because he had been blackmailed or because he truly believed it, he had indeed been a victim of the Great Game of espionage. None of the intelligence agencies Gillman and Midolo had scrutinised were innocent. The KGB was exploiting Holden to penetrate the Middle East, a dangerous job that had cost him his life. The Egyptians had him killed, with his murder cementing their alliance with the Saudis and the Americans. The British had tried to derail the *Sunday Times* investigation and covered everything up, to avoid yet another Cambridge spy scandal. And the CIA still pretended it knew nothing about it.

'I don't know, it's all a world of smoke and mirrors,' Peter said as he stood up, signalling to his visitors that their conversation was nearing its end. Midolo recalled the last lines of *Farewell to Arabia*: 'For better or worse, what has happened has happened … All that remains is to say farewell to innocence and gird ourselves to understand the shape of things to come.'

They thanked Peter and he led them to the front door. As he opened it, they saw something they had not noticed when they arrived. Halfway up the door, which was painted scarlet red, was a brass letterbox bearing the single word HOLDEN. They said goodbye and then, as they turned away, they heard the door close behind them.

NOTES AND REFERENCES

PART ONE

The principal source for much of Part One was the 110-page internal report on the *Sunday Times* (*ST*) inquiry into David Holden's death, written by Peter Gillman in December 1978 and never previously published. We also drew on documents and reports that have survived from the original inquiry. In some cases, we have amplified the previous information with research and interviews conducted for this book. This includes information from the personnel files held by the Times Newspapers archives. We are grateful to the archivists, Anne Jensen and Michael-John Jennings, who have welcomed us and provided us with everything we needed, including sharp pencils. We were also assisted by the recollections of two members of the original research team, Isabel Hilton and John Barry, and those of the former *ST* New York correspondent, Peter Pringle, and former Beirut correspondent, Helena Cobban. Further information came from Gillman's continuing research during the 1980s and 1990s. Some detailed notes follow.

PROLOGUE
The description of Holden on the flight to Cairo is based on the

interview with Mrs Bonnette conducted in 1977 by the *ST* New York correspondent, Peter Pringle, as related in the Holden report (HR).

CHAPTER 1

We obtained further details of Holden's last trip from internal *ST* memos and correspondence as well as interviews with first-hand witnesses as quoted in the HR. Harold Evans's reaction to Holden's disappearance and death draws on his memoir, *My Paper Chase*. Our thanks go to Bob Jobbins, whom we interviewed in 2023.

CHAPTERS 3 AND 4

We benefited especially from detailed notes written in 1978 by Cal McCrystal, plus copies of the telexes sent by the investigating team to the *ST* in London. John Barry kindly relayed his impressions of his meeting with General Hassan in a memo in September 2023.

CHAPTERS 7, 8, 9 AND 10

The account of Holden's life draws on the HR and on new material obtained during the research for this book. We are grateful to Tessa Snowdon for her archival research into Holden's early writings for his school magazine and for the Ayton Old Scholars' Association reports for former pupils at Great Ayton. Ian Sherlock, digital lead at the Sunderland Libraries Service, gave us meticulous assistance with the career of Holden's father, Thomas. Jason Nargis of the McCormick Collection at Northwestern University, Evanston (Illinois), gave us exceptional help in providing material from the collection archives, invaluable in enabling us to describe Holden's time at Northwestern. We also obtained new material about Leo Silberman, where we were generously assisted by Lisa Larsson, who had conducted extensive research into the L. S. Mayer company; and by James Harte at the National Library of Ireland who kindly shared with us copies of Silberman's letters to the poet John Jordan. Declassified memos from the CIA, which can be accessed online via the agency's FOI reading room, provided us with further information about Silberman and his mysterious trips across Africa. We met Celia Adams at her home in Devon in 2022 and we thank her for sharing her memories of her late husband Michael.

CHAPTER 11

For the reconstruction of the legal battle between the *ST* and the CIA, we relied on court documents as well as internal communications held by Times Newspapers' legal archives. We are grateful to Pia Sarma for opening up the archives to us and to Donna Boultwood and Tracy Graves for assisting us with our research over many weeks. We interviewed Sir David Blatherwick, who went on to become the British ambassador in Cairo (1991–95), at his home near Cambridge in 2023.

CHAPTERS 12 AND 13

Information about Alexandra Johnson draws on Gillman's notes and recollections, as well as some subsequent research, which confirmed that everything Johnson had told Gillman was true and accurate. This book is a testament to her courage, determination and commitment to the truth.

PART TWO

CHAPTER 14

The reconstruction of David Halton's visit to Cairo in 1974 is based on two interviews with Halton in 2022. For some of the details and for the exact date of the incident, we relied on what Halton told the Insight team in 1978, as relayed in the HR.

CHAPTER 16

Jan Morris's description of Holden comes from her memoir, *Pleasures of a Tangled Life*. We are grateful to our interviewees, who shared their memories of Holden: David Hirst, Don McCullin, Roger Matthews, Tim Llewellyn, Bernd Debusmann, Charles Glass, Rosemary Sayigh, Seymour Hersh, Jon Swain, Magnus Linklater, Rosie Atkins, Clive Irving and Peter Kellner. The Palestinian academic Ahmed Rahman (not his real name) first refused to talk to us, then said he didn't remember anything about these matters. The memoir of the CIA station chief in Amman is *King's Counsel* by Jack O'Connell and Vernon Loeb. The *Documents from the US Espionage Den* are available online at the Internet Archive.

CHAPTER 17

We are grateful to Jim Fine and his wife Debbie for their recollections of Jean de Muralt. De Muralt's friend did not wish to be named. To reconstruct Jim Fees's life and career, we relied vastly on his daughter Paula's recollections, which she shared with us during two interviews in 2023 and 2024, as well as what she said to the *True Spies* podcast (Spyscape Studios). More details of Fees's career and times with the CIA emerged from newspaper clippings, archival material and books such as Tom Bower's *The Perfect English Spy*, Uri Bar-Joseph's *The Angel*, Owen Sirrs's *A History of the Egyptian Intelligence Service*, Mohamed Heikal's *Autumn of Fury* and Wilbur Eveland's *Ropes of Sand*. We conducted interviews with Renato Casaro, Uri Bar-Joseph, Vernon Loeb and Tom Bower, as well as a number of former CIA operatives who did not wish to be named. For the description of the war in Yemen, we benefited from books such as Anthony Verrier's *Through the Looking Glass*, David Smiley's *Arabian Assignment*, Stephen Dorril's *MI6* and Sirrs's history of the Egyptian mukhabarat. For the description of Egypt under Sadat, we relied largely on Heikal's books, Sirrs's history, Bar-Joseph's

NOTES AND REFERENCES

The Angel, David Hirst's *Sadat*, Bob Woodward's *Veil*, Joe Trento's *Prelude to Terror* and Hazem Kandil's *Soldiers, Spies and Statesmen*. Owen Sirrs was generous in showing us his notes on Kamal Adham and helping us reconstruct the relationships between the US, the USSR and Egypt.

CHAPTER 18

The three dossiers on Holden's murder (FCO 93/1467, FCO 93/1964, FCO 93/2393) were declassified by the Foreign Office in 2008, 2010 and 2011 and can be viewed at the National Archives in Kew. Arnaud de Borchgrave's proximity to Henry Kissinger, the CIA and James Angleton in particular is evident from declassified documents that can be found within the CIA archives online, including the confidential assessment, *Of Moles and Molehunters: A Review of Counterintelligence Literature, 1977–92*, from May 1992. For the history of the Lavender Scare, we relied on James Kirchick's *Secret City* and on Trento's *The Secret History of the CIA*, as well as declassified material from the CIA, the FBI and the US State Department. For Angleton's life and career, we relied extensively on Jefferson Morley's *The Ghost*, Tom Mangold's *Cold Warrior*, David Wise's *Molehunt* and David Martin's *Wilderness of Mirrors*. The source of the information about Iverach McDonald and MI6 comes from an interview with Anthony Cavendish in June 1989.

CHAPTER 19

We are grateful to Joe Trento for his recollections of his liquid lunches and long phone conversations with Angleton, which he shared with us during the course of many interviews. Besides the essential books on Angleton by Morley, Mangold, Martin and Wise, we are indebted to Seymour Hersh's groundbreaking reporting for the *New York Times* in the 1970s about Angleton, the CIA Family Jewels and the agency's clandestine operations. We are grateful to

Carl Bernstein for agreeing to discuss 'The CIA and the Media' with us at the Sir Harry Evans Investigative Journalism Summit in 2023. We quoted from volume one of the Church committee's final report, 'Foreign and Military Intelligence'. We have published a verbatim account of our conversation with a CIA official in 2023 even though the official asked that it be 'off the record'. This is usually interpreted to mean that the information cannot be quoted or reported directly and is a fundamental principle of journalism. However, most journalists consider that the implicit agreement becomes invalid if the journalists learn that they have been lied to. In this case, the employee told us that the CIA did not hold a file on Holden, which we know to be untrue. This repeated the same claim the CIA made to the *ST* forty-five years earlier. It still raises the question of what the CIA wants to conceal.

CHAPTER 20

For Tony Terry's biography, we relied on Judith Lenart's fascinating book, *Berlin to Bond and Beyond*, interviews with Lenart, as well as Ian Fleming's two biographies by Andrew Lycett and Nicholas Shakespeare. We interviewed a number of former *ST* journalists and staffers about Frank Giles, some of whom did not want to be named. We are grateful to the StB archives in Prague for their help. Geoffrey Tantum's biography comes from newspaper clippings and open sources. We interviewed Sir Geoffrey at his home in Bath in April 2023. He died in February 2024, aged eighty-three. We are thankful to him and his wife, Carin, for their hospitality.

CHAPTER 21

We are grateful to our interviewees: Rana Kabbani Seale, Ben Macintyre, Afif Aburish, Susan Griggs and James Barr, who was especially generous in helping us navigate the diaries of John Slade-Baker and sharing his own remarkable findings. Details of Richard Beeston's life and of his dealings with Kim Philby are taken from Beeston's memoir, *Looking for Trouble*. Said Aburish's book *Beirut Spy* provided us with the sketches of the British correspondents at the St George Hotel Bar who all also happened to be spies. Angleton's last words to Trento are quoted in his book, *The Secret History of the CIA*. We are grateful to Debbie Usher, the archivist of the Middle East Centre at Oxford, for welcoming us over multiple visits and unfailingly offering us tea.

CHAPTER 22

For the interviews with David Halton see note to Chapter 14. We relied on a number of books to reconstruct Egypt's relationship with the USSR, among which invaluable to us were Heikal's *The Sphinx and the Commissar* and *Autumn of Fury*, Sirrs's history of the Egyptian intelligence services and Bar-Joseph's *The Angel*. Mark Perry, in his book *Eclipse*, wrote that the young CIA officer who met Ashraf Marwan was Thomas Twetten, who later became head of the CIA Near East division and deputy director of operations. However, Twetten denied this in a phone interview to us in September 2023. For Kamal Adham's life and details of the Safari Club operations, we relied on Heikal's books, Bar-Joseph, Sirrs, as well as a number of books on the BCCI scandal, including Mark Potts, Nicholas Kochan and Robert Whittington's *Dirty Money* and James Adams and Douglas Frantz's *A Full Service Bank*. Richard Johns, who completed Holden's book on Saudi Arabia, told Gillman in the 1980s that Holden had been 'taken care of' by Adham and his nephew Prince Turki bin Faisal during his first visits to the kingdom. Johns said that he was surprised to see that the Saudis had shown no interest in Holden's fate. The interview with Prince Turki was conducted in September 2024.

CHAPTER 23

Rachel is a pseudonym. Giulio Regeni's story comes from newspaper clippings and, in particular, from a long report by Declan Walsh in the *New York Times* on 15 August 2017.

CHAPTER 24

The story of Heikal's arrest and of Sadat's assassination is taken mainly from Heikal's *Autumn of Fury*. The interview with Isis Elten was conducted at her home in Acqualoreto, Italy, in July 2023.

CHAPTER 25

We interviewed Roger Hardy at Oxford in March 2024 and in several subsequent telephone calls. Jeremy Wolfenden's story is taken from Phillip Knightley's *The Second Oldest Profession*, Sebastian Faulks's *The Fatal Englishman* and Andrew Lownie's *Stalin's Englishman*. Michael Straight wrote about Silberman in his suspiciously partial autobiography, *After Long Silence*. The assessment of Philby's usefulness to the KGB as a correspondent in Beirut comes from Tim Milne's book *Kim Philby*. We are grateful to the archivists of the BnF in Paris. Kenizé Mourad responded in February 2025. The quote from Graham Greene is from *The Quiet American*.

EPILOGUE

The interview with Peter Holden, David Holden's nephew, was conducted at his house in Cirencester in March 2024.

BIBLIOGRAPHY

Aburish, Said, *Beirut Spy: The St George Hotel Bar* (Unicorn, London, 2022)

Aburish, Said, *The House of Saud* (Bloomsbury, London, 1994)

Adams, James; Frantz, Douglas, *A Full Service Bank: How BCCI Stole Billions Around the World* (Simon & Schuster, New York, 2000)

Adams, Michael, *The Untravelled World* (Quartet, London, 1994)

Al Faisal Al Saud, Turki, *The Afghanistan File* (Arabian Publishing, London, 2021)

Andrew, Christopher; Gordievsky, Oleg, *KGB: The Inside Story* (Hodder & Stoughton, London, 1990)

Andrew, Christopher; Mitrokhin, Vasili, *The World Was Going Our Way: The KGB and the Battle for the Third World* (Basic Books, London, 2006)

Bar-Joseph, Uri, *The Angel: The Spy Who Saved Israel* (HarperCollins, London, 2017)

Barr, James, *Lords of the Desert* (Simon & Schuster, London, 2018)

Beeston, Richard (sr), *Looking for Trouble* (Tauris Parke Paperbacks, London, 2006)

de la Billière, Peter, *Looking for Trouble: SAS to Gulf Command* (HarperCollins, London, 1995)

Bird, Kai, *The Good Spy: The Life and Death of Robert Ames* (Crown, New York, 2015)

de Borchgrave, Arnaud; Moss, Robert, *The Spike* (Crown, New York, 1980)

Bower, Tom, *The Perfect English Spy: Sir Dick White and the Secret War 1935–1990* (St Martin's Press, London, 1995)

Carter, Miranda, *Anthony Blunt: His Lives* (Pan Macmillan, London, 2001)

Cavendish, Anthony, *Inside Intelligence: The Revelations of an MI6 Officer* (Collins, London, 1990)

Cobban, Helena, *The Palestinian Liberation Organisation* (Cambridge Middle East Library, Cambridge, 1984)

Cockburn, Leslie, *Out of Control* (Bloomsbury, New York, 1988)

Colby, William, *Honorable Men: My Life in the CIA* (Simon & Schuster, New York, 1978)

Coll, Steve, *Ghost Wars: The Secret History of the CIA, Afghanistan and Bin Laden from the Soviet Invasion to September 10, 2001* (Penguin, New York, 2004)

Corn, David, *Blond Ghost: Ted Shackley and the CIA's Crusades* (Simon & Schuster, New York, 1994)

Davenport-Hines, Richard, *Enemies Within: Communists, the Cambridge Spies and the Making of Modern Britain* (William Collins, London, 2018)

Dennett, Charlotte, *Follow the Pipelines: Uncovering the Mystery of a Lost Spy and the Deadly Politics of the Great Game for Oil* (Chelsea Green, Chelsea, 2022)

Dorril, Stephen, *MI6: Fifty Years of Special Operations* (Fourth Estate, London, 2001)

Evans, Harold, *Good Times, Bad Times* (Weidenfeld & Nicolson, London, 1983)

Evans, Harold, *My Paper Chase: True Stories of Vanished Times* (Hachette, London, 2009)

Eveland, Wilbur Crane, *Ropes of Sand: America's Failure in the Middle East* (W. W. Norton & Co., New York, 1980)

Faulks, Sebastian, *The Fatal Englishman: Three Short Lives* (Hutchinson, London, 1990)

Fistere, Isobel and John, *Jordan, the Holy Land* (Middle East Export Press, 1964)

Freedman, Robert O., *Soviet Policy Toward the Middle East Since 1970* (Praeger, New York, 1978)

Giles, Frank, *Sundry Times: Autobiography* (John Murray, London, 1986)

Greene, Graham, *The Quiet American* (William Heinemann, London, 1955)

Grey, Stephen, *Ghost Plane: The True Story of the CIA Torture Program* (St Martin's Press, New York, 2006)

Halliday, Fred, *Arabia Without Sultans* (Penguin, London, 1974)

Hanning, James, *Love and Deception: Philby in Beirut* (Corsair, London, 2021)

Heikal, Mohamed, *Autumn of Fury: The Assassination of Sadat* (HarperCollins, London, 1983)

Heikal, Mohamed, *Return of the Ayatollah* (Andre Deutsch, London, 1984)

Heikal, Mohamed, *Road to Ramadan* (HarperCollins, London, 1975)

Heikal, Mohamed, *The Sphinx and the Commissar* (HarperCollins, London, 1978)

Hersh, Seymour, *The Dark Side of Camelot* (Little, Brown & Co., Boston, 1988)

Hersh, Seymour, *The Price of Power* (Faber & Faber, New York, 1983)

Hersh, Seymour, *Reporter* (Allen Lane, London, 2018)

Hirst, David, *Sadat* (Faber & Faber, London, 1981)

Hobson, Harold; Knightley, Phillip; Russell, Leonard, *The Pearl of Days: An Intimate Memoir of the Sunday Times 1822–1972* (Hamish Hamilton, London, 1972)

Holden, David, *Farewell to Arabia* (Faber & Faber, London, 1966)

Holden, David, *Greece Without Columns: The Making of Modern Greeks* (Lippincott, London, 1972)

Holden, David; Johns, Richard, *The House of Saud* (Sidgwick & Jackson, London, 1981)

Hollingsworth, Mark, *Agents of Influence: How the KGB Subverted Western Democracies* (Oneworld, London, 2023)

Insight team (various authors), *The Sunday Times Investigates: Reporting That Made History* (Times Books, London, 2021)

Jacobsen, Annie, *Surprise, Kill, Vanish: The Definitive History of Secret CIA Assassins, Armies and Operators* (Little, Brown & Co., Boston, 2019)

Jordan, Eric (aka Fees, James), *Operation Hebron* (International Media Group, London, 2000)

Kandil, Hazem, *Soldiers, Spies and Statesmen: Egypt's Road to Revolt* (Verso, London, 2012)

Kinzer, Stephen, *Poisoner in Chief: Sidney Gottlieb and the CIA Search for Mind Control* (Henry Holt & Co., New York, 2019)

Kirchick, James, *Secret City: The Hidden History of Gay Washington* (Henry Holt & Co., New York, 2022)

Knightley, Phillip, *The First Casualty: The War Correspondent as Hero, Propagandist and Myth Maker* (Andre Deutsch, London, 1975)

Knightley, Phillip, *The Second Oldest Profession* (Andre Deutsch, London, 1986)

Lacey, Robert, *Inside the Kingdom* (Viking, New York, 2009)

Lashmar, Paul, *Spies, Spin and the Fourth Estate: British Intelligence and the Media* (Edinburgh University Press, Edinburgh, 2020)

Lenart, Judith, *Berlin to Bond and Beyond: The Story of a Fleming Man* (Athena Press, Twickenham, 2007)

Lycett, Andrew, *Ian Fleming* (Weidenfeld & Nicolson, London, 1995)

Lynam, Ruth (ed.), *Paris Fashion* (Michael Joseph, London, 1972)
Maas, Peter, *Manhunt: The Incredible Pursuit of a CIA Agent Turned Terrorist* (Random House, New York, 1986)
Macintyre, Ben, *A Spy Among Friends: Kim Philby and the Great Betrayal* (Bloomsbury, London, 2014)
Macintyre, Ben, *The Spy and the Traitor: The Greatest Espionage Story of the Cold War* (Viking, London, 2018)
Mangold, Tom, *Cold Warrior – James Jesus Angleton: The CIA's Master Spy Hunter* (Simon & Schuster, New York, 1991)
Martin, David C., *Wilderness of Mirrors: Intrigue, Deception and the Secrets that Destroyed Two of the Cold War's Most Important Agents* (Harper & Row, New York, 1980)
Milne, Tim, *Kim Philby: A Story of Friendship and Betrayal* (Biteback, London, 2014)
Moll, Hermann; Leapman, Michael, *Brokers of Death: An Insider's Story of the Iran Arms Deals* (Macmillan, London, 1988)
Morley, Jefferson, *The Ghost: The Secret Life of CIA Spymaster James Jesus Angleton* (St Martin's Press, New York, 2017)
Morris, Jan, *Pleasures of a Tangled Life* (Random House, London, 1989)
Moscrop, Andrew, *The Camel's Neighbour: Travel and Travellers in Yemen* (Signal, London, 2020)
Newton, Verne, *The Cambridge Spies: The Untold Story of Maclean, Philby and Burgess in America* (University Press of America, Lanham, 1991)
Noel-Clarke, Michael (ed./translator), *Memories of a Bygone Age: Qajar Persia and Imperial Russia 1853–1902* (Gingko, London, 2016)
O'Connell, Jack; Loeb, Vernon, *King's Counsel: A Memoir of War, Espionage and Diplomacy in the Middle East* (W. W. Norton & Co., New York, 2011)
O'Shaughnessy, Hugh, *Pinochet: The Politics of Torture* (Latin America Bureau, London, 1980)

Page, Bruce; Leitch, David; Knightley, Phillip, *Philby: The Spy Who Betrayed a Generation* (HarperCollins, London, 1968)

Perry, Mark, *Eclipse: The Last Days of the CIA* (William Morrow & Co., New York, 1992)

Perry, Roland, *Last of the Cold War Spies: The Life of Michael Straight – The Only American in Britain's Cambridge Spy Ring* (Da Capo Press, Boston, 2005)

Philby, Charlotte, *Edith and Kim* (Borough Press, London, 2022)

Philby, Kim, *My Silent War* (MacGibbon & Kee, London, 1968)

Pilger, John (ed.), *Tell Me No Lies* (Vintage, London, 2005)

Potts, Mark; Kochan, Nicholas; Whittington, Robert, *Dirty Money: BCCI: The Inside Story of the World's Sleaziest Bank* (National Press Books, Bethesda, 1992)

Quandt, William B., *The United States and Egypt* (Brookings Institution, Washington, 1990)

Ranelagh, John, *The Agency: Rise and Decline of the CIA* (Simon & Schuster, New York, 1986)

Riad, Mahmoud, *The Struggle for Peace in the Middle East* (Quartet, London, 1981)

Risen, James, *The Last Honest Man: The CIA, the FBI, the Mafia and the Kennedys – and One Senator's Fight to Save Democracy* (Little, Brown & Co., New York, 2023)

Robert, Denis; Backes, Ernest, *Révélations* (Les Arènes, Paris, 2001)

Sakharov, Vladimir; Tosi, Umberto, *High Treason* (Robert Hale, New York, 1981)

Saunders, Frances Stonor, *Who Paid the Piper? The CIA and the Cultural Cold War* (Granta, London, 1999)

Sayigh, Rosemary, *The Palestinians* (Zed Books, London, 2007)

Seale, Patrick, *Abu Nidal: A Gun for Hire* (Random House, London, 1992)

Seale, Patrick; McConville, Maureen, *Philby: The Long Road to Moscow* (Hamish Hamilton, London, 1973)

Seale, Patrick; McConville, Maureen, *The Hilton Assignment* (Maurice Temple Smith, London, 1973)

Secord, Richard, *Honored and Betrayed: Irangate, Covert Affairs and the Secret War in Laos* (Wiley, New York, 1992)

Shakespeare, Nicholas, *Ian Fleming: The Complete Man* (Harvill Secker, London, 2023)

Silberman, Fred, *Jungles and Skyscrapers* (Private publication, 1941)

Sirrs, Owen L., *A History of the Egyptian Intelligence Service* (Routledge, London, 2011)

Smiley, David, *Arabian Assignment: Operations in Oman and the Yemen* (Cooper, London, 1975)

Smith, Chris, *The Last Cambridge Spy: John Cairncross, Bletchley Codebreaker and Soviet Double Agent* (History Press, London, 2019)

Straight, Michael, *After Long Silence* (HarperCollins, New York, 1983)

Trento, Joseph J., *Prelude to Terror* (Carroll & Graf, New York, 2005)

Trento, Joseph J., *The Secret History of the CIA* (Prima, New York, 2001)

Trento, Joseph J; Trento, Susan B; Corson, William R., *Widows* (Crown, New York, 1989)

Truell, Peter; Gurwin, Larry, *BCCI: The Inside Story of the World's Most Corrupt Financial Empire* (Bloomsbury, London, 1992)

von Tunzelmann, Alex, *Blood and Sand: Suez, Hungary and the Crisis That Shook the World* (Simon & Schuster, London, 2017)

Vatikiotis, P. J. ('Taki'), *The History of Modern Egypt: From Muhammad Ali to Mubarak* (Littlehampton Book Services, London, 1986)

Weiner, Tim, *Legacy of Ashes: The History of the CIA* (Doubleday, New York, 2007)

Whipple, Chris, *The Spymasters: How the CIA Directors Shape History and the Future* (Simon & Schuster, New York, 2020)

Wilford, Hugh, *America's Great Game: The CIA's Secret Arabists and the Shaping of the Modern Middle East* (Basic Books, New York, 2013)

Wilford, Hugh, *The CIA: An Imperial History* (Basic Books, New York, 2024)

Wilford, Hugh, *The Mighty Wurlitzer: How the CIA Played America* (Harvard University Press, Cambridge, 2008)

Wise, David, *Molehunt: The Secret Search for Traitors That Shattered the CIA* (Random House, New York, 1992)

Woodward, Bob, *Veil: The Secret Wars of the CIA 1981–1987* (Simon & Schuster, New York, 1987)

Wright, Peter; Greengrass, Paul, *Spycatcher: The Candid Autobiography of a Senior Intelligence Officer* (Heinemann, Sydney, 1987)

ACKNOWLEDGEMENTS

We are indebted to a large number of people who generously gave us their time and their memories, illuminating aspects of our quest in ways which proved invaluable. We have thanked many of them in our 'Notes and references' section, and we do so again. We also wish to offer our particular thanks to the following:

The remaining participants in the original Insight Holden inquiry, namely John Barry and Isabel Hilton, as well as Peter Pringle, former *Sunday Times* New York correspondent, and Helena Cobban, *Sunday Times* correspondent in Beirut at the time.

Harry Evans, the greatest newspaper editor, who set the original inquiry in motion and then inspired us to take it up again as we reflected on his regret that this was 'the one that got away'. His pursuit of truth serves as a model for all of journalism.

Tina Brown, who took an immediate interest in our quest, despite having lived with her late husband Harry Evans's obsession with the case for four decades, and revealed the many theories she had discussed with him. We are especially grateful that Tina wrote her wonderful introduction to this book.

Peter Holden, David's nephew, and his wife, Joanne, for their hospitality and for sharing Holden's letters to his father Geoffrey – David's brother.

Paula Fees, who answered all our questions about her father Jim, even though some were uncomfortable for her.

Celia Adams, for her recollections of her late husband Michael's pursuit of the Holden case and the crucial tale involving Mohamed Heikal. Celia also introduced us to several people, including the remarkable Isis Elten in Italy.

David Halton for sharing his memories of his incredible near miss with Egyptian hit men at Cairo Airport.

Roger Hardy for revealing the tantalising details of his last phone call with Fred Halliday.

The family of Mohamed Heikal, in particular Hassan Heikal and Hedayat Heikal, for being the most generous hosts as well as the bravest champions of investigative journalism.

Paul Lashmar for his help with the Information Research Department and Tony Terry's stepdaughter, Judith Lenart, for her insight into her stepfather's activities and her investigative acumen.

Gabriel Pogrund, inspirational journalist and dear friend, who suggested we embark on this project.

Andrew Holgate for his incisive edits to our proposal and insightful suggestions regarding the structure of this book.

Manu's editor at *The Times* and the *Sunday Times*, Carol Lewis, for her unwavering support.

Also at *The Times* and the *Sunday Times*: Ben Taylor, John Witherow, Pia Sarma, Helen Davies, Ian Brunskill, Michael Binyon, Roger Boyes, Tom Calver, Venetia Menzies and Claire Patchett.

David Walmsley, editor-in-chief of the *Globe and Mail* in Canada, for his close interest in our project since the start and for his priceless encouragement and practical help.

The following three copyright holders for generously giving us permission to quote at length from the respective works: Mark Morris, for *Pleasures of a Tangled Life* by Jan Morris; Afif Aburish,

ACKNOWLEDGEMENTS

for *Beirut Spy* by Said Aburish; and Carl Bernstein, for his article about the CIA and the media.

The readers of our manuscript at various stages, who gave us many key comments and suggestions: Simon Creasey, Gian Volpicelli, Fabio Bottari, Alessio Ghirlanda, Leni Gillman and Alessandra Cardile.

Alberto and Julia Nania for their precious help translating Leo Silberman's letters.

Stephen Grey for sharing the findings of his own investigation of Holden's murder two decades ago.

Mark Hollingsworth for opening up his archive of ex-MI6 agents and providing continuous help.

Phil Green, former *Sunday Times* illustrator, for his superb map of Holden's last journey.

Matthew Cole, our agent and tireless advocate.

At House Productions: Juliette Howell and Charlie Silver. After a chance meeting between Charlie and Manu, they grasped the story from the very start and encouraged us throughout.

Olivia Beattie and Ella Boardman at Biteback for giving a home to the outcome of our investigation.

Peter's family, in particular Blake, Seth and Orla, for their support in difficult circumstances during the final stages of writing the book.

Manu's family, not only for tolerating his childhood dream of becoming a writer but for giving him what he needed so that the dream could come true.

Finally, most importantly, our partners Leni and Sandra, who supported our quest and were vital in helping us see it through. This book is for you.

INDEX

Abu Jihad 64, 65
Aburish, Afif 303, 304
Aburish, Said 214, 302–4
Adams, Celia 101, 297, 331–2, 358, 360, 403
Adams, Michael 96, 101, 314, 331–2, 334, 360, 403
Adham, Kamal 227, 232, 326–8, 330, 349, 401
Adorno, Theodor 388
Akhbar el-Yom 217
Al-Ahram 207, 333, 341
Al Fajr 33
Alalawi, Brigadier 29–30, 34, 57–8
Allen, Robert S. 271
Allende, Salvador 127–8, 129, 253, 264, 369
Alsop, Joseph 265, 282, 375
Alsop, Mary 282
Alsop, Stewart 265
Amin, Ali 217, 218–19, 362
Amin, Mustafa 123, 136, 217–19, 235, 343, 351, 397
Amin, Safia 343–4
Anderson, Jack 260
Angleton, James Jesus 141, 245, 250–1, 253, 259–60, 261, 266–7, 300, 305–7, 399–400
Anstey, John 114, 122
Applewhite, Ed 305
Arab News Agency (ANA) 94–5
Arabia Without Sultans (Halliday) 366, 369
Arabiyat, Ghazi 34, 39
Arran, Lord 274
Asner, Ed 178
al-Assad, Hafez 3, 208
Associated Press 18
Attenborough, David 104
Austin, Anthony 109, 135
Avedon, Richard 259

Baer, Bob 401
Baldwin, Hanson 271
Barr, James 308, 309, 311, 312
Barry, John
    investigation of Holden's murder 10, 21, 22–7, 31–2, 37–9, 40–41
    early career 21–2
    remains in Cairo 44, 47
    continued investigation of Holden's murder 50–51, 52–60, 64–6, 147
    and thefts at *Sunday Times* 61, 67, 68
    and Holden as an intelligence agent 138, 139, 140–41, 142, 143
    and report on *Sunday Times* Holden inquiry 156
Barry, Pat 44
Batista, Fulgencio 84
Battle, John 170
BBC 102, 123–4, 131, 274–5
Bede College Boys' School 72
Beedham, Brian 370–71
Beeley, Sir Harold 126
Beeston, Moyra 301
Beeston, Richard 'Dick' 299–301, 314, 362
Begin, Menachem 4, 19
Behan, Brendan 111
Belfast Telegraph 21
Benjamin, Walter 387, 388
Bergman, Lewis 109
Berlin to Bond and Beyond: The Story of a Fleming Man (Lenart) 276, 278
Bernstein, Carl 114, 172, 262–5, 266–7, 400, 404
Binyon, Michael 246–9, 284, 285, 340, 343, 345, 347, 349, 353–5, 373

Bisharat, Mr 50, 149–50
Bitar, Afif 303
Bitar, Ali 302
Blake, George 246–7, 274
Blatherwick, David 143–4
Blundy, David 298
Blunt, Anthony 251, 380–81
Bonnette, Barbara xvii–xviii, 47–8
Bonnette, James 47–8
Bootham School 72–3
de Borchgrave, Arnaud 244–5
Boyd, Ruth 24, 51
Boyd, Steve 21, 23–4, 38
Boyes, Roger 245–6, 339–40, 375
Bradlee, Ben 167, 172–3, 174, 306
Brandon, Henry 274, 275, 276
Brecht, Bertolt 387
Browne, Martina 377
Buchan, Sir Alastair 284
Buckley, William 'Bill' 232, 237, 238, 348
Buist, John 102, 103
Bunney, John 59
Bunney, Pamela 59
Burgess, Guy 88, 91, 251–2, 276, 299, 378
Bush, George H. W. 265–6
Byline Times 367

Cameron, James 49, 51–2
le Carré, John 74
Carter, Jimmy 19, 234, 349
Casaro, Renato 238
Casey, Bill 289
Casino Royale (Fleming) 280
Castro, Fidel 84
Cavendish, Anthony 275–6, 289, 296
Chisholm, Roderick 377
Church, Frank 265–6
CIA
    and Domestic Operations Division 113–14
    Holden as an agent for 140–43, 155–6, 160, 179–82, 196, 208, 261–2, 264–71
    observation on Kim Philby 150, 214
    suspected involvement in Holden's death 182, 217, 406
    and Bob Pelletreau 212
    and Ahmed Rahman 213–14
    and John Fistere 214, 303–5
    and storming of US Embassy in Tehran 215–16
    and Kenizé Mourad 216
    and Bruce Taylor Odell 218
    plot to remove Nasser 219
    and James Fees 220, 221, 224, 225–39, 321, 326, 327, 348, 373, 398–401, 406–7
    operations in Jordan 230, 292–3

support for Anwar Sadat 231–3
and Arnaud de Borchgrave 244–5
Lavender Scare in 249–51
use of journalists by 260–67, 361
taps on journalists 270–71
and Le Cercle 289
and Anwar Sadat 322, 324, 325, 348–9
Close, Raymond 236
Cobban, Helena 21, 39–40, 50, 63–4
Cody, Ed 173–4
Colby, William 265, 266, 270, 289
Collar the Lot! (Gillman) 176
Colvin, Ian 276
Comben, Tony 49–50, 57, 68, 69, 243
Conundrum (Morris) 130
Cooper, Robert Wright 90
Copeland, Miles 141, 150, 305
Correspondents Worldwide 284–5
CounterSpy (magazine) 214
Courvoisier, Jean 19–20, 58–9
Crankshaw, Edward 284, 375
Cranswick, Harold 74
Critchfield, James 227
Crookston, Peter 122, 131
Crozier, Brian 289

Daily Telegraph 229–30, 376, 377
Darwish, Mahmoud 296
Deakin, Ralph 248
Debusmann, Bernd 211–12
Dench, Judi 68
Directorate of Military Intelligence 253
Documents from the US Espionage Den 215–16
Domestic Operations Division 114
Douglas-Home, Charles 177
Dulles, Allen 307
Dulles, John Foster 91, 249, 262, 263
Dulwich College 121
Duns High School 74

Economist, The 87, 88, 229, 252–3, 289, 295
Eddy, Paul
    investigation of Holden's murder 10, 11, 21, 31, 34, 39, 40–41, 44
    early career of 18
    investigation of Israeli torture of Palestinian prisoners 18–19, 132, 162
    and thefts at *Sunday Times* 62, 63, 66–7, 68–70
    continued investigation of Holden's murder 70, 224
    on Insight team 131
    and report on *Sunday Times* Holden inquiry 148, 149, 154, 156
Eden, Anthony 95, 97, 219, 312
Eichelberger, James 219, 234–5

INDEX

Eilts, Hermann 195, 234, 244
Eisenstein, Sergei 386
Elizabeth II, Queen 110, 120
Elkins, Michael 33, 213, 214
Elliott, Nicholas 289, 298, 305–6
Elten, Isis 358–63
Elten, Jorg Andrees 360
Emmanuel College, Cambridge 73–4
Encounter (magazine) 127–8, 253, 261, 264, 371, 395, 400
Epstein, Ed 141
Evans, Sir Harold
    and Insight team xi–xiii, 18, 131, 191, 192–3
    and death of Holden xiii–xiv, 10
    and disappearance of Holden 4–6, 405
    investigation of Holden's murder 44, 286
    and thefts at *Sunday Times* 62, 63, 66, 68, 69–70, 286
    joins *Sunday Times* 119
    and Holden as an intelligence agent 137–8, 140, 141
    and report on *Sunday Times* Holden inquiry 148, 161, 286, 298
    and investigation of Israeli torture of Palestinian prisoners 167
    becomes editor of *The Times* 176, 282
    ousted as editor of *The Times* 177, 282
    death of 191–3
    and Ahmed Rahman 213
    continued interest in Holden case 396
Evans, Timothy xii

Fairlie, Henry 253
Faisal, King 229, 283
Farewell to Arabia (Holden) 113–14, 128, 213, 229, 361, 381, 405
Fatah, Mohammed Abdul 145
FBI
    file on Holden 138–40
    and Cambridge spies 251, 394–5
    mentions Holden in report 254–5
    report on Leo Silberman 255–7, 380
    surveillance of Holden 398, 399
Feather, Vic 78
Fees, James 220, 221, 224, 225–39, 321, 326, 327, 348, 373, 395, 398–401, 405, 406–7
Fees, Paula 231, 234, 235, 236, 405–6
Fine, Debbie 223
Fine, Jim 169, 223
Fischer, Benjamin 306
Fisk, Robert 207
Fistere, Isobel 40, 41, 48–9, 50, 53, 149–50
Fistere, John 40, 41, 48–9, 50, 53, 149–50, 212–13, 214, 303–5

Fleming, Ian xii, 117, 118, 275, 276–7, 278, 279, 280, 281, 282, 285, 286, 299, 309
Follett, Ken 322
Foot, Michael 370
Ford, Gerald 181
Forty Thousand Against the Arctic: Russia's Polar Empire (Smolka) 254
Forum World Features 289
Fox, James 283–4
Friends' School 72, 87

Gaddafi, Colonel 8, 234
Galizia, Daphne Caruana 343, 396
al Gawhary, Fuad 8–9
Gershkovich, Evan 405
Gibson, Archie 299
Giles, Frank 117–19, 159–61, 176, 177, 243–4, 281–4, 285–6
Gillman, Danny 41
Gillman, Leni 20–21, 35, 44, 67–8, 81, 121, 122, 172, 281, 368, 409
Gillman, Peter
    and disappearance of Holden 6–7, 10
    investigation of Holden's murder 10–11, 17, 19–21, 27, 29–31, 34–5, 39, 41
    and Emanuele Midolo on new investigation 13, 193–7, 199–201, 205–6, 208, 209, 210, 213–14, 220, 221–6, 245, 273, 353
    in Insight team 18, 131–3, 176
    investigation of Israeli torture of Palestinian prisoners 18–19, 132–3, 162–7, 169, 170, 171–3, 174–5
    return home 44–5
    and flight manifest of Holden's flight to Cairo 47–9
    continued investigation of Holden's murder 52–60, 64–5, 68–9, 70
    and thefts at *Sunday Times* 61, 66–8, 69, 70
    research into Holden's early life 71, 72, 73–4, 75, 76–7, 78, 79–80, 81–2, 83, 94
    and Leo Silberman 76–7, 79–81, 84, 140, 153–4, 155, 156, 160, 224, 295, 379–80, 382, 394
    research into Holden's career 89, 90, 114, 124, 125, 126, 128, 129, 133
    early life and career 120–23
    and Holden as an intelligence agent 138, 139, 140–41, 288–9, 290–91, 292, 375
    meetings with Cairo police 143–8
    continued investigation of Holden's life 143–8, 178–83, 304–5, 334–5, 343, 366–70, 371, 376, 395, 399, 400, 401, 403, 404, 406
    report on *Sunday Times* Holden inquiry 148–57

Gillman, Peter *cont.*
  continued work with Insight team 176–7
  meeting with Alexandra Johnson 178–83
  and death of Sir Harold Evans 192–3
  interview with Anthony Cavendish 276
  and David Halton 317, 319, 320
  at Anwar Sadat press conference 356–7
  meeting with Peter Holden 409–12
Gillman, Seth 44
Good Times, Bad Times (Evans) 191
Gordievsky, Oleg 323, 370, 371–2, 373, 382
Greece Without Columns (Holden) 133–4, 366
Greene, Graham 405
Grey, Stephen 395–402
Griggs, Susan 304–5
Grimsley, Ed 138–9
Guardian, The xi, 101, 274, 281, 297, 314, 372, 376
  Holden as foreign correspondent with 107–8, 111–13, 152–3, 229
Guevara, Ernesto 'Che' 84

Haley, William 103, 107
Halliday, Fred 128, 334–5, 365–73, 399
Halton, David 187–9, 317–20, 347–8
Hamilton, Sir Denis 161, 282
Hankin, Muriel 148
Hanning, James 297
Hardy, Roger 365–7, 369
Harper's Bazaar 115, 125
Harvey, Bill 306
Hassan, Ahmed 25, 26, 37–8, 55–6
Heartfield, John 387
Heikal, Ahmed 357
Heikal, Hassan 340, 342–3, 350
Heikal, Hedayat 350–51
Heikal, Mohamed 331, 332, 333–4, 341–2, 347, 350–51, 355, 356, 357, 358
Helms, Richard 307
Hersh, Seymour 213, 270
Heseltine, Michael 122
Hetherington, Alastair 107
High Treason (Sakharov) 325
Hilton, Isabel
  investigation of Holden's murder 70, 72
  continued investigation of Holden's murder 143–4, 145, 147
  and report on *Sunday Times* Holden inquiry 156
  investigation of Israeli torture of Palestinian prisoners 165, 166–7, 170, 174–5
Hipkins, Dominic 257–8, 287
Hirst, David 155, 206–8
Hodson, Harry 309–10, 313
Holden, David
  arrival in Cairo xvii–xix

  concerns over disappearance 3–7
  death of 7–11
  first article on last trip in *Sunday Times* 41–4
  post-mortem examination 49, 51–2
  Scotland Yard investigation of 49–50
  childhood of 71–3
  at Cambridge University 73–4
  working for intelligence services 73–4, 90, 137–43, 152, 153, 155–6, 160–62, 179–82, 208, 211–12, 261–2, 264–71, 283–4, 285–6, 287–93, 295, 297–302, 303, 313, 334–5, 394–5, 366–8, 374–5, 382, 394, 397, 398, 399, 400
  teaching career 74–5, 152
  at Northwestern University, Illinois 75, 81–3, 152
  sexuality of 76, 249, 375
  relationship with Leo Silberman 76–7, 81, 82, 83–4, 88, 89, 99–101, 103, 104–5, 152, 160, 256, 296, 404
  in Mexico 83–4
  starts work for *The Times* 87–9
  in Washington for *The Times* 89–91
  as Middle East correspondent 92–9, 101–3
  and Kim Philby 98, 208, 295, 298, 307–8, 314
  as African correspondent 103–4
  resigns from *The Times* 105–6
  as foreign correspondent for *The Guardian* 107–8, 111–13, 152–3, 229
  works for *New York Times* 108–9, 124, 130, 135–6, 266
  marriage to Ruth 109–11, 115, 401, 403
  and *Farewell to Arabia* 113–14, 213, 229
  with *Sunday Times* 118, 119–21, 123–5, 126–33, 135–6, 153
  works for BBC 123–4
  social life of 125–6
  and *Greece Without Columns* 133–4
  and *The House of Saud* 134, 327, 330
  final *Sunday Times* report on last trip 148–57, 159–61, 179, 202, 208, 217, 264, 319, 347, 400
  David Halton mistaken for 187–9, 317–20, 347–8
  Foreign Office records on 241–5
  in FBI report 254–5
  parallels with Tony Terry 278–9
  and Kamal Adham 327–8
  and Fred Halliday 365–8
  and Jeremy Wolfenden 376
Holden, Ethel 71, 85
Holden, Freda 101
Holden, Geoffrey 71, 73, 82, 85, 91, 96–7, 101, 111, 131, 409, 411
Holden, Joanne 409
Holden, Peter 409–12

INDEX

Holden, Ruth 33, 39, 51, 109–11, 114–15, 122, 125, 130–31, 134, 161–2, 205, 402–3, 410
Holden, Simon 412
Holden, Thomas 71, 74, 85
Honourable Men: My Life in the CIA (Colby) 265
Hoover, J. Edgar 251, 254
House of Saud, The (Holden) 134, 327, 330
Hughes, Richard 276
Hull, Edmond 170
Hunt, Howard 114
Hussein, King 3, 32, 41, 230, 244, 304

Imbert, Peter 20
Independent, The 224, 289, 372
Information Research Department (IRD) 94–5
Inside Intelligence (Cavendish) 275
Insight team
    under Sir Harold Evans xi–xiii, 131, 191, 192–3
    Peter Gillman in 18, 131–3, 176, 192–3
    investigation of Israeli torture of Palestinian prisoners 18–19, 132–3, 162–7, 169, 170, 171–3, 174–5, 221
    creation of 118–19
    reports from Northern Ireland 123
    final report on Holden's death 148–57, 159–61, 167, 179, 202, 208, 217, 264, 319, 347, 400
    and Kim Philby 297, 361
    in Stephen Grey's investigation 395–9
International Committee of the Red Cross (ICRC) 19, 58–9, 132–3, 169–70, 171, 174, 222
Iran–Contra affair 237–8
al-Islambuli, Khalid 358
Ismail, Brigadier 31–2, 39, 57
Ismail, Mohammed Hafez 232
Izvestia 274

Jobbins, Bob 8–9
Johns, Richard 153, 312
Johnson, Alexandra 163–7, 169–71, 172, 173–5, 177–83, 221, 222, 223–4, 225, 231–2, 402
Johnson, Boris 199
Jones, J. D. F. 125, 126
Jordan, John 82
Jordan Times 29

Kalugin, Oleg 239, 373–4
Kamal, Mustafa 25, 50–51
Kassem, Abdul 107–8
Kellner, Peter 131
Kemp, Chris 16
Kemsley, Lord 118, 275, 309
Kennedy, John F. 84
Key to Rebecca, The (Follett) 322
KGB
    and Kim Philby 5, 229, 301, 306, 374, 382

Holden as an agent for 84, 152, 182, 208, 254–5, 299, 335, 349, 366, 368, 369, 381–2, 394–5, 397, 398, 400, 404, 406
    and Leo Silberman 84, 152, 257, 394
    and Patrick Seale 153, 208, 295, 296, 399
    involvement in thefts at *Sunday Times* 181
    and George Blake 246–7
    and James Angleton 259, 306
    and Sami Sharaf 323, 324
    plot to remove Sadat 325–6
    Sunday Times article on 370–71
    and Fred Halliday 370–72
    and Jeremy Wolfenden 375–8
Khashoggi, Adnan 283, 327, 328
Khashoggi, Jamal 328
Khomeini, Ayatollah 215
Khouri, Rami 58
Killing Fields, The 5
Kissinger, Henry 164, 225, 231, 244–5, 270, 289, 327, 357
Knight, David 288
Knightley, Phillip 98, 150, 153, 275, 276, 377–8, 382
Kobaladze, Yuri 370, 371–2
Kosygin, Alexei 323–4
Kraft, Joe 23
Kruse, Donald 169, 171, 178, 179

Labovitch, Clive 122
Lack, Alastair 124
Lasdun, Denys 125
Lawrence, Anita 48
Lawrence, T. E. 212, 226, 310
Le Cercle 289, 292
Le Nouvel Observateur 27
Leitch, David 98
Leith Academy 74–5
Lenart, Judith 276–7, 278, 286–7
Leonov, Nikolai 84
Life (magazine) 109–10
Llewellyn, Tim 211
Looking for Trouble (Beeston) 301
Lords of the Desert (Barr) 312
Love and Deception: Philby in Beirut (Hanning) 297
Löwenthal, Richard 315
Luce, Henry 304
Lumumba, Patrice 128–9
Lycett, Andrew 278

Macbeth (Shakespeare) 68
McCarthy, Joseph 249, 254
McCormick, Donald 276, 286
McCrystal, Cal 135
    and disappearance of Holden 6, 7, 405
    reaction to death of Holden 9

McCrystal, Cal *cont.*
  investigation of Holden's murder 10, 21, 22–7, 31–4
  early career 21
McCullin, Don 209–10, 283
McDonald, Iverach 89, 90, 97, 102, 103–4, 253–4
Macintyre, Ben 298–9, 306, 373
McKellen, Ian 68
Maclean, Donald 88, 91, 276, 301, 378
Macrae, Diana 132, 162, 163, 171
Malone, David 319
Mansour, Adly 355–6
Mantovani, Sergio 143
Margaret, Princess 120, 125, 126
Marsden, Eric 132, 162
Marwan, Ashraf 231, 232, 233, 324, 325, 400
Mathew, Francis 89, 90, 92
Matthews, Roger 211
Maxwell, Robert 284–5
Meisel, Edmund 386
Menzies, Robert 94
Mercer, Derrick 6
MI6
  and Holden as an agent for 208, 211–12, 261–2, 264–71, 283–4, 285–6, 287–93, 367–8
  plot to remove Nasser 219, 235
  and Tony Terry 224
  and James Fees 230
  use of journalists by 273–90, 302, 309–15
  operations in Jordan 292
  and John Slade-Baker 309–15
Middle East Centre for Arab Studies (MECAS) 246–7
Midolo, Emanuele
  investigation of Holden's murder 13–16, 193–7, 199–220, 241–6, 252, 257–8, 273, 330–32, 335–7, 339–44, 345–63, 373–4, 375, 376, 393, 394–403
  and death of Sir Harold Evans 191–3
  and James Fees 221–6, 228–9, 237, 238
  and Michael Binyon 245, 246, 248–9
  and Leo Silberman 256, 378, 380, 382, 383, 385, 386–7, 389, 391, 394–6
  and Holden's involvement with intelligence services 260, 261, 264, 267–70, 287–93, 349, 375, 382
  and MI6's use of journalists 277, 278, 281–2, 284, 285, 286, 287
  investigation of Kim Philby 295–9, 300, 303, 307–15
  and David Halton 317, 318, 319, 320
  and plots against Anwar Sadat 324
  and Jeremy Wolfenden 378
Morley, Jefferson 306

Morris, Jan (James) 53–4, 92, 93, 124, 130, 150, 179, 180, 203–5, 404
Morris, Joe Alex Jr 301, 362
Morsi, Mohamed 355–6
Mortimer, Edward 23, 32–4, 51, 53, 179
Mosaddegh, Mohammad 133, 141
Mossad 10, 17, 211–12, 228, 235, 285, 347, 348, 398, 399, 401, 406, 407
Mourad, Kenizé 27–9, 31, 32, 41, 151, 214–15, 216, 217, 383–6, 397
Mubarak, Hosni 233, 235, 336, 351, 400–401
Muir, Jean 125
de Muralt, Jean 169–70, 171–2, 178, 179, 221–3
Murdoch, Rupert 176, 177
My Paper Chase (Evans) xii, xiii, 194, 367, 396
My Silent War (Philby) 361

Nasser, Gamal Abdel 93, 94, 95, 108, 112, 119, 124–5, 219, 227, 230, 235, 312, 313, 321, 323, 333, 347
Neil, Andrew 177
New York Times 42, 108–9, 124, 130, 135–6, 266, 267, 270, 337, 338
Newsweek (magazine) 177–8
Nicholson, Evelyn 72
Nixon, Richard 231, 270
Nockolds, Harold 89
Norman, Gerald 90, 92, 99, 100
Northern Echo xi, xii, 119
Northwestern University, Illinois 75, 81–3, 152
Nutting, Anthony 95

Obote, Milton 129, 209
Odell, Bruce Taylor 217–18
Offie, Carmel 250, 307
One Pair of Eyes (TV series) 123–4
Operation Hebron (Fees) 238
Osnos, Peter 173
Oswald, Lee Harvey 84

Page, Bruce 98
Paisley, Ian 123
Paisley, John Arthur 261
Palestine Liberation Organization (PLO) 54, 60, 63–5, 164–5, 178, 230, 231
Paper Palace, The (Harling) 286
Pawley, S. R. 'Pop' 229
Pedley, Robin 72, 75, 76
Pelletreau, Bob 59, 212, 217
Perry, Mark 325
Philby, Eleanor 304
Philby, Josephine 304
Philby, Kim xi–xii, 5, 87–8, 98, 150, 153, 208, 214, 227, 247, 250–52, 254, 295–301, 303–8, 309, 312–15, 320, 361, 374, 381–2, 394, 398

INDEX

Philby, St John 312
Pinochet, Augusto 127, 253
Pleasures of a Tangled Life (Morris) 203
Powell, Charles 241–2
Press Gazette 246
Pringle, Peter 47–8
Putin, Vladimir 373–4, 381

Qabbani, Nizar 296
Qasim, Abd al-Karim 218

Radio Times 131
Rahman, Ahmed 41, 53, 150, 170, 179, 181–2, 212, 213–14, 217
Rashid, Ali 144–7
Reagan, Ronald 237
Reed, Tom 173, 174
Regeni, Giulio 15, 336–9
Regler, Gustav 387
Rice, Michael 126
Rolling Stone (magazine) 262
Roosevelt, James 222
de la Rosa, Javier 239
Royal Opera House 110
Rusbridger, Alan xi

Sackville, Lady Katherine 117, 283
Sadat, Anwar 3, 4, 43, 125, 126, 134–5, 136, 144, 155, 206–7, 218, 219, 225, 231–3, 235, 245, 315, 328–19, 321–6, 329–31, 333–4, 347, 348, 349, 356–8, 400
Sadat, Jehan 236
Safari Club 326–7, 328, 329, 333, 349, 395, 401
Saguer, Louis 385, 386–7, 392, 393, 394
Sakharov, Vladimir 324, 325, 382
Salameh, Ali Hassan 64–5
Salazar, António 108
Sassoon, Vidal 125, 403
Saud, King 227
al-Sayyid, Ma'amoun 33
Scott, Gavin 23
Scott, Paul 271
Seale, Patrick 153, 208, 295–7, 395, 397, 399
Seale, Rana 295–7
Secord, Richard 235
Sharaf, Sami 323, 325
Sharett, Moshe 311
Sherman, Alfred 371
Silberman, Fred 77–8
Silberman, Freddy 76, 77, 78, 81, 83, 104–5, 160, 256, 394
Silberman, Gordon 77
Silberman, Hilda 77
Silberman, Leo 75–85, 88, 89, 99–101, 103, 138, 139, 140, 152, 160, 196, 224, 255–7, 269, 295,
296, 378–80, 381, 382–3, 385–95, 399, 404, 410–11
Silberman, Moyra 76
Simoni, Wolfgang 385, 386–7, 392, 393, 394
Singer, Norman 169
Sirrs, Owen 219, 325
al-Sisi, Abdul Fattah 15, 336, 337, 339–40, 341
Skripal, Sergei 373
Slade-Baker, John 96, 302, 307–15, 322
Slade-Baker, Robert 308–9
Small, Ray 49–50, 57, 68, 69, 243
Smiley, David 229
Smith, Ian 120
Smolka, Hans Peter 254
Snowden, Lord 120, 125, 126
Spectator (magazine) 370
Spencer, Richard 341–2
Spice, Betty 79
Spy Among Friends, A (Macintyre) 298
Spy Who Betrayed a Generation, The (Knightley et al.) 98
Stacey, Tom 284–5
Stalin, Joseph 391
Stern, Larry 173, 175
Stewart, James 48
Stirling, David 227
Straight, Michael 379–82
Stuart, Douglas 313
Suez Crisis 93–4, 95–6, 312, 360, 361
Sulzberger, C. L. 264–5
Sunday Mirror 18
Sunday Times
  Insight team at xi–xiii
  thefts in xiv, 61–3, 66–70
  concerns over Holden's disappearance 3–7
  investigation of Holden's murder 10–11
  first article on Holden's last trip 41–5
  Holden with 118, 119–21, 123–5, 126–33, 135–6, 153
  under Denis Hamilton 118–19
  Peter Gillman joins 122–3
  closure during 1978 159
  changes at after Murdoch purchase 176, 177
  Foreign Office obstruction of 241–6
  and MI6 links 275, 276–7, 309–15
  investigation of KGB 370
Sundry Times (Giles) 281–2
Svendsen, Leroy 'Swede' 235, 237
Swain, Jon 5
Swinburn, James 94

Tantum, Geoffrey 57, 289–93
Tantum, Laura 289
Tarantino, Quentin 238
TASS (news agency) 273–4

Tawil, Raymonda 30–31
Taylor, Elisabeth Russell 394
Terry, Rachel 278–9, 280
Terry, Tony 21, 30–31, 40, 41, 224–5, 243, 276–81, 285, 286–7, 309
Thomas, Jacques Leon 235
Thomson, Lord 285
Thornhill, Michael T. 308
Tiger, Life, The (Gainham) 280
Time (magazine) 177–8
Times, The
    Holden at 87–106
    closure during 1978 159
    changes at after Murdoch purchase 176, 177, 282
    MI6 and journalist links 273–4, 299
Times Educational Supplement (TES) 248
Timken, Ernest 216
Tinker Tailor Soldier Spy (le Carré) 74
Tomalin, Nick 5
Town Magazine 121–2
Trento, Joseph 259, 260–62, 267, 307
Trevelyan, Humphrey 125–6
Trotsky, Leon 84
Truman, Harry 248
Tucker, Emma 405
Turki bin Faisal, Prince 328–9, 352
Turner, Stansfield 236
Tyerman, Donald 87–8, 252–3, 371
Tzara, Tristan 387

de Valois, Ninette 110
Vassall, John 375
Vatikiotis, P. J. ('Taki') 334–5, 369
Viall, H. G. 111

Walker, Charles 113–14
Wall Street Journal 405
Ward, Ronald 402
Washington Post 114, 167, 172–5, 239, 306, 328
Watson, John 75
Webster, David 110
Weekend Telegraph 114, 122
White, Dick 227, 228
White Mischief (Fox) 283
WikiLeaks 194–5, 222
Wilsher, Peter 6, 41–4, 135
Wilson, Harold 279
Wilton, Sir John 247
Wisner, Frank 250, 307
Witherow, John 340, 341, 345, 346–7, 349, 350, 353–4, 383, 397
Wolfenden, Jeremy 375–8
Woodhouse, C. M. 133
Woodward, Bob 114, 172, 232

Wooley, Geoffrey 248–9, 253
World Tonight, The (news programme) 124
Worsthorne, Peregrine 252–3, 371
Wrangel Clarke, Dudley 299
Wynne, Greville 377

Young, George Kennedy 279

Zacki, Said 144
Zaza, Izadeen 58